THE ARCHAEOLOGICAL GAZETTEER SERIES, VOLUME 2

Archaeology in Greater London, 1965–1990

A guide to records of excavations by the Museum of London

Museum of London Archaeological Gazetteer Series

1   Archaeology in the City of London, 1907–1991: a guide to records of excavations by the Museum of London and its predecessors, eds. John Schofield with Cath Maloney

ISBN 0 904818 81 0

2   Archaeology in Greater London, 1965–1990: a guide to records of excavations by the Museum of London, eds. Alan Thompson, Andrew Westman and Tony Dyson

ISBN 0 904818 80 2

3   Post-War Archaeology in the City of London, 1946–1972: a guide to records of excavations by Professor W F Grimes held by the Museum of London, ed. John Shepherd

ISBN 0 904818 82 9

THE ARCHAEOLOGICAL GAZETTEER SERIES, VOLUME 2

Archaeology in Greater London 1965–1990

a guide to records of excavations by the Museum of London

Edited by Alan Thompson, Andrew Westman and Tony Dyson

Museum of London 1998

First published in Great Britain in 1998 by the Museum of London, 150 London Wall, London EC2Y 5HN

British Library Cataloguing in Data. A catalogue record for this book is available from the British Library

ISBN 0 904818 80 2

Project co-ordination: John Shepherd

Editorial: Monica Kendall, Mandi Gomez and Katie Frederick

Design: Tracy Wellman

Typesetting and layout: Jeannette van der Post

Index: Susanne Atkin

Printed and bound by Valente UK

A complete catalogue of Museum of London publications is available on request. This book is published to coincide with the opening of the Museum of London Archive.

Front cover: view showing excavation of the medieval bridge at Kingston upon Thames.

C O N T E N T S

ACKNOWLEDGEMENTS

The project of compiling the present archive guide was initiated in the DGLA by Peter Hinton, with the collaboration of Alan Thompson, Michael Jones and Susan Hurman, and with the advice of Gill Andrews and Roger Thomas, for English Heritage. Many DGLA staff helped to collate records and compile summaries in 1990–1. The bulk of the work of producing this *Guide* has been accomplished jointly by MoLAS and the Museum of London archaeological archive, with a generous grant made by English Heritage towards the printing of this volume. The editors of the *Guide* were Alan Thompson (MoL Archaeological Records Officer), Andrew Westman (MoLAS project manager) and Tony Dyson (MoLAS editor). Our very special thanks to Monica Kendall who has tirelessly copy-edited all three volumes. Most of the maps were drawn by Michael Jones (MoLAS), and some by Susan Hurman; the material was put together by Helen Jones. Bibliographical lists were compiled by Cheryl Thorogood (MoL). Computing assistance was given by Majella Egan and Ian Riddler (MoLAS), and the late Des Woods. SMR numbers were obtained by Sophie Upstone (MoLAS), with the help of Ian Greig (EH). Typesetting was done by Jeannette van der Post, who also prepared all of the artwork for publication. The series was designed by Tracy Wellman. In the course of the project, advice has been gratefully received from Peter Hinton, Gill Andrews, Roger Thomas, Quita Mould and Ellen Barnes. The editors would also like to thank Nina Crummy and John Shepherd (successive MoL Archaeological Archive Managers) for their help, Peter Hinton for supplying substantial text on historical matters incorporated in the Introduction, and Harvey Sheldon and Jon Cotton for their advice on the history of the DGLA and its predecessors (for the account of which the editors, of course, remain solely responsible).

ABBREVIATIONS

The following abbreviations, including those for certain archaeological societies (see also *London Archaeologist*, 1, 15, 1972), are used in this *Guide*. In the indexes and maps the names of boroughs are abbreviated to their first four letters.

Archaeol J *Archaeology Journal*

BC&WAS Beddington, Carshalton and Wallington Archaeological Society

Bull Counc Brit Archaeol Churches Comm *Bulletin of the Council of British Archaeology Churches Committee*

Bull Inst Archaeol Univ London *Bulletin of the Institute of Archaeology, University of London*

Bull of the Wandle Group *Bulletin of the Wandle Group*

c century or centuries

c circa

CBA Council for British Archaeology

CEU Central Excavation Unit (see **EH**)

Current Archaeol *Current Archaeology*

DGLA Department of Greater London Archaeology (of MoL)

DGLA(N) Department of Greater London Archaeology (North)

DGLA(S&L) Department of Greater London Archaeology (Southwark and Lambeth)

DGLA(SW) Department of Greater London Archaeology (South-West)

DGLA(W) Department of Greater London Archaeology (West)

DoE Department of Environment (of UK government)

DUA Department of Urban Archaeology (of Guildhall Museum and MoL)

E east

EAS Enfield Archaeological Society

EH English Heritage

EH(CEU) English Heritage (Central Excavation Unit)

FARG Fulham Archaeological Research Group

GIS Geographical Information System

GLC Greater London Council

GLSMR Greater London Sites and Monuments Record

HADAS Hendon and District Archaeological Society

HBMC Historical Buildings and Monuments Commission for England

HBMC AM Lab Historical Buildings and Monuments Commission for England: Ancient Monuments Laboratory

ILAU Inner London Archaeological Unit

Int J Naut Archaeol & Underwater Exploration *International Journal of Nautical Archaeology & Underwater Exploration*

KARU Kent Archaeological Rescue Unit

Kingston upon Thames Archaeol Soc Newsletter *Kingston upon Thames Archaeological Society Newsletter*

KUTAS Kingston upon Thames Archaeological Society

LAMAS London and Middlesex Archaeological Society

London Archaeol *London Archaeologist*

m metres

Medieval Archaeol *Medieval Archaeology*

MoL Museum of London

MoLAS Museum of London Archaeology Service

N north

NGR National Grid Reference (Ordnance Survey)

NMS Newham Museum Service

OS Ordnance Survey

PEM Passmore Edwards Museum

PHELHAS Pinner and Hatch End Local History and Archaeology Society

PHS Pinner Historical Society

Post-Medieval Archaeol *Post-Medieval Archaeology*

RCHM Royal Commission on the Historical Monuments (of England)

RN&ELHS Ruislip, Northwood and Eastcote Local History Society

S south

SAEC Southwark Archaeological Excavation Committee

SAFG Sutton Archaeological Field Group

SAM Scheduled Ancient Monument

SAS Surrey Archaeological Society

SEHHS Stanmore, Edgware and Harrow Historical Society

SLAEC Southwark and Lambeth Archaeological Excavation Committee

SLAS Southwark and Lambeth Archaeological Society

SMR Sites and Monuments Record

Surrey Archaeol Coll *Surrey Archaeological Collections*

Surrey Archaeol Soc Bull *Surrey Archaeological Society Bulletin*

SWLAU South-West London Archaeological Unit

SWLT South-West London Team

Trans London Middlesex Archaeol Soc *Transactions of the London and Middlesex Archaeological Society*

W west

WHS Wandsworth Historical Society

WLAFG West London Archaeological Field Group

WL&SAFG West London and Spelthorne Archaeological Field Groups

WLAU West London Archaeological Unit

WLT West London Team

World Archaeol *World Archaeology*

WRTBA Worcester Rescue Trust for British Archaeology

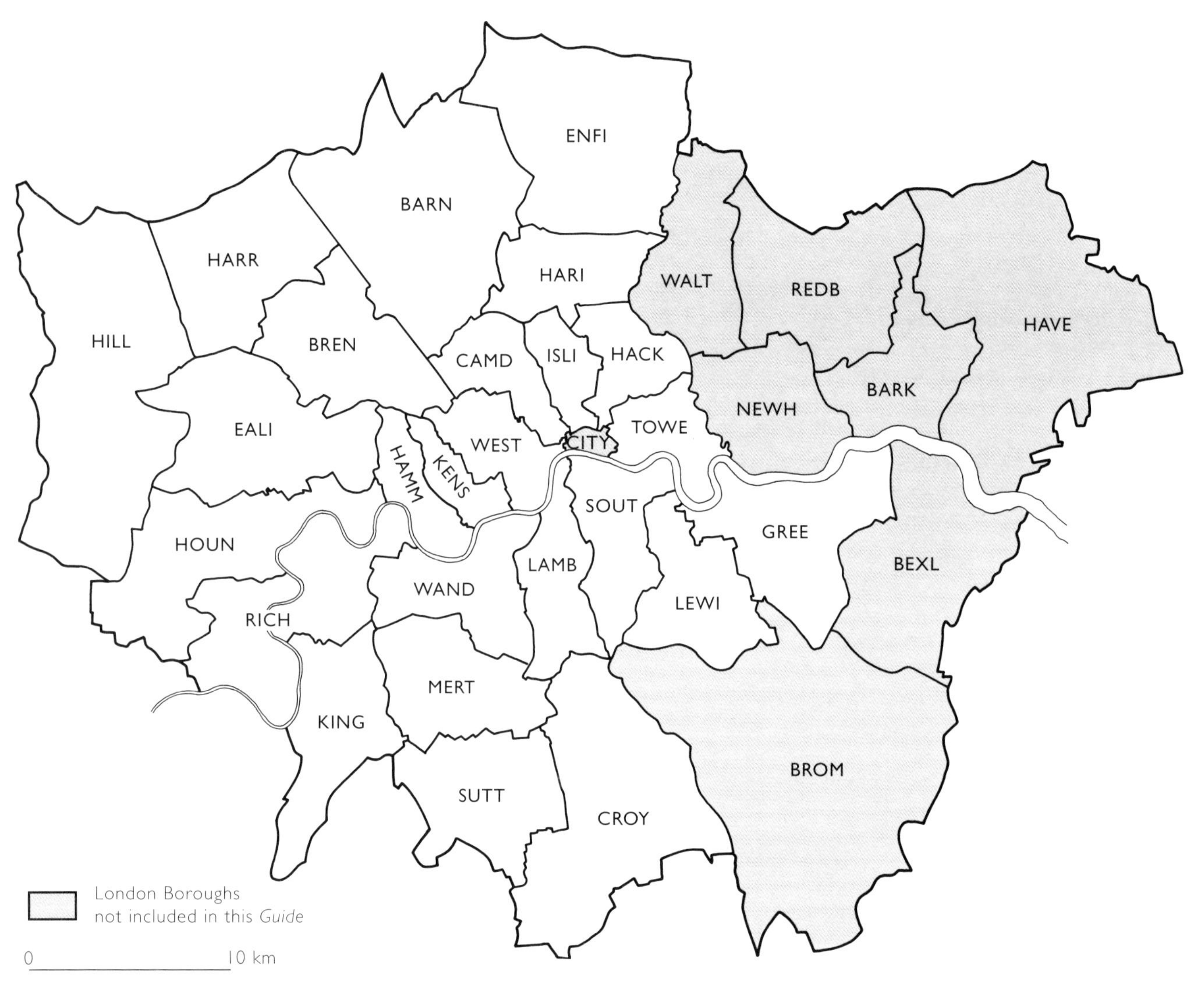

BARK	Barking	HACK	Hackney	LEWI	Lewisham
BARN	Barnet	HAMM	Hammersmith and Fulham	MERT	Merton
BEXL	Bexley	HARI	Haringey	NEWH	Newham
BREN	Brent	HARR	Harrow	REDB	Redbridge
BROM	Bromley	HAVE	Havering	RICH	Richmond upon Thames
CAMD	Camden	HILL	Hillingdon	SOUT	Southwark
CITY	City of London	HOUN	Hounslow	SUTT	Sutton
CROY	Croydon	ISLI	Islington	TOWE	Tower Hamlets
EALI	Ealing	KENS	Kensington and Chelsea	WALT	Waltham Forest
ENFI	Enfield	KING	Kingston upon Thames	WAND	Wandsworth
GREE	Greenwich	LAMB	Lambeth	WEST	Westminster

INTRODUCTION

This is a guide to most of the records of archaeological investigations conducted by the Museum of London's former Department of Greater London Archaeology (DGLA) and by some of its contemporary and predecessor organisations between 1965 and 1990 (and mainly from 1972 to 1990). By the latter date these organisations had investigated nearly 1,000 sites in 25 of the 33 modern London boroughs in Greater London. In this *Guide* archaeological sites are indexed by site code, by address or site name, and by location on maps of their respective boroughs; for many sites the results of fieldwork are summarised, and for certain sites a more detailed location plan is added.

This *Guide* excludes records derived from archaeological sites in several London boroughs not investigated by the DGLA. In some cases the Museum's archive nevertheless holds such records, most notably records of sites in the City of London (regarded for this purpose as another borough) excavated by the Museum's former Department of Urban Archaeology (DUA) and its predecessors. Essential information about most of these City sites is given in two companion guides to the present volume, one being *Archaeology in the City of London, 1907–1991: a guide to records of excavations by the Museum of London and its predecessors* (Schofield & Maloney 1998), and the other giving fuller details of the sites in the City investigated by W F Grimes between 1946 and 1972 (Shepherd 1998). The present *Guide* excludes the archaeological work of the Passmore Edwards Museum (later the Newham Museum Service) in five north-eastern London boroughs, and that of the Kent Archaeological Rescue Unit in four south-eastern boroughs.

A guide such as this can serve only as a preliminary introduction to the contents of the archaeological archive produced by the DGLA and its predecessors, with the purpose of aiding the understanding and use of that archive. This *Guide*, with its inevitable limitations of size and in geographical and temporal coverage, should not be regarded as anything like a thorough survey of the archaeology of London. It is one of several publications, funded by English Heritage, dealing with a specific backlog of unpublished archaeological information from Greater London. The results of some of the fieldwork described here are in the process of being assessed, analysed and published. For many sites, however, the statement of results contained in this volume may be the fullest form of publication they will receive, no further work being considered necessary at the present time.

How to use this *Guide*

All the contents of the Museum's archaeological archive are related to one or other particular site. An intending user of the archive therefore needs to know which site or sites are relevant to his or her enquiries.

In this *Guide* each site can be identified by means of various indexes. If possible, the location of each site is also shown on a map of the borough in which it is situated and a brief summary is given of its archaeological results. Two main indexes come directly after the Introduction, and thereafter the borough maps and summaries are arranged borough by borough.

Identifying sites

Sites are identified in the indexes and summaries by:

1 Address or site name

This *Guide* identifies almost 1,000 addresses or site names, but these do not always represent separate investigations or separate sites. Redevelopment — which occasions archaeological investigation — may go in fits and starts, with successive bouts of archaeological work on the same site covering different areas, and the address or name by which a site is called can sometimes vary: a site may be known for the duration of its development by an ephemeral name, or the name of a property may be changed after its redevelopment; numbers in street addresses may run with obscure logic along a street and, where properties are amalgamated, grouped numbers especially can cause confusion; and archaeologists may know a site by the name of only one of several adjacent streets (where the site entrance happened to be, for instance).

2 Site code

Fieldwork produces site records and also, usually, finds and environmental materials. Each investigation described in this *Guide* used a site code to identify its particular records, finds and environmental materials.

Site codes were created in several different ways by the several different constituent branches of the DGLA and their predecessor organisations, variously combining letters and numbers. Most site codes, however, have initial letters, or numbers and letters, that represent a location, and two final digits that represent the year in which fieldwork began, for example ELS83 or 199BHS74. Exceptionally, certain site codes consist of a serial number prefixed by letters representing a district or borough, with two year digits added, such as LAM203/78 or UX85vi. In the former case, LAM (for Lambeth) is abbreviated in this *Guide* to L. In the latter case (Uxbridge site code) the final Roman numerals, which would be converted to Arabic numerals for computer use, remain in their original form.

In this *Guide* site codes are listed, firstly, as far as possible in alphabetical order. Some site codes happen to share the same combination of letters but can be distinguished from each other by having different numbers. The latter site codes are therefore put, secondly, in numerical order relative to each other.

3 Map site number

This is a serial number applied to nearly every site within a particular borough, locating it on the respective borough map. A total of over 800 sites can be located with enough accuracy to place them on such a map. These numbers form a separate series running from 1 onwards in each borough, generally in order of site code, as explained above. An equivalent series of numbers, roughly in the order in which fieldwork took place, exists for DUA sites in the City of London (MoL 1987). These maps show major eastings and northings of the Ordnance Survey national grid.

For the purposes of this *Guide*, borough boundaries are taken to be as they were at the time of fieldwork. The boundaries of the City of London, in particular, which separated the areas covered by the DGLA and the DUA, were changed in 1994. Some sites now inside the City were not so at the time of fieldwork; they were therefore investigated by the DGLA, which explains their inclusion here. Conversely, a few sites now in boroughs adjoining the City are excluded from this *Guide* because at the time of fieldwork they were within the City, and therefore were investigated by the DUA.

4 Ordnance Survey (OS) national grid reference

This refers to the approximate centre of a site and is given, if possible, to eight figures. This allows a grid reference to be located on the national grid to the nearest 10m, independently of the maps in this *Guide*. For some sites it has not been possible, for the present, to determine a grid reference as precisely as this.

5 Sites and Monuments Record (SMR) number(s)

These are reference numbers allocated to sites included in the Greater London Sites and Monuments Record (GLSMR). The GLSMR is a computerised record of information relating to archaeological sites and historic (mainly listed) buildings in Greater London. It is now funded and managed by English Heritage and was compiled initially in co-operation with the Museum of London, Passmore Edwards Museum and the Royal Borough of Kingston upon Thames. The GLSMR is updated as information becomes available. Each entry contains a range of information including location of the site, find or building (both address and OS national grid reference), its date and original function, the statutory protection it may have, and bibliographical references. Each entry is identified by a six-digit number. Some sites have more than one entry, separately numbered and usually cross-referred. In this *Guide* consecutive numbers referring to a single site are run together. Enquiries concerning SMR information in London should be addressed directly to the Greater London Sites and Monuments Record, in the care of English Heritage.

Indexes

Besides the general index at the back of this volume, there are three indexes to the sites in this *Guide*. The first two indexes appear after this Introduction and are arranged as follows:

1 Site address (in alphabetical order of the first street name) > borough (name abbreviated to the first four letters) > map site number > site code > page number.
2 Site code (in alphabetical–numerical order explained above) > site address or name > borough > map site number.

The third form of index is divided borough by borough, and appears after each borough map, arranged as follows:

Map site number > site code > site address or name.

It should therefore be possible for a user of this *Guide* to find a site summary so long as some item of information is known about the site: its site code, its address or name, or the borough in which it lay. For example, to search for sites in a certain area, use a borough map or maps to identify relevant sites by their map site numbers, and use the index after the borough map to identify the corresponding site codes. Then look up the summaries under the appropriate site codes, borough by borough.

Site summaries

The summaries of results are arranged in order of site code (as explained above), for each borough separately. Note, however, that the results of some fieldwork may not have been summarised, especially if these results were negative or, alternatively, if they led to a more extensive investigation which is summarised. Each summary is preceded by a site code, site address or name and, if applicable, a map site number, OS grid reference, SMR number(s), the name of the organisation responsible for fieldwork, and the name(s) of person(s) in charge of fieldwork.

The names of site supervisors or directors in charge of fieldwork are reproduced here from the archived records and are correct to the best of the editors' knowledge. It is possible, however, that responsibility for supervising sites has been attributed to some people incorrectly, and not attributed to others as it should be, for which the editors apologise.

Summaries of archaeological results are written, ideally, in chronological order (or, at least they indicate briefly that results pertain to particular periods). In many cases these summaries were originally written, usually by the site supervisor or director, soon after fieldwork ended. Often these are the summaries in the annual round-up of excavated sites published in *London Archaeologist* (1973 to date). Where this has not been so, the summary will have been compiled from other sources, usually by one of the editors of this *Guide*. It cannot be emphasised too strongly that in the former cases, at least, it has not been possible to check the accuracy of these statements of results and the editors cannot take full responsibility for what these summaries do or do not say.

Usually a summary will include a few words describing how fieldwork was carried out, indicating the conditions under which records were made and their likely scope. The summaries use different terms to describe the conditions of fieldwork. Fieldwork took (and takes) basically three different forms: (1) preliminary work to test and evaluate the archaeological potential of a site (now usually called 'evaluation'; there may have been prior assessment of archaeological potential by documentary means and visual inspection only, which is now usually called 'assessment'); (2) controlled excavation in favourable conditions ('excavation'); and (3) recovery of archaeological information under less favourable conditions, during demolition and building works for example ('watching brief').

In this *Guide* the summaries use the following terms:

1   For evaluation: 'trial excavation', 'evaluation excavation', 'survey and excavation', 'archaeological survey', 'trial trenching', 'trial work', 'testpit survey', 'site assessment'.
2   Full-scale excavation is usually described as 'excavation', but it should be appreciated that limitations of funding and access, under rescue conditions, very rarely permitted anything approaching full-scale excavation under archaeologists' exclusive control.
3   For watching brief: 'observation', 'salvage work', 'site watching', 'emergency excavation', 'investigation', 'limited excavation'.

A bibliography of published works directly relevant to a site follows a summary. The editors have not been able to search for and check these references exhaustively, and must warn users of this *Guide* that these references may therefore not be correct and up to date. In any case, minor references to a site have not been sought.

For the more notable sites, at least, a site location plan also accompanies the summary. This shows the nearest streets and landmarks, such as railway lines and canals, as well as the limits of the site (shown hatched) and of any trenches and areas of excavation within it (shown solid). North is to the top in all these plans. While great efforts have been made to ensure the accuracy of these plans (as at the time of fieldwork), this is necessarily limited by the small scale of mapping and by the fact that, in many cases, no thorough post-excavation work has yet taken place, when such plans would be drawn and checked at a relatively large scale. The location plans in this *Guide* are therefore intended to be indicative rather than definitive.

One major item of information omitted from the summaries is the name of the sponsor or funder of particular pieces of fieldwork. The original records from which these summaries have been compiled contain the names of most, but not all, sponsors and funders (as do the SMR records and published summaries in journals). Although it would be very desirable to include these names in the summaries it would be extremely difficult to identify those at present unrecorded. In these circumstances, rather than name some and omit others invidiously, the editors think it best to thank here all sponsors and funders generally.

The archive

Principles

The Museum of London's archaeological archive contains stratigraphic site records, finds and environmental materials, and associated data, derived from many, although not all, recent archaeological sites in the London area. These 'site data' correspond to a 'site archive' in the terms of the Museum's own guidelines (MoL 1995), English Heritage specifications (English Heritage 1991), and the Cunliffe Report (CBA & DoE 1982), and to a 'Level II Archive' in the terms of the Frere Report (DoE 1975). It should be noted that, of course, it was the principles enunciated in the two latter documents that, in general, applied to the investigations referred to in this *Guide* at the time site records were made and archived.

At that time the site archive ('Level II') was to be augmented by 'archive reports', intended to contain the results of an initial and comprehensive interpretation of the site data. Such reports ('Level III') were too big and detailed to be published themselves; indeed, in an urban situation, their value was expected to be realised only cumulatively, as nearby or comparable sites were investigated in an order dictated by redevelopment. It was expected that only syntheses of information from one or more sites and at a high level of interpretation would be published in the normal way ('Level IV').

Such principles, in which research aims, fieldwork, archiving, interpretation and publication operated in a continual cycle, were suited to a single archaeological unit investigating a single historic town. Their successful application demanded, however, a level of systematisation and cohesion, not to mention funding, which the circumstances of the DGLA made it difficult, or impossible, to attain.

Site records

In the archive a site code is the key to all records, finds and environmental materials, and the contents of the archive are labelled, stored and catalogued by site code. Most of the information in this *Guide* comes, as mentioned, from stratigraphic site records. These are records made on site during fieldwork, recording the nature and layout of what is exposed and excavated. Most of these records consist of plans on film or paper, descriptions of units of stratigraphy ('contexts') written on preprinted paper sheets, on cards or in notebooks; drawings of sections and elevations on film or paper; other lists, notes and diagrams — especially diagrams ('matrices') of the stratigraphic sequence of contexts — on film or paper; and photographic contact prints. These records are to be distinguished from others, such as those recording the kinds and quantities of artefacts recovered and environmental materials sampled. Records may also be in electronic form; among records made on site these might include surveying data. This *Guide* does not attempt to show what kind of records may exist for any particular site; such information is, of course, indexed and available in the archive.

All DGLA site records are in the process of being copied on microfilm and copies deposited with the National Archaeological Record (NAR, formerly the National Monuments Record), administered by RCHME.

The Museum's archive may contain further documentation related to a site, additional to the site archive. Papers and digital data generated in the course of post-excavation work — notably 'archive reports', 'developer reports', the products of assessment and analysis, and drafts for publication — constitute a 'research archive'. These materials are indexed in the archive but are not referenced in this *Guide*.

Obviously it is important that anyone consulting the original records of a site should know what further work has been done with them. The Museum's archaeological records officers will normally be in a position to help. In this *Guide*, bibliographical information about published works that deal wholly or mainly with a site has been added to that site's summary. For the time being, this is probably the simplest way of keeping these summaries up to date.

Access

The Museum's archaeological archive is open to the public, researchers and students on weekdays, by appointment. Appointments can be made by applying to the Museum of London, London Wall, London EC2Y 5HN.

The facilities in the archive include a research room containing a photocopier, a microfiche reader-photocopier, and a limited library.

Records from certain sites may temporarily be with the Museum of London Archaeology Service (MoLAS), for assessment and analysis preparatory to publication.

Copyright in the contents of the archive, as a rule, is held by the Museum of London. The Museum's policy statement on copyright and intellectual property rights is available.

How sites were investigated and records made

The circumstances in which site records were produced naturally influence the form that such records take, and these circumstances therefore merit a brief description. The DGLA's dates of operation and territorial scope — and the dates and scope of its predecessors, which became the constituent parts of the DGLA — are here traced in very broad outline (see also Chitty *et al* 1985; Hinton, Haynes & Evans 1991).

The archaeology of London has naturally tended to be concentrated on its historic core, which lies largely within the modern boundaries of the City of London and immediately adjacent parts of the boroughs of Southwark, Tower Hamlets and Camden, as well as much of the City of Westminster. The Guildhall Museum was established in 1826 to serve the City's history; it was not until 1912 that the London Museum was founded to cater specifically for the history of the whole of the capital. The London Museum was from its inception a museum of social history and under directors such as Mortimer Wheeler and W F Grimes it also actively supported archaeology. The two museums were amalgamated in 1975 to form the present Museum of London and the history of these museums has been written by Francis Sheppard (1991).

The archaeology of the relatively vast area of London outside the City has always been heavily dependent on the energy and enthusiasm of the members of local historical and archaeological societies. The two principal societies are the oldest and have the widest geographical scope. The Surrey Archaeological Society (SAS) was founded in 1854, at a time when the county of Surrey embraced most of London south of the Thames, including Southwark. London north of the Thames was the province of the London and Middlesex Archaeological Society (LAMAS), inaugurated in 1855, when the now-defunct county of Middlesex comprised most of London to the west and north of the City, and the western boundary of the county of Essex was on the River Lea.

There was virtually no modern professional archaeological fieldwork in London outside the City before the end of the Second World War. Starting in 1945 SAS funded a three-year campaign of excavations on bombed sites in Southwark, under the direction of Kathleen Kenyon (Kenyon 1959). In 1962 SAS was a prime mover in establishing the Southwark Archaeological Excavation Committee (SAEC), with which LAMAS was also associated. In 1965 the Southwark and Lambeth Archaeological Society (SLAS) was set up, organising archaeological work in the boroughs jointly with SAEC (the latter becoming SLAEC after Lambeth began to sponsor fieldwork in 1975). The SLAEC's professional unit was formed under Harvey Sheldon, and managed in later years by Eric Ferretti, Michael Hammerson and Laura Schaaf.

In the early 1960s Roy Canham, Archaeological Field Officer at the London Museum, identified appreciable prehistoric and Roman remains at Brentford, in west London. The many volunteers who helped in Canham's excavations in Brentford formed in 1967 the West London Archaeological Field Group (WLAFG), also known as the West London Archaeological Unit (WLAU) or West London Team (WLT). This unit, managed at first by Canham and later by Alison Laws and Jon Cotton, functioned with the London Museum's support, and when the London Museum was absorbed into the Museum of London, WLAFG continued its relationship with the new museum. In 1974 Harvey Sheldon succeeded Canham as the London Museum's Archaeological Field Officer.

LAMAS set up an Inner London Archaeological Unit (ILAU) in 1974, initially covering the boroughs of Camden, Hackney, Hammersmith, Fulham, Islington, Kensington, Chelsea, Tower Hamlets and eventually Westminster. This unit was led at first by John Hinchcliffe, then by Graham Black and Irene Schwab, and later by David Whipp.

SAS set up a South-West London Archaeological Unit (SWLAU) or South-West London Team (SWLT), also in 1974, operating in Wandsworth, Merton, Kingston and Richmond, under the direction of Scott McCracken.

In these and other parts of London a number of relatively small archaeological societies were also active locally to varying degrees.

This was the situation until 1983. The Museum of London had taken over the Guildhall Museum's Department of Urban Archaeology (DUA), which had been operating in the City of London since 1973. In 1983 the Museum of London established a second archaeological department: the Department of Greater London Archaeology (DGLA), in effect an amalgamation of the four existing units described above, operating outside the City. Harvey Sheldon, who had become the Museum of London's Greater London Field Officer, was instrumental in setting up the DGLA and he directed it throughout its existence. At the same time the Greater London Council (GLC) set up the London Archaeological Service to provide for full-time archaeological coverage in all 32 London boroughs outside the City. This service provided establishment funds to the DGLA (covering 23 boroughs), the Passmore Edwards Museum (PEM), later Newham Museum Service (NMS), covering Barking and Dagenham, Havering, Newham, Redbridge and Waltham Forest, and the Kent Archaeological Rescue Unit (KARU), operating partly on an agency basis for the DGLA in Bexley, Bromley, Greenwich and Lewisham. After the abolition of the GLC in 1986 the establishment-funding of this service in Greater London was effected through English Heritage (itself established in 1983).

The DGLA encompassed, as mentioned, the four existing archaeological units: SLAEC, WLAU (or WLT), ILAU and SWLT. The WLAU became DGLA(W), covering Hammersmith and Fulham, Hillingdon, Hounslow, Ealing and Brent, with headquarters in Brentford. The ILAU became DGLA(N), with headquarters in Islington, and added to its geographical coverage the boroughs of Harrow, Barnet, Enfield and Haringey. SWLT, as DGLA(SW), with headquarters in Richmond, added to its coverage the boroughs of Sutton and Croydon. The work of the DGLA, like that of its predecessors, was closely connected with the membership and activities of local archaeological societies, and the names of societies that appear in this *Guide* will be found above (under Abbreviations).

With the exception of the West London Team, these units had been financed independently of the London Museum and its successor museum. They had operated very largely on their own, and this had naturally affected the selection of sites, the scope of fieldwork, the obtaining of funds, methods of making records and, not least, the archiving and the survival or accessibility of records. In an urban or suburban environment, theirs was generally 'rescue archaeology'; the opportunity, and need, for fieldwork arose nearly always as a consequence of commercial redevelopment, and archaeological operations were nearly always constrained by this fact. This fundamental constraint continued of course to condition the work of the DGLA.

In the 1980s, and especially in 1989–91 when a merger of the DGLA and the DUA was being planned, concerted efforts were made to standardise fieldwork methods and records. Field staff moved between units anyway, being exchanged between, for example, DGLA, DUA and Passmore Edwards Museum; this was not done for the express purpose of standardisation, but by 1991 that was undoubtedly an effect.

An economic recession that began in 1990 greatly slowed down redevelopment and forced the Museum's two archaeological departments to be severely reduced in size, with numerous lay-offs. The Museum of London Archaeology Service (MoLAS) came into existence at the end of 1991 as a self-financing organisation within the Museum of London, absorbing the DGLA, the DUA and the Greater London Environmental Archaeology Service.

Publishing the archaeological results and the origin of this *Guide*

In view of the rapid growth in the amount of archaeological work in Greater London from the early 1970s onwards and the limited extent of dependable core funding to the region's archaeological units, it is not surprising that the structures and techniques needed to deal effectively with the results of fieldwork evolved only gradually. As a result it was perhaps inevitable that the post-excavation processing and publication of results did not keep pace with excavation.

Summary results of the DGLA's fieldwork were customarily published in *London Archaeologist*, *Surrey Archaeological Collections* and *Transactions of the London and Middlesex Archaeological Society*, and then in the main period journals (*Britannia*, *Medieval Archaeology* and *Post-Medieval Archaeology*). Such summaries tended to be compiled without much attempt to attain, or rather success in attaining, systematic consistency of terminology, coverage, level of detail and so on. A gazetteer of sites in Southwark and Lambeth was published in 1988 (Swain). Results of archaeological investigations and research have, of course, been published more fully and in more detail, as will be evident from the bibliographical lists after the relevant summaries in this *Guide*.

A brief survey of the DGLA's work was published in 1990, unfortunately without a bibliography (Blackmore, Cotton & Sheldon). Published thematic surveys included Roman sites in Greater London (Sheldon & Schaaf 1978). The main scholarly publications of work in Southwark and Lambeth are Sheldon (1974), Bird *et al* (1978) and Hinton (1988). Numerous articles on results of archaeological work in other boroughs have been published in *London Archaeologist*, as well as in the societies' journals and the period journals mentioned above.

In 1990, thanks to English Heritage funding, it was possible to take stock of the discoveries to date. The archive of written, drawn and photographic records and of artefacts and environmental samples derived from this work was rich and extremely large. A preliminary survey at this time indicated that there were records from some 1,000 excavations and watching briefs, and an estimated 150 metric tons of finds and environmental samples. It was also apparent that the amount of attention given to both site records and excavated material had varied considerably from site to site; although post-excavation work was routinely undertaken on site records and excavated material, resources were seldom enough to produce a well-ordered, secure and accessible archive. The unpublished data included material of high scholarly importance, sometimes in great quantity.

In 1990, at a time of recession and severe contraction of the DGLA, several publication projects that were in progress had to be suspended. It was evident that, in addition to the material in these projects, there was a very large backlog of other post-excavation work and publication that derived from the work of the DGLA and its predecessors. In 1990, however, English Heritage approved and began to fund a concerted programme that would permit this mass of archival material to be rationalised, completed to a minimum standard and systematically put in order, with a view to selective publication, a programme described in more detail by Hinton and Thomas (1998). The approach to this task applied, and indeed tested, the principles of *Management of archaeological projects* (frequently called 'MAP2': English Heritage 1991). The latter document was written while the Greater London publication programme was being formulated, and drew on that experience.

It was clear from the outset of the Greater London publication programme that the resources available would not be enough to publish in full the results of all interventions, even if this were desirable. The approach adopted was therefore to try and ensure that the limited resources were applied to best effect. The programme had the following objectives and products:

1   Compile an elementary database of basic information about all fieldwork and order the resulting archives, making these both secure and accessible.
2   Publish this archive guide as a reference to almost every piece of fieldwork, enabling future researchers to identify material of potential interest. Compilation of the *Guide* naturally created an opportunity to assess the quality and quantity of the data recovered from individual sites, and appraise the scholarly value of these data; priorities could be determined, and the extent of more detailed analysis and publication decided. Of the 1,000 or so interventions, some 700 were felt not to be worth further study beyond a basic ordering of their archives and the summary publication of their results in the present volume.
3   Assess, analyse and publish the results of the most important data in an academically coherent manner. The remaining 300 interventions were grouped together to form 65 analysis and publication projects, based on research themes. Thus, any one publication project could draw on the results of a number of different interventions, and the results from any one of these interventions could contribute to a number of different thematic publication projects.
4   Evolve better and more cost-effective methods for completing archives, assessing their potential for further research, and publishing the results of that research.

This *Guide* itself is modelled in part on the examples of the *DUA archive catalogue* (MoL 1987) and the City of Lincoln Archaeological Unit's archive guide (Vince & Jones 1990). The present guide is one of the first of these Greater London backlog publications. The Greater London publication programme seeks to produce some two dozen monographs and 19 major journal articles; two are already published (Brigham *et al* 1995; Thomas, Sloane & Phillpotts 1997) and the others are either nearing publication or are well advanced.

This *Guide* stops with sites investigated in 1990, a limit set by the start of the English Heritage-funded backlog publication programme, the DGLA continuing until its absorption into MoLAS in 1991.

The creation of such a large archive of material, permitting the development of a very ambitious publication programme, is a tribute to the many paid and unpaid excavators, site supervisors, finds processors and specialists, environmental archaeologists, illustrators, photographers and documentary researchers who worked with or for the DGLA and its predecessors between 1965 and 1990. That resources were forthcoming to recover the archaeological material, and to begin work on analysing and publishing it, is largely thanks to the vision and tenacity of Harvey Sheldon and his management team, who have been named above. This team was supported in its project management by Planning and Negotiation Officers and Deputy Area Officers: Dave Beard, Carrie Cowan, George Dennis, Robin Densem, John Dillon, Duncan Hawkins, Steve Haynes, Mike Hutchinson, John Mills, Peter Mills, Eric Norton, Derek Seeley, Ken Whittaker and Rob Whytehead. Post-excavation in DGLA was managed by Scott McCracken assisted by Peter Hinton, Lyn Blackmore and Hedley Swain. For MoLAS, Peter Hinton, with John Schofield's assistance, supervised implementation of the publication programme; Dick Malt, Derek Seeley and Andrew Westman managed individual projects; Hedley Swain oversaw finds work, and James Rackham and Jane Sidell oversaw environmental archaeology; Andy Chopping was responsible for photography, and Alison Hawkins, Anne Jenner and Tracy Wellman were responsible for graphics and illustrations. Gill Andrews, Ellen Barnes, Brian Kerr, Quita Mould, Roger Thomas and Tim Williams gave advice or monitored the programme for English Heritage.

The archaeological value of the evidence in the archive

The historic core of London comprises the modern City of London, the nearest parts of Southwark, Tower Hamlets and Camden, and much of Westminster. The City and the northern part of Southwark contain the site of the Roman town of Londinium, on both sides of the River Thames: the 'first London'. Westminster contains, firstly, the site of the Middle Saxon settlement of *Lundenwic* on the north bank of the River Thames upstream of the Roman town, constituting the 'second London', the existence of which was proved by the DGLA in the 1980s; secondly, the Late Saxon and medieval royal palace and abbey established on Thorney Island, further up the river; thirdly, medieval suburbs and the earliest post-medieval expansion outwards from the City, the last phenomenon constituting the 'fourth London' (the 'third London' in this highly simplified chronology being the early medieval reoccupation of the walled site of the Roman town).

The distribution of sites in this volume reflects the location of archaeological activity, which in turn was substantially dictated by the pattern of modern redevelopment. There are concentrations in Southwark, on the borders of the City and in the gravel extraction areas of west London. The sites have allowed the development of an archaeology of Greater London from late glacial to post-medieval date, with important discoveries in every period.

Prehistoric

Prehistoric activity is widely attested in the archive, particularly on the gravel terraces in the middle and upper Thames valleys. Perhaps the most interesting discoveries have been in west London. There have been records of Palaeolithic finds since the 19th century; and excavations by the ILAU at Northwold Road, Stoke Newington, and by the DGLA at Creffield Road, Acton, have re-examined two prolific sites. One of the most significant sites is at Three Ways Wharf, Uxbridge (Hillingdon: UX86viii, UX88viii), where excavation revealed an undisturbed sequence of sediments in which about 10,000 flint artefacts and associated faunal remains were found *in situ*. One scatter of material produced horse bones radio-carbon-dated to 10,270 ± 100 BP and 10,010 ± 120 BP, and another a piece of burnt flint dated by thermoluminescence to 8000 ± 800 BP. Approximately 2,800 environmental and debitage samples were recovered from these and other scatters, study of which has permitted the study of the dating and character of the late Devensian/early Flandrian transition. Spatial analysis of flint and bone fragments, coupled with flint refitting, has led to the identification of a number of activity areas. A similar but less well-preserved site was discovered in the Old Kent Road in 1990 (Southwark: BAQ90).

The wealth of excavations has allowed archaeologists, for the first time, to build up a picture of the developing landscape of west London. The sites in the archive have much to tell of the settlement, economy and environment on the Thames gravels in the prehistoric, Roman and Saxon periods. Of particular importance is the emergence of evidence for a ritual Late Neolithic/Early Bronze Age occupation, indicated by a hengiform monument, a cursus, apparently ritual deposits of Peterborough and Grooved ware, and the site of an aurochs 'kill' (Hillingdon: HL87). There is evidence for settlement, land division and agriculture in the Middle and Late Bronze Age and in the Iron Age.

Southwark and Lambeth have also produced copious evidence for prehistoric settlement in the lower Thames Valley. Discoveries include a Bronze Age ring ditch containing a cremation burial (Southwark: FW84), a Bronze Age 'burnt mound' of flints and a rectangular pit thought to be associated with food preparation or ritual bathing, and ard-plough marks indicating Bronze Age agriculture (Southwark: PHW88). Round-houses and an apparent inhumation of Iron Age date have been found (Southwark: CO87, CO88, 124BHS77).

Roman (AD50–410)

A large proportion of the sites in the archive contain information about Roman London and its environs (outside the modern City of London), our understanding of which has changed almost beyond recognition since the 1960s. Perhaps the greatest wealth of information comes from Southwark. Here excavations have revealed an important area of Roman London built on islands and reclaimed land in the marshy area to the south of the Thames, at the easternmost point at which the river could be bridged. The town contained a wide variety of public, domestic, industrial and dockside buildings, including an exceptionally well-preserved timber building or warehouse (CO88), a high-status, possibly public or military, building (WP83: Stave and Rosing's Wharves), and a likely *mansio* (15SKS80). There is also evidence for a possible shrine or mausoleum (SCC77). Timber waterfronts marked the edges of channels running through the settlement and associated wharves. The archive now contains enough data to analyse the changing topography and environment of the settlement in Southwark and to explore its economic and political relationship with the rest of the town on the opposite bank of the Thames.

Excavations in Southwark have also uncovered a large cemetery area, but the best evidence for funerary activity — and the human population of Roman London — comes from the Roman cemetery to the east of Londinium (Tower Hamlets: MSL87, HOO86, HOO88, etc). Here over 800 inhumations and cremations spanning the 1st to 5th centuries AD have been recorded on a total of 12 separate excavations.

Further from the centre, several roadside settlements have been excavated, for example in Bow (Tower Hamlets: ROM80, etc), close to where the Roman road between London and Colchester crossed the River Lea, and from Kingston (EDE89), which developed into an important medieval royal town. A Roman villa, overlying an Iron Age settlement, has been excavated at Beddington (Sutton: BSF81, BSF82). The prehistoric sites in Hillingdon (eg HL87) also gave evidence of early Roman rural prosperity, followed by a possible relative decline in fortune in the 2nd century, succeeded in turn by renewed prosperity late in the Roman period.

Saxon (AD410–1100)

Few Early Saxon settlements have been found, apart from in Hammersmith (HAM90) and, possibly, Lambeth (L448/80).

When the DGLA was set up, the location of the Middle Saxon settlement and trading port of *Lundenwic* was unknown, though there was much debate about it in the 1970s and early 1980s (Vince 1984; Biddle 1984). In the mid-1980s conclusive archaeological evidence for the settlement was discovered in Covent Garden (Westminster: JUB85), and since then a large and valuable archive of records and material has been accumulated, permitting study of the size, development economy and infrastructure of the settlement. Other possible Middle Saxon occupation has been located in Battersea (Wandsworth: AG75).

Excavations have also produced an Early to Middle Saxon settlement near Harmondsworth (eg HL82, MFH87, MFH88 and MFH89).

Medieval (1100–1500)

In the medieval period London's population growth from 1100 onwards was checked only temporarily by the Black Death in 1348–9; the City recovered as a flourishing trading centre in the later 14th century. Evidence for London's changing fortunes and social needs can be found in the many monuments founded and expanded during the medieval period, of which the religious houses are a striking example. Six excavated houses lay just outside the City: the Priory and Hospital of St Mary Spital, Bishopsgate (Tower Hamlets: NRF88); the Nunnery of St Mary de fonte, Clerkenwell (Islington: NEW81, etc), the London Charterhouse (Islington: GSW90, MED89, etc), the Convent of the Minoresses of St Clare (eg Tower Hamlets: HAY86), St Mary Graces, from which a substantial assemblage of skeletal material has been recovered from a Black Death cemetery (Tower Hamlets: MIN86, etc), and the Priory of the Order of St John of Jerusalem, Clerkenwell (Islington: ALB89, etc). Further afield lay Westminster Abbey and two establishments that were extensively excavated and produced important assemblages of human skeletal remains: Bermondsey Abbey (Southwark: BA84) and the Priory of St Mary, Merton (MPY). These sites have produced a massive archive of information, unique in Europe, with which to study the development, economy, function and environment of religious institutions in the medieval city and its hinterland.

The archive includes records from excavations in and around the standing Great Barn at Manor Farm, Harmondsworth (MFH87, MFH88 and MFH89), as well as of a non-conventual priory founded on the site in the late 11th/early 12th century. A series of excavations further up the Colne Valley sought to unravel the origins and subsequent development of the medieval market town of Uxbridge, on the main road between London and Oxford (eg UX83iv, UX88viii and UX88ix).

The archive of excavation data includes information on several medieval royal, aristocratic and episcopal residences on the south bank of the Thames. They include parts of the Tower of London (Tower Hamlets: TOL79), the palace of the bishops of Winchester in Southwark and its associated waterfronts (WIN85, the WP83 sites and WP84). There are excavation records, too, from Edward II's 14th-century house in Southwark, known as 'The Rosary' (GAS88, MOR86, MOR87, MOR88, SYM88), and the adjacent residence of Sir John Fastolf (the inspiration for Shakespeare's Falstaff), built in the mid-15th century (BFN88, BFS88, BTH88, MOR86, MOR87, MOR88). These sites produced evidence for the earlier topography and development of the south bank of the Thames, and the history and functioning of the house and its estate, its mills and water management, and subsequent industrial use. An excavation downstream at Rotherhithe revealed the 14th-century moated residence of Edward III, converted in the 17th century into a tin-glaze-ware factory (Southwark: PW86, PW89, PW90).

Two medieval Thames bridges have been excavated. From Southwark there are records and material from the southern abutment of the celebrated 12th-century London Bridge, and from Kingston upon Thames from the excavation of Kingston Bridge (HOR86).

The archive is a valuable resource for the study of London's industries, particularly the manufacture of ceramics. There is a large assemblage of Roman tile waste from Canons Park, Edgware (Harrow: CPE79, CPK88). Medieval wasters have been found in great quantity from a 13th-century South Hertfordshire grey-ware kiln at Potter Street Hill, Pinner (Harrow: PIN75) and from a mid-14th-century Whiteware kiln at Bankside (Southwark: BKS81, BS81).

Post-medieval (1500–1900)

There is copious information, including a massive amount of artefactual data, relating to London's industrial production in the post-medieval period. Once again ceramics are well represented, especially tin-glaze ware, often referred to as delftware. This pottery was first produced in England in 1567 at Norwich, and in London in 1571 at Aldgate, by refugee potters from Antwerp. During the 17th, 18th and 19th centuries, 19 tin-glaze potteries were established on the south bank of the Thames, and the archive contains evidence either for structures or for products of 12 of these sites. Excavations at the Limehouse porcelain factory (1744–6) have produced many forms not previously recognised as being Limehouse porcelain (Tower Hamlets: LLK89). Other excavated industries include stoneware, clay pipe and glass manufacture, tanning, clothmaking and brushmaking.

Very small portions of two Shakespearean theatres, the Globe and the Rose, have been excavated on Bankside, Southwark (ACT89, SBH88). Details of theatre design in this period are not adequately covered by documentary evidence, and the archive contains information of importance to archaeologists, theatre historians and actors.

The DGLA has recorded archaeologically a number of standing buildings, an approach complementing that of the well-known and invaluable Survey of London, begun in 1894 and now carried out by the Royal Commission on the Historical Monuments of England (RCHM) (Hobhouse 1994).

The future

The Museum of London's archaeological archive is expected to receive additions continually, from MoLAS, the successor to the DGLA, and from other bodies. Standards are set for admitting material so that it can be safely stored and, above all, efficiently used. These standards are documented in published guidelines (MoL 1998) and a fieldwork manual (MoL 1994).

This guidance does not simply endorse 'best practice'; standardisation, consistency and uniformity are required in certain essential matters in order to understand archaeological information from London as well as to archive material efficiently. Indeed, it might be said that as the understanding and integration of data have increased, so also have the advantages of standardisation become more appreciated (or its previous absence has come to be felt more painfully).

For example, how well are sites located? Post-excavation assessment and analysis of multi-period sites in a densely occupied urban environment require that individual sites be located with great accuracy, independently of the present-day street layout and building-lines. Experience shows that even among small clusters of sites in distinct localities this fundamental need could, in the past, be neglected; smaller pieces of fieldwork and casual observations may not have been located at all accurately.

How well are the results of fieldwork summarised, indexed and disseminated? This *Guide*, and other work now being undertaken in the Museum's archive, represent perhaps the first attempts to undertake these tasks systematically and comprehensively, surely a *sine qua non* of a cumulative urban archaeological archive.

This *Guide* is a portable, 'hard copy' version of an electronic database of site information. This information is being continually updated (so that in some respects this *Guide* must already be out of date), and in future will be available to be searched and read electronically. No new hard-copy edition of this *Guide*, as such, is therefore anticipated, although there might be a supplement to bring this *Guide* up to 1991, at least, and the end of the DGLA as a separate unit (as well as to correct mistakes).

An important corollary of such greater accessibility is worth emphasising here, that the value of easier searching and reading depends crucially on the systematic collection, summarising and indexing of data in the first place. The combination of relatively simple data about sites and graphical information locating these sites would seem to lend itself admirably to a simple form of geographical information system (GIS).

The apparent omission of a summary, a site code or indeed a site from this *Guide* may mean that the site records have not been archived, and their present whereabouts are unknown. Most of the summaries in this *Guide* were originally written for the annual excavation round-up in *London Archaeologist*, a local, privately run periodical, starting with the round-up for 1972, appearing in 1973. It may be imagined what the task of compiling this *Guide* would have been had these summaries not existed.

In compiling a guide such as this, there is always the possibility of unwittingly perpetrating or perpetuating errors: determining the same item of information more than once, each time with a different result (OS grid references, for example); 'hyper-correction' (something may appear anomalous, and be corrected, when in fact it is true); and the simple repetition of information without the opportunity to check it systematically and thoroughly. The editors apologise for all such errors and omissions, and would like readers to bring instances to the Museum archaeological records officers' attention.

References

Anon, 1972 'List of local societies', *London Archaeol*, 1, 15, 356–7

Biddle, M, 1984 'London on the Strand', *Popular Archaeol*, 6, No. 1, 23–7

Bird, J, Graham, A H, Sheldon, H L, & Townend, P (eds) [SLAEC], 1978 *Southwark excavations 1972–74*, London Middlesex Archaeol Soc & Surrey Archaeol Soc joint publication 1

Blackmore, L, Cotton, J, & Sheldon, H L, 1990 *Recent archaeological excavations in Greater London: the work of the department of Greater London Archaeology* (MoL Annual Archaeology Lecture 1986)

Brigham, T, Goodburn, D, & Tyers, I, with Dillon, J, 1995 'A Roman timber building on the Southwark waterfront, London', *Archaeol J*, 152, 1–72

CBA & DoE 1982 *The publication of archaeological excavations* (Council for British Archaeology and Department of Environment: the 'Cunliffe Report')

Chitty, G, Clubb, N, Greenwood, P, Hammerson, M, Mills, J, Mills, P, Orton, C, & Sheldon, H, 1985 'Greater London's rescue archaeology service: a *Rescue News* special report', *Rescue News*, 37, supplement

DoE, 1975 *Principles of publication in rescue archaeology* (Department of Environment: the 'Frere Report')

DoE, 1990 *Planning policy guidance 16: archaeology and planning* (London HMSO: 'PPG16')

English Heritage, 1991 *The management of archaeological projects*, 2nd edn: 'MAP2'

Hinton, P (ed), 1988 *Excavations in Southwark 1973–76, Lambeth 1973–79*, London Middlesex Archaeol Soc & Surrey Archaeol Soc joint publication 3

Hinton, P, & Thomas, R, 1998 'The Greater London publication programme', *Archaeol J*, (1997) 154, 196–213

Hinton, P, Haynes, S, & Evans, G, 1991 'The Department of Greater London Archaeology: a self-portrait', *Current Archaeol*, 124, 163–4

Hobhouse, H, 1994 *London survey'd: a history of the Survey of London 1894–1994* (RCHM)

Kenyon, K M, 1959 *Excavations in Southwark*, Surrey Archaeol Soc Res Pap 5

MoL, 1987 *DUA archive catalogue*

MoL, 1994 *Archaeological site manual*, 3rd edn

MoL, 1998. *General standards for the preparation of archaeological archives deposited with the Museum of London*

Schofield, J, with Maloney, C (eds), 1998 *Archaeology in the City of London, 1907–1991: a guide to records of excavations by the Museum of London and its predecessors*

Sheldon, H L, 1974 'Excavations at Toppings and Sun Wharves, Southwark, 1970–1972' *Trans London Middlesex Archaeol Soc*, 25, 1–116

Sheldon, H L, & Schaaf, L, 1978 'A survey of Roman sites in Greater London', in Bird, J, Chapman, H, & Clark, J (eds), *Collectanea Londiniensia: studies presented to Ralph Merrifield*, London Middlesex Archaeol Soc Spec Pap 2, 59–88

Shepherd, J (ed), 1998 *Post-War archaeology in the City of London, 1946–1972: a guide to records of excavations by Professor W F Grimes held by the Museum of London*

Sheppard, F, 1991 *The treasury of London's past*

Swain, H, 1988 'Gazetteer of sites', in Hinton, P, 479–88

Thomas, C, Sloane, B, & Phillpotts, C, 1997 *Excavations at the Priory and Hospital of St Mary Spital, London*, MoLAS monograph 1

Vince, A G, 1984 'The Aldwych: Mid-Saxon London discovered', *Current Archaeol*, 98, 310–12

Vince, A G, & Jones, M J, 1990 *Lincoln's buried archaeological heritage: a guide to the archive of the City of Lincoln Archaeological Unit*

Citation and copyright

This *Guide* may be cited and listed bibliographically as: Thompson, A, Westman, A, & Dyson, T (eds), 1998 *Archaeology in Greater London, 1965–1990: a guide to records of excavations by the Museum of London.*

Copyright: © Museum of London 1998

INDEX OF SITE CODES

site code	site name/address	borough	map site number
105GRA77	105–106 Grange Rd, SE1	SOUT	1
106BHS73	106–114 Borough High St, SE1	SOUT	2
107BHS81	107–115 Borough High St, SE1	SOUT	3
109BR87	109–115 Blackfriars Rd, SE1	SOUT	4
10SS81	10–16 Southwark St, SE1	SOUT	5
11STS77	11–19 St Thomas St, SE1	SOUT	6
120BHS89	120–124 Borough High St, SE1	SOUT	7
124BHS77	124–126 Borough High St, SE1	SOUT	8
128BHS74	128–132 Borough High St, SE1	SOUT	10
128SS76	128–130 Southwark St, SE1	SOUT	9
134BHS72	134–138 Borough High St, SE1	SOUT	11
15SKS80	15–23 Southwark St (Calverts Buildings), SE1	SOUT	13
154US82	154 Union St (railway arch), SE1	SOUT	12
169BHS74	169B Borough High St, SE1	SOUT	14
170BHS79	170–194 Borough High St, SE1	SOUT	15
170GRA89	170–176 Grange Rd, SE1	SOUT	16
175BHS76	175–177 Borough High St, SE1	SOUT	17
175LL81	175–177 Long Lane, Weston St, SE1	SOUT	18
179BHS89	179–191 Borough High St, SE1	SOUT	19
179SBR80	179 Southwark Bridge Rd, SE1	SOUT	20
180LL80	180–196 Long Lane, SE1	SOUT	21
199BHS74	199 Borough High St, SE1	SOUT	22
1STS74	1–7 St Thomas St, SE1	SOUT	23
201BHS75	201–205 Borough High St, SE1	SOUT	24
207BHS72	207–211 Borough High St, SE1	SOUT	25
209BHS69	209–215 High St, Brentford, TW8	HOUN	1
20LBS75	20–26 London Bridge St, SE1	SOUT	26
210BHS90	210–212 Borough High St, SE1	SOUT	27
213BHS77	213 Borough High St, SE1	SOUT	28
218BHS79	218–224 Borough High St, SE1	SOUT	29
223BHS68	219–223 High St, Brentford, TW8	HOUN	2
223BHS81	223–237 Borough High St, SE1	SOUT	30
22BHS88	22 Borough High St, SE1	SOUT	31
235US80	235–241 Union St, SE1	SOUT	32
239BHS87	239 Borough High St, SE1	SOUT	33
244BHS65	244–246 Borough High St, SE1	SOUT	34
245BR87	245 Blackfriars Rd, SE1	SOUT	35
289BHS90	289–299 Borough High St, SE1	SOUT	36
28PS84	28 Park St, SE1	SOUT	37
2SSBS85	2 Southwark St, 1A Bedale St, SE1	SOUT	38
30SLR89	30–60 South Lambeth Rd, SW8	LAMB	1
37BS87	37–46 Bankside, SE1	SOUT	39
38ALB89	38–46 Albert Embankment, SE1	LAMB	2
38BHS79	38 Borough High St, SE1	SOUT	40
38SBR79	38–42 Southwark Bridge Rd, SE1	SOUT	41
42BS86	42–44 Bermondsey St, SE1	SOUT	42
44TS86	44–46 Tooley St, SE1	SOUT	43
48SS89	48 Southwark St, SE1	SOUT	44
4STS82	4–26 St Thomas St, SE1	SOUT	45
52SOS89	52–54 Southwark St, SE1	SOUT	46
57BHS82	57 Borough High St (shaft outside), SE1	SOUT	47
5BS87	5–15 Bankside, SE1	SOUT	48
5SS73	5–7 Southwark St, SE1	SOUT	49
60STS82	60–68 St Thomas St, SE1	SOUT	50
64BHS74	64–70 Borough High St, SE1	SOUT	51
64SS74	64 Southwark St, SE1	SOUT	52
66BHS75	66 Borough High St, SE1	SOUT	53
684OKR86	684–698 Old Kent Rd, SE15	SOUT	54
6MSRD88	6–8 Marshalsea Rd, SE1	SOUT	55
78BHS73	78–80 Borough High St, SE1	SOUT	56
806OKR82	806–814 Old Kent Rd, SE15	SOUT	57
84BHS74	84–86 Borough High St, SE1	SOUT	58
85BHS90	85–87 Borough High St, SE1	SOUT	59
88BHS74	88 Borough High St, SE1	SOUT	60
89BHS75	89 Borough High St, SE1	SOUT	61
8US74	8–10 Union St, SE1	SOUT	62
92BHS74	92–104 Borough High St, SE1	SOUT	63
93BHS74	93–95 Borough High St, SE1	SOUT	64
93LR84	87–100 London Rd, SE1	SOUT	65
96BHS74	96–104 Borough High St, SE1	SOUT	66
97BHS74	97–99 Borough High St, SE1	SOUT	67
99SBR78	99–103 Southwark Bridge Rd, SE1	SOUT	68
AB78	Arcadia Buildings, Silvester St, Great Dover St, SE1	SOUT	69
ABB86	Abbots Lane, Tooley St, SE1	SOUT	70
ABB87	Abbots Lane, Tooley St, SE1	SOUT	71
ABB88	Abbots Lane, Tooley St, SE1	SOUT	72
ABST85	Anchor Brewhouse, Shad Thames (Mill House), SE1	SOUT	73
ACT89	Park St (Anchor Terrace car park), SE1	SOUT	74
ADB89	Aldenham Bus Overhaul Works, Watford-By-Pass, Elstree Hill South, Elstree, HA7	HARR	1
AG75	Althorpe Grove, Westbridge Rd, SW11	WAND	1
AGA81	49–51 Avenue Gardens, W3	EALI	1
AGA85	36 Avenue Gardens, W3	EALI	2
AGH90	72A Armagh Rd, 91–93 Parnell Rd, E3	TOWE	1
AKW90	Athelstan Rd, Kingston, KT1	KING	1
ALA88	19 Albert Embankment, SE1	LAMB	3
ALB89	2 Albemarle Way, EC1	ISLI	1
ALS88	28 Alie St, E1	TOWE	2
AP72	Angel Place, 207 Borough High St, SE1	SOUT	75
ARL76	37–39 Artillery Lane, E1	TOWE	3
ART76	27–33 Artillery Lane, E1	TOWE	4
ASC89	Churchfield Rd (Acton Shopping Centre), W3	EALI	3
ASH87	24 Alie St, E1	TOWE	5
ASS90	159–173 St John St, 8–15 Aylesbury St, EC1	ISLI	2
ASY75	Asylum Rd, SE15	SOUT	76
ATW89	Atwood Primary School, Limpsfield Rd, Sanderstead, South Croydon, CR2	CROY	1
ATW90	Atwood Primary School, Limpsfield Rd, Sanderstead, South Croydon, CR2	CROY	2
AW89	Alaska Works, Grange Rd, SE1	SOUT	77
AYL90	Aylands Allotments, Aylands Rd, Enfield, EN3	ENFI	1
BA76	38 Burleigh Avenue, Wallington, SM6	SUTT	1
BA84	Bermondsey Abbey, Abbey Buildings, Long Walk, SE1	SOUT	78
BAD89	Badger Yard, 12–13 St John's Square, EC1	ISLI	3
BAD90	6–9 Briset St, 12–13 St John's Square, EC1	ISLI	4
BAG89	1–6 Barge House St, SE1	SOUT	79
BAQ90	Old Kent Rd, Bowles Rd (B and Q Depot), SE1	SOUT	80
BAR76	14 Barter St, WC1	CAMD	1
BCL88	95–105 Back Church Lane, E1	TOWE	6
BCRE79	Bulls Cross Ride, Enfield, EN2	ENFI	2
BCS84	Copthall Field Sports Centre, Great North Way, NW4	BARN	1
BDF89	21–26 Bedford St (Moss Bros site), WC2	WEST	1
BDL89	Bedlesford, 1 Wheatfield Way, Kingston, KT1	KING	2
BDPS84	Bank End, Park St, SE1	SOUT	81
BDS89	39–40 Bedford St (outside), WC2	WEST	2
BED88	36 Beddington Lane (Ariston Alloys), CR0	SUTT	2
BEF89	Battersea Wharf, Queenstown Rd, SW8	WAND	2
BEN87	Bentall's Redevelopment, Wood St, Kingston, KT1	KING	3
BEN88	Bentall's Redevelopment, Wood St, Kingston, KT1	KING	4
BEN90	Bentall's Department Store, West St, Fife Rd, Clarence St, Kingston, KT1	KING	5
BER88	39–45 Bermondsey St, SE1	SOUT	82
BER90	100–104 Bermondsey St, SE1	SOUT	83
BEV79	42 Bevenden St (opposite), N1	HACK	1
BEV90	Bradbank Sports Ground, Beverley Way, New Malden, KT3	MERT	1
BFD88	20–22 Bedfordbury, WC2	WEST	3
BFN88	Butter Factory (north), Tooley St, SE1	SOUT	84
BFR86	Bury Farm, 123 Bury St, Ruislip, HA4	HILL	1
BFS88	Butter Factory (south), Tooley St, SE1	SOUT	85
BGR88	103 Stockwell Rd, Broomgrove Rd, SW9	LAMB	4
BHM88	12 Buckingham St, WC2	WEST	4

BARNET

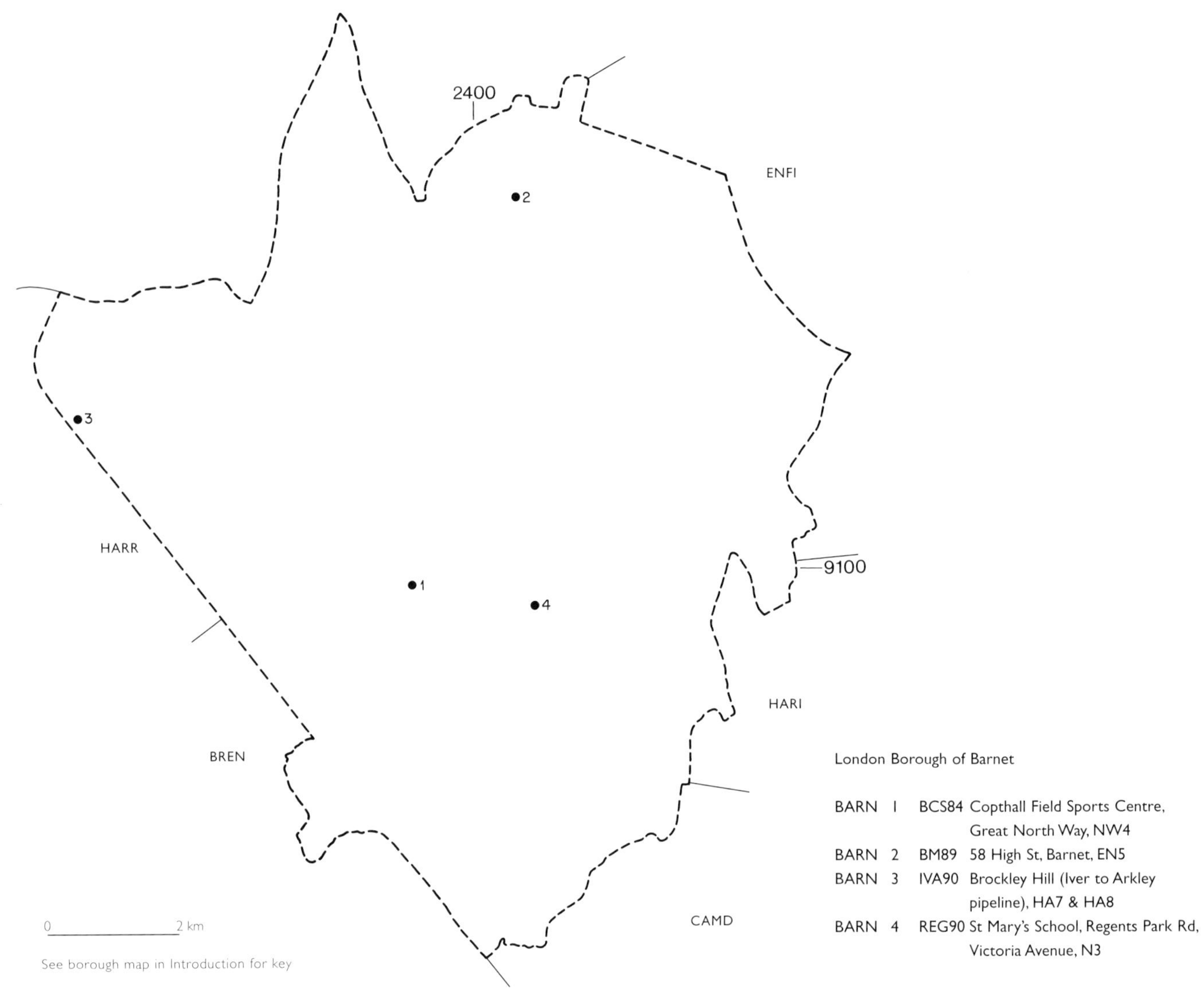

BCS84

Map site: 1
DGLA(N): Paul Falcini
NGR: TQ 230 910
SMR: 081971

Copthall Field Sports Centre, Great North Way, NW4

A trial excavation in 1984 revealed no archaeological features: only disturbed topsoil containing modern glazed pottery was found above natural.

BM89

Map site: 2
HADAS: Stewart Hoad
NGR: TQ 2480 9648
SMR: 082276–7

58 High Street, Barnet, EN5

Excavation in 1989 revealed a series of five walls, built of red tile and running E–W, perhaps the foundations for a suspended floor. They truncated layers of dark, humic soil which contained pottery not yet dated but thought to be medieval. (SMR gives site code as BN89.)

Iver to Arkley pipeline, Brockley Hill, HA7, HA8

IVA90

A watching brief in 1990 recorded the profile of a gravel road, together with its ditches, in a trench to the E of the modern A5 highway. It almost certainly represents part of Watling Street. The E ditch was apparently recut at least once, though no dating evidence was found.

London Archaeol, 6, 1991, 301; *Britannia,* 22, 1991, 272

Map site: 3
DGLA(N): Trevor Cox
NGR: TQ 1780 9350
SMR: 082281

St Mary's School, Regents Park Road, Victoria Avenue, N3

REG90

An evaluation excavation in 1990 revealed evidence of early medieval occupation in the form of post-holes, beam-slots and two hearths. Assemblages of sherds from cooking pots and domestic vessels in local or S Herts fabrics and of flint-tempered wares of uncertain source, suggest that the most intensive period of occupation was *c* 1150–1250.

London Archaeol, 6, 1991, 301; *Medieval Archaeol,* 35, 1991, 148

Map site: 4
DGLA(N): Bruno Barber
NGR: TQ 2510 9065
SMR: 082280

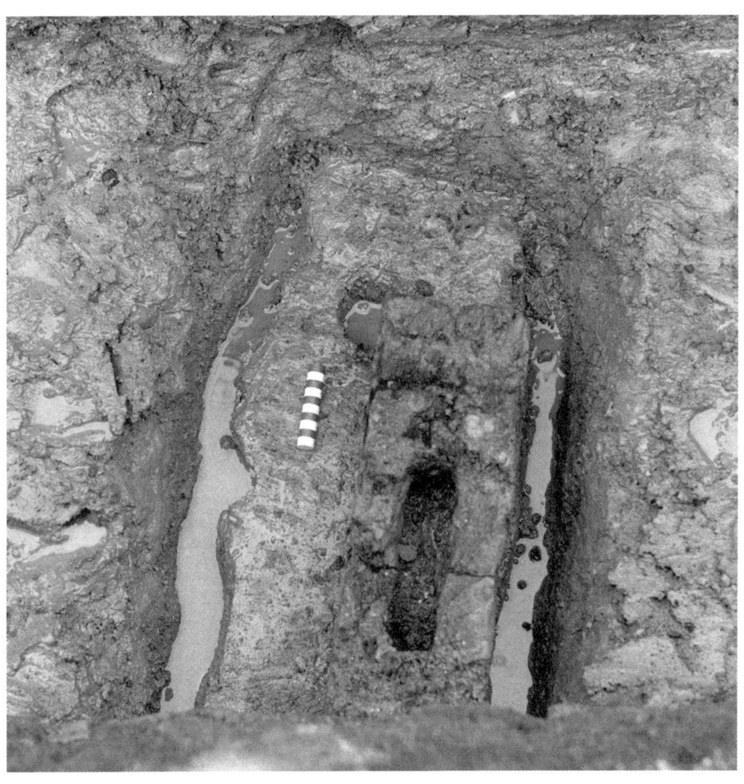

Brent SWW86 South Way, Wembley, HA9. Waterlogged timber footings of a long narrow building – undated.

BRENT

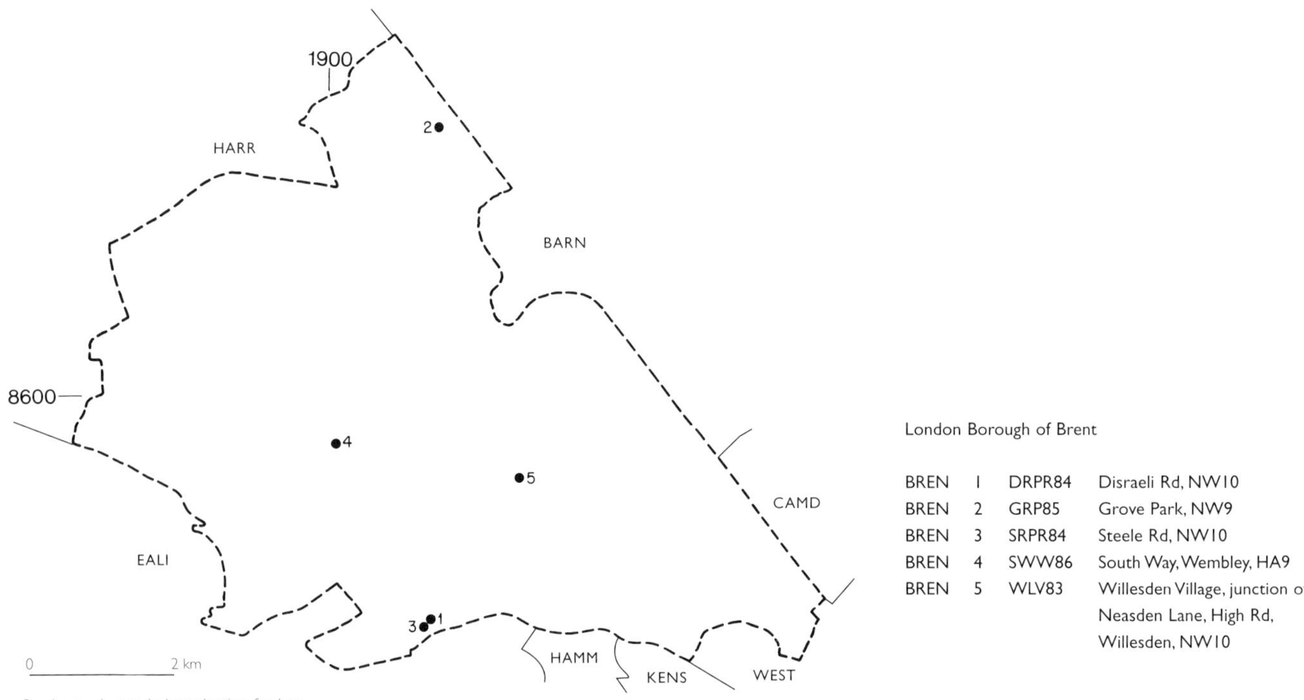

DRPR84, SRPR84

Map site: 1, 3
DGLA, WLAFG: John Mills
NGR: TQ 204 830
SMR: 050937

Disraeli Road, Steele Rd, NW10

A watching brief in 1984, close to the site of a Late Bronze Age hoard recovered in 1975, revealed no definite prehistoric features. Several pits containing 13th-c pottery were examined, perhaps associated with the former village of East Twyford.

London Archaeol, 5, 1985, 47

GRP85

Map site: 2
ILAU: Robert Whytehead,
Gavin Evans
NGR: TQ 205 895

Grove Park, NW9

A watching brief on a pipe trench in 1975 recorded several layers, one of them consisting of compacted grey sand and pebbles and believed to be the make-up for a Roman road.

SWW86

Map site: 4
DGLA(W): John Mills
NGR: TQ 191 854
SMR: 050935

South Way, Wembley, HA9

A trial excavation in 1986 on the supposed site of the medieval free chapel of St Michael, Tokyngton, revealed a few apparently medieval features — mostly shallow scoops — together with the waterlogged timber footings of a long narrow building referred to as 'dog kennels' on early 19th-c maps, but otherwise undated. No trace was found of the chapel itself, which probably lay a little further N, under the modern road.

London Archaeol, 5, 1987, 270

Willesden Village, junction of Neasden Lane, High Road, Willesden, NW10

WLV83

Map site: 5
DGLA(W): Jon Cotton
NGR: TQ 216 848

A trial excavation in 1983 revealed the foundations for a late 17th–early 18th-c brick-built house cut into a thick deposit of sticky grey-black clay which overlay the natural London Clay. No trace was located of structures or deposits relating to the medieval village of Willesden.

London Archaeol, 4, 1984, 386

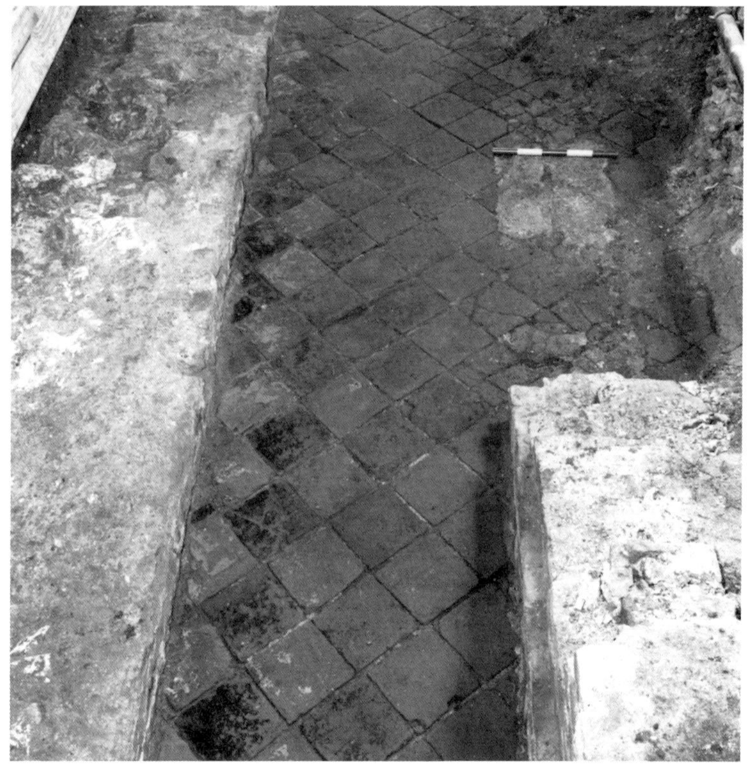

Camden ELY85 St Etheldreda's church, Ely Place, EC1. Part of the cloister floor, tiled with Flemish tiles.

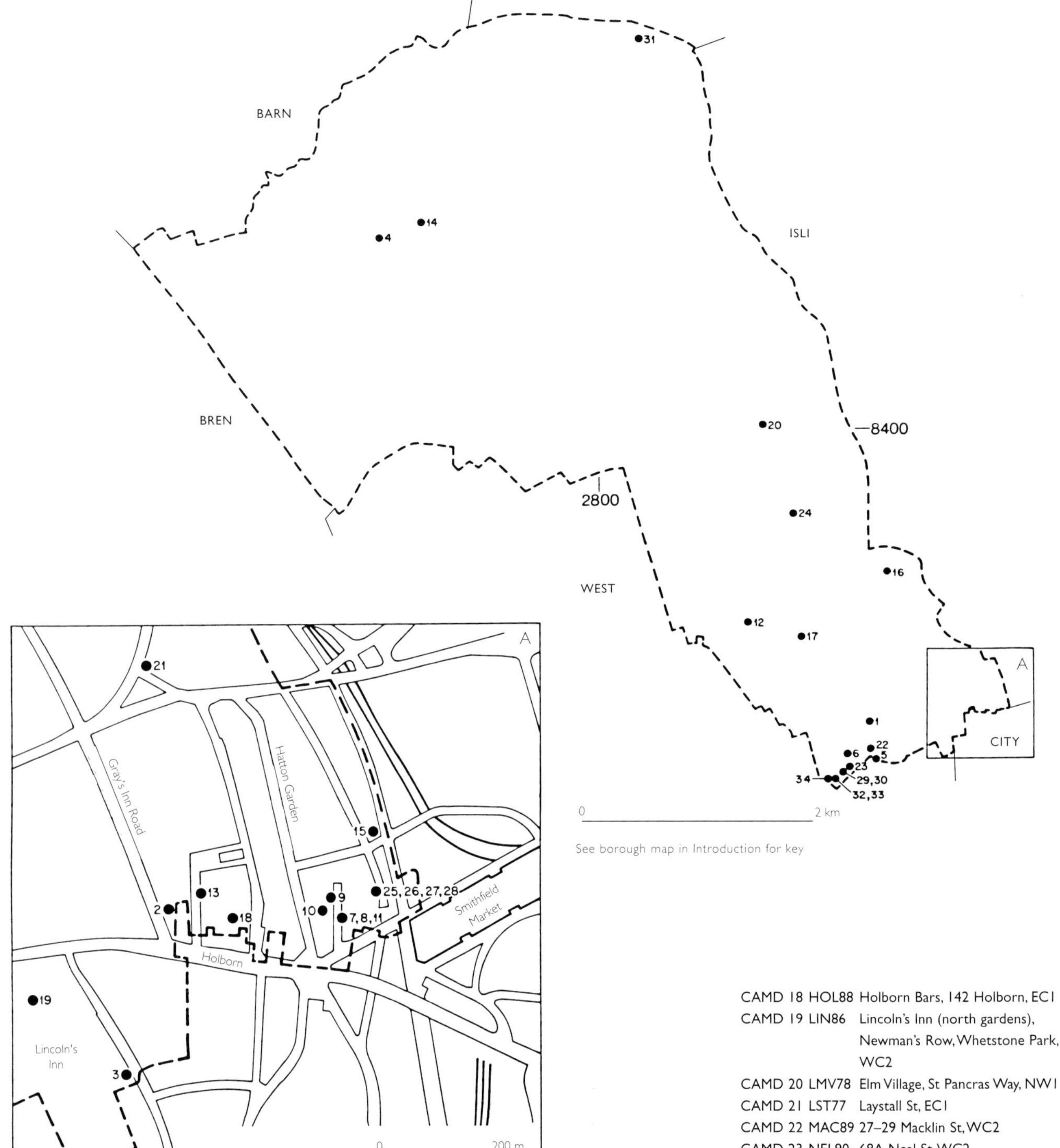

London Borough of Camden

CAMD 1   BAR76   14 Barter St, WC1

CAMD 2   BRK80   30–40 Brooke St, 143–150 High Holborn, 2–12 Gray's Inn Rd, EC1

CAMD 3   CHC88   78–87 Chancery Lane, 8–14 Bishop's Court, 1–17 & 2–12 Chichester Rents, WC2

CAMD 4   CRO76   13 Church Row (land adjoining), NW3

CAMD 5   DRL75   Drury Lane, WC2

CAMD 6   DUD78   Dudley House, Endell St, WC2

CAMD 7   EEL90   31–32 Ely Place, EC1

CAMD 8   ELP90   34 Ely Place, EC1

CAMD 9   ELY83   St Etheldreda's Clergy House, Ely Place, EC1

CAMD 10   ELY85   St Etheldreda's (church), Ely Place, EC1

CAMD 11   ELY90   33 Ely Place, EC1

CAMD 12   EUR79   Tottenham Court, 250 Euston Rd, NW1

CAMD 13   FCT75   Fox Court, adjacent to Brooke St, Holborn, EC1

CAMD 14   FLK90   Flask public house, 14 Flask Walk, NW3

CAMD 15   FRR79   22–25 Farringdon Rd, EC1

CAMD 16   GIR76   267–275 Gray's Inn Rd, WC1

CAMD 17   GOD90   Gordon Square, WC1

CAMD 18   HOL88   Holborn Bars, 142 Holborn, EC1

CAMD 19   LIN86   Lincoln's Inn (north gardens), Newman's Row, Whetstone Park, WC2

CAMD 20   LMV78   Elm Village, St Pancras Way, NW1

CAMD 21   LST77   Laystall St, EC1

CAMD 22   MAC89   27–29 Macklin St, WC2

CAMD 23   NEL90   68A Neal St, WC2

CAMD 24   PLT77   18–22 Platt St (rear of), NW1

CAMD 25   SFR75   Ukrainian church site, 147–152 Saffron Hill, 11–21 Charterhouse St, EC1

CAMD 26   SFR77   Afsil House, 147–152 Saffron Hill, EC1

CAMD 27   SFR78   141–145 Saffron Hill, EC1

CAMD 28   SFR81   Saffron Hill, EC1

CAMD 29   SGA89   2–26 Shorts Gardens, 19–41 Earlham St, WC2

CAMD 30   SHG89   2–26 Shorts Gardens, 19–41 Earlham St, WC2

CAMD 31   SOG86   South Grove, N6

CAMD 32   TGA88   Texaco Garage, Seven Dials, WC2

CAMD 33   TGX88   Texaco Garage, Seven Dials, WC2

CAMD 34   TOW8822   Tower St, WC2

14 Barter Street, WC1

Trial excavation in 1976 to establish the lines of two Roman roads revealed that all archaeological deposits had been removed by basements.

London Archaeol, 3, 1977, 37

BAR76

Map site: 1
ILAU: Graham Black
NGR: TQ 304 815
SMR: 082074

30–40 Brooke Street, 143–150 High Holborn, 2–12 Gray's Inn Road, EC1

Observations in 1980 recorded traces of two pits of probable 16th-c date in the centre of the site. Redeposited Roman pottery was also recovered.

BRK80

Map site: 2
ILAU: Robert Whytehead
NGR: TQ 312 816

78–87 Chancery Lane, 8–14 Bishop's Court, 1–17 & 2–12 Chichester Rents, WC2

A watching brief in 1988 on 13 testpits and others excavated by developers revealed evidence of cut features, probably post-medieval refuse pits, some of them cutting into a soil layer of uncertain character. A brick floor and layer of debris were also noted. There was extensive modern truncation.

CHC88

Map site: 3
DGLA(N): Stewart Hoad
NGR: TQ 308 813

Land adjoining 13 Church Row, NW3

Trial trenching in 1976 on a site within the medieval settlement area of Hampstead showed that all archaeological deposits had been removed by modern site levelling.

London Archaeol, 3, 1977, 37

CRO76

Map site: 4
ILAU: Graham Black
NGR: TQ 261 856
SMR: 082071

Drury Lane, WC2

Observation of a work trench in 1975 recovered finds only.

DRL75

Map site: 5
ILAU
NGR: TQ 3145 8115

DUD78

Map site: 6
ILAU: Robert Whytehead
NGR: TQ 3019 8128

Dudley House, Endell Street, WC2

Observation in 1978 recorded evidence mainly of a topographical character, though a human bone was reportedly found by workmen at the E end of the site.

EEL90, ELP90, ELY90

Map site: 7, 8, 11
DGLA(N): Bruno Barber, Gordon Malcolm
NGR: TQ 3145 8165
SMR: 081799, 082283–6

31–32 Ely Place, EC1 (EEL90)
34 Ely Place, EC1 (ELP90)
33 Ely Place, EC1 (ELY90)

Excavation and observation during the refurbishment of a Georgian terrace in 1990 recorded substantial remains of the hall and E range of the London residence of the bishops of Ely, documented *c* 1290. Human burials included two thought to date to the Civil War period, when the site was used as a prison and hospital. Several other features were noted, including a possible Roman ditch. Most deposits will be preserved *in situ*.

London Archaeol, 6, 1991, 301; *Medieval Archaeol*, 35, 1991, 148; *Post-Medieval Archaeol*, 25, 1991, 131

ELY83

Map site: 9
ILAU: Peter Mills
NGR: TQ 3141 8168

St Etheldreda's Clergy House, Ely Place, EC1

A watching brief in 1983 recorded the relieving arch of a 13th-c crypt.

ELY85

Map site: 10
DGLA(N): Peter Mills
NGR: TQ 3141 8165
SMR: 081799

St Etheldreda's (church), Ely Place, EC1

Excavation in 1985 to examine the N portion of the W cloister of the town house (*c* 1290–1300) of the bishops of Ely exposed a 9m length of the cloister floor, at one point to its full width of 3m. It was tiled with green-glazed and yellow-slipped Flemish tiles, laid in a diagonal chequerboard pattern. To the W a substantial cloister wall, about 0.9m wide, was uncovered, aligned askew to the chapel and crypt of the palace and constructed of ragstone with a white plaster facing.

London Archaeol, 5, 1986, 158; *Medieval Archaeol*, 30, 1986, 137

Tottenham Court, 250 Euston Road, NW1

Excavation and observation in 1979 at the junction of Euston Road and Tolmers Square on the site of the medieval manor house of Tottenhall revealed a stone garderobe pit containing 16th-c deposits, and also yard surfaces and fragments of walls. There was modern disturbance.

London Archaeol, 3, 1980, 385

Blackmore, L, 1983 'The Anglo-Saxon and medieval pottery', in Whytehead, R, & Blackmore, L, 81–91

Whytehead, R, & Blackmore, L, 1983 'Excavations at Tottenham Court, 250 Euston Road, NW1', *Trans London Middlesex Archaeol Soc,* 34, 73–92

EUR79

Map site: 12
ILAU: Robert Whytehead
NGR: TQ 2930 8240
SMR: 081795, 082072

Fox Court, adjacent to Brooke Street, Holborn, EC1

A trial excavation in 1975 uncovered a brick-lined pit containing pottery of the first half of the 17th c. The basement had wholly removed the stratigraphy.

London Archaeol, 2, 1976, 370; *Post-Medieval Archaeol,* 10, 1976, 162

FCT75

Map site: 13
ILAU: J Hinchcliffe
NGR: TQ 312 817
SMR: 082077

Flask public house, 14 Flask Walk, NW3

Excavation in 1990 encountered 18th-c walls, apparently part of a rear cellar of the earlier Flask Tavern.

London Archaeol, 6, 1991, 301; *Post-Medieval Archaeol,* 25, 1991, 131

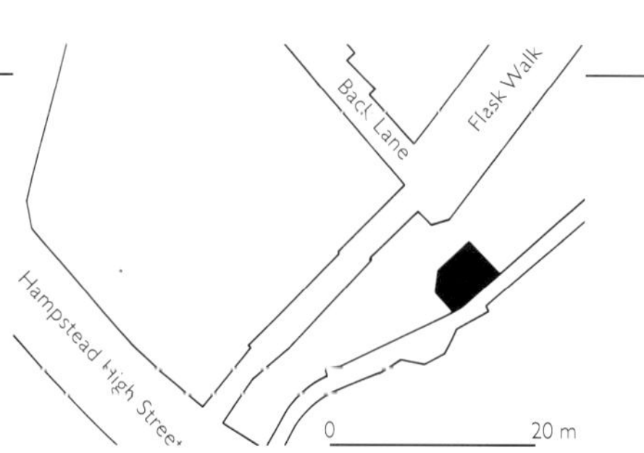

FLK90

Map site: 14
DGLA(N): Aileen Connor,
Stewart Hoad
NGR: TQ 2646 8575
SMR: 082287

22–25 Farringdon Street, EC1

For details of this site see Schofield & Maloney 1998.

FRR79

Map site: 15

267–275 Gray's Inn Road, WC1

Excavation in 1976 revealed a cylindrical brick structure identified as a 19th-c earth closet.

GIR76

Map site: 16
ILAU: David Whipp
NGR: TQ 3050 8280
SMR: 082076

GOD90

Map site: 17
DGLA(N): Gordon Malcolm,
Christopher Thomas
NGR: TQ 2950 8240
SMR: 082288

Gordon Square, WC1

Observation in 1990 recorded an irregular channel interpreted as a minor tributary of the River Fleet.

London Archaeol, 6, 1991, 301

HOL88

Map site: 18
DGLA(N): Eric Norton
NGR: TQ 3118 8162

Holborn Bars, 142 Holborn, EC1

A trial excavation in 1988 revealed mainly backfilling of demolition debris and redeposited post-medieval refuse.

LIN86

Map site: 19
DGLA(N)
NGR: TQ 308 814

Lincoln's Inn (north gardens), Newman's Row, Whetstone Park, WC2

Observation in 1988 of a trench across an embankment at the N boundary wall recorded beneath the garden soil building rubble overlying brick footings; three clay pipe bowls suggest that the demolition occurred in the late 17th c. Beneath the modern debris in a second trench was found redeposited brickearth from which sherds of medieval pottery were recovered.

LMV78

Map site: 20
ILAU: J Siegel
NGR: TQ 295 840

Elm Village, St Pancras Way, NW1

A watching brief in 1978 recorded no archaeological features, though post-medieval pottery was recovered.

LST77

Map site: 21
ILAU: E Platts
NGR: TQ 311 820

Laystall Street, EC1

A watching brief in 1977 revealed extensive tips of 16th–17th-c garden soil.

MAC89

Map site: 22
DGLA(N): Stewart Hoad
NGR: TQ 3041 8140
SMR: 082186–7

27–29 Macklin Street, WC2

Excavation in 1989 recorded no archaeological features, though a sherd of Saxon pottery was recovered and a layer of organic soil examined.

Cowie, R, 1988 'A gazetteer of Middle Saxon sites and finds in the Strand/Westminster area', *Trans London Middlesex Archaeol Soc*, 39, 43 (43)

68A Neal Street, WC2

A watching brief in 1990 on a site close to an area of Middle Saxon settlement recorded deep cut features, at present undated.

London Archaeol, 6, 1991, 301

NEL90

Map site: 23
DGLA(N): Gordon Malcolm
NGR: TQ 3021 8121
SMR: 082289

Rear of 18–22 Platt Street, NW1

Excavation in Platt Yard in 1977 revealed evidence of heavy waterlogging dated no later than the 17th c.

London Archaeol, 3, 1978, 160

PLT77

Map site: 24
ILAU: Graham Black
NGR: TQ 297 833
SMR: 082073

Ukrainian church site, 147–152 Saffron Hill, 11–21 Charterhouse Street, EC1

Trial trenching in 1975 showed that any archaeological levels had been removed by basements.

London Archaeol, 2, 1976, 370

SFR75

Map site: 25
ILAU: David Whipp
NGR: TQ 315 817

Afsil House, 147–152 Saffron Hill, EC1

A watching brief in 1977 recorded the filled-in bed of the River Bourne. Much of the site was disturbed by modern basements however.

SFR77

Map site: 26
ILAU: Graham Black
NGR: TQ 315 817
SMR: 082075

141–145 Saffron Hill, EC1

Excavation in 1978 revealed topographical data, and the foundations of the Ukrainian church.

London Archaeol, 3, 1979, 262

SFR78

Map site: 27
ILAU: Irene Schwab
NGR: TQ 315 817
SMR: 082079

Saffron Hill, EC1

Examination in 1981 of a wooden tree-trunk pipe, one of several apparently encountered by the contractor.

SFR81

Map site: 28
ILAU: Robert Whytehead
NGR: TQ 315 817

SGA89

Map site: 29
DGLA(N): Aileen Connor
NGR: TQ 3013 8112
SMR: 082184–5

2–26 Shorts Gardens, 19–41 Earlham Street, WC2

Excavation in 1989 produced evidence of six hearths, at least one of them used for smelting. A collapsed wattle and daub wall about 8m long, extensive slag deposits and more than 150 iron objects, including blades, tools and furniture fittings of Middle Saxon date, were found (see SHG89 below).

London Archaeol, 6, 1990, 188; *Medieval Archaeol*, 34, 1990, 175; 35, 1991, 148; *Post-Medieval Archaeol*, 25, 1991, 130
Cowie, R, 1988 'A gazetteer of Middle Saxon sites and finds in the Strand/Westminster area', *Trans London Middlesex Archaeol Soc*, 39, 42–3 (33)

SHG89

Map site: 30
DGLA(N)
NGR: TQ 3014 8113
SMR: 082184–5

2–26 Shorts Gardens, 19–41 Earlham Street, WC2

A trial excavation in 1989 (preceding SGA89) revealed extensive archaeological deposits, largely undated on account of site restrictions. The recovery of part of a loom weight suggests some form of Saxon occupation on the site, and a fragment of human skull may be of similar date. Much pitting and rubbish disposal appears to have occurred in the medieval and post-medieval periods.

SOG86

Map site: 31
DGLA(N): Robert Ellis
NGR: TQ 283 873

South Grove, N6

Excavation in 1986 revealed a linear feature containing fragments of decorated wall plaster. To the N of this, post-holes in circular formation were located, though no direct association was established. Segments of a brick feature, possibly a path or similar, were recorded in the NE corner of the site.

TGA88, TGX88

Map site: 32, 33
DGLA(N): Stephen Haynes
NGR: TQ 3005 8107

Texaco Garage, Seven Dials, WC2

An archaeological assessment and evaluation in 1988 concluded that survival of archaeological strata was limited and truncation precluded further investigation.

TOW88

Map site: 34
DGLA(N): Martin Brown
NGR: TQ 3003 8106

22 Tower Street, WC2

A watching brief in 1988–90 recorded evidence of marsh deposits only.

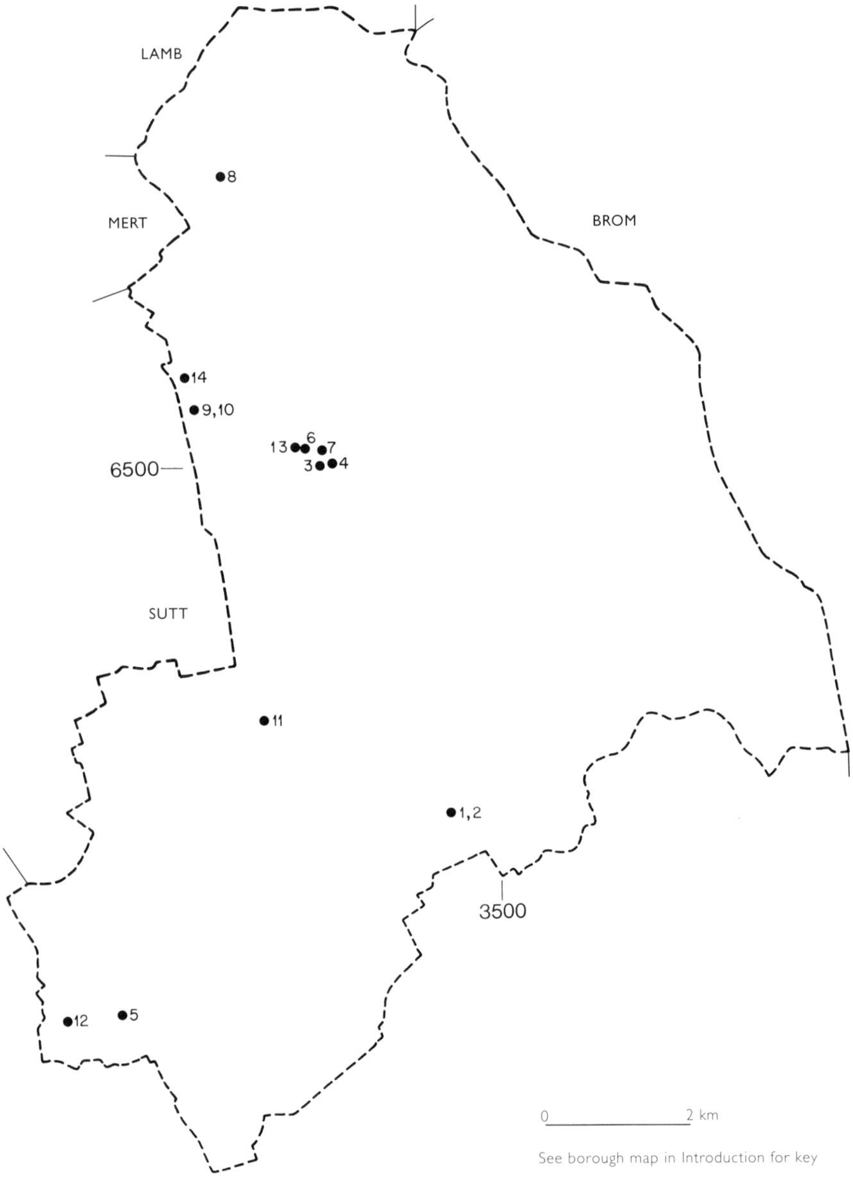

London Borough of Croydon

CROY 1   ATW89   Atwood Primary School, Limpsfield Rd, Sanderstead, South Croydon, CR2
CROY 2   ATW90   Atwood Primary School, Limpsfield Rd, Sanderstead, South Croydon, CR2
CROY 3   CHP89   113–121 High St, Croydon, CR0
CROY 4   EDG89   5–25 Edridge Rd, Croydon, CR0
CROY 4   EDR89   5–25 Edridge Rd, Croydon, CR0
CROY 5   FAD90   Farthing Down, Ditches Lane, Coulsdon, CR5
CROY 6   GBS88   Grants Redevelopment, Middle St, Surrey St, Croydon, CR0
CROY 7   MTW90   Mint Walk, Croydon, CR0
CROY 8   NLR88   London Rd, Ederline Avenue, SW16
CROY 9   PCB90   Philips Factory site, Beddington Farm Rd, Croydon, CR0
CROY 10   PFC90   Philips Factory site, Beddington Farm Rd, Croydon, CR0
CROY 11   PUH90   112–114 High St, Purley, CR8
CROY 12   STK89   9–11 Starrock Rd, Coulsdon, CR5
CROY 13   SYC90   35–36 Surrey St, Croydon, CR0
CROY 14   VAP89   Valley Park Development site, Purley Way, Beddington Farm Rd, Croydon, CR0

See borough map in Introduction for key

ATW89

Atwood Primary School, Limpsfield Road, Sanderstead, South Croydon, CR2

Map site: 1
DGLA(SW): Gill Batchelor
NGR: TQ 3427 6051
SMR: 020263

Excavation in 1960 located a Romano-British settlement of the 1st/2nd c AD; fresh excavation in 1989 produced more than 200 archaeological features, including at least 60 post-holes, six large ditches, and chalk and ash surfaces or floors. One cut feature may represent a dewpond relating to the surface water drainage of the settlement. Finds included a La Tène III Late Iron Age-style bronze brooch and two almost complete early Roman pottery vessels.

London Archaeol, 6, 1990, 188; *Surrey Archaeol Coll*, 80, 1990, 217
Batchelor, G, 1990 '"Friends, Romans, Schoolchildren!" — archaeology and education in Croydon', *London Archaeol*, 6, 199–205

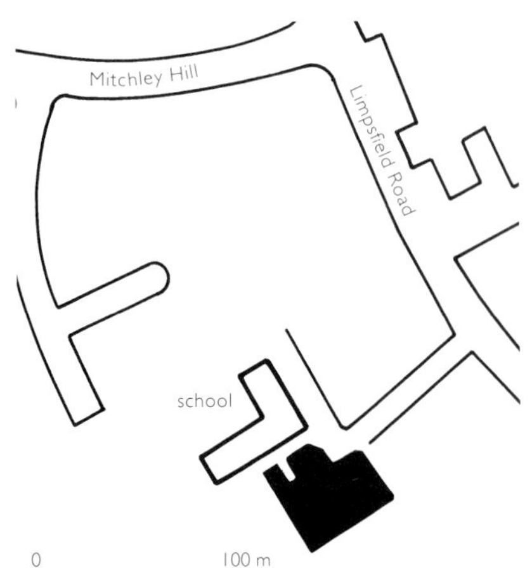

Atwood Primary School, Limpsfield Road, Sanderstead, South Croydon, CR2

Further excavation in 1990 proved to be of limited success. Four cut features were observed, none of them yielding dating evidence.

London Archaeol, 6, 1992, 416

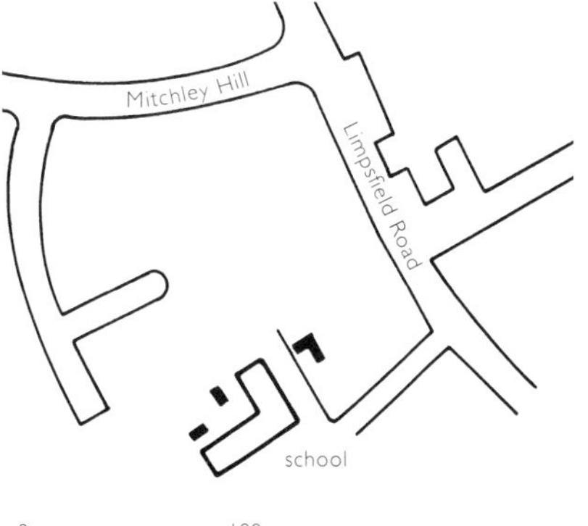

ATW90

Map site: 2
DGLA(SW): Penny Bruce
NGR: TQ 3424 6055
SMR: 020263

113–121 High Street, Croydon, CR0

Excavation in 1989 took place in three parts of the site. In the first, to the E, a small Roman ditch and a post-medieval well were exposed. In the second, to the S, post-medieval features were located, including a cobbled flint surface possibly related to Wrencote, an 18th-c building at 123 High Street. In the third area, closest to the High Street, the N end of a sequence of late medieval buildings was revealed. The earliest was a flint and mortar structure provisionally dated to the 14th–15th c; a copper-alloy havette or shearman's hook found in the floor layers suggests that the building may have been a fuller's workshop. This was demolished and succeeded by a flint, Reigate stone, chalk and mortar structure of slightly larger plan and probably 15th-c date, its interior divided into two rooms at the N end, and plastered. The building remained in use into the 16th c when it was refurbished as a dwelling, possibly of a smallholding. Probably it was part of the property referred to as Coombe or Mortimers which is documented as early as 1546, when it was described as 'a messuage or tenement, curtilage, garden and also one barn'. The present building was probably demolished to make way for the construction of Wrencote.

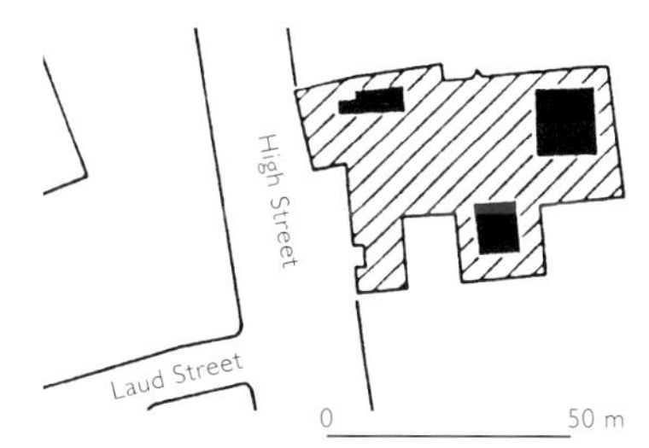

London Archaeol, 6, 1990, 188; *Medieval Archaeol,* 34, 1990, 181; *Post-Medieval Archaeol,* 24, 1990, 177; *Surrey Archaeol Coll,* 80, 1990, 217

CHP89

Map site: 3
DGLA(SW): Pat Miller
NGR: TQ 3239 6515
SMR: 021164–6

5–25 Edridge Road, Croydon, CR0

Though close to an area of Saxon burial, excavation in 1989 (EDR89: TQ 3249 6516) produced no clear evidence of early occupation; Roman and medieval pottery was residual.

London Archaeol, 6, 1990, 188; *Surrey Archaeol Coll,* 80, 1990, 217

EDG89, EDR89

Map site: 4
DGLA(SW): Pat Miller
NGR: TQ 3260 6500
SMR: 021162–3

FAD90

Map site: 5
DGLA(SW): Pat Miller
NGR: TQ 2980 5820
SMR: 021300

Farthing Down, Ditches Lane, Coulsdon, CR5

A watching brief on a pipe trench in 1990 encountered a small oval pit within the edges of the trench. Subsequent excavation revealed a dark orange-brown soil fill with chalk inclusions. A number of flint-tempered pottery fragments, including a rim sherd, have been provisionally dated to the Neolithic/Bronze Age.

London Archaeol, 6, 1991, 301; Surrey Archaeol Coll, 81, 1991–2, 157

GBS88

Map site: 6
DGLA(SW): Stephen Haynes
NGR: TQ 3228 6546
SMR: 021312

Grants Redevelopment, Middle Street, Surrey Street, Croydon, CR0

Trial excavation in 1988 revealed extensive modern truncation over most of the area, but located an apparently rectangular feature constructed of chalk blocks set in mortar, and also the chalk wall of a medieval building abutting Oak Alley.

London Archaeol, 6, 1990, 188; Surrey Archaeol Coll, 80, 1990, 217

MTW90

Map site: 7
DGLA: Mark Barratt
NGR: TQ 323 653
SMR: 021303–6

Mint Walk, Croydon, CR0

Trial excavation in 1990–1 produced prehistoric and early Roman finds, as well as a medieval pit and material from a nearby 19th-c pipe kiln.

London Archaeol, 6, 1991, 302; Medieval Archaeol, 35, 1991, 153; Surrey Archaeol Coll, 81, 1991–2, 157

NLR88

Map site: 8
DGLA(SW): Robin Nielsen
NGR: TQ 3093 6889
SMR: 021167

London Road, Ederline Avenue, SW16

An evaluation excavation in 1988 alongside the supposed line of the Roman road from London to Portslade produced traces of post-medieval ploughing but no evidence of the road.

Surrey Archaeol Coll, 80, 1990, 217

Philips Factory site, Beddington Farm Road, Croydon, CR0

Excavation in 1990 produced, in one area, Late Bronze Age pottery and flints in silt and gravel, and a series of Mesolithic cores and flakes. In another area a linear ditch feature of V-shaped profile was revealed, possibly of Late Iron Age or Roman date although no dating evidence was found.

London Archaeol, 6, 1991, 302; Surrey Archaeol Coll, 81, 1991–2, 157

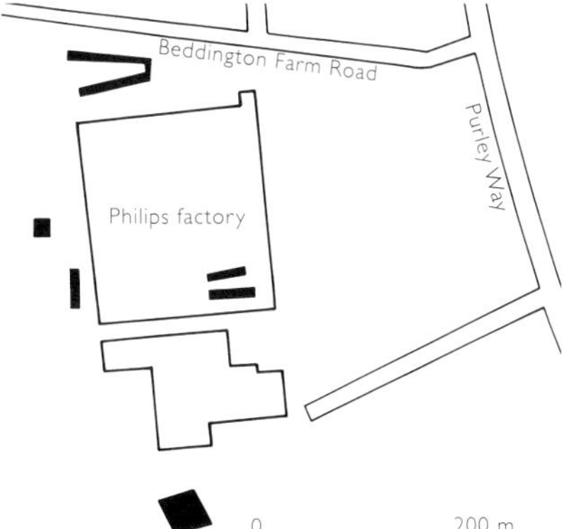

PCB90

Map site: 9
DGLA: Steve Tucker
NGR: TQ 3070 6560
SMR: 021296–7

Philips Factory site, Beddington Farm Road, Croydon, CR0

Excavation in three areas was carried out in 1990 (further to PCB90). The first, within an existing building, indicated severe truncation of archaeological deposits. A small N–S linear feature, observed cutting into the low-lying gravels, is thought to be Late Iron Age, though no dating evidence was recovered. The second area, also severely truncated, produced a few struck flints. The third area revealed a series of shallow, intercutting linear features, without dating evidence but thought to indicate Late Bronze Age/Iron Age farming activity. A large shallow linear feature containing post-medieval material was also recorded.

London Archaeol, 6, 1991, 302; Surrey Archaeol Coll, 81, 1991–2, 157

PFC90

Map site: 10
DGLA: Steve Tucker
NGR: TQ 3070 6560
SMR: 021296–7

112–114 High Street, Purley, CR8

A trial excavation in 1990 produced prehistoric finds only, with ploughsoil of the medieval and post-medieval periods.

London Archaeol, 6, 1991, 302; Medieval Archaeol, 35, 1991, 153; Post-Medieval Archaeol, 25, 1991, 158; Surrey Archaeol Coll, 81, 1991–2, 157

PUH90

Map site: 11
DGLA: Bob Bazely
NGR: TQ 3158 6177
SMR: 021298–9

9–11 Starrock Road, Coulsdon, CR5

Excavation in 1989 on the slope of the N Downs, across the valley from the prehistoric site of Farthing Down and in the vicinity of known Saxon cemeteries, produced no evidence of occupation. Two periglacial deposits cut the chalk. Plough marks and pottery, still to be dated, were located. No other archaeological features were noted, but a local resident presented the excavators with two stone tools found in his garden; one was a Lower Palaeolithic hand axe (Wymer 'Ficron' type M), and the other a worked flint flake of Mesolithic or later date.

London Archaeol, 6, 1989, 73; 6, 1990, 188; Surrey Archaeol Coll, 80, 1990, 216

STK89

Map site: 12
DGLA: Gill Batchelor
NGR: TQ 2918 5794
SMR: 021155

SYC90

Map site: 13
DGLA: Gill Batchelor
NGR: TQ 3225 6549
SMR: 021301–2

35–36 Surrey Street, Croydon, CR0

Excavation in 1990 recovered a prehistoric worked flint tool but produced no evidence of ancient settlement or occupation.

London Archaeol, 6, 1991, 302; *Medieval Archaeol,* 34, 1990, 181; *Surrey Archaeol Coll,* 81, 1991–2, 157

VAP89

Map site: 14
DGLA(SW): Bob Bazely,
Steve Tucker
NGR: TQ 3050 6625
SMR: 021154

Valley Park Development site, Purley Way, Beddington Farm Road, Croydon, CR0

Excavation in 1989 within a 104 acre (42ha) site on the Wandle gravels was conducted in five phases. The first of these involved five distinct areas, only one of which produced archaeological remains: a number of pit-like features, of which one is datable to the Late Neolithic on the evidence of a piece of Mortlake ware. A series of ditches, two of them roughly parallel, may have been related to a droveway: pottery from them indicates Late Bronze/Early Iron Age dates. In the second phase of excavation, two parallel ditches were again found, one of them overlying an earlier ditch containing burnt flint. A third ditch lay at right angles to these two, and a few pits were also encountered. Dating evidence was poorer than for the first phase, but would again seem to indicate Late Bronze/Early Iron Age.

London Archaeol, 6, 1990, 188; *Surrey Archaeol Coll,* 80, 1990, 216

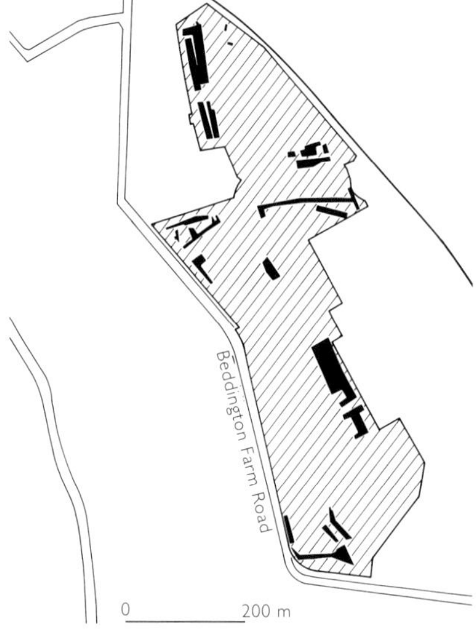

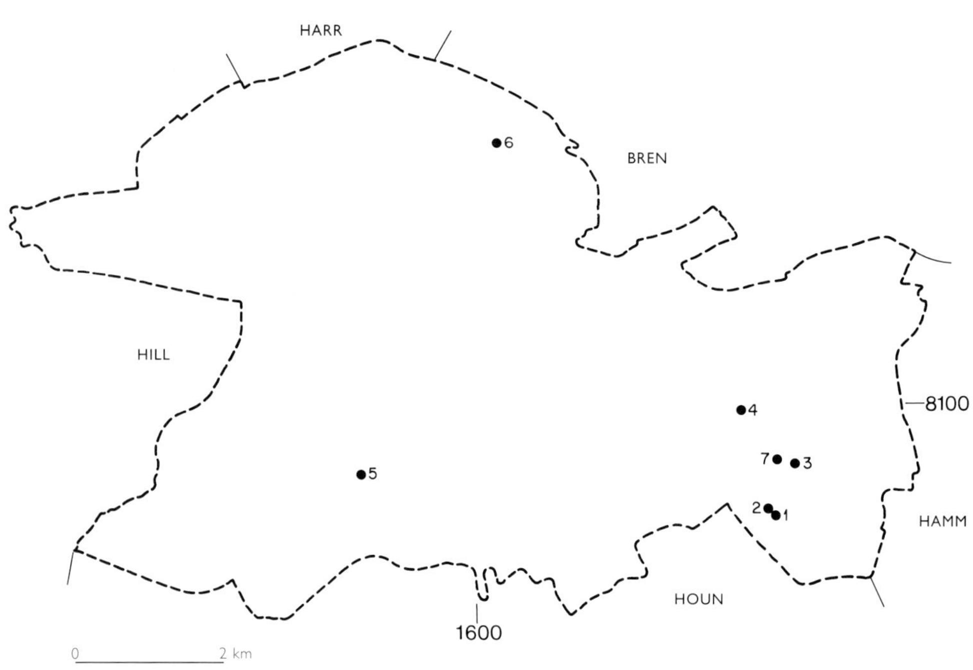

See borough map in Introduction for key

London Borough of Ealing

EALI	1	AGA81	49–51 Avenue Gardens, W3
EALI	2	AGA85	36 Avenue Gardens, W3
EALI	3	ASC89	Churchfield Rd (Acton Shopping Centre), W3
EALI	4	CRA88	Creffield Rd (Japanese School), W3
EALI	5	EAL90	St Bernard's Hospital, Uxbridge Rd, Windmill Lane, Southall, UB2
EALI	6	HH87	Horsenden Hill, Horsenden Lane North, Perivale, Greenford, UB6
EALI	7	KSA88	King St, W3

AGA81

Map site: 1
MoL, WLAFG: Jon Cotton
NGR: TQ 1985 7966
SMR: 050939–42

49–51 Avenue Gardens, W3

A trial excavation in 1981, adjacent to the site of a Middle Bronze Age flat grave cemetery found in 1883, revealed traces of intercutting Roman ditches whose fills produced, in addition to Roman finds, much residual material including flint blades and a microlith of Mesolithic type, together with sherds of probable prehistoric pottery (see AGA85 below). Notable Roman finds included a bronze finger-ring and an almost complete decorated samian bowl (Dragendorf form 30), dated to c 100–130.

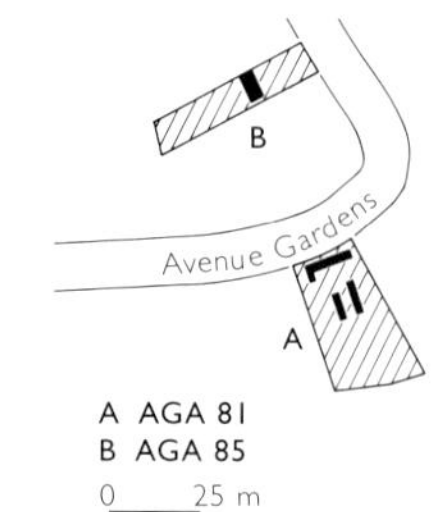

London Archaeol, 4, 1982, 163

Bird, J, 1993 'Samian', in Cotton, J, 10–11

Cotton, J, 1993 'Excavations and observations of a Bronze Age cemetery and Roman site in Avenue Gardens, Acton, Middlesex 1882 and 1981–5', Trans London Middlesex Archaeol Soc, 44, 1–22

Davis, B, 1993 'Coarseware', in Cotton, J, 11–12

Degnan, S, 1993 'Building material', in Cotton, J, 13

Mills, J, 1993 'Appendix: Mill Hill Park Estate and the discoveries of 1882', in Cotton, J, 19–21

Rackham, J, & Wooldridge, M, 1993 'Animal bones', in Cotton, J, 13

36 Avenue Gardens, W3

AGA85

Map site: 2
DGLA: Jon Cotton
NGR: TQ 1984 7971
SMR: 050939–42

A watching brief in 1985 revealed traces of presumably linear features of prehistoric or Roman date, from one of which some 80 sherds of a large bucket-shaped urn of Deverel-Rimbury type were recovered, similar to those found during construction of the house in 1882. The finds complement those recovered during trial work in 1981 (see AGA81 above). (For plan, see AGA81.)

London Archaeol, 5, 1986, 161
Bird, J, 1993 'Samian', in Cotton, J, 10–11
Cotton, J, 1993 'Excavations and observations of a Bronze Age cemetery and Roman site in Avenue Gardens, Acton, Middlesex 1882 and 1981–5', Trans London Middlesex Archaeol Soc, 44, 1–22
Davis, B, 1993 'Coarseware', in Cotton, J, 11–12
Degnan, S, 1993 'Building material', in Cotton, J, 13
Mills, J, 1993 'Appendix: Mill Hill Park Estate and the discoveries of 1882', in Cotton, J, 19–21
Rackham, J, & Wooldridge, M, 1993 'Animal bones', in Cotton, J, 13

Acton Shopping Centre, Churchfield Road, W3

ASC89

Map site: 3
DGLA(W): Caroline Pathy-Barker
NGR: TQ 202 802
SMR: 051133–4

An evaluation excavation in 1989 revealed heavy disturbance with little or no archaeological survival, apart from two Roman pits, 18th-c quarry pits and mid-19th-c pits and brick walls, probably representing backyard activity.

London Archaeol, 6, 1990, 189; Post-Medieval Archaeol, 24, 1990, 177

Japanese School, Creffield Road, W3

CRA88

Map site: 4
DGLA(W), WLAFG: Bob Bazely
NGR: TQ 195 808
SMR: 051105

A trial excavation in 1988 uncovered a small quantity of Mesolithic and Palaeolithic flint implements, as well as topographical and geological information.

London Archaeol, 6, 1989, 73
Bazely, R, Green, C, & McGregor, D, 1991 'Excavation of an early prehistoric site at Creffield Road, Acton', Trans London Middlesex Archaeol Soc, 42, 17–32
Collcutt, S, 1991 'Structural geology', in Bazely, R, Green, C, & McGregor, D, 21–5
Green, C, & McGregor, D, 1991 'Sediment analysis', in Bazely, R, Green, C, & McGregor, D, 25–8
Merriman, N, 1991 'The flintwork', in Bazely, R, Green, C, & McGregor, D, 28–9

St Bernard's Hospital, Uxbridge Road, Windmill Lane, Southall, UB2

EAL90

Map site: 5
DGLA(W): Helen Jones
NGR: TQ 1445 8000
SMR: 052243

An evaluation excavation of the Lynch Hill gravels in 1990 revealed in two of the areas examined a dispersed assembly of Late Bronze Age pottery fragments and flints. A ditch with sloping sides and a vertical-sided, flat-bottomed central channel was located to the E of the scatters; its date is uncertain.

London Archaeol, 6, 1991, 302

HH87

Map site: 6
DGLA(W): J Bruce
NGR: TQ 163 844
SMR: 050981–6

Horsenden Hill, Horsenden Lane North, Perivale, Greenford, UB6

A survey and excavation of a Scheduled Ancient Monument in 1987 suggested that banks and ditches on the W, S and E slopes are unlikely to be manmade, but the result of natural downslope slumping of the London Clay. None the less, considerable quantities of prehistoric struck flint and pottery were recovered from a deep ploughsoil layer, shown by augering to cover much of the summit of the hill.

London Archaeol, 5, 1988, 411

KSA88

Map site: 7
DGLA(W): Caroline Pathy-Barker
NGR: TQ 198 803
SMR: 051027

King Street, W3

Excavation in 1988 located the western branch of Stamford Brook, and recorded medieval and later fills. A pebbled floor and beam slot yielded pottery dated to *c* 1740–50.

London Archaeol, 6, 1989, 73

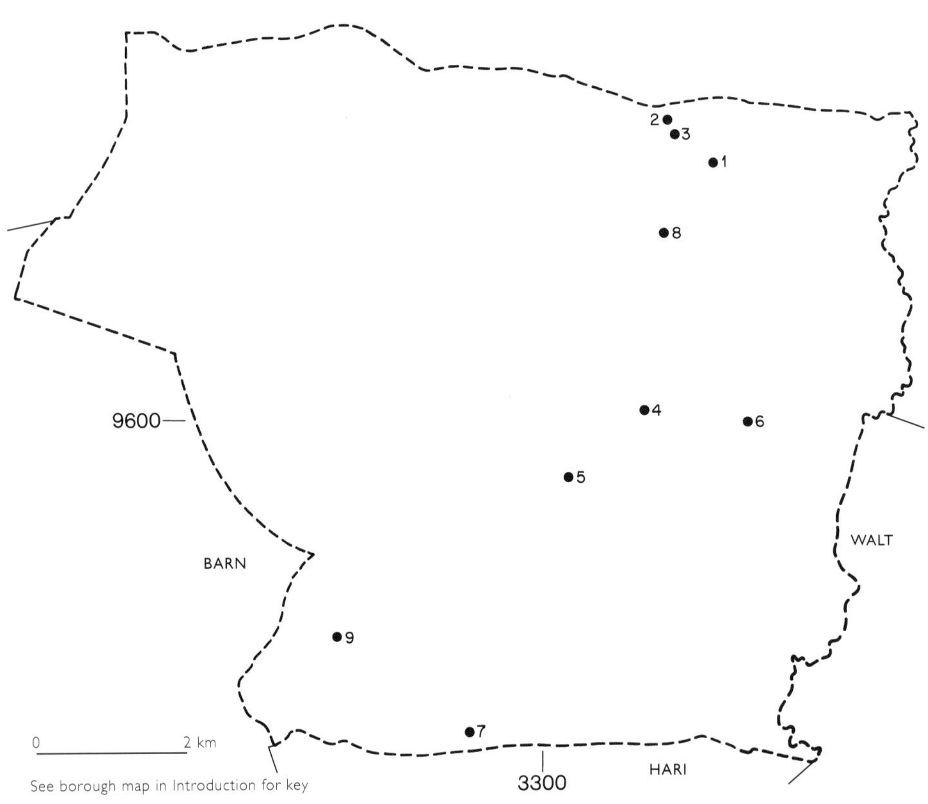

London Borough of Enfield

ENFI 1 AYL90 Aylands Allotments, Aylands Rd, Enfield, EN3
ENFI 2 BCRE79 Bulls Cross Ride, Enfield, EN2
ENFI   BRM85 Broomfield House, Broomfield Lane, N13
ENFI 3 CAP90 Capel Manor, Bullsmoor Lane, Enfield, EN1
ENFI 4 ELR76 Lincoln Rd, Enfield, EN1
ENFI 5 ERH86 20 Village Rd, Enfield, EN1
ENFI 6 GAR89 Garfield Rd, Ponders End, Enfield, EN3
ENFI 7 GTH90 Greentrees Hospital, Tottenhall Rd, N13
ENFI 8 HOE90 Hoe Lane, Enfield, EN1
ENFI 9 SOU90 Southgate House, Cannon Hill, N14

AYL90

Map site: 1
DGLA(N): Patricia Allan
NGR: TQ 353 991
SMR: 082190–3

Aylands Allotments, Aylands Road, Enfield, EN3

Excavation in 1990 revealed that the site consisted almost entirely of shallow, irregular features cut into the natural subsoil, none of them directly related stratigraphically. Three phases of activity were indicated by the finds evidence. The earliest occupation occurred during the Late Mesolithic/Early Neolithic period and was apparent over the entire site. This was followed by a second phase of activity in the Late Bronze/Early Iron Age, which was confined to the gravel at the crest of the hill and may have involved settlement. The third phase occurred during the Early Saxon period and included settlement, indicated by the presence of two sunken-featured buildings. There is no documentary evidence of subsequent settlement until the present day.

London Archaeol, 6, 1991, 302; Medieval Archaeol, 35, 1991, 153

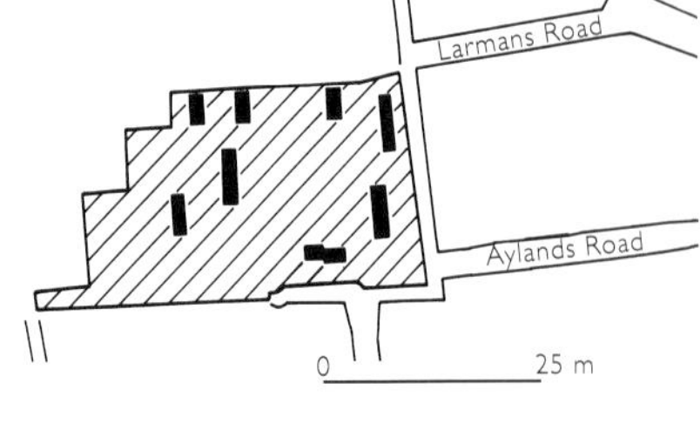

Bulls Cross Ride, Enfield, EN2

A trial excavation in 1979 on the line of Ermine Street revealed features of geological rather than archaeological significance, although sherds of medieval pottery were recovered from the ploughsoil.

London Archaeol, 3, 1980, 386; *Britannia,* 11, 1980, 381

BCRE79

Map site: 2
WLAFG: Jon Cotton
NGR: TQ 3441 9999
SMR: 081481

Broomfield House, Broomfield Lane, N13

An archaeological survey was made in 1985 of a standing building recently damaged by fire. This was originally a large country house, begun at least as early as the 16th c as a two-storey building of timber-framing with lath and plaster infill; its upper floor was partly jettied. The jetty was superseded when the ground-floor walls were rebuilt and a large brick chimney stack was inserted. At the same time or slightly later, the house was extended to the N over a brick-lined cellar. This extension was of timber-frame construction around another, smaller brick chimney stack. Further extensions or partial rebuilds were of timber-framing infilled with brick nogging, also partly over additional brick-lined cellars, and at about this time sash windows of 17th-c type were inserted. The roof of the main part of the building was raised and realigned, probably when a two-storey entrance hall containing an oak staircase was built within the first extension to the original house. A mural painting in the hall, signed by Lanscroon and dated 1726, provided a *terminus ante quem* for this development. The ground-floor room in the S part of the original house was probably a kitchen, and rooms added to its E were built to stay cool and well ventilated as larders, and were connected with the existing cellars by a basement passage. A range of service rooms was built subsequently, filling in the E front, perhaps at the same time as the principal rooms were panelled and a portico was added to the main entrance in the W front. A suite of spacious rooms was added to the N, probably early in the 19th c, built of place bricks faced internally with lath and plaster and externally with stock bricks. Later modifications, such as installation of waterpipes (some of which ran behind fireplaces to be heated) and drains, culminated in the early 20th c in the refacing of most of the exterior in imitation of timber-framing.

London Archaeol, 5, 1986, 161
Lea, R, 1994 'Broomfield House, Enfield: the structural development of the house', English Heritage Archive Report

BRM85

Map site: not shown
DUA: Richard Lea, Andrew Westman
NGR: TQ 3045 9265
SMR: 222042

Capel Manor, Bullsmoor Lane, Enfield, EN1

A watching brief in 1990 examined various post-medieval features possibly associated with Capel House, though no evidence of the house itself was found.

London Archaeol, 6, 1991, 302; *Post-Medieval Archaeol,* 25, 1991, 147

CAP90

Map site: 3
DGLA(N): Trevor Cox
NGR: TQ 3440 9970
SMR: 080664

Lincoln Road, Enfield, EN1

Excavation in 1976 revealed Roman occupation and 4th-c industrial activity.

London Archaeol, 3, 1977, 37
Gentry, A, Ivens, J, & McClean, H, 1977 'Excavations at Lincoln Road, London Borough of Enfield, November 1974–March 1976', *Trans London Middlesex Archaeol Soc,* 28, 101–89
McClean, H, & Deal, G, 1977 'Site-watching at Lincoln Road, October 1975–March 1976', in Gentry, A, Ivens, J, & McClean, H, 121–4

ELR76

Map site: 4
ILAU, EAS, WLAFG: H McClean, G Deal
NGR: TQ 3408 9607

ERH86

Map site: 5
DGLA(N): Paul Falcini
NGR: TQ 332 958
SMR: 082157

20 Village Road, Enfield, EN1

A trial excavation conducted in 1986 to ascertain the presence of Roman burials, previously located in the vicinity, revealed no trace of Roman activity.

GAR89

Map site: 6
DGLA(N): Trevor Cox
NGR: TQ 353 960
SMR: 082230

Garfield Road, Ponders End, Enfield, EN3

An evaluation excavation in 1989 revealed two boundary ditches aligned E–W and a gravel pathway, all relating to fields of c 17th-c date.

London Archaeol, 6, 1990, 189; Post-Medieval Archaeol, 24, 1990, 195

GTH90

Map site: 7
DGLA(N): Vaughan Birbeck
NGR: TQ 317 919
SMR: 082290–2

Greentrees Hospital, Tottenhall Road, N13

Excavation in 1990 located several redeposited flints, and a ditch of probably agricultural character dating to AD1070–1100.

London Archaeol, 6, 1991, 302; Medieval Archaeol, 35, 1991, 153

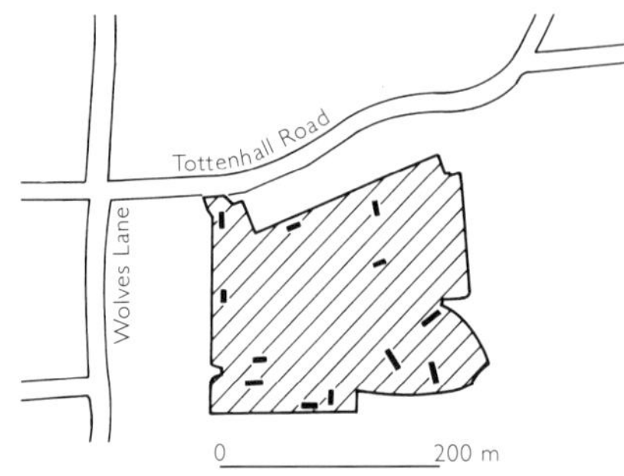

HOE90

Map site: 8
DGLA(N): Trevor Cox
NGR: TQ 3430 9810
SMR: 082296

Hoe Lane, Enfield, EN1

Excavation in 1990 located no archaeological features.

London Archaeol, 6, 1991, 302

SOU90

Map site: 9
DGLA(N): Vaughan Birbeck
NGR: TQ 2995 9320
SMR: 082293–5

Southgate House, Cannon Hill, N14

An evaluation excavation in 1990 revealed redeposited flint 'waste flakes' and burnt flint, together with a large quantity of redeposited 12th-/13th-c pottery sherds. A ditch or ha-ha aligned E–W was examined, as was a similarly aligned brick and tile drain, possibly of 17th–18th-c date. Both appear to be part of the gardens of the house.

London Archaeol, 6, 1991, 302; Post-Medieval Archaeol, 25, 1991, 147

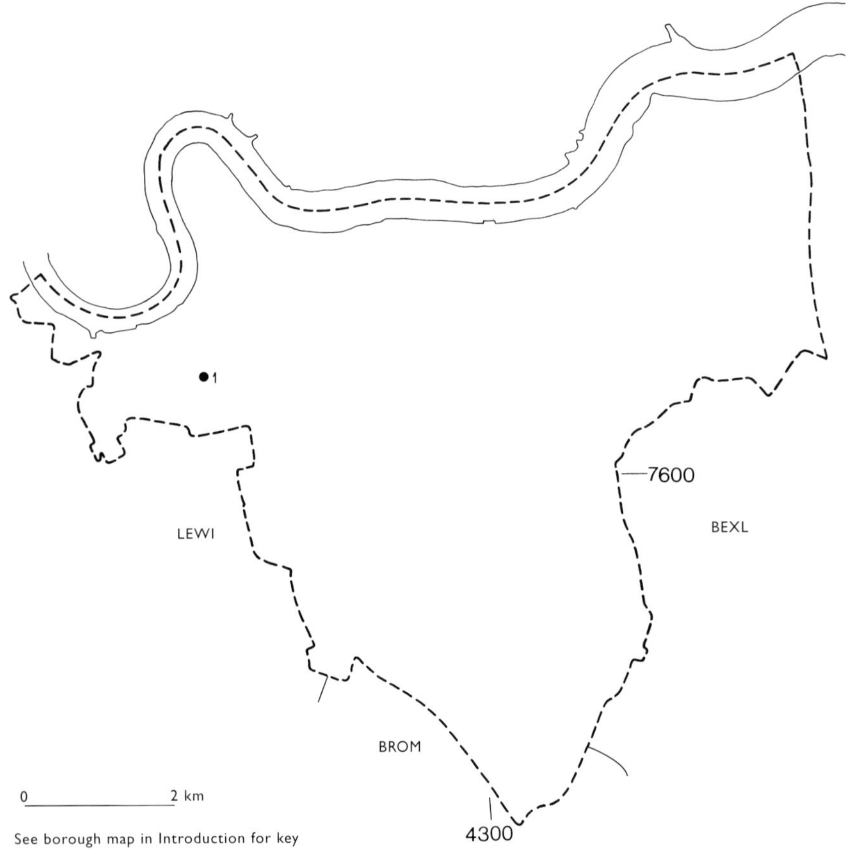

GP78

Map site: 1
SLAEC: Harvey Sheldon,
Brian Yule, Eric Ferretti
NGR: TQ 3930 7740
SMR: 070247

Greenwich Park, Maze Hill, SE10

The re-examination in 1978 of a Roman stone building and adjacent area, first reported in 1902 and now considered to be part of a temple complex, revealed two superimposed structures, including a tessellated floor belonging to the later structure. The masonry foundations of an E–W wall, probably the main S wall of the later structure, were also located; these foundations had been robbed out, but not before the mid-4th c. A considerable part of the site had clearly been destroyed in previous excavations, notably in 1902.

London Archaeol, 3, 1979, 262; *Britannia,* 10, 1979, 317
Sheldon, H, & Yule, B, 1979 'Excavations at Greenwich Park, 1978–9', *London Archaeol,* 3, 311–17

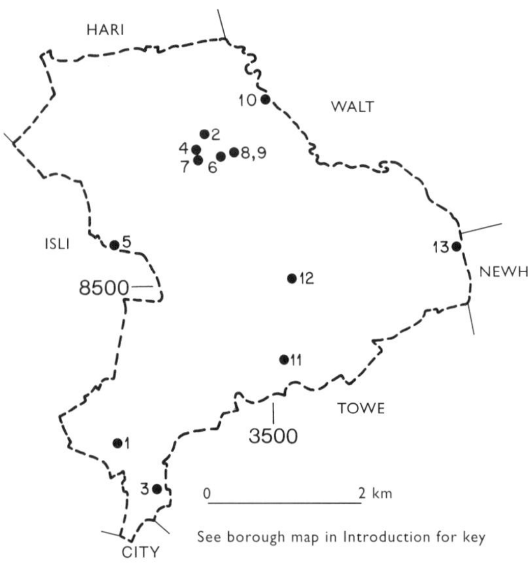

London Borough of Hackney

HACK	1	BEV79	42 Bevenden St (opposite), N1
HACK	2	CAZ76	65–69 Cazenove Rd, N16
HACK	3	HLP89	Holywell Priory, 183–185 Shoreditch High St, Holywell Lane, E1
HACK	4	KYV87	14 Kyverdale Rd, N16
HACK	5	NGR88	54 Newington Green, N16
HACK	6	NOR76	66–76 Northwold Rd, E5
HACK	7	NWR81	55 Northwold Rd, N16
HACK	8	ROT85	Rossington St (council depot), E5
HACK	9	RST82	Rossington St (council depot), E5
HACK	10	SFP87	Springfield Park, Spring Lane, E5
HACK	11	SHR78	18 Shore Rd, E9
HACK	12	SUT90	Sutton House, 2–4 Homerton High St, E9
HACK	13	TML75	Temple Mills Lane, E15

BEV79

Map site: 1
ILAU: David Whipp
NGR: TQ 328 828

Opposite 42 Bevenden Street, N1

Observation in 1979 revealed no archaeological features.

CAZ76

Map site: 2
ILAU: David Whipp
NGR: TQ 341 869
SMR: 080048

65–69 Cazenove Road, N16

A trial excavation in 1976 within a Palaeolithic working floor exposed soil horizons more than 360,000 years old. The lack of flints from the site has proved important in establishing the extent of the floor.

London Archaeol, 3, 1977, 37

HLP89

Map site: 3
DGLA(N): Barney Sloane
NGR: TQ 3342 8235
SMR: 080141, 082194

Holywell Priory, 183–185 Shoreditch High Street, Holywell Lane, E1

A trial excavation in 1989 within the precinct of the Augustinian priory of St John the Baptist, Holywell, produced evidence of Roman activity in the lowest levels, and agricultural soil established before the foundation of the nunnery (documented 1133–62). Much of the reconstruction of the priory based on documentary evidence was confirmed, including the location of the S aisle and chapels of the church. Despite the robbing of many of the walls, two or three phases of rebuilding were identified. At least one 15th-c floor surface was found, as were burials within the church and to the S of it, where the cemetery would be expected.

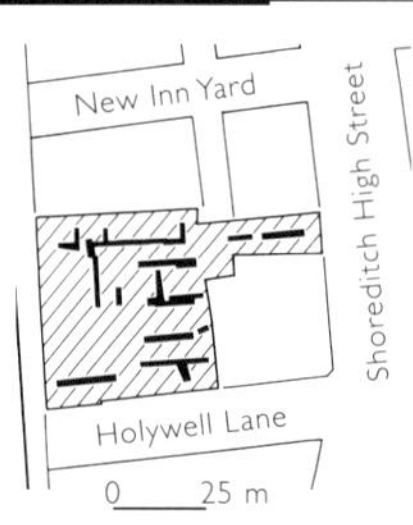

London Archaeol, 6, 1990, 189; *Medieval Archaeol,* 34, 1990, 181

14 Kyverdale Road, N16

KYV87

Map site: 4
DGLA(N): Kevin Wooldridge
NGR: TQ 3396 8672

An evaluation excavation in 1987 revealed no archaeological features.

54 Newington Green, N16

NGR88

Map site: 5
DGLA(N): Gordon Malcolm
NGR: TQ 3282 8536

A watching brief in 1988 produced no evidence of prehistoric or Roman features, though the former may be sealed beneath the recorded deposits. The discovery of a previously unrecorded building is consistent with documentary evidence of late medieval settlement at Newington Green.

66–76 Northwold Road, E5

NOR76

Map site: 6
ILAU: Graham Black
NGR: TQ 344 868
SMR: 080153

An evaluation excavation in 1976 indicated that most of the archaeological stratigraphy had been removed by the digging of 19th-c brickearth pits.

London Archaeol, 3, 1977, 37

55 Northwold Road, N16

NWR81

Map site: 7
ILAU: Philip Harding, Philip Gibbard
NGR: TQ 3398 8663
SMR: 080068–72, 080157

Excavation in 1981 in an area where many Lower Palaeolithic flint hand axes were found in the 19th c located a prehistoric river channel from which large quantities of pollen were recovered for analysis. A complete Acheulian-type hand axe was found, together with the tip of another and considerable quantities of flint waste.

London Archaeol, 4, 1982, 163
Blackmore, L, 1983 'The pottery', in Harding, P, & Gibbard, P, 'Excavations at Northwold Road, Stoke Newington, North-East London, 1981', *Trans London Middlesex Archaeol Soc, 34, 17–18*

Rossington Street (council depot), E5

ROT85

Map site: 8
DGLA: Gavin Evans, Rob Ellis, Paul Falcini
NGR: TQ 3447 8670

A watching brief in 1985 observed no evidence of the expected Palaeolithic working floor, but recorded a post-medieval pit.

Rossington Street (council depot), E5

RST82

Map site: 9
ILAU: Rob Ellis
NGR: TQ 3440 8669

A watching brief in 1982 showed that no archaeological features survived.

SFP87

Map site: 10
DGLA: Dave Whipp, Robert Whytehead
NGR: TQ 3495 8750
SMR: 082121

Springfield Park, Spring Lane, E5

A watching brief in 1987 resulted in the recovery of a wooden boat 4m long, located at a depth of about 6m in waterlogged ground, which precluded further investigation. The boat is dated by dendrochronology to AD950–1050, its position suggesting that it had been abandoned as a wreck to silt up on the W bank of the River Lea: later land reclamation and the canalisation of the Lea account for its land-locked location.

London Archaeol, 5, 1988, 411–12; *Medieval Archaeol,* 32, 1988, 250
Marsden, P (ed), 1989 'A late Saxon logboat from Clapton, London Borough of Hackney', *Int J Naut Archaeol & Underwater Exploration,* 18, 89–111

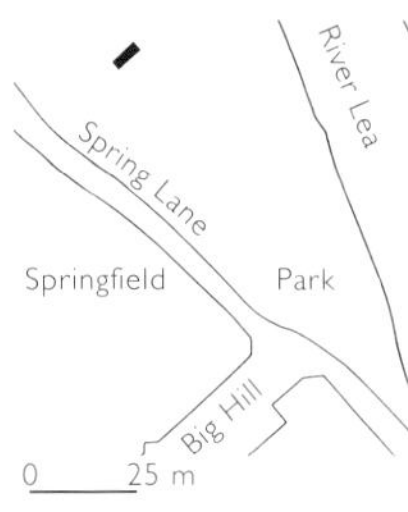

SHR78

Map site: 11
ILAU: Irene Schwab
NGR: TQ 351 841
SMR: 080179

18 Shore Road, E9

Excavation in 1978 revealed part of the medieval manor house known as Shoreditch Place. Wall foundations of chalk, ragstone and tile were located; in the initial phase of the house (13th–14th c) a revetted stream flowed beneath it. This was later blocked off, and floors of packed gravel and chalk were laid over the stream channel.

London Archaeol, 3, 1979, 263; *Medieval Archaeol,* 23, 1979, 270
Blackmore, L, & Schwab, I, 1989 'From the Templars to the tenement — a medieval and post-medieval site at 18 Shore Road, London, E9', *Trans London Middlesex Archaeol Soc,* 37, 147–86

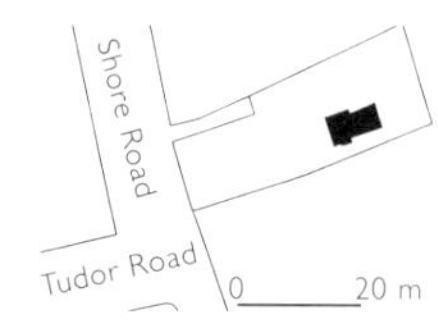

SUT90

Map site: 12
DGLA(N): Christopher Phillpotts
NGR: TQ 3527 8507
SMR: 080171, 220295

Sutton House, 2–4 Homerton High Street, E9

Excavations for the National Trust in 1990 within a 16th-c house and its courtyard revealed evidence of occupation and structural alterations from c 1535 to modern times, and included outbuildings, a 16th-c well, boundary walls, floor surfaces and hearths. Analysis of the standing structure by English Heritage was co-ordinated with the work of excavation.

London Archaeol, 6, 1991, 302
Blackburn, A, & Gray, M, 1992 *Sutton House, Hackney: an illustrated souvenir,* National Trust

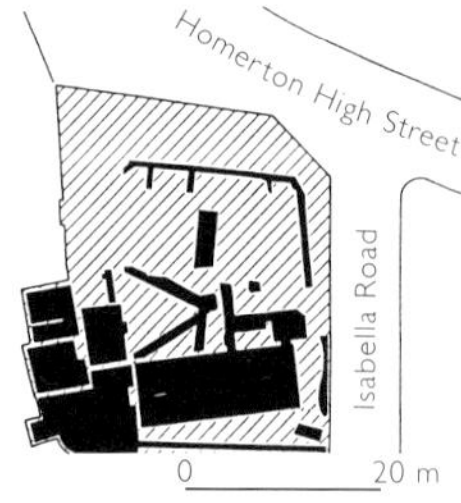

TML75

Map site: 13
ILAU: J Hinchcliffe
NGR: TQ 375 855
SMR: 081692–3

Temple Mills Lane, E15

Salvage work in 1975 in a sewer trench cut through Hackney Marsh produced human bone and a quantity of undated timber structures.

London Archaeol, 2, 1976, 371

HAMMERSMITH AND FULHAM

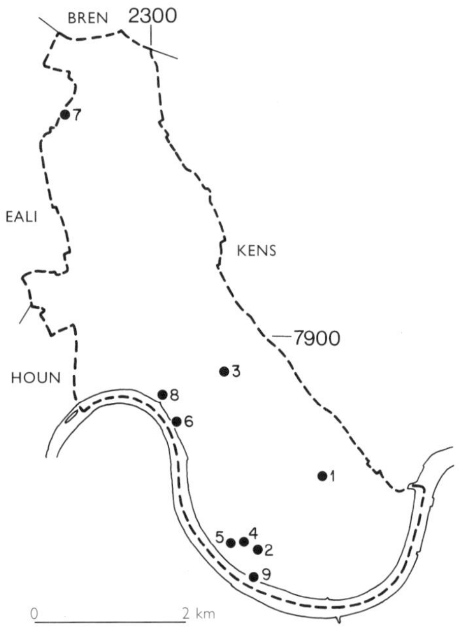

See borough map in Introduction for key

London Borough of Hammersmith and Fulham

HAMM	1	BRC76	30 Barclay Rd, SW6
HAMM	2	BUR78	Burlington Rd, SW6
HAMM	3	CLG76	St Paul's School, Colet Gardens, Hammersmith Rd, Edith Rd, Talgarth Rd, W14
HAMM	4	FPA90	Fulham Palace (walled gardens and playground), Bishop's Avenue, SW6
HAMM	5	FPGM87	Fulham Palace, Bishop's Avenue, SW6
HAMM	6	HAM90	Winslow Rd (distillery site), W6
HAMM	7	NPD88	North Pole British Rail Depot, off Old Oak Common Lane, Wormwood Scrubs, W12
HAMM	8	QCS76	51 Queen Caroline St (rear of), W6
HAMM	9	SWW78	Swan Wharf, Willow Bank, SW6

BRC76

Map site: 1
ILAU: J Siegel
NGR: TQ 2528 7712
SMR: 052251

30 Barclay Road, SW6

A watching brief in 1976 revealed two small lenses of burnt material; no dating evidence was recovered.

BUR78

Map site: 2
ILAU: Peter Mills
NGR: TQ 2443 7625
SMR: 050946

Burlington Road, SW6

Excavation in 1978, intended to assess the extent of the medieval village of Fulham, located no tenements, although a series of pits dating from the 17th–18th c indicated that the site lay within the area of the settlement.

London Archaeol, 3, 1979, 263
Blackmore, L, 1984 'The medieval and post-medieval pottery', in Mills, P S, 'Excavations at Burlington Road, Fulham, London, SW6', *Trans London Middlesex Archaeol Soc, 35, 101–8*

CLG76

Map site: 3
ILAU: J Siegel
NGR: TQ 239 786

St Paul's School, Colet Gardens, Hammersmith Road, Edith Road, Talgarth Road, W14

Observation in 1976 recorded no archaeological features, though post-medieval finds were recovered.

FPA90

Map site: 4
DGLA: Fiona Walker, John Mills
NGR: TQ 2420 7630

Fulham Palace (walled gardens and playground), Bishop's Avenue, SW6

A watching brief in 1990 revealed post-medieval build-up and garden soil, with clay pipes, brick and tile.

London Archaeol, 6, 1991, 302; Post-Medieval Archaeol, 25, 1991, 131

Fulham Palace, Bishop's Avenue, SW6

A watching brief in 1987 to the NW of the palace, within the area of the Scheduled Ancient Monument, located part of the substructure of the moat bridge, usually considered to be early 19th c, consisting of mortared brick, chalk and reused blocks of ragstone. Between the bridge and the W quadrangle of the palace a culturally sterile garden soil was exposed to a depth of 0.5–0.6m over a distance of some 75–80m along the palace driveway. A deep, backfilled feature, undated, was observed immediately adjacent to the gate of the W quadrangle. Within the E corner of the latter, the top of a linear brick structure, running ENE–WSW and possibly a drain, was observed at a depth of 0.2m.

London Archaeol, 5, 1988, 411; *Post-Medieval Archaeol,* 22, 1988, 217

FPGM87

Map site: 5
DGLA, FARG: John Mills,
K R Whitehouse
NGR: TQ 239 762

Distillery site, Winslow Road, W6

Excavations in 1990 exposed three rectangular sunken-featured buildings of Early Saxon date, aligned E–W and with post-holes set at the mid-points of the two short sides. Other associated post-holes were also located.

London Archaeol, 6, 1991, 302; *Medieval Archaeol,* 35, 1991, 154
Anon, 1990 'Early Saxon settlement in Hammersmith', Mosaic, *London Archaeol,* 6, 224

HAM90

Map site: 6
DGLA: Neil Bugler
NGR: TQ 233 779

North Pole British Rail Depot, off Old Oak Common Lane, Wormwood Scrubs, W12

Excavations in 1988 showed that the channel of Stamford Brook had been cleaned out early in the 20th c, and that no archaeological deposits survived.

London Archaeol, 6, 1989, 74

NPD88

Map site: 7
DGLA(SW): Caroline
Pathy-Barker
NGR: TQ 218 819
SMR: 051106

Rear of 51 Queen Caroline Street, W6

Excavations in 1976 to investigate the medieval settlement of Hammersmith located only large-scale 18th-c dumping.

London Archaeol, 3, 1977, 37

QCS76

Map site: 8
ILAU: Graham Black
NGR: TQ 231 783
SMR: 050945

Swan Wharf, Willow Bank, SW6

A trial excavation in 1978 revealed the brick foundations of a malthouse probably built in the late 17th c.

London Archaeol, 3, 1979, 263

SWW78

Map site: 9
ILAU: David Whipp
NGR: TQ 243 758

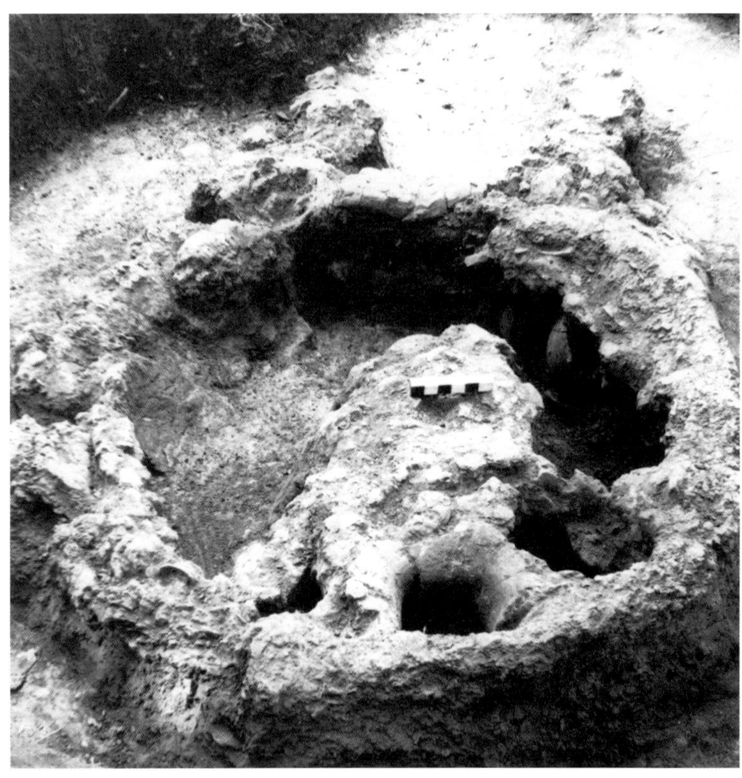

Haringey   HW70   Highgate Wood, Muswell Hill Road, N6 & N10. Round foundation of a Roman pottery kiln, built of clay and occasional tiles, and dated to the late 1st–early 2nd c.

HARINGEY

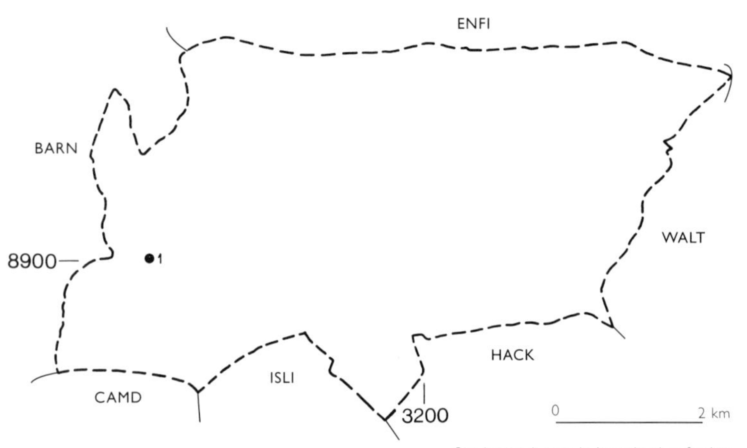

London Borough of Haringey

HARI   I   HW70   Highgate Wood, Muswell Hill Rd,
N6 & N10

See borough map in Introduction for key

HW70

Map site: I
Tony Brown, Harvey Sheldon
NGR: TQ 282 890
SMR: 080276

Highgate Wood, Muswell Hill Road, N6 & N10

Field survey in 1962 produced evidence of Roman pottery manufacture, confirmed by trial trenching in 1966. Subsequent excavation, which continued until 1971, disclosed eight kilns built of clay and occasional tiles, bounded by a ditch to the E, and several clay pits, rubbish pits and large dumps of pottery wasters. The pottery industry is dated to the late 1st–early 2nd c.

London Archaeol, 2, 1973, 41; 2, 1974, 134; 2, 1975, 257
Brightwell, A, Demetriou, G, Massey, M, & Neacy, N, 1972 'The Horniman Museum kiln experiment at Highgate Wood', *London Archaeol,* 2, 12–17
Brown, A E, & Sheldon, H L, 1969 'Early Roman pottery factory in North London', *London Archaeol,* 1, 39–44
Brown, A E, & Sheldon, H L, 1969 'Post-excavation work on pottery from Highgate', *London Archaeol,* 1, 60–5
Brown, A E, & Sheldon, H L, 1970 'Highgate 1969', *London Archaeol,* 1, 150–4
Brown, A E, & Sheldon, H L, 1971 'Highgate 1970–1971', *London Archaeol,* 1, 300–3
Brown, A E, & Sheldon, H L, 1974 'Highgate Wood: the pottery and its production', *London Archaeol,* 2, 222–31
Butterworth, P, 1969 'Moving a Roman kiln', *London Archaeol,* 1, 75–9
Orton, C R, 1970 'Pottery associated with Pit 3 and Kiln 3 in Highgate Wood' (privately circulated)
Orton, C R, 1970 'The production of pottery from a Romano-British kiln site: a statistical investigation', *World Archaeol,* 1 (part 3), 343–58
Orton, C R, 1971 'Some pottery from Ditch 1 in Highgate Wood' (privately circulated)
Orton, C R, 1972 'Pottery from the Dump Area in Highgate Wood' (privately circulated)
Orton, C R, 1974 'An experiment in the mathematical reconstruction of the pottery from a Romano-British kiln site at Highgate Wood', *Bull Inst Archaeol Univ London,* 11, 41–73
Robertson, B, 1970 & 1971 'Resistivity surveying', *London Archaeol,* 1, 195–8 & 232–5
Sheldon, H, 1987 'The Roman pottery', in *Highgate Wood* (City of London centenary booklet), 24–5
Tyers, P A, 1977 'The Highgate Wood Roman pottery industry and its origins', BSc Thesis, University College, Cardiff

LONDON BOROUGH OF

HARROW

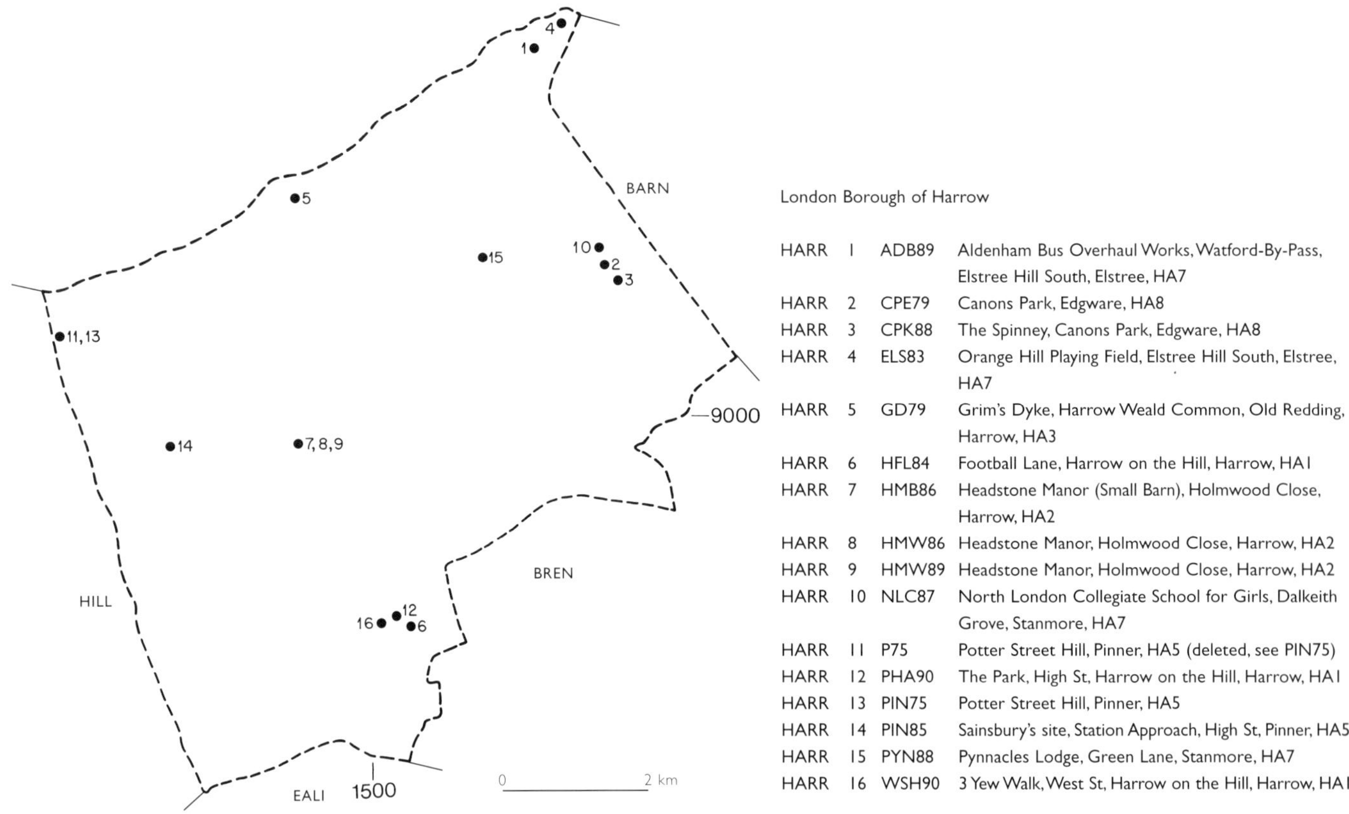

London Borough of Harrow

HARR	1	ADB89	Aldenham Bus Overhaul Works, Watford-By-Pass, Elstree Hill South, Elstree, HA7
HARR	2	CPE79	Canons Park, Edgware, HA8
HARR	3	CPK88	The Spinney, Canons Park, Edgware, HA8
HARR	4	ELS83	Orange Hill Playing Field, Elstree Hill South, Elstree, HA7
HARR	5	GD79	Grim's Dyke, Harrow Weald Common, Old Redding, Harrow, HA3
HARR	6	HFL84	Football Lane, Harrow on the Hill, Harrow, HA1
HARR	7	HMB86	Headstone Manor (Small Barn), Holmwood Close, Harrow, HA2
HARR	8	HMW86	Headstone Manor, Holmwood Close, Harrow, HA2
HARR	9	HMW89	Headstone Manor, Holmwood Close, Harrow, HA2
HARR	10	NLC87	North London Collegiate School for Girls, Dalkeith Grove, Stanmore, HA7
HARR	11	P75	Potter Street Hill, Pinner, HA5 (deleted, see PIN75)
HARR	12	PHA90	The Park, High St, Harrow on the Hill, Harrow, HA1
HARR	13	PIN75	Potter Street Hill, Pinner, HA5
HARR	14	PIN85	Sainsbury's site, Station Approach, High St, Pinner, HA5
HARR	15	PYN88	Pynnacles Lodge, Green Lane, Stanmore, HA7
HARR	16	WSH90	3 Yew Walk, West St, Harrow on the Hill, Harrow, HA1

ADB89

Map site: 1
DGLA(N): Aileen Connor
NGR: TQ 1681 9482
SMR: 052166

Aldenham Bus Overhaul Works, Watford-By-Pass, Elstree Hill South, Elstree, HA7

An evaluation excavation in 1989 produced no archaeological evidence apart from two sherds of medieval pottery.

CPE79

Map site: 2
MoL, WLAFG: Jon Cotton, Alison Laws
NGR: TQ 184 917
SMR: 052033

Canons Park, Edgware, HA8

An evaluation excavation in 1979, carried out to investigate a spread of Roman tiles uncovered during drainage work, located alternating layers of tile and clay, apparently dumped on an old turf-line. Since many of the tiles were misfired, they would seem to form part of a manufacturing waste heap. Initial augering of the immediate area indicated that the dump was extensive, while the presence of further dumps was indicated as a result of fieldwalking in Canons Park. The site lies only a mile to the S of Brockley Hill, whose pottery products date to the late 1st and 2nd c.

London Archaeol, 3, 1980, 386; *Britannia,* 11, 1980, 381

CPK88

Map site: 3
DGLA(N): Barney Sloane
NGR: TQ 1845 9165

The Spinney, Canons Park, Edgware, HA8

An archaeological survey in 1988 revealed several layers containing varying quantities of Roman tile fragments. No features were located, except for a possible cut seen in section, but it is likely that a Roman tile kiln lay on this site.

Orange Hill Playing Field, Elstree Hill South, Elstree, HA7

Site watching in 1983 observed a hearth and probable ditch of 13th-c date, suggesting limited activity, perhaps in part occupational. Much of the pottery recovered appeared to be waste material, though no evidence of a kiln was observed.

London Archaeol, 4, 1984, 387; Medieval Archaeol, 28, 1984, 229

ELS83

Map site: 4
ILAU: Rob Ellis
NGR: TQ 1765 9515

Grim's Dyke, Harrow Weald Common, Old Redding, Harrow, HA3

Excavation in 1979 revealed a hearth with potential evidence for dating the earthwork. Two sherds of possibly Early Iron Age pottery, probably residual, were found within the bank.

London Archaeol, 3, 1980, 386
Ellis, R, 1982 'Excavations at Grim's Dyke, Harrow, 1979', *Trans London Middlesex Archaeol Soc, 33, 173–6*

GD79

Map site: 5
ILAU: Rob Ellis
NGR: TQ 1416 9288

Football Lane, Harrow on the Hill, Harrow, HA1

Site watching in 1984 revealed no archaeological features.

HFL84

Map site: 6
ILAU: Rob Ellis
NGR: TQ 1559 8734
SMR: 052248

Headstone Manor (Small Barn), Holmwood Close, Harrow, HA2

A survey of the post-medieval framework of the barn and excavation within its standing structure in 1986, prior to restoration, showed, despite severe fire damage, that all the timbers in the common post and truss cross-frame oak construction had been salvaged from other timber-framed buildings, and that not all of them were reused as originally intended. The barn had developed from a much smaller structure to the NE which was later extended SW by the addition of a larger building of similar construction, the two parts then sharing a single roof. Evidence of other alterations and repairs was found. Excavation revealed a series of chalk and rammed pebble floors with associated post-holes from an earlier post-medieval building, apparently on the same alignment as the existing structure. At the NE end were the remains of a red-brick hearth and drainage channel. Artefacts indicated that this development had occurred in the medieval and post-medieval periods. However, redeposited prehistoric and Roman pottery suggest much earlier activity on the site.

London Archaeol, 5, 1987, 275; Post-Medieval Archaeol, 21, 1987, 283
Tucker, S, 1987 'Excavations and survey of the Small Barn, Headstone Manor, Harrow, Middlesex', *Trans London Middlesex Archaeol Soc, 38, 151–8*

HMB86

Map site: 7
DGLA(N): Stephen Tucker
NGR: TQ 1410 8970
SMR: 052146–8

Headstone Manor, Holmwood Close, Harrow, HA2

A watching brief on the site of the medieval manor house of Headstone in 1986, followed by an evaluation excavation in 1989, revealed the presence of stratified deposits consisting of a series of undated dumps, whose position within the monument would suggest that they are of medieval or later date.

HMW86: *Post-Medieval Archaeol, 21, 1987, 283*
HMW89: *Post-Medieval Archaeol, 25, 1991, 147*

**HMW86,
HMW89**

Map site: 8, 9
DGLA(N): Michael Hutchinson, Stephen Haynes
NGR: TQ 1410 8970
SMR: 052249

NLC87

Map site: 10
DGLA(N): Gordon Malcolm
NGR: TQ 1830 9220

North London Collegiate School for Girls, Dalkeith Grove, Stanmore, HA7

Excavation in 1987 produced no findings of importance, apart from fragments of oolitic limestone used as field drain packing and derived from earlier buildings of unknown date.

PHA90

Map site: 12
DGLA: Fiona Walker
NGR: TQ 1550 8750
SMR: 052244

The Park, High Street, Harrow on the Hill, Harrow, HA1

A watching brief in 1990 recorded post-medieval deposits or topsoil.

London Archaeol, 6, 1991, 303; Post-Medieval Archaeol, 25, 1991, 131

PIN75

Map site: 13
MoL, WLAFG: Alison Laws
NGR: TQ 1071 9121
SMR: 052083

Potter Street Hill, Pinner, HA5

Excavation in 1975 located part of a medieval kiln, probably 13th c in date, its contents including jars and bowls with applied decoration as well as jugs with slashed and thumb-impressed handles and curfews, mostly in a hard grey fabric containing large quantities of small flint grits. P75 (map site 11) was given incorrectly to this site, and has now been deleted.

London Archaeol, 2, 1976, 371
Sheppard, R, 1977 'A medieval pottery kiln at Pinner', *London Archaeol, 3, 31–5*

PIN85

Map site: 14
DGLA(N), PHS: Peter Mills
NGR: TQ 1220 8953

Sainsbury's site, Station Approach, High Street, Pinner, HA5

A watching brief in 1985 showed that much of the stratigraphy had been truncated in recent times, though one structure of uncertain purpose was identified: the N end of a finished and rounded wall, perhaps part of an open-sided outbuilding with later alterations. Also examined was a large ditch aligned E–W, continued recutting of which would imply that it functioned as a drain or boundary. A small quantity of medieval material was recovered.

PYN88

Map site: 15
DGLA(N): Niall Roycroft
NGR: TQ 1669 9232
SMR: 052250

Pynnacles Lodge, Green Lane, Stanmore, HA7

A watching brief in 1988 observed natural clays sloping gently from E to W. Sectioning indicated two large round-bottomed pits filled with gravel and clay, apparently the earliest features on the site, though no dating evidence was forthcoming.

3 Yew Walk, West Street, Harrow on the Hill, Harrow, HA1

Excavation in 1990 revealed a ditch containing possible Saxon abraded sherds, and a smaller ditch and a pit containing medieval pottery. Post-holes and pits of 19th-c date, and a brick drain and well, were also found.

London Archaeol, 6, 1991, 303; Medieval Archaeol, 35, 1991, 154

WSH90

Map site: 16
DGLA: Heather Fear, Brian Pye
NGR: TQ 1520 8755
SMR: 052245

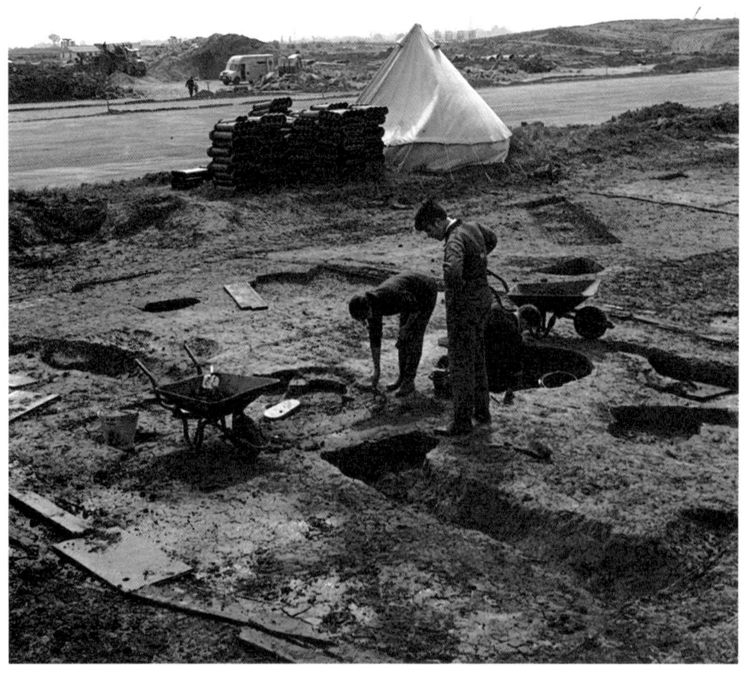

Hillingdon HEA69 Heathrow Airport, Runway 1, Western Perimeter Road, Hounslow, TW6.
Work in progress, examining evidence of prehistoric to Roman date.

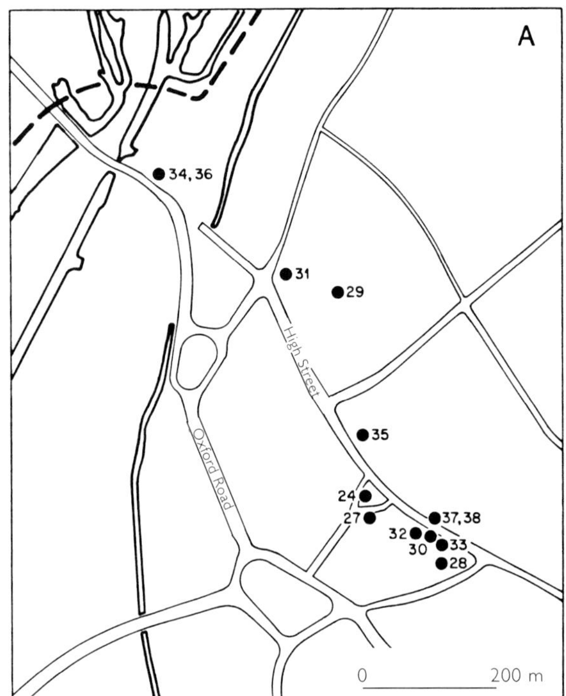

London Borough of Hillingdon

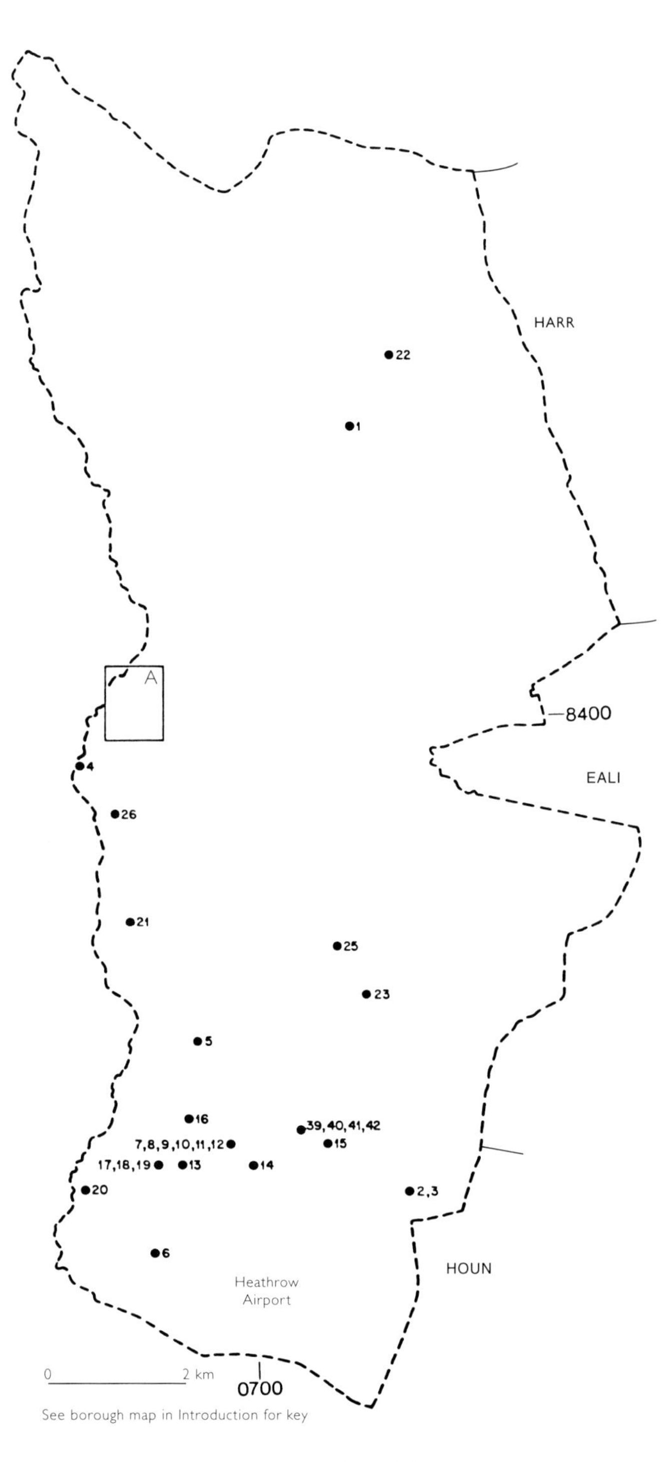

See borough map in Introduction for key

HILL 1   BFR86   Bury Farm, 123 Bury St, Ruislip, HA4

HILL 2   CLH89   Cranford Lane, Harlington, Hayes, UB3

HILL 3   CLH90   Cranford Lane, Harlington, Hayes, UB3

HILL 4   CMU89   Cowley Mill Rd (former Auto Diesels
                  site), Uxbridge, UB8

HILL 5   GNWD79   Gate House Nurseries, Church Rd,
                  West Drayton, UB7

HILL 6   HEA69   Heathrow Airport, Runway 1, Western
                  Perimeter Rd, Hounslow, TW6

HILL 7   HL80   Holloway Lane, Harmondsworth,
                  West Drayton, UB7

HILL 8   HL81   Holloway Lane, Harmondsworth,
                  West Drayton, UB7

HILL 9   HL82   Holloway Lane, Harmondsworth,
                  West Drayton, UB7

HILL 10 HL83   Holloway Lane, Harmondsworth,
                  West Drayton, UB7

HILL 11 HL85   Holloway Lane, Harmondsworth,
                  West Drayton, UB7

HILL 12 HL87   Holloway Lane, Harmondsworth,
                  West Drayton, UB7

HILL 13 HLL89   15 Holloway Lane (rear of),
                  Harmondsworth, West Drayton, UB7

HILL 14 HOM88   Home Farm, off Harmondsworth
                  Lane, Sipson, West Drayton, UB7

HILL 15 ICSG86   Imperial College Sports Ground,
                  Sipson Lane, Harlington, Hayes, UB3

HILL 16 M4W84   M4 Widening Scheme, West Drayton,
                  UB7

HILL 17 MFH87   Manor Farm, off Holloway Lane,
                  Harmondsworth, West Drayton, UB7

HILL 18 MFH88   Manor Farm, off Holloway Lane,
                  Harmondsworth, West Drayton, UB7

HILL 19 MFH89   Manor Farm, off Holloway Lane,
                  Harmondsworth, West Drayton, UB7

HILL 20 MLW82   Accommodation Lane, Moor Lane
                  (west), Harmondsworth, West
                  Drayton, UB7

HILL 21 PBL89   Packet Boat Lane (former George
                  Hopton site), Cowley, Uxbridge, UB8

HILL 22 PWR84   Park Wood, Bury St, Ruislip, HA4

HILL 23 RLS90   Rigby Lane, Dawley Rd (Stockley
                  Park Development), Hayes, UB3

HILL 24 SMC87   St Margaret's church, Belmont Rd,
                  Uxbridge, UB8

HILL 25 SPD85   Stockley Park, fronting Dawley Rd,
                  Hayes, UB3

HILL 26 TSC89   Trys site (rear of), High St, Cowley,
                  Uxbridge, UB8

HILL 27 UX83i   2–3 Windsor St, Uxbridge, UB8

HILL 28 UX83ii   5–6 High St, Uxbridge, UB8

HILL 29 UX83iii 126 High St, Uxbridge, UB8

HILL 30 UX83iv   15–17 High St, Uxbridge, UB8

HILL 31 UX85v   118 High St, Uxbridge, UB8

HILL 32 UX85vi   20 High St, Uxbridge, UB8

HILL 33 UX85vii 12–14 High St, Uxbridge, UB8

HILL 34 UX86viii 101–105 Oxford Rd, Uxbridge, UB8

HILL 34 UX88viii Three Ways Wharf, 101–105 Oxford
                  Rd, Uxbridge, UB8

HILL 35 UX88ix   155–156 High St, Uxbridge, UB8

HILL 36 UX90viii 101–105 Oxford Rd, Uxbridge, UB8

HILL 39 WGF79   Wall Garden Farm, Sipson Lane,
                  Harlington, West Drayton, UB7

HILL 40 WGF80   Wall Garden Farm, Sipson Lane,
                  Harlington, West Drayton, UB7

HILL 41 WGF81   Wall Garden Farm, Sipson Lane,
                  Harlington, West Drayton, UB7

HILL 42 WGF84   Wall Garden Farm, Sipson Lane,
                  Harlington, West Drayton, UB7

Bury Farm, 123 Bury Street, Ruislip, HA4

During renovation in 1985, a brick building dated to the early 17th c was found to include the wall of a timber-framed open hall house dated to the 15th c. Excavation in 1986 uncovered features of 13th–18th-c date, including flint-rubble wall footings, probably part of the solar of the 15th-c building, and brick foundations, perhaps from an outhouse of 17th-c date.

London Archaeol, 5, 1987, 275

BFR86

Map site: 1
DGLA(W), WLAFG,
RN&ELHS: John Mills
NGR: TQ 087 882
SMR: 050964

Cranford Lane, Harlington, Hayes, UB3

An evaluation S of Cranford Lane in 1989 revealed features that were predominantly of Late Bronze–Early Iron Age date (c 900–500BC) and late Roman date (early–mid-4th c). Finds recovered from the latter point to the presence in the vicinity of a substantial late Roman building.

London Archaeol, 6, 1990, 189

CLH89

Map site: 2
DGLA(W): Andrew Boucher
NGR: TQ 093 772
SMR: 051098–9

Cranford Lane, Harlington, Hayes, UB3

Following an evaluation in 1989 (CLH89), site watching and excavation in 1990 revealed later prehistoric and Roman features. The former, provisionally dated to the Late Bronze Age, consisted of a series of field boundary ditches and some pits. The Roman features, dated to the 3rd and 4th c AD, comprised one corner of an enclosure containing a series of pits and ditches. Part of a part-polished Neolithic axe was found in a late Roman feature.

London Archaeol, 6, 1991, 303; Britannia, 22, 1991, 272

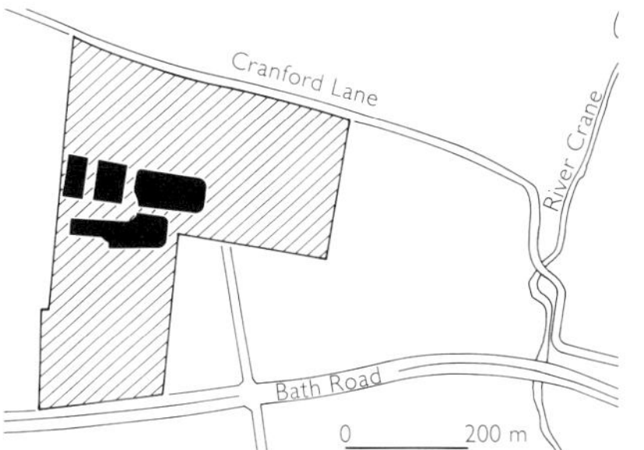

CLH90

Map site: 3
DGLA(W): Ian Stewart,
Fiona Walker
NGR: TQ 0900 7750
SMR: 051098–9

Former Auto Diesels site, Cowley Mill Road, Uxbridge, UB8

Excavation in 1989 of a site near the River Colne, on a river terrace gravel covered locally with a layer of organic peaty silt to varying depths, revealed parts of two scatters of flintwork. These were at the interface of the gravel and organic layers, and are dated to the Early Mesolithic period.

London Archaeol, 6, 1990, 189

CMU89

Map site: 4
DGLA: Ian Stewart
NGR: TQ 0462 8344
SMR: 051142

Gate House Nurseries, Church Road, West Drayton, UB7

Excavations were undertaken in 1979 to determine the location of a manor house built in the vicinity in the 1540s by the Tudor statesman William Paget. A series of pits and ditches, containing pottery dated to the 11th or 12th c, was sealed by the surfaces of a late medieval courtyard, perhaps pertaining to a manor owned by the canons of St Paul's. These surfaces were superseded in turn by the remains of what is identified as the S wing of Paget's building. Evidence was found for a drainage system, and for one phase of alteration before demolition of the building. A feature on an 18th-c survey, identified hitherto as a porch, is reinterpreted as a clock tower.

London Archaeol, 3, 1980, 387; 4, 1981, 47; Post-Medieval Archaeol, 14, 1980, 209
Cotton, J, 1981 'Excavations in Church Road, West Drayton, 1979–80', London Archaeol, 4, 121–9

GNWD79

Map site: 5
MoL, WLAFG: Jon Cotton,
Alison Laws
NGR: TQ 062 795

HEA69

Map site: 6
London Museum, WLAFG:
Roy Canham
NGR: TQ 0555 7651
SMR: 050217–21

Heathrow Airport, Runway I, Western Perimeter Road, Hounslow, TW6

Excavations in 1969 revealed evidence of settlement from the Bronze Age to the late Roman period. Two ring ditches were exposed by contractors' groundworks, one of which was divided into segments by causeways. Emergency fieldwork was concentrated on a site of Iron Age and Roman date, much of which appeared to have been destroyed already. Some Early Iron Age pottery contained unusual forms, dated to the 6th or 5th c BC.

Anon, 1969 'Heathrow Airport excavations', Mosaic, *London Archaeol*, 1, 96
Bird, J, 1978 'The samian', in Canham, R, 36
Canham, R, 1978 'Excavations at London (Heathrow) Airport 1969', *Trans London Middlesex Archaeol Soc*, 29, 1–44
Hartley, K F, 1978 'A mortarium stamp from Heathrow', in Canham, R, 36–7
Laws, A, 1978 'Historical background', in Canham, R, 3–4
Laws, A, 1978 'The Roman pottery', in Canham, R, 29–36
Sutton, M, 1978 'The bone evidence', in Canham, R, 38–43

HL80

Map site: 7
MoL, WLAFG: Jon Cotton
NGR: TQ 067 781
SMR: 051154

Holloway Lane, Harmondsworth, West Drayton, UB7

Observation in 1980 during the initial stages of gravel extraction confirmed the presence of prehistoric activity in the area. Features noted during their destruction included two pits containing Late Neolithic flints and pottery, part of a probably later Bronze Age ring-gully and a series of possible late prehistoric ditches.

London Archaeol, 4, 1981, 47

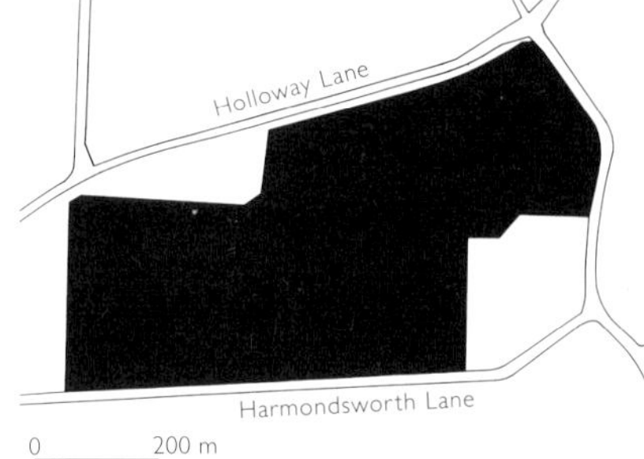

HL81

Map site: 8
MoL, WLAFG, SAFG: Jon Cotton
NGR: TQ 067 781
SMR: 051158

Holloway Lane, Harmondsworth, West Drayton, UB7

An emergency excavation in 1981 recovered evidence of later prehistoric activity covering several acres. Features included a number of pits and ditches containing Late Iron Age or early Roman pottery, and quantities of possible slag.

London Archaeol, 4, 1982, 164

HL82

Map site: 9
MoL, WLAFG: Jon Cotton, John Mills
NGR: TQ 067 780
SMR: 051152–64

Holloway Lane, Harmondsworth, West Drayton, UB7

Excavation in 1982 of an area of more than 2000sq m to the S and W of previous work (see HL80 and HL81 above) exposed, among the earliest features, a small series of Late Neolithic pits and clearance hollows, some of them apparently cut by a narrow, irregularly dug double-ditched trackway running N–S. This was succeeded by a substantial double-ditched track or droveway of later Bronze Age date, running E–W. A group of small rubbish-filled pits, probably to be associated with this phase, produced pottery of post-Deverel-Rimbury type. A small group of later Iron Age pits was dug to the S of this trackway, and was partly overlain by a sub-oval Romano-British enclosure of probably mid-1st-c AD date, which delimited an area of intercutting pits and hollows. This enclosure appears to have continued in use into the 2nd c, and may be associated with an interrupted and much recut boundary ditch and part of a two-phase rectilinear field-system. No evidence of late Roman occupation was recovered, though the area was reoccupied in the Middle Saxon period when a small two-post sunken-floored hut was constructed in a small enclosure on the edge of the Roman field-system.

London Archaeol, 4, 1983, 288; *Medieval Archaeol*, 27, 1983, 195

Holloway Lane, Harmondsworth, West Drayton, UB7

HL83

Map site: 10
MoL, WLAFG: John Mills
NGR: TQ 065 781
SMR: 051157, 051161

Excavation in 1983 to the N and W of previous work (see HL80, HL81 and HL82 above) revealed further features of prehistoric and Roman date. In particular, the later Bronze Age double-ditched track or droveway noted previously was found to continue to the W beyond the area of current excavation, bringing its recorded length to more than 600m. An unusual, probably late Hallstatt, brooch with two sets of skeuomorphic spring-coils wound around iron pins was recovered from the base of secondary silting in the S ditch. In addition, a small series of later Roman features was uncovered, including a small oven and possible accompanying windbreak.

London Archaeol, 4, 1984, 387

Holloway Lane, Harmondsworth, West Drayton, UB7

HL85

Map site: 11
DGLA, WLAFG: Jon Cotton,
John Mills
NGR: TQ 068 782
SMR: 051156

Further excavation in 1985 revealed a series of prehistoric pits and scoops assigned to the later Neolithic period and Late Bronze Age. Part of a rectangular enclosure was also recovered, perhaps of later prehistoric date. Excavation continued in 1986, when pits, hearths and lengths of a shallow gully producing Late Bronze Age pottery were located at one end of the site. Investigation of an apparently rectilinear enclosure with opposed entrance, located the previous year, produced Late Bronze Age pottery from primary and secondary ditchfills.

London Archaeol, 5, 1986, 162; 5, 1987, 275

Holloway Lane, Harmondsworth, West Drayton, UB7

HL87

Map site: 12
DGLA, WLAFG: John Lewis,
Jon Cotton
NGR: TQ 070 783
SMR: 051155

Excavations and a watching brief in 1987 to the E of the area examined previously (see HL85 above) revealed a series of pits and scoops of both Late Neolithic/Early Bronze Age and Late Bronze Age date, cut into the natural brickearth. One shallow scoop was cut through by a large vertically sided oval pit; the dismembered carcass of a young aurochs accompanied by six barbed and tanged flint arrows was revealed just above the floor of the pit. The bone was poorly preserved, but the animal was clearly of considerable size. It is dated to the Early Bronze Age on the basis of the arrowheads.

London Archaeol, 5, 1988, 412

Rear of 15 Holloway Lane, Harmondsworth, West Drayton, UB7

HLL89

Map site: 13
DGLA: Heather Fear
NGR: TQ 059 778
SMR: 051143–4

An evaluation excavation in 1989 revealed a possible late glacial stream channel, and a sub-rectangular feature containing a small quantity of probable Saxon pottery, together with pits and a gully of 12th–13th-c date.

London Archaeol, 6, 1990, 189; Medieval Archaeol, 34, 1990, 182

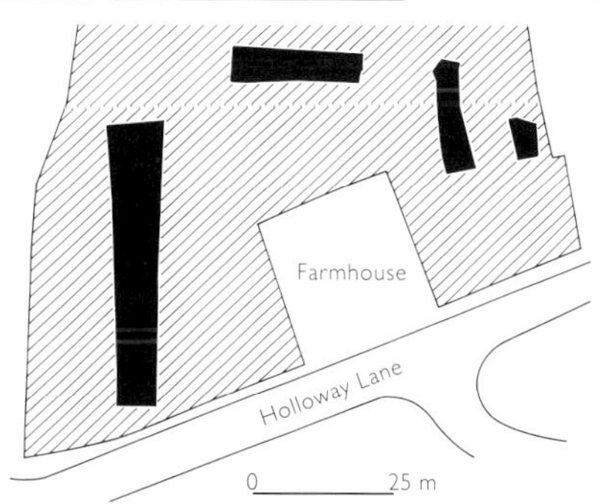

HOM88

Map site: 14
DGLA: Andrew Boucher
NGR: TQ 071 777
SMR: 051107–10

Home Farm, off Harmondsworth Lane, Sipson, West Drayton, UB7

Excavation in 1988 revealed much worked flint, including a Mesolithic adze, and two ditches and two pits of Neolithic date. Most of the excavated features were of Late Bronze Age date and included linear ditches and rubbish pits. An Early Saxon feature containing fragments of loom weight was also found.

London Archaeol, 6, 1989, 74

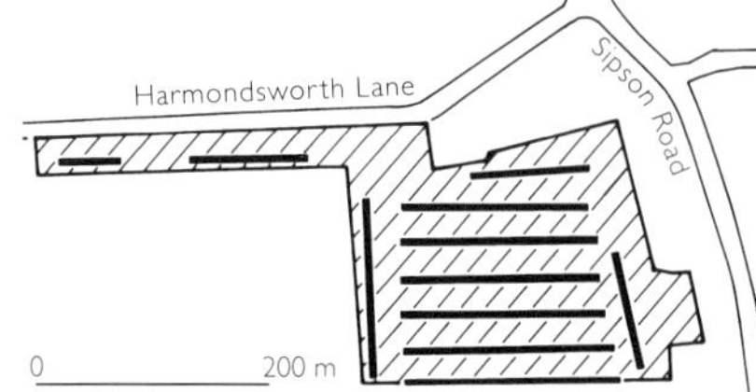

ICSG86

Map site: 15
DGLA: Jon Cotton
NGR: TQ 082 780
SMR: 051126

Imperial College Sports Ground, Sipson Lane, Harlington, Hayes, UB3

Site watching in 1986 revealed a series of features, mostly undated, comprising N–S gullies and a scoop containing much burnt flint. The upper silts of a large oval feature dug into the natural terrace gravel produced a few sherds of probable Late Bronze Age pottery; the lower, waterlogged, silts contained a few small fragments of wood.

London Archaeol, 5, 1987, 275

M4W84

Map site: 16
DGLA(W): John Mills
NGR: TQ 0607 7836
SMR: 050962, 051045

M4 Widening Scheme, West Drayton, UB7

Excavation in 1984 revealed Late Bronze Age pits and a Saxon *gruebenhaus*.

MFH87

Map site: 17
DGLA: John Mills
NGR: TQ 056 777–056 778
SMR: 050963, 051119–22

Manor Farm, off Holloway Lane, Harmondsworth, West Drayton, UB7

A watching brief in 1987 on a developer's trial inspection pits around and S of a Scheduled tithe barn revealed medieval gullies, ditches and a pit, dating to the late 12th or 13th c. Part of an unidentified deep feature of 18th–19th-c date was exposed, and sherds of chaff-tempered, probably Saxon, pottery were recovered. Trial pits within the barn showed that the present floor consists of apparently undisturbed natural brickearth, and that the dwarf walls supporting the sill-beams of the barn are very shallowly founded. Three dendrochronological samples taken from timber beams within the barn produced a felling date of 1420–30.

London Archaeol, 5, 1988, 412; Medieval Archaeol, 32, 1988, 250

Manor Farm, off Holloway Lane, Harmondsworth, West Drayton, UB7

MFH88

Map site: 18
DGLA: John Mills
NGR: TQ 056 778
SMR: 051123–4

Excavation in 1988 uncovered several small pits and scoops, probably prehistoric, cut into the natural brickearth. A right-angled ditch, possibly part of a rectangular enclosure, and a shallow rectangular scoop, thought to be part of a two-post sunken building, can be dated to the Early/Middle Saxon period. A series of post-holes and possible beam slots appears to represent the remains of rectangular buildings of probably 11th-/early 12th-c date. Several of the beam slots had been cut by a substantial 12th-c ditch, an apparent change of use which may be associated with the acquisition of the site by the Norman abbey of St Catherine, Rouen, in 1069, and with the subsequent foundation of a non-conventual priory during the late 11th/early 12th c.

London Archaeol, 6, 1989, 74; Medieval Archaeol, 33, 1989, 184; 34, 1990, 181

Manor Farm, off Holloway Lane, Harmondsworth, West Drayton, UB7

MFH89

Map site: 19
DGLA: John Mills
NGR: TQ 055 777
SMR: 051136–40

Excavation near the tithe barn in 1989, a short distance to the N of the previous year's site (MFH88), revealed a single shallow pit containing flints of probable Early Mesolithic date, and several other pits with animal bone and pottery of possible Neolithic date. A series of large pits and two post-holes containing early Romano-British pottery was located at the N end of the site. A number of pits, post-holes and several N–S gullies, dated to the Early/Middle Saxon period, were also found. Other pits examined could be dated to the late 11th–12th c.

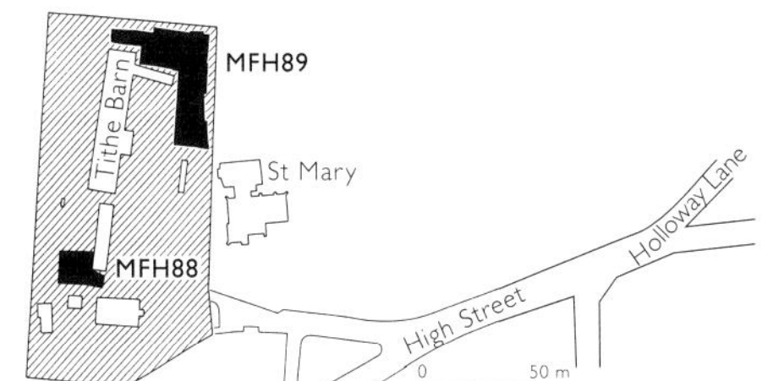

London Archaeol, 6, 1990, 189; Britannia 21, 1990, 344

Accommodation Lane, Moor Lane (west), Harmondsworth, West Drayton, UB7

MLW82

Map site: 20
MoL, WLAFG: Jon Cotton
NGR: TQ 045 774
SMR: 050961

A two-day salvage excavation in 1982 of two large parallel ditches 21m apart, uncovered during gravel extraction N of the Colnbrook by-pass, produced a number of pieces of struck flint. Further stretches of the same ditches, discovered to the S at Stanwell by the Surrey Archaeological Unit, have been interpreted as forming part of a Late Neolithic cursus or ceremonial avenue.

London Archaeol, 4, 1983, 288

Former George Hopton site, Packet Boat Lane, Cowley, Uxbridge, UB8

PBL89

Map site: 21
DGLA: John Lewis
NGR: TQ 053 812
SMR: 051145–6

An evaluation excavation in 1989 revealed a probable stream channel of prehistoric date, and a linear ditch and other features of probable Late Bronze/Early Iron Age date.

London Archaeol, 6, 1990, 189

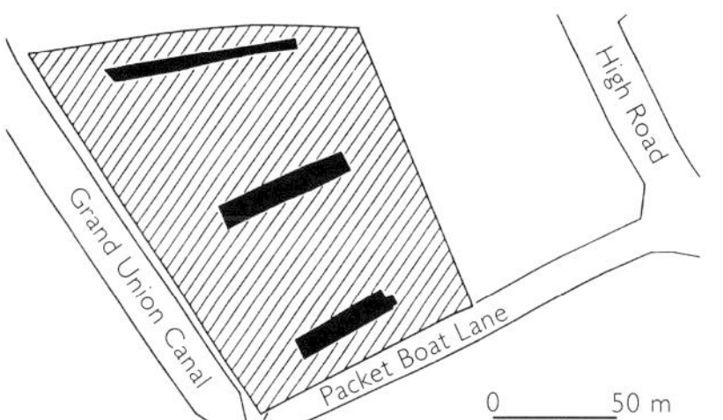

PWR84

Map site: 22
MoL, WLAFG, RNELHS: Jon
Cotton
NGR: TQ 094 889
SMR: 050207

Park Wood, Bury Street, Ruislip, HA4

Following the recovery of a Late Bronze Age socketed spearhead by metal-detection, excavation in 1984 revealed two phases of activity in the form of shallow scoops cut into the natural London Clay.

London Archaeol, 5, 1985, 52
Cotton, J, 1986 'A Late Bronze Age barbed spearhead and associated find from Park wood, Ruislip', *Trans London Middlesex Archaeol Soc,* 37, 1–16

RLS90

Map site: 23
DGLA: John Lewis
NGR: TQ 087 801
SMR: 051196

Stockley Park Development, Rigby Lane, Dawley Road, Hayes, UB3

Excavation in 1990 failed to locate scatters of Middle Palaeolithic flint artefacts at the interface of brickearth and natural gravel, but samples were taken for brickearth particle size analysis and thermoluminescence dating in order to characterise the sediments in this area.

London Archaeol, 6, 1991, 303

SMC87

Map site: 24
DGLA(N), WLAFG:
John Lewis
NGR: TQ 0550 8404
SMR: 050555

St Margaret's church, Belmont Road, Uxbridge, UB8

Refurbishment revealed late 18th–early 19th-c vaults.

London Archaeol, 5, 1988, 412; *Post-Medieval Archaeol,* 22, 1988, 189

SPD85

Map site: 25
DGLA: Jon Cotton
NGR: TQ 083 808
SMR: 050760

Stockley Park, fronting Dawley Road, Hayes, UB3

Excavation in 1985 on a surviving acre of Fourth Terrace gravel recovered several Palaeolithic flakes from its surface. A single Neolithic pit contained struck flints and sherds of possible Fengate ware. Also examined was a small unenclosed Iron Age settlement comprising four circular huts and a number of post-built granary structures. A considerable quantity of pottery was also recovered, including triangular loom weights and a spindle-whorl. Metal slag was present in a number of features, and there was an indication of copious carbonised cereal grain in certain of the soil samples.

London Archaeol, 5, 1986, 162
Cotton, J, 1985 'Iron Age settlement at Dawley, West London', Mosaic, *London Archaeol,* 5, 140

TSC89

Map site: 26
DGLA: James Bennett
NGR: TQ 051 828
SMR: 051032

Rear of Trys site, High Street, Cowley, Uxbridge, UB8

An evaluation excavation in 1989 on a gravel river terrace site adjoining the River Colne and capped by a thin layer of alluvial brickearth showed that lenses of organic silts resting upon the brickearth were archaeologically sterile. However, two parallel shallow gullies some 20–30m apart and running NW–SE were revealed. They are of probable Late Bronze Age date and perhaps represent a linear field boundary or trackway.

London Archaeol, 6, 1990, 189

2–3 Windsor Street, Uxbridge, UB8

Excavation in 1983 on the site of a 17th-c inn established an occupation sequence from the prehistoric
to the modern period. The earliest feature was a short stretch of a large ditch of V-section, cut into the
natural gravels. Running roughly N–S, it contained fragments of probable Bronze Age/Iron Age pottery
and struck flints. The site appears subsequently to have lain open until brought into cultivation in the
early medieval period. Shortly after *c* 1200 a series of timber-floored buildings was constructed, fronting
the market square. Associated with these were a number of rubbish-filled pits, stake-holes and a
pitched-tile hearth. Footings of the 17th-c building, composed of flint rubble, brick and roof tile, survived
at the N end of the site, together with a pitched-tile hearth and soak-away. Late 18th–19th-c alterations
included the addition of a Regency frontage, brick outbuildings and an internal rammed chalk floor.

London Archaeol, 4, 1984, 387; *Medieval Archaeol*, 28, 1984, 230

U X 8 3 i

Map site: 27
MoL, WLAFG: John Mills
NGR: TQ 0553 8406
SMR: 050243, 050695–700

5–6 High Street, Uxbridge, UB8

Excavation in 1983 revealed evidence of prehistoric activity in the form of a N–S ditch, examined in
section, parallel to that located at 2–3 Windsor Street (see UX83i above). Other features, mainly pits
and shallow scoops, lay to the W and contained sherds of probable Bronze Age/Iron Age pottery and
struck flint. A sequence of medieval and post-medieval rubbish pits was also discovered.

London Archaeol, 4, 1984, 387

U X 8 3 i i

Map site: 28
MoL, WLAFG: John Mills
NGR: TQ 056 840
SMR: 050243

126 High Street, Uxbridge, UB8

Excavation in 1983 of two small areas in Beasley's Yard, close to the site of Uxbridge School (founded
1790), suggested that the area was under cultivation until the building of the school and nearby Meeting
House (now Watts Hall) in the 18th c. A remnant ploughsoil was found to overlie the natural London
Clay, and produced a small group of Mesolithic-type flintwork and also medieval pottery. This was in
turn sealed beneath a series of compacted gravel surfaces, presumably relating to the schoolyard, from
which were recovered several Uxbridge School tokens, and sherds of 18th–19th-c pottery.

London Archaeol, 4, 1984, 387

U X 8 3 i i i

Map site: 29
MoL, WLAFG: John Mills
NGR: TQ 055 844
SMR: 050244, 051014–15

15–17 High Street, Uxbridge, UB8

Recording in 1983 of a probably mid-16th-c three-bay timber-framed building was followed, after its
demolition, by excavation. Finds from a series of clay floors at the front of the building plot suggest that
it had been continuously occupied since the medieval period.

London Archaeol, 4, 1984, 387; *Medieval Archaeol*, 28, 1984, 229; 29, 1985, 176; *Post-Medieval Archaeol*, 18, 1984, 311
Mills, J, 1984 'Excavations at Uxbridge 1983–4', *London Archaeol*, 5, 3–11

U X 8 3 i v

Map site: 30
MoL, WLAFG: John Mills,
Jon Cotton
NGR: TQ 056 841
SMR: 050701–6

UX85v

Map site: 31
MoL, WLAFG: Jon Cotton
NGR: TQ 054 844
SMR: 051016–18

118 High Street, Uxbridge, UB8

A trial excavation in 1985 at the rear of a 17th-c house at the N end of the town recovered pottery of 13th–15th-c date, but no medieval features.

London Archaeol, 5, 1986, 162; *Medieval Archaeol,* 30, 1986, 142

UX85vi

Map site: 32
DGLA, WLAFG: John Mills
NGR: TQ 055 841
SMR: 051019–21

20 High Street, Uxbridge, UB8

Following the demolition of the 19th-c rear wing of a Tudor timber-framed inn, excavation in 1985 revealed traces of medieval and 17th-c rear extensions and gravelled yard surfaces. Among the structures recovered were a well-preserved tile-built keyhole oven and a chalk-lined well, both probably of late medieval date. A rectangular brick-lined cesspit, probably associated with the inn, produced a large assemblage of post-medieval pottery, mainly of near-complete vessels tentatively dated to *c* 1770–90. Recording by DGLA and RCHM of the Tudor frontage prior to refurbishment suggests that the core of the building, of two bays with an adjacent covered cross-passage, may date to *c* 1500. Fragmentary red and blue paintings of foliage were observed on one wall of a first-floor chamber. Other notable features included pits and scoops datable to the prehistoric period and the 13th–15th c.

London Archaeol, 5, 1986, 162; *Medieval Archaeol,* 30, 1986, 142
Mills, J, 1986 'Buildings and excavations: 20 High Street, Uxbridge', *Hillingdon Conservation News,* 2

UX85vii

Map site: 33
DGLA(W): John Mills

12–14 High Street, Uxbridge, UB8

Currently there is no further information for this site.

UX86viii

Map site: 34
MoL, WLAFG: John Lewis
NGR: TQ 052 846
SMR: 051187–8

101–105 Oxford Road, Uxbridge, UB8

Excavation in 1986 recovered large quantities of struck flint tools, together with bones of horse and reindeer, from a series of horizontal sediments overlying natural river gravels. The material may represent the remains of a hunter-gatherers' camp. The flints are of the 'long-blade' industry, and date to *c* 8000 ± 800 BP. Also located were the remains of a 16th-c brick-built octagonal tower, originally forming half of the Treaty House gate lodge. Several ditches and pits have been exposed, some dating from the 13th and 16th c. See also UX88viii and UX90viii below.

London Archaeol, 5, 1987, 275; 5, 1988, 412; *Medieval Archaeol,* 31, 1987, 130; 32, 1988, 250; *Post-Medieval Archaeol,* 21, 1987, 283; 22, 1988, 208; 23, 1989, 53; 25, 1991, 131; 32, 1988, 250
Lewis, J, 1987 'Excavations at 105 Oxford Road, Uxbridge', *Hillingdon Conservation News,* 2
Lewis, J, in prep. 'Excavations of a late glacial/Mesolithic site at Uxbridge, Middlesex', MoLAS Monograph series

Three Ways Wharf, 101–105 Oxford Road, Uxbridge, UB8

Excavation in 1988, intended to test the existence of settlement in the town area before the grant of a market in the late 12th c, and to record subsequent development, produced evidence of a series of horizontal sediments overlying the natural river gravels beneath 105 Oxford Road. This comprised many struck flint tools, including flakes, blades and a core, together with bones of horse and deer; the assemblage apparently representing the undisturbed remains of a hunter-gatherers' camp dated, on the basis of the flints, to *c* 8000 ± 800 BP (Upper Palaeolithic). The site is of unique importance to the study of late glacial prehistory in Britain. The next phase of activity was medieval, represented by a large ditch and several smaller gullies across the site. These produced the largest group of 13th-c pottery yet found in Uxbridge, and suggest intensive occupation in the immediate area. In the late 16th or early 17th c a gatehouse comprising two hexagonal brick-built towers was constructed as the entrance to a Tudor mansion, part of which still stands as the Crown and Treaty public house. Trial excavations uncovered the E tower, which appears to have stood until the 1850s. See also UX86viii above and UX90viii below.

London Archaeol, 6, 1989, 74

UX88viii

Map site: 34
DGLA: John Lewis
NGR: TQ 052 846
SMR: 051023–5

155–156 High Street, Uxbridge, UB8

Excavation in 1988 revealed part of a gravelled yard and pits, dated by pottery to the 13th c, later medieval and Tudor pits, and a well.

London Archaeol, 6, 1989, 74; 6, 1990, 189; Medieval Archaeol, 33, 1989, 184; 34, 1990, 181; Post-Medieval Archaeol, 24, 1990, 178

UX88ix

Map site: 35
DGLA: Deborah Mattocks
NGR: TQ 0550 8417
SMR: 051026, 051187–8

101–105 Oxford Road, Uxbridge, UB8

Excavation in 1990 revealed Upper Palaeolithic/Mesolithic flint artefacts within sediments; a backfilled channel, possibly a shire ditch of post-medieval date, along with two other ditches; and an E–W aligned ditch of medieval or post-medieval date. See also UX86viii and UX88viii above.

London Archaeol, 6, 1991, 303; Post-Medieval Archaeol, 25, 1991, 131

UX90viii

Map site: 36
DGLA: Andrew Boucher
NGR: TQ 0525 8463
SMR: 051102, 051189

Rear of 194–195 High Street, Uxbridge, UB8

Excavation to the rear in 1990 revealed a pit of probable late 17th–early 18th-c date. A brick-built trough or tank, probably of the late 18th c, was also recorded.

London Archaeol, 6, 1991, 303; Post-Medieval Archaeol, 25, 1991, 131

UX90x

Map site: 37
DGLA: Fiona Walker
NGR: TQ 0569 8403
SMR: 052241–2

Rear of 175–222 High Street, Uxbridge, UB8

Excavation to the rear in 1990 in the form of testpits located medieval and later garden soil and ploughsoil.

London Archaeol, 6, 1991, 303; Medieval Archaeol, 35, 1991, 154

UX90xi

Map site: 38
DGLA: Fiona Walker
NGR: TQ 0570 8400
SMR: O51195

WGF79

Map site: 39
MoL, WLAFG: Jon Cotton,
Alison Laws
NGR: TQ 077 782
SMR: 050456

Wall Garden Farm, Sipson Lane, Harlington, West Drayton, UB7

Site watching and excavation in 1979 produced evidence of
part of a probable field-system and occupation of Roman
date, and traces of possible Neolithic activity.

London Archaeol, 3, 1980, 387

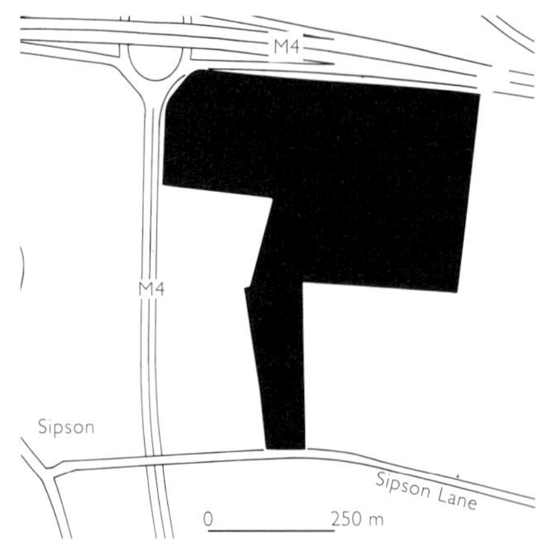

WGF80

Map site: 40
MoL, WLAFG: Jon Cotton
NGR: TQ 077 782
SMR: 050456, 051167

Wall Garden Farm, Sipson Lane, Harlington, West Drayton, UB7

Salvage excavation in 1980 revealed a series of features of Late Bronze/Early Iron Age date, including
several pits and gullies. Some of the features may have been associated with iron-smelting.

London Archaeol, 4, 1981, 47

WGF81

Map site: 41
MoL, WLAFG: Jon Cotton
NGR: TQ 077 782
SMR: 050456

Wall Garden Farm, Sipson Lane, Harlington, West Drayton, UB7

Site watching and limited salvage work in 1981 recovered further traces of prehistoric activity to the
E of those already recorded (see WGF79 and WGF80 above). Struck flint from the interface of topsoil
and natural brickearth would appear to be of later Neolithic date, while a small number of pits and
scoops dug into the brickearth contained struck flint and sherds of Late Neolithic (?Mortlake-style)
pottery. The latter invite comparison with those recovered at Heathrow, a mile to the SSE, in 1944.

London Archaeol, 4, 1982, 164

WGF84

Map site: 42
MoL, WL&SAFG: Jon Cotton,
John Mills
NGR: TQ 078 784
SMR: 050463, 051165–9

Wall Garden Farm, Sipson Lane, Harlington, West Drayton, UB7

Site watching in 1984 to the N and W of previous work (see WGF81 above) revealed a complex
sequence of features ranging in date from the later Neolithic to the Early/Middle Saxon period. Notable
finds include a small Mousterian hand axe recovered from the base of the natural brickearth; conjoining
fragments of a single polished flint axe from two shallow Neolithic scoops; and a considerable quantity
of Deverel-Rimbury pottery from the upper fill of a wide shelving ditch. Most of the features appeared
to be of Romano-British date, and included a large sub-oval gravel quarry. An interesting group of
wooden objects, including part of a ladder, was recovered from the waterlogged lower fill of the quarry.

London Archaeol, 5, 1985, 52; *Medieval Archaeol*, 29, 1985, 176
Cotton, J, 1984 'A Mousterian handaxe from West London', *Lithics*, 5, 40–3
Cotton, J, 1985 'Roman woodwork from West London', Mosaic, *London Archaeol*, 5, 84

LONDON BOROUGH OF

HOUNSLOW

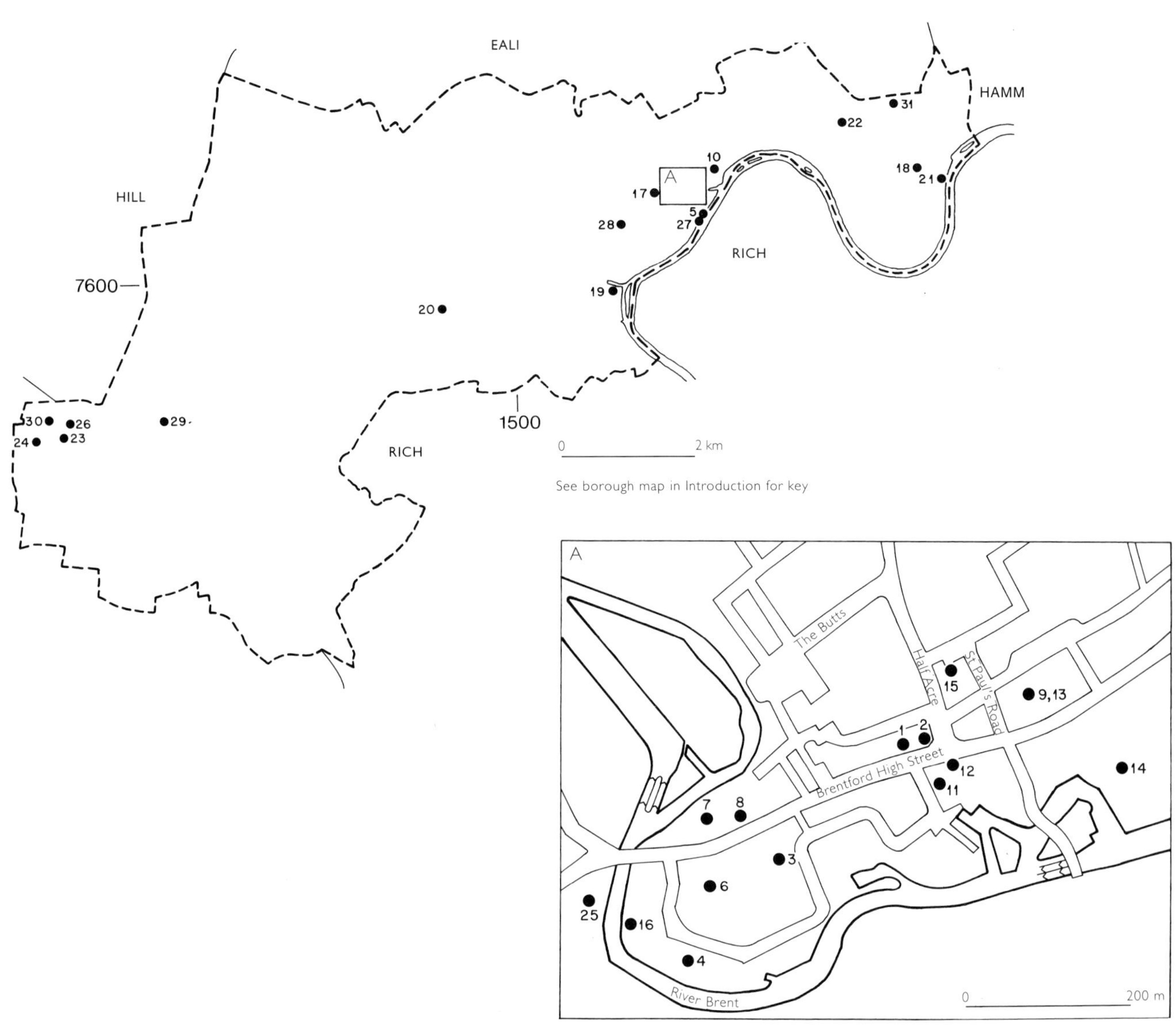

London Borough of Hounslow

HOUN 1 209BHS69 209–215 High St, Brentford, TW8
HOUN 2 223BHS68 219–223 High St, Brentford, TW8
HOUN 3 BREi/68 135–136 High St, Brentford, TW8
HOUN 4 BRE66 The Ham Recreation Ground, The Ham, Brentford, TW8
HOUN 5 BRE66A Syon Reach foreshore, River Thames, Brentford, TW8
HOUN 6 BRE67A 141–147 High St, Brentford, TW8
HOUN 7 BRE67B 175 High St, Brentford, TW8
HOUN 8 BRE68A 184–187 High St, Brentford, TW8
HOUN 9 BRE70 233–246 High St, Brentford, TW8
HOUN 10 BRE72A 285–289 High St, Brentford, TW8
HOUN 11 BRE72B Catherine Wheel House, 88–97 High St, Brentford, TW8
HOUN 12 BRE74 231–232 High St, Brentford, TW8
HOUN 13 BRE77 9–14 New Spring Gardens, High St, Brentford, TW8

HOUN 14 BRE79 Montgomery's Wharf, 74–76 High St, Brentford, TW8
HOUN 15 BRE82 St Paul's Rd (International Supermarket), High St, Brentford, TW8
HOUN 16 BRE87 152–158 High St, Brentford, TW8
HOUN 17 BRF89 2–10 London Rd, Brentford, TW8
HOUN 18 CH82 Chiswick House, Burlington Lane, W4
HOUN 19 CSI86 3–23 Church St, Isleworth, TW7
HOUN 20 DRH85 1–3 Douglas Rd, High St, Hounslow, TW3
HOUN 21 LEP89 LEP Depot, Pumping Station Rd, Corney Reach, W4
HOUN 22 LRT89 Chiswick High Rd (former LRT Bus Works), W4
HOUN 23 MFEB87 Mayfield Farm, Great South-West Rd, Stanwell Rd, East Bedfont, Feltham, TW14

HOUN 24 MFEB88 Mayfield Farm, Great South-West Rd, Stanwell Rd, East Bedfont, Feltham, TW14
HOUN 25 NW74 Northumberland Wharf, London Rd, Brentford, TW8
HOUN 26 PIP89 Pioneer Plastics Container Factory, Stanwell Rd, East Bedfont, Feltham, TW14
HOUN 27 SF78 Syon Reach foreshore, Isleworth, TW7
HOUN SHE67 Rose Acre Nurseries, south of Briar Rd, Shepperton Green, Shepperton, TW17
HOUN 28 SL75 Syon Lodge, Busch Corner, London Rd, Isleworth, TW7
HOUN 29 SRB90 413–419 Staines Rd, Bedfont, Feltham, TW14
HOUN 30 STA76 Stanwell Rd, Bedfont, Feltham, TW14
HOUN 31 TGB90 Turnham Green Bus Garage, Belmont Rd, W4

209–215 High Street, Brentford, TW8

Excavation in 1969 recovered fragments of Patch Grove-type pottery. Other sherds of early Roman pottery were also recovered.

Canham, R, 1978 *2000 years of Brentford*, 23–4

209BHS69

Map site: 1
London Museum: Roy Canham
NGR: TQ 1764 7742
SMR: 050268

219–223 High Street, Brentford, TW8

Excavation in 1968 revealed a considerable accumulation of dark soil resting on the natural brickearth and containing Roman pottery sherds; at one or two points in the sections post-holes or refuse pits were observed. An E–W ditch was noted running parallel to the High Street, the pottery from its fill dating mainly to the 1st c AD. When the ditch was almost full with dark soil, a gravel surface was laid down, its long axis lying E–W across the site and parallel with the ditch. This appeared to have sealed the ditch and to have subsided slightly into it as the filling became compacted.

Canham, R, 1978 *2000 years of Brentford*, 23

223BHS68

Map site: 2
London Museum: Roy Canham
NGR: TQ 1767 7744
SMR: O50274, 050319–20

135–136 High Street, Brentford, TW8

Excavation in 1968 opened nine trenches in a N–S line, one of them revealing the foundation of a small timber building probably dating to AD50–100. Sealing this was a deposit containing sherds of mid–late Roman date, and a large quantity of 14th-c material. The first masonry structure on the site was apparently erected in the 16th c, its remains consisting of an L-shaped wall, which formed the W side and rear of a building fronting the High Street. The original construction was of brick nodules set in mortar, but the W arm was subsequently rebuilt in brick. It is very likely that this was a dwarf wall supporting a timber-framed superstructure. Following demolition, the area was paved at the end of the 16th c with a mixture of regularly set bricks, tiles and rough patches of brick and stone, the surface sloping evenly downwards to a flattened central gutter. Refuse pits and post-holes of a large timber structure obliterated much of this surface in the first half of the 17th c, and much domestic refuse and soil were allowed to accumulate. A minor street of granite setts presumably dates from the 19th c, though it was probably first established c 1700.

Canham, R, 1978 *2000 years of Brentford*, 22

BREi/68

Map site: 3
London Museum: Roy Canham
NGR: TQ 1748 7730
SMR: 050269–73

The Ham Recreation Ground, The Ham, Brentford, TW8

Trial excavation in 1966 revealed nothing earlier than c 1800, the date at which the deep stratigraphy of mainly clay and gravel lenses was dumped on the site, probably during the digging or subsequent dredging of the Grand Union Canal. The hard-packed gravel encountered was wholly blackened and capped by marshy material, indicating that before the dumping the area had long been uninhabitable.

Canham, R, 1978 *2000 years of Brentford*, 17

BRE66

Map site: 4
London Museum: Roy Canham
NGR: TQ 1740 7715
SMR: 050998

BRE66A

Map site: 5
London Museum:
Roy Canham
NGR: TQ 1785 7695
SMR: 050275

Syon Reach foreshore, River Thames, Brentford, TW8

An investigation was undertaken in 1966–7 into one of the alleged Romano-British huts noted on the foreshore since at least 1928, and accessible only at the lowest tides. The hut structure examined consisted of two separate segments, the earlier of which was constructed of parallel hazel saplings resting on a number of small planks intended to limit subsidence. This most probably represented the floor of a small hut, from which pieces of tile, pottery and a coin of Diocletian dated 292–3 are assigned to the Roman period. The edge of the later segment was constructed of hazel saplings woven around a single plank and this possibly represents a wall rather than a floor. The two structures may therefore be interpreted either as the floor and wall of a single hut or possibly as the floors of two separate huts, both of Roman date.

Canham. R, 1978 *2000 years of Brentford*, 32–4

BRE67A

Map site: 6
London Museum:
Roy Canham
NGR: TQ 1739 7725
SMR: 050310–18, 050733,
050934

141–147 High Street, Brentford, TW8

A trial excavation in 1967 revealed undisturbed Pleistocene gravel in the NW corner of the site. Elsewhere layers of silt and loose earthy gravel were encountered, apparently the infilling of a former channel of the River Brent. Resting upon and cutting into this infill were traces of Romano-British occupation. The earliest feature was an E–W ditch containing a few pottery sherds of the 2nd c. Another ditch, narrower and steeper sided, produced little pottery but was dated by a coin of 385–402. Further late Roman activity was indicated by a 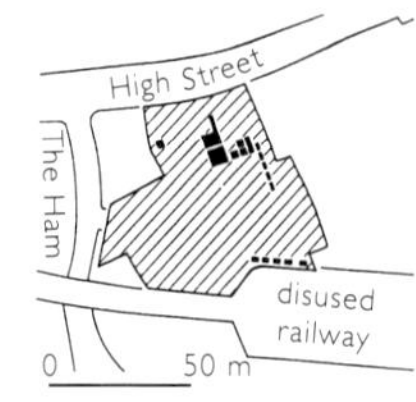

small refuse pit and two post-holes, all dug into the ditch silt and sealed in turn by a dark occupation layer containing 4th-c pottery found widely in the excavation. Above the Roman horizon was evidence of shallow medieval features of the 13th c. Elsewhere on the site were indications of a 14th-c building: a shallow L-shaped trench filled with a mixture of soil, chalk and Reigate stone fragments and decayed mortar marked the position of a robbed-out wall. The post-holes on the High Street frontage of the building were roughly contemporary but probably belonged to an entirely separate building. Excavation on the line of Church Alley revealed gravel layers and a drainage gully from an earlier street.

Canham, R, 1978 *2000 years of Brentford*, 17–19

BRE67B

Map site: 7
London Museum: Roy
Canham
NGR: TQ 1740 7732
SMR: 050956

175 High Street, Brentford, TW8

Excavation in 1967 proved that the Roman occupation did not extend in this direction, nor was there any evidence of an infilled channel of the River Brent (see BRE67A above); the geology here was disturbed brickearth. The site was generally barren, except in the vicinity of the High Street, where layers of Stuart domestic refuse were excavated.

Canham, R, 1978 *2000 years of Brentford*, 19

184–187 High Street, Brentford, TW8

BRE68A

Map site: 8
London Museum:
Roy Canham
NGR: TQ 1745 7733
SMR: 050171, 050955

Excavation in 1968 produced little evidence on the W side of the site. On the E side the earliest feature was a small gully of prehistoric date, above which was a layer containing struck flints, including blades and a few cores, and pottery in a fabric tempered with flint grits. A few sherds of Roman pottery were found in a soil resting on a distinct surface formed by a layer of rammed earth and gravel. A group of early pottery sherds, much of it coarse native ware but also samian dated AD50–100, was recovered from a narrow band of brown soil sealed between the rammed gravel and the top of the brickearth. Post-holes of a large timber building constructed in the 19th c were also recorded.

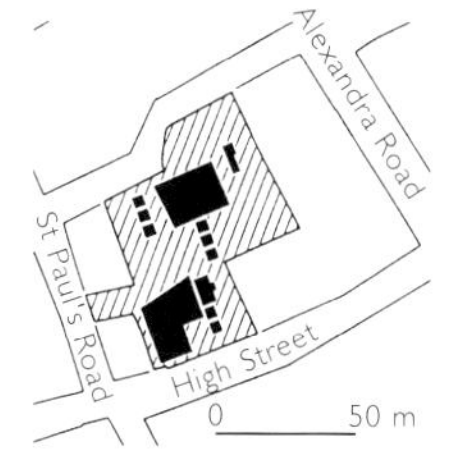

Canham, R, 1978 *2000 years of Brentford*, 19–22

233–246 High Street, Brentford, TW8

BRE70

Map site: 9
London Museum:
Roy Canham
NGR: TQ 1780 7750
SMR: 050335, 050342–3,
050571, 050732

Excavation in 1970, designed to establish the line of a possible Roman road in the area, revealed an extensive manmade surface with patches of repair and reconstruction, the earliest feature encountered. It was well preserved and extended beyond the N limit of excavation. An identical surface located close by was cut by a shallow channel containing sherds of the 2nd c and apparently part of the same feature, with a proven width of 24m. Other features, ranging in date to the later Roman period, included scoops and gullies as well as post-holes and small building trenches. Saxon pottery was recovered from the filling of a shallow feature which was cut into the natural and was distinguished by the presence of numerous small stake-holes and a few larger post-holes, possibly the location of a *gruebenhaus*. It is probable that any building of the 17th–18th c was obliterated by the redevelopment of the High Street in the 19th c, to which all the brick structures encountered belong. A small number of pits, presumably cesspits, were found scattered over the area.

Canham, R, 1978 *2000 years of Brentford*, 24–31

285–289 High Street, Brentford, TW8

BRE72A

Map site: 10
London Museum:
Roy Canham
NGR: TQ 1798 7762
SMR: 050994

Excavation in 1972 established the absence of Roman and medieval settlement. In the NE corner of the site a sequence of 18th-c cesspits was excavated and proved a rich source of finds, especially of pottery and animal bone.

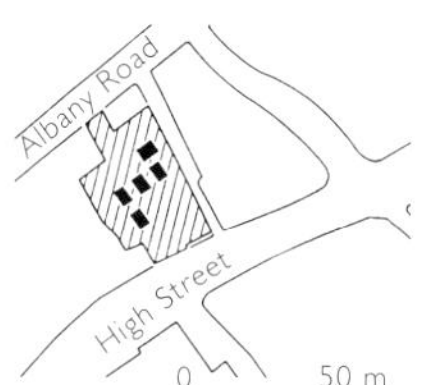

London Archaeol, 2, 1973, 41
Canham, R, 1978 *2000 years of Brentford*, 31–2 [address given incorrectly as 181–189 High St]

Catherine Wheel House, 88–97 High Street, Brentford, TW8

BRE72B

Map site: 11
London Museum, WLAFG:
Roy Canham
NGR: TQ 1768 7738
SMR: 050277–8

Excavation in 1972 revealed a partially disturbed infant burial in association with Roman pottery. In the extreme S of the site was found the edge of a scoop containing sherds of 1st-c pottery.

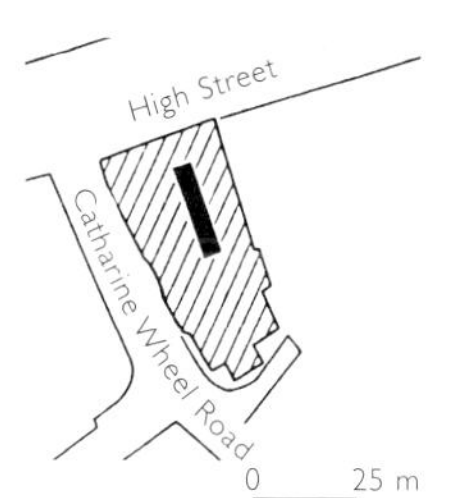

London Archaeol, 2, 1973, 41
Canham, R, 1978 *2000 years of Brentford*, 24

BRE74

Map site: 12
London Museum, WLAFG:
Roy Canham
NGR: TQ 1773 7746
SMR: 050954

231–232 High Street, Brentford, TW8

Excavation in 1974 located a substantial proportion of the Roman road from London to Silchester, represented by a hard-packed gravel surface about 12m wide. On the S side was a road ditch a little over 2m wide and 1m deep, and dated to the 1st c AD. This was deliberately filled in towards the end of the 1st c, and several periods of occupation have been encountered on both sides of the road. Traces of post-holes, clay floors and collapsed clay walls belonging to this roadside settlement all date to the late 1st and 2nd c. At some time in the late 2nd or 3rd c this area of the settlement was apparently abandoned, and the road went out of use. Several large pits of later Roman date were encountered, cutting through the hard-packed gravel road surface.

London Archaeol, 2, 1975, 257–8; Britannia, 6, 1975, 268

BRE77

Map site: 13
London Museum, WLAFG:
Alison Parnum
NGR: TQ 1780 7751

9–14 New Spring Gardens, High Street, Brentford, TW8

Excavation revealed the remains of an 18th-c clay pipe kiln, and a further section of the London–Silchester (Roman) road with associated ditch. A gully sealed beneath the road ditch contained pottery, probably of pre-conquest date.

London Archaeol, 3, 1978, 161; 3, 1979, 263
Parnum, A, & Cotton, J, 1983 'Recent work in Brentford: excavations and observations 1974–82', *London Archaeol, 4, 318–25 & 336*

BRE79

Map site: 14
MoL, WLAFG: Jon Cotton,
Alison Laws
NGR: TQ 1790 7740
SMR: 050995 .

Montgomery's Wharf, 74–76 High Street, Brentford, TW8

A trial excavation in 1979 on a site between the High Street and the River Brent failed to locate any stratigraphy earlier than the 18th–19th c. The natural brickearth was found to drop away steeply immediately S of the High Street, while the discovery of a thick grey clay-sand layer underlying the modern make-up suggests that much of the N part of the site remained unusable marshland until its reclamation in the 19th c. Borehole data corroborate these observations.

London Archaeol, 3, 1980, 387

BRE82

Map site: 15
MoL, WLAFG: Jon Cotton
NGR: TQ 1771 7746
SMR: 050328–34

International Supermarket, St Paul's Road, High Street, Brentford, TW8

Site watching and limited excavation in 1982 revealed evidence of the prehistoric and Roman settlement of the area. The first complete section through the Roman road running W from the City was obtained, and the alignment of its N ditch established. Small groups of Roman material, struck flint and fragmentary sherds of Neolithic pottery were recovered from the brickearth beneath the road.

London Archaeol, 4, 1983, 289

152–158 High Street, Brentford, TW8

A trial excavation in 1987 revealed extensive post-medieval cellaring throughout the site area.
No material of earlier than 17th-c date was recovered.

London Archaeol, 5, 1988, 412

BRE87

Map site: 16
DGLA: John Mills
NGR: TQ 1733 7727
SMR: 050993

2–10 London Road, Brentford, TW8

An evaluation excavation in 1989 revealed a series of
ditches representing Iron Age property boundaries running
E–W and containing pottery and struck flint. A number of
4th-c Roman ditches were located, including a large one
initially thought to be the N ditch of the Roman road from
London to Silchester; an interpretation favoured by
evidence of compacted gravel to the S. Roman post-holes
lacking any obvious relation to each other were also
recorded. Two medieval post-holes were found with large
quantities of packing material, including worked stone.

London Archaeol, 6, 1990, 189; Britannia, 21, 1990, 344

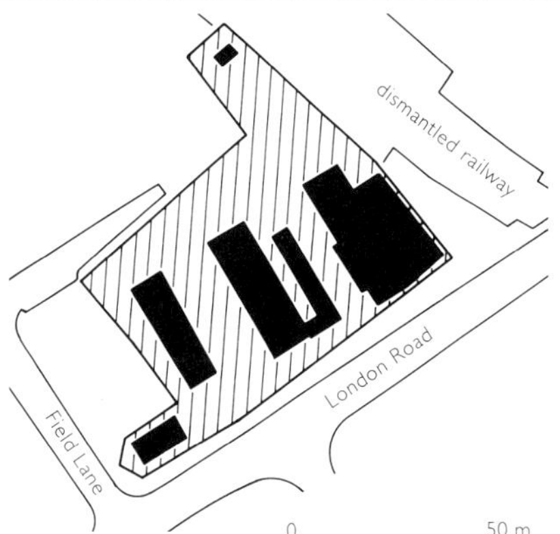

BRF89

Map site: 17
DGLA(W): Neil Bugler
NGR: TQ 1715 7726
SMR: 051095–7

Chiswick House, Burlington Lane, W4

Excavation in 1982 of part of the original Jacobean house to the NW of Burlington's villa revealed a
sequence of post-medieval gardening and building activity. The earliest recorded features consisted of a
series of shallow bedding trenches provisionally dated to the 17th–18th c, possibly representing part
of a small kitchen garden NW of the Jacobean house. The area was subsequently enclosed by several
phases of brick wall and was used as a small, metalled courtyard later provided with a centrally placed
well. Following the demolition of the Jacobean house in 1788, a wide, curving corridor was laid out
across the area to link the present Chiswick House (Burlington's villa) with the original stable block.
(The site records are held by EH.)

London Archaeol, 4, 1983, 289; 4, 1984, 387; Post-Medieval Archaeol, 18, 1984, 316

CH82

Map site: 18
MoL, WLAFG: Jon Cotton
NGR: TQ 212 775
SMR: 050958–60

3–23 Church Street, Isleworth, TW7

Trial excavation in 1986 on the site of the moated medieval manor house of
Richard, earl of Cornwall, revealed a series of possible pre-moat ditches, perhaps
of 12th–13th-c date, cut into natural sands and gravels. Other features examined
included the moat, over 10m wide and 4–6m deep, and substantial foundations
of iron conglomerate, provisionally interpreted as the footings of Earl Richard's
great hall. Traces of further, apparently medieval, buildings and floors were located,
though most had suffered much post-medieval disturbance, particularly during
the 17th c when the area was levelled and the moat partially backfilled to
accommodate Sir John Offley's new brick house, the cellar range of which was
also revealed.

London Archaeol, 5, 1987, 275; Medieval Archaeol, 31, 1987, 130; Post-Medieval Archaeol, 21, 1987, 283

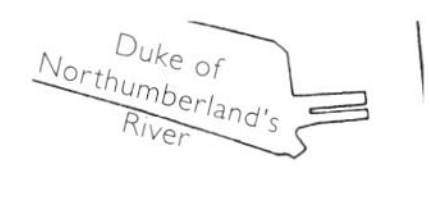

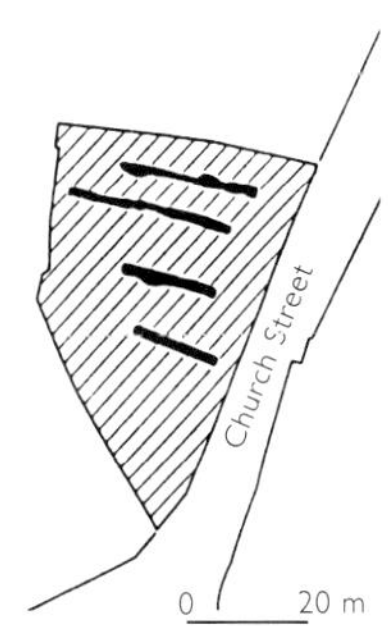

CSI86

Map site: 19
DGLA, WLAFG: John Mills
NGR: TQ 165 759
SMR: 051128–32

DRH85

Map site: 20
DGLA, WLAFG: John Mills
NGR: TQ 1385 7575
SMR: 050952

1–3 Douglas Road, High Street, Hounslow, TW3

Trial excavation in 1985 to the rear of properties fronting onto the High Street failed to locate the Roman road between London and Silchester, but revealed evidence of late medieval/early post-medieval gravel-quarrying.

London Archaeol, 5, 1986, 162

LEP89

Map site: 21
DGLA: John Lewis
NGR: TQ 2145 7765
SMR: 051147–50

LEP Depot, Pumping Station Road, Corney Reach, W4

Excavation in 1989 next to a meander of the Thames on the W edge of old Chiswick revealed that alluvial silts in the N area of the site had been cut by ancient watercourses, containing artefacts dating from the late prehistoric, until the levelling and revetting of the land to form the grounds of Corney House in the late 17th c. A small pit and gully of Late Neolithic date containing Peterborough ware and flint artefacts were also found, close to the location of a 15th–16th-c timber-lined drain within the silts of one of the water channels. To the W of this, the remains of a timber-floored cellar and an underground passage were uncovered. These may well have formed part of Corney House.

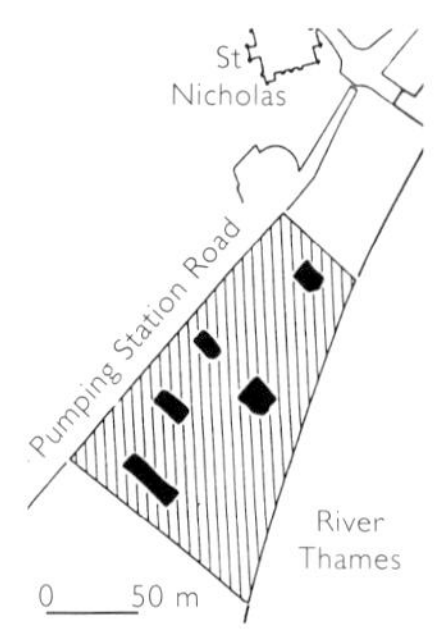

London Archaeol, 6, 1990, 189–90; *Post-Medieval Archaeol,* 24, 1990, 188

LRT89

Map site: 22
DGLA: Andrew Boucher
NGR: TQ 198 787
SMR: 051090–4

Former LRT Bus Works, Chiswick High Road, W4

Trial trenching in 1989 revealed a series of 18th–19th-c pits and ditches in the N part of the site. To the S a complex of post-holes, pits and ditches dating to the Late Bronze Age was uncovered, although one of the ditches may be Deverel-Rimbury in date, and some of the later pits contained Early Iron Age pottery in their fills.

London Archaeol, 6, 1990, 190

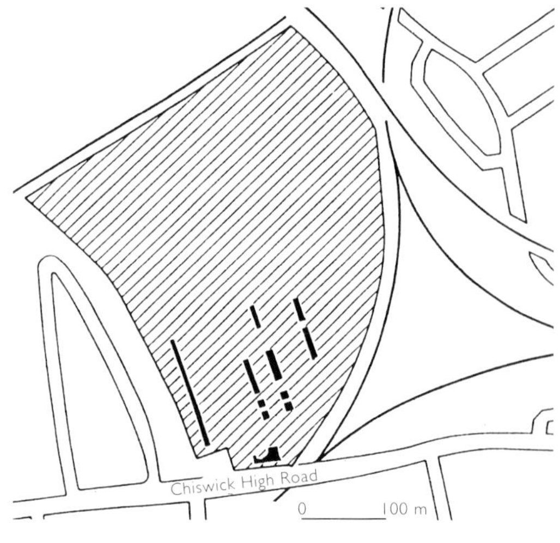

MFEB87

Map site: 23
DGLA, WLAFG, HBMC AM
Lab: John Lewis, A David,
Jon Cotton
NGR: TQ 081 737

Mayfield Farm, Great South-West Road, Stanwell Road, East Bedfont, Feltham, TW14

A geophysical survey and fieldwalking programme in 1987 on the Scheduled double-ditch cropmark site (SAM 62) preceded a trial excavation (see MFEB88 below). Magnetometer scanning and topsoil magnetic susceptibility measurement were largely unsuccessful in defining archaeological features, though fieldwalking revealed a scatter of struck flint of probable Late Neolithic/Early Bronze Age type, with a concentration towards the edge of the Third Terrace at the S end of the field.

London Archaeol, 5, 1988, 412

Mayfield Farm, Great South-West Road, Stanwell Road, East Bedfont, Feltham, TW14

MFEB88

Map site: 24
DGLA: Caroline Pathy-Barker
NGR: TQ 075 736
SMR: 051028–31

Excavation in 1988 of a double-ditched enclosure (see MFEB87 above) produced a provisional dating to the Late Bronze Age, on the basis of pottery from the secondary silts of its inner ditch. Other features located inside and outside the enclosure suggested a complex settlement history.

London Archaeol, 6, 1989, 74

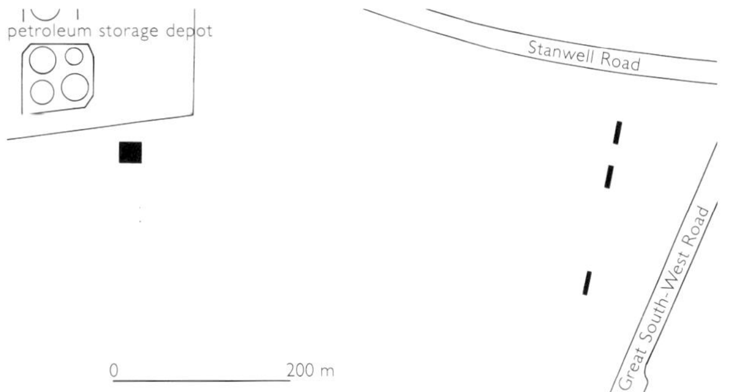

Northumberland Wharf, London Road, Brentford, TW8

NW74

Map site: 25
London Museum, WLAFG:
Roy Canham
NGR: TQ 1725 7720
SMR: 050321–6

Excavation in 1974 located a series of pits and ditches providing evidence of occupation throughout most of the Roman period. A series of stake-holes indicated a small circular enclosure, possibly an animal pen.

London Archaeol, 2, 1975, 258; Britannia, 6, 1975, 269

Pioneer Plastics Container Factory, Stanwell Road, East Bedfont, Feltham, TW14

PIP89

Map site: 26
DGLA: Fiona Walker
NGR: TQ 083 739
SMR: 051100

Excavation in 1989 opposite a Scheduled Late Bronze Age defended site and other prehistoric monuments (SAM 61 and 62) encountered no further prehistoric remains.

London Archaeol, 6, 1990, 190

Syon Reach foreshore, Isleworth, TW7

SF78

Map site: 27
MoL: Alison Laws
NGR: TQ 178 769

Observation in 1978 revealed a few sherds of Roman pottery as well as post-medieval pottery and clay pipes (see BRE66A above).

Rose Acre Nurseries, south of Briar Road, Shepperton Green, Shepperton, TW17

SHE67

Map site: not shown
London Museum: Roy Canham
NGR: TQ 0705 6770

Excavations in 1967 and 1973 revealed traces of a succession of circular timber structures, probably prehistoric, and evidence for settlement, including burials, ditches, pits and a *gruebenhaus*, of Saxon and medieval date.

Canham, R, 1979 'Excavations at Shepperton Green 1967 and 1973', *Trans London Middlesex Archaeol Soc*, 30, 97–124

SL75

Map site: 28
MoL, WLAFG: Alison Laws
NGR: TQ 1667 7682
SMR: 050327, 050868

Syon Lodge, Busch Corner, London Road, Isleworth, TW7

Excavation in 1975 revealed much 19th-c ground disturbance, though a deposit of brickearth resting upon the gravel produced flint flakes and implements in association with a quantity of prehistoric pottery sherds. A small scatter of abraded late Roman pottery sherds was also recovered.

London Archaeol, 2, 1976, 371

SRB90

Map site: 29
DGLA: Robert Cowie
NGR: TQ 0960 7400
SMR: 051190

413–419 Staines Road, Bedfont, Feltham, TW14

An evaluation excavation in 1990 exposed no archaeological features.

London Archaeol, 6, 1990, 303

STA76

Map site: 30
MoL, WLAFG: Alison Laws
NGR: TQ 0770 7400
SMR: 050377

Stanwell Road, Bedfont, Feltham, TW14

Trial trenching in 1976 located an E–W ditch, visible on aerial photographs, of probable prehistoric date, and also a ditch system of late 18th-c date. There was no evidence of the prehistoric occupation encountered in fields to the S of Stanwell Road.

London Archaeol, 3, 1977, 38

TGB90

Map site: 31
DGLA(W): Andrew Boucher
NGR: TQ 2067 7866
SMR: 051193–4

Turnham Green Bus Garage, Belmont Road, W4

Excavation in 1990 located a feature containing several pieces of struck flint, charcoal and burnt clay or daub, for which there was no definite dating evidence but presumably it was prehistoric.

London Archaeol, 6, 1990, 303

LONDON BOROUGH OF

ISLINGTON

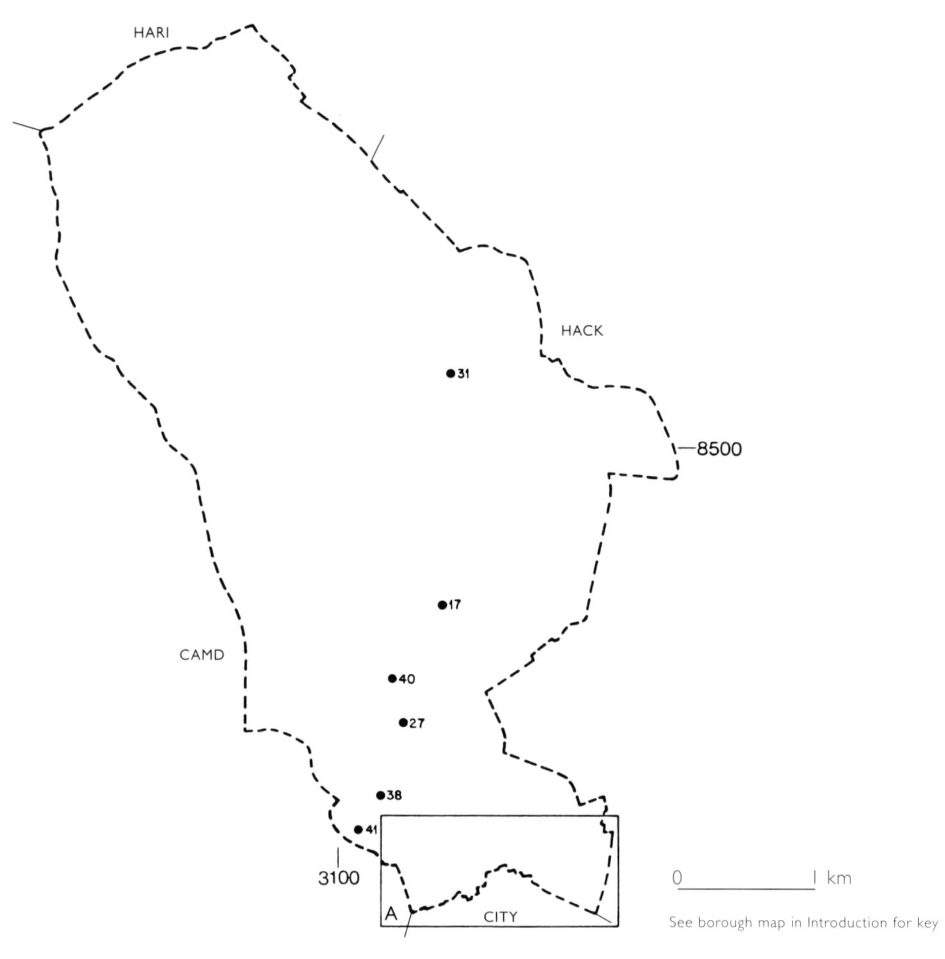

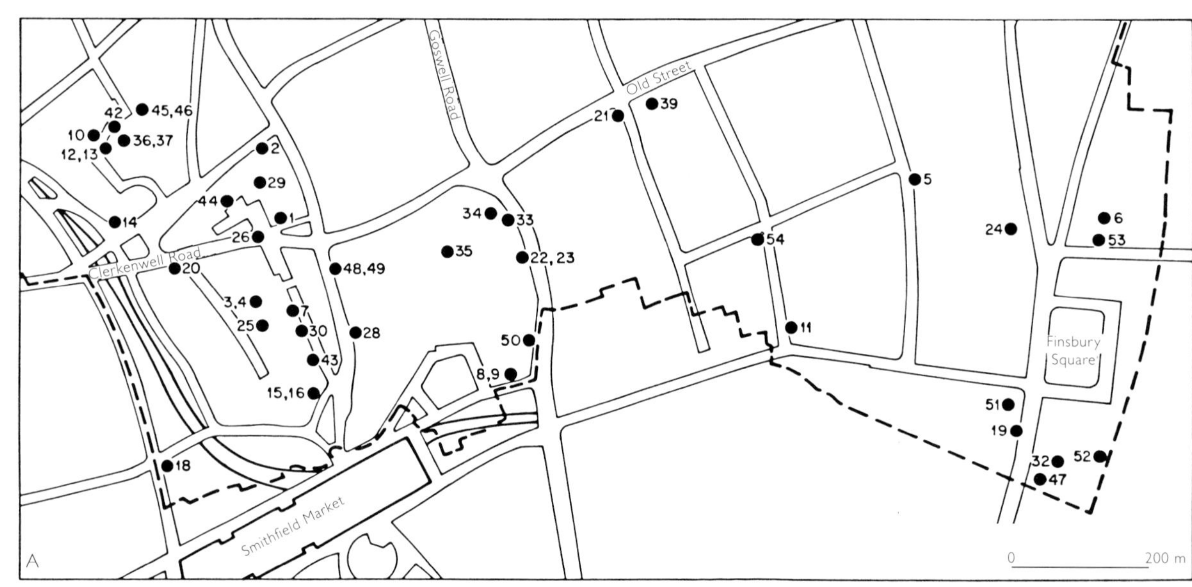

London Borough of Islington

ISLI 1	ALB89	2 Albemarle Way, EC1
ISLI 2	ASS90	159–173 St John St, 8–15 Aylesbury St, EC1
ISLI 3	BAD89	Badger Yard, 12–13 St John's Square, EC1
ISLI 4	BAD90	6–9 Briset St, 12–13 St John's Square, EC1
ISLI 5	BNH88	Gravelle House, 2–14 Bunhill Row, EC1
ISLI 6	BON76	Triton Grange, Bonhill St, EC2
ISLI 7	BRI86	16–21 St John's Lane, EC1
ISLI 8	CAR89	7–8 Carthusian St, EC1
ISLI 9	CAR90	7–8 Carthusian St, EC1
ISLI 10	CCL79	25–26 Clerkenwell Close, EC1
ISLI 11	CET86	Chiswell St, Whitecross St, EC1
ISLI 12	CLK86	42–46 Clerkenwell Close, EC1
ISLI 13	CLL79	25–26 Clerkenwell Close, EC1 (deleted site code)
ISLI 14	CLW82	14–16 Farringdon Lane, EC1
ISLI 15	COW88	Cowcross St (redevelopment), EC1
ISLI 16	COW89	20–26 Cowcross St, 9–13 Peter's Lane, 35a St John St, 1–4 St John's Lane, 8–10 Eagle Court, 37–39 Britton St, EC1
ISLI 17	DAG77	282 Dagmar Terrace, N1
ISLI	ENG84	8–13 Clerkenwell Close, 33–36 Clerkenwell Green (engineers' car park), EC1
ISLI 18	FAR75	Farringdon Rd, Clerkenwell Rd, EC1
ISLI 19	FINP78	101–117 Finsbury Pavement, EC2
ISLI 20	GIN90	55 Clerkenwell Rd, EC1
ISLI 21	GOL90	125 Golden Lane, EC1
ISLI 22	GOS89	7–21 Goswell Rd, EC1
ISLI 23	GSW90	7–21 Goswell Rd, EC1
ISLI 24	HAC90	Honourable Artillery Company, City Rd, EC1

ISLI 25 JAN90   1–7 Albion Place, EC1
ISLI 26 JER83   Clerkenwell Rd (British Telecom trench), EC1
ISLI 27 JOE90   394–416 St John St, EC1
ISLI 28 JOH88   52–54 St John St, EC1
ISLI 29 JON89   47–49 St John's Square, EC1
ISLI 30 KEE90   14 St John's Lane, EC1
ISLI 31 LEI86   Christ Church Hall, Leigh Rd, N5
ISLI 32 LIG88   Ling House, 10–13 Dominion St, EC2
ISLI 33 LIT89   Litton House, 27 Goswell Rd, EC1
ISLI 34 MED89   St Bartholomew's Hospital Medical College, Clerkenwell Rd, EC1

ISLI 35 MED90   St Bartholomew's Hospital Medical College, Clerkenwell Rd, EC1
ISLI 36 NEW81   Newcastle Row, rear of 36 Clerkenwell Close, EC1
ISLI 37 NEW87   6 Newcastle Row, EC1
ISLI 38 NTB77   Northampton Buildings, Skinner St, Corporation Row, Rosoman St, EC1
ISLI 39 OLD89   76–78 Old St, EC1
ISLI 40 PKF77   Parkfield St, N1
ISLI 41 ROS88   Rosebery Avenue, Topham St, EC1
ISLI 42 SCT87   36–41 Scotswood St, EC1
ISLI 43 SJL90   6–7 St John's Lane, EC1
ISLI 44 SJS86   49–52 St John's Square, EC1

ISLI 45 SNS86   Sans Walk, St James's Row (National Car Park), EC1
ISLI 46 SNS87   Sans Walk, St James's Row (National Car Park), EC1
ISLI 47 SOP77   South Place, EC2
ISLI 48 STJ88   94–100 St John St, EC1
ISLI 49 STJ89   94–100 St John St, EC1
ISLI 50 TEZ88   Teziac House, 110–115 Aldersgate St, EC1
ISLI 51 VER90   Veritas House, 119–125 Finsbury Pavement, EC2
ISLI 52 WIL89   31–35 Wilson St, EC2
ISLI 53 WOP88   19–23 Worship St, EC2
ISLI 54 WTC76   Whitbread's Brewery, Whitecross St, EC1

2 Albemarle Way, EC1

ALB89

Map site: 1
DGLA(N): Ken Pit
NGR: TQ 3171 8213

A small watching brief was conducted after contractors digging underpinning holes for refurbishment of a standing building had uncovered human skeletons. Natural gravels and brickearth, and possible agriculturally worked soils, were succeeded by soils into which two inhumation burials were inserted. One was surrounded by a coffin stain, and a medieval shroud pin was recovered from the other. The site was within the inner precinct of the priory of St John Clerkenwell. At least one rubbish pit was also found, probably of medieval date. The burials and pits were truncated by the 18th-c brick cellar of the standing building.

Sloane, B, & Malcolm, G, in prep. *St John of Jerusalem, London: excavations at the priory, 1900–1994*, MoLAS Monograph series

159–173 St John Street, 8–15 Aylesbury Street, EC1

ASS90

Map site: 2
DGLA(N): Mark Atkinson
NGR: TQ 3165 8217
SMR: 080436, 082199

An evaluation excavation in 1990 of a site to the N of the site of the church of St John's Priory, Clerkenwell, showed that there had been little truncation by modern buildings, and that survival of medieval masonry fragments and layers of soft stratigraphy was good. At the W edge of the site a series of Tudor brick vaults was uncovered, thought to have been cellars along Jerusalem Passage. Finds include a significant group of 13th-c Kingston ware and 18 fragments of carved sandstone.

London Archaeol, 6, 1991, 304; *Medieval Archaeol*, 35, 1991, 154; *Post-Medieval Archaeol*, 25, 1991, 132

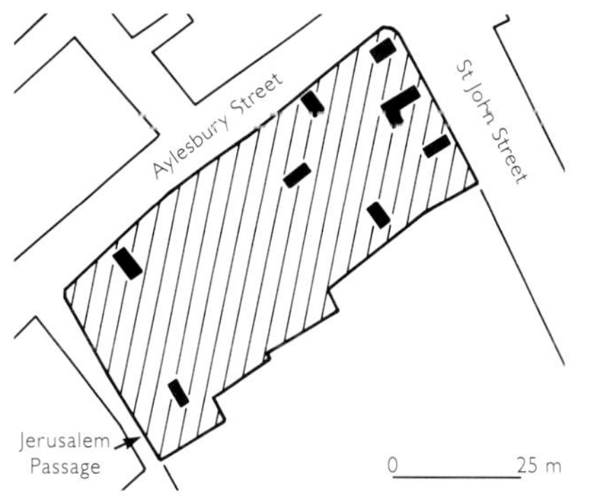

BAD89, BAD90

Map site: 3, 4
DGLA(N): John Roche
NGR: TQ 3168 8201
SMR: 080436, 082304–5

Badger Yard, 12–13 St John's Square, 6–9 Briset Street, EC1

Excavation in 1989–90 revealed a
Roman ground surface containing
sherds of pottery, and a steep-sided
linear ditch aligned N–S, possibly a
storm drain and part of St John's
Priory. There was also evidence of
demolition within the lifetime of
the priory. Two 16th-c brick wall
foundations running E–W across the
site and joined by a N–S party wall
formed the footings of two buildings.
The N wall was founded on two
courses of faced freestone blocks,
obtained from the demolition of part of the priory.

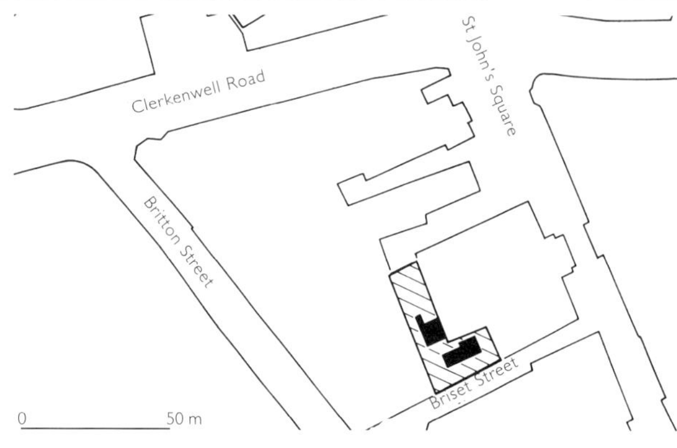

London Archaeol, 6, 1991, 303; Britannia, 22, 1991, 272; Post-Medieval Archaeol, 25, 1991, 131

BNH88

Map site: 5
DGLA(N): Peter McCrone
NGR: TQ 3264 8199

Gravelle House, 2–14 Bunhill Row, EC1

A watching brief in 1988 revealed deposits of sand and gravel with a covering layer of brickearth. In the
southern-most section various cuts in the lower layers may be the result of sand and gravel extraction,
most probably before the local build-up of marsh deposits which followed the construction of the
Roman city wall to the S in *c* AD200. The clay layers above the brickearth probably resulted from
deposition under waterlogged conditions, and indicate that the Moorfields marsh extended as far N as
the Bunhill area. A thick upper layer of dark ash, sand and clay may represent landfilling intended to
reclaim the damp ground during the laying out of the area for gardens and fields in the 17th c.

BON76

Map site: 6
ILAU: Graham Black
NGR: TQ 329 821
SMR: 080384, 080485

Triton Grange, Bonhill Street, EC2

Rescue excavation in 1976 included a section through the Moorfields marsh which revealed deposits
to a depth of some 10m, and showed that the construction of buildings was preceded by large-scale
reclamation by dumping in the 16th c. A quantity of well-preserved leather of that date was recovered.

London Archaeol, 3, 1977, 38; Post-Medieval Archaeol, 11, 1977, 90

BRI86

Map site: 7
DGLA(N): Rob Whytehead
NGR: TQ 3172 8200

16–21 St John's Lane, EC1

A watching brief in 1986, within the outer precinct of the priory of St John Clerkenwell, produced
evidence of medieval pits and garden soil. This was followed by the brick walls of part of the late 16th-c
Berkeley House, and cellars and wall footings of 18th- and 19th-c buildings.

Sloane, B, & Malcolm, G, in prep. St John of Jerusalem, London: excavations at the priory, 1900–1994, MoLAS Monograph series

7–8 Carthusian Street, EC1

A trial excavation in 1989 revealed a number of features which were almost certainly rubbish pits of later medieval or post-medieval date. Archaeological survival was exceptionally good and indicated continuous and intense occupation over several c. The deposits possibly represent the dumping of material from yards and gardens at the rear of the properties that abutted the Charterhouse wall, which was not itself located.

CAR89

Map site: 8
DGLA: Martin Brown
NGR: TQ 3204 8191
SMR: 082310

7–8 Carthusian Street, EC1

An evaluation excavation in 1990 established that the earliest evidence on the site consisted of shallow cut features containing Roman tile and pottery. Medieval or Tudor pits which produced pottery and glazed floor tiles were also located.

London Archaeol, 6, 1991, 303; *Britannia,* 22, 1991, 272

CAR90

Map site: 9
DGLA: David Bowsher
NGR: TQ 3205 8192

25–26 Clerkenwell Close, EC1

Examination of contractors' pits revealed the lower part of a brick-lined well, probably of 17th-c date.

CCL79

Map site: 10
ILAU: Rob Whytehead,
Wendy McIsaac
NGR: TQ 3145 8225

Chiswell Street, Whitecross Street, EC1

Site watching in 1986 showed that the site had been quarried for sand and gravel to varying depths in the medieval period. The area was truncated by basements, except along the N edge of the site where stratigraphy survived to ground level, over the medieval quarry pits, and produced pottery sherds of the 16th–18th c.

CET86

Map site: 11
DGLA(N): Rob Whytehead
NGR: TQ 3238 8200

42–46 Clerkenwell Close, EC1

Excavation in 1986, some 20m N of the cloisters of the nunnery of St Mary Clerkenwell, revealed deposits attributed to the nunnery kitchen. The walls had been destroyed by later intrusions, but floors, occupation debris and hearths survived. The building appeared to have been in use over a long period, the floors and hearths having been repaired several times and replaced at least once. The occupation deposits contained large quantities of fish bones and food waste (see ENG84, NEW81 below).

London Archaeol, 5, 1988, 412

CLK86

Map site: 12
DGLA(N): Michael Hutchinson
NGR: TQ 3146 8224
SMR: 080437

CLL79

Map site: 13

25–26 Clerkenwell Close, EC1

This site code is no longer in use and has been deleted (see CCL79 above).

CLW82

Map site: 14
ILAU: Peter Mills
NGR: TQ 3146 8213

14–16 Farringdon Lane, EC1

A watching brief (on the site of the clerks' well that gave Clerkenwell its name) revealed a refacing, possibly 16th c, of the medieval precinct wall of the nunnery of St Mary, forming a tank or cistern against the wall. In the 17th c this was rebuilt in ragstone, and in the 18th or 19th c a brick well shaft was sunk.

Sloane, B, in prep. *Excavations at the nunnery of St Mary de fonte, Clerkenwell*, MoLAS Monograph series

COW88

Map site: 15
DGLA(N): Catherine Gillard
NGR: TQ 3163 8184

Cowcross Street (redevelopment), EC1

A trial excavation in 1988 indicated the existence of post-medieval tenement buildings.

COW89

Map site: 16
DGLA(N): Mark Atkinson,
Gordon Malcolm
NGR: TQ 3163 8184
SMR: 080436, 082201

20–26 Cowcross Street, 9–13 Peter's Lane, 35a St John Street, 1–4 St John's Lane, 8–10 Eagle Court, 37–39 Britton Street, EC1

Excavation in 1989 following trial work (see COW88 above) revealed, some 150m S of the gatehouse of St John Clerkenwell, substantial chalk footings and clay floor surfaces of between four and ten buildings of medieval date, and several post-Dissolution Tudor structures. Three phases of chalk-founded medieval buildings were identified, and traces of earlier, timber constructions. Structures to the W included a chalk-lined well and several cesspits. There was also evidence of milling and baking in the form of Rhineland quernstone fragments associated with a crushed chalk floor and, in the adjoining room, a tiled oven complex. A few medieval burials were also excavated to the W of the chalk buildings.

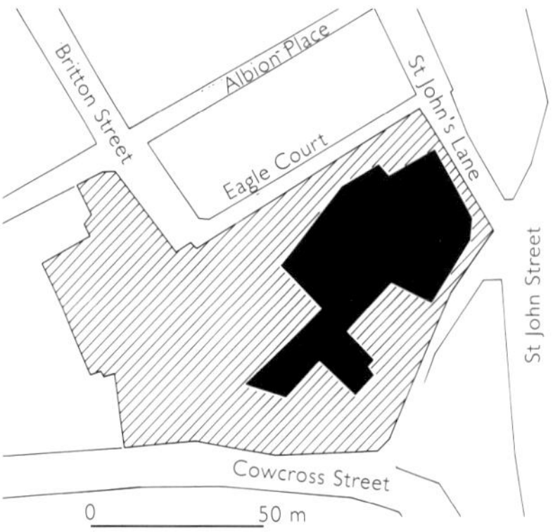

London Archaeol, 6, 1990, 190; *Medieval Archaeol,* 34, 1990, 182
Atkinson, M, & Malcolm, G, 1990 'Recent excavations at St John's Priory in Cowcross Street, EC1', *London Archaeol,* 6, 171–8

DAG77

Map site: 17
ILAU: Irene Schwab
NGR: TQ 3178 8392

282 Dagmar Terrace, N1

Excavation in 1977 revealed two linear features cutting the natural gravel and containing 14th–15th-c material. Above them was a packed gravel surface of similar date.

London Archaeol, 3, 1978, 161

Engineers' car park, 8–13 Clerkenwell Close, 33–36 Clerkenwell Green, EC1

Excavations in 1984 in the SW corner of the former precinct of the nunnery of St Mary Clerkenwell (founded c 1195) revealed Iron Age, medieval and post-medieval remains in an area shown by 16th-c maps to have been occupied by tenements belonging to the nunnery. A sub-circular Iron Age feature 1m deep, from which a large quantity of pottery was recovered, extended about 4m N–S by 2m E–W, and probably represented the end of a ditch. The remains of three substantial medieval buildings were found standing to a height of about 2.5m, two of them constructed of coursed chalk blocks and the other of Kentish ragstone; built into the last was a stone-lined cesspit, possibly contemporary. The remains of three possibly late medieval kilns were also exposed. A tile-built post-medieval hearth and numerous rubbish pits reflected the intensive use of the site since the Dissolution (see also CLK86 above, NEW81 below).

London Archaeol, 5, 1985, 63–4

Sloane, B, in prep. *Excavations at the nunnery of St Mary de fonte, Clerkenwell,* MoLAS Monograph series

ENG84

Map site: not shown
DGLA: R Ellis
NGR: TQ 314 821
SMR: 080358, 080437, 080491–2

Farringdon Road, Clerkenwell Road, EC1

A trial excavation in 1975 showed that any archaeological levels had been removed by post-medieval intrusion.

London Archaeol, 2, 1976, 371

FAR75

Map site: 18
ILAU: David Whipp
NGR: TQ 314 821

101–117 Finsbury Pavement, EC2

A trial excavation in 1978, intended to recover information about the Moorfields marsh, showed that the site apparently occupied an island within the marshy area.

London Archaeol, 3, 1979, 263

FINP78

Map site: 19
ILAU: Irene Schwab
NGR: TQ 328 818
SMR: 080494

55 Clerkenwell Road, EC1

An evaluation excavation in 1990 within the precinct of the priory of St John of Jerusalem showed that most archaeological deposits had been destroyed by modern intrusion. Most of the surviving deposits consisted of 17th-c garden soils and rubbish pits. The only early feature was the base of a Tudor barrel-well, comprising two complete waterlogged barrels, their joints reinforced with reused fragments of Caen stone.

London Archaeol, 6, 1991, 303; *Post-Medieval Archaeol,* 25, 1991, 131

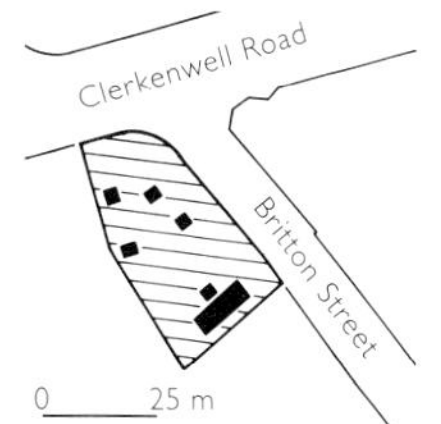

GIN90

Map site: 20
DGLA(N): Mark Atkinson
NGR: TQ 3158 8206
SMR: 082303

125 Golden Lane, EC1

An evaluation excavation in 1990 located a block of dressed sandstone, possible Tudor pottery and a post-medieval yellow-glazed tile, as well as layers containing small Reigate stone fragments.

London Archaeol, 6, 1991, 303

GOL90

Map site: 21
DGLA(N): Mark Atkinson
NGR: TQ 3221 8228
SMR: 082314

GOS89

Map site: 22
DGLA(N): Mark Barratt
NGR: TQ 3208 8207

7–21 Goswell Road, EC1

An archaeological assessment in 1989 indicated undisturbed stratigraphy in the basement at the N end of the site.

GSW90

Map site: 23
DGLA(N): Christopher Kirby
NGR: TQ 3208 8207
SMR: 080482, 082306–7

7–21 Goswell Road, EC1

Excavation in 1990 revealed a possible road drainage ditch containing residual human bone, and pottery and tile dated to the 1st–3rd c. Evidence that the area had once been used as a garden was provided by a terrace cut at right angles to a chalk wall which, though badly truncated, seems likely to have been part of the Charterhouse precinct wall. A series of post-medieval dumpedlayers with a related ditch, group of pits, two brick-lined cesspits, a wall and a very large pit was located.

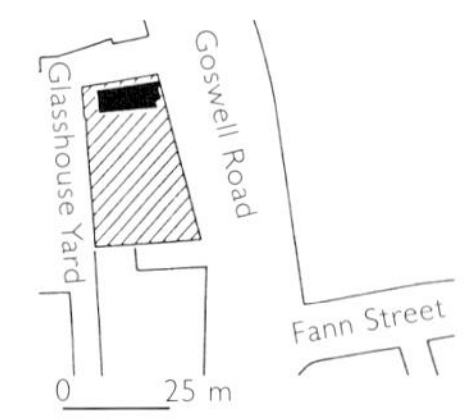

London Archaeol, 6, 1991, 303; *Britannia,* 22, 1991, 272; *Post-Medieval Archaeol,* 25, 1991, 131

HAC90

Map site: 24
DGLA(N): Gordon Malcolm
NGR: TQ 3277 8212
SMR: 082315

Honourable Artillery Company, City Road, EC1

A watching brief in 1990 revealed probable medieval deposits.

London Archaeol, 6, 1991, 304; *Medieval Archaeol,* 35, 1991, 154

JAN90

Map site: 25
DGLA(N): Gordon Malcolm
NGR: TQ 3169 8195
SMR: 080436, 082302

1–7 Albion Place, EC1

Excavation in 1990 on the E edge of a large site in the outer precinct of St John's Priory, Clerkenwell, followed an evaluation examination in which a number of 18th-c Delft tiles were recovered. Four 18th-c tenement buildings were recorded as overlying extensive 16th- and 17th-c structures belonging to Berkeley House and another, earlier building. The large number of early 16th-c moulded bricks associated with this building suggests that it was probably part of the mansion of Sir Thomas Docwra, prior of the Order of St John in 1501–27.

London Archaeol, 6, 1991, 303; *Post-Medieval Archaeol,* 25, 1991, 115

JER83

Map site: 26
ILAU: Rob Whytehead
NGR: TQ 3167 8212
SMR: 080504

British Telecom trench, Clerkenwell Road, EC1

Observations in 1983 noted the remains of a stone rubble wall, composed mainly of green Reigate stone, which ran N–S and then returned E.

394–416 St John Street, EC1

Excavation in 1990 revealed brick walls probably of early 19th-c date, and square pits with straight sides dug through natural brickearth. These were backfilled with soil and a small quantity of domestic refuse, and are interpreted as 19th-c quarry pits for the extraction of gravel.

London Archaeol, 6, 1991, 304

JOE90

Map site: 27
DGLA(N): James Hunter
NGR: TQ 3170 8280

52–54 St John Street, EC1

A watching brief in 1988 revealed the site (within the precincts of the priory of St John Clerkenwell) to be badly truncated by modern basements, and deposits which did survive suggested medieval and later rubbish pitting and gravel-quarrying. Pottery types were broadly similar to those recorded elsewhere in the priory precinct, and were apparently Tudor in date with the exception of sherds from beneath a chalk wall, which are earlier and include a body sherd of Coarse Border ware dated *c* 1350–1550.

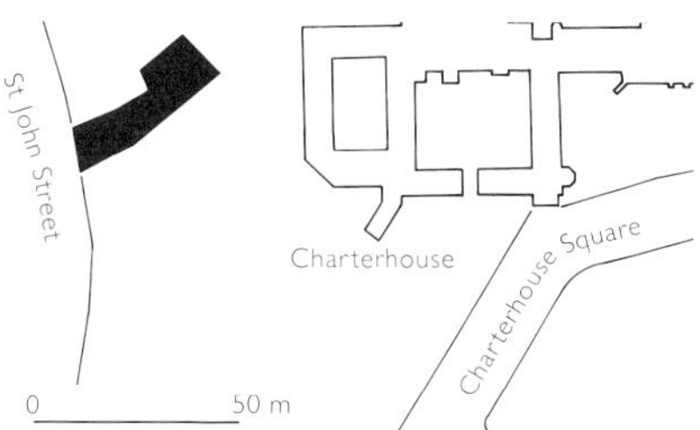

JOH88

Map site: 28
DGLA(N): Mark Barratt
NGR: TQ 3182 8196

47–49 St John's Square, EC1

Excavations in 1989 revealed a doorway and later light well in the N wall of the crypt of the church of the priory of St John and associated basements; both were blocked, and the light well overlay the very fragmentary remains of a building of medieval date, possibly part of the prior's apartments. Near the N wall of the later 14th-c nave was located a lay cemetery from which 13 skeletons were recovered from a very clear sequence of grave cuts of 14th- to probably 16th c date. Beneath the cemetery were the remnants of an earlier church wall, which in turn cut through a ditch left by the robbing of the 12th-c round nave. In the area of the 17th-c mansion of the earls of Aylesbury floor surfaces of tile, clay and brick were located, along with the remains of joists from a wooden platform; a gateway was recorded leading into a gravelled yard surface with wheel ruts at the point of entry. The mansion reused many of the priory walls.

London Archaeol, 6, 1989, 190; *Medieval Archaeol,* 34, 1990, 182; *Post-Medieval Archaeol,* 24, 1990, 189
Sloane, B, & Malcolm, G, in prep. *St John of Jerusalem, London: excavations at the priory, 1900–1994,* MoLAS Monograph series

JON89

Map site: 29
DGLA(N): Barney Sloane
NGR: TQ 317 821
SMR: 080436

14 St John's Lane, EC1

Excavation in 1990 in two areas within the outer precinct of St John's Priory, Clerkenwell, produced evidence in one area of 16th-c occupation and of several domestic animal burials, including that of a horse, semi-articulated, in rubbish pits cut into the natural gravel. The other area featured a number of 15th–17th-c wall footings and a brick garderobe belonging to Berkeley House. At a later stage a 15th-c ceramic watering-can was found within a barrel-lined well.

London Archaeol, 6, 1991, 304; *Medieval Archaeol,* 35, 1991, 154; *Post-Medieval Archaeol,* 25, 1991, 132

KEE90

Map site: 30
DGLA(N): Gordon Malcolm
NGR: TQ 3169 8195
SMR: 080436, 082299

LEI86

Map site: 31
DGLA(N): Rob Whytehead
NGR: TQ 317 855

Christ Church Hall, Leigh Road, N5

A watching brief in 1986 revealed evidence of the medieval manor house, traces of chalk wall foundations of probable outbuildings, which clearly extended onto the neighbouring site of Eton House, the traditional site of the manor house. Gravel yard surfaces were also noted, and a single pottery sherd dated to the period *c* 1275–1350, predating the destruction of the manor house in the Peasants' Revolt of 1381.

LIG88

Map site: 32
DGLA(N): Alex Mackie
NGR: TQ 3287 8180
SMR: 082069–70, 082092

Ling House, 10–13 Dominion Street, EC2

Excavation in 1988 investigated known marsh deposits previously dated to the Roman and medieval periods. The marsh material, up to 0.3m thick, is interpreted as pond deposits in the bottom of clay quarries, overlain by layers of dumped material probably representing post-medieval land reclamation.

London Archaeol, 6, 1989, 74

LIT89

Map site: 33
DGLA(N): Christopher Phillpotts
NGR: TQ 3200 8210

Litton House, 27 Goswell Road, EC1

Excavation in 1989 located no trace of the Charterhouse buildings or of its precinct wall, nor found any indication of Roman activity. The area appears to have been used for quarrying, probably in the post-medieval period.

MED89, MED90

Map site: 34, 35
DGLA(N): Mark Barratt
NGR: TQ 3200 8214, 3196 8209
SMR: 080514, 082200

St Bartholomew's Hospital Medical College, Clerkenwell Road, EC1

Excavation in 1989 exposed extensive refuse pits containing a large quantity of 17th-c pottery. A layer cut by a substantial ragstone and green Reigate stone wall produced the earliest dating evidence on site in the form of pottery of the period 1350–1550. The site was occupied by the London Charterhouse between 1371 and 1537, and the wall and pits appear to relate to occupation by Lord North after the Dissolution. Excavation on the site of the cloister garth in 1990 revealed *in situ* walls and floor levels of the period, and a large quantity of plain yellow- and black-glazed Flemish floor tiles of the 14th–15th c recovered from robber trenches of the Dissolution period, when the Charterhouse was converted to a residence.

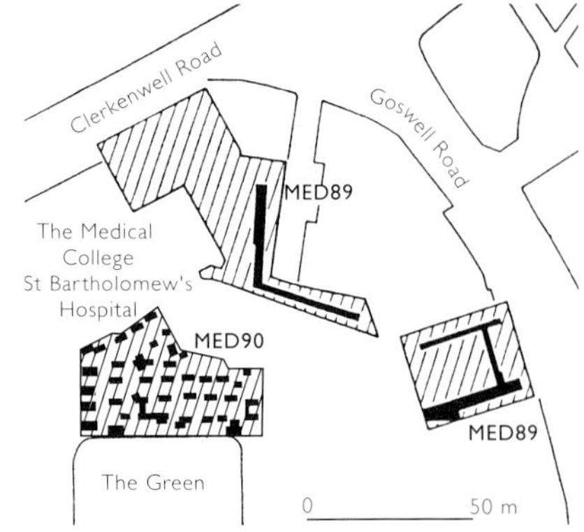

A substantial wall of this period, constructed from robbed materials, was found to traverse the site for a distance of more than 50m.

London Archaeol, 6, 1990, 190; 6, 1991, 304; *Medieval Archaeol,* 34, 1990, 182; 35, 1991, 154; *Post-Medieval Archaeol,* 24, 1990, 186
Barratt, M, & Thomas, C, 1991 'The London Charterhouse', *London Archaeol,* 6, 283–91

Newcastle Row, rear of 36 Clerkenwell Close, EC1

Excavation in 1981 on the W side of Newcastle Row on the supposed site of the N range of the cloister of St Mary's Nunnery, Clerkenwell, identified two phases of medieval occupation. The first comprised part of a building of possible 12th–13th-c date with an associated yard surface of rammed gravel; a much repaired mortar floor may also relate to this phase. The second phase was represented by a chalk cellar or undercroft, possibly of the 15th c, inserted within the walls of the earlier building and including part of a window or chute and a recess. The remains have been provisionally interpreted as part of the building referred to in the 18th c as the 'Nuns' Hall', and may have formed part of the infirmary. See also CLK86, ENG84 above, NEW87, SCT87 below.

London Archaeol, 4, 1982, 164; *Post-Medieval Archaeol*, 16, 1982, 228
Sloane, B, in prep. *Excavations at the nunnery of St Mary de fonte, Clerkenwell*, MoLAS Monograph series

NEW81

Map site: 36
ILAU: Peter Mills
NGR: TQ 3148 8226

6 Newcastle Row, EC1

Excavation in 1987 within the N cloister of St Mary's Nunnery, Clerkenwell, located substantial building remains identified as those of the 'Nuns' Hall', perhaps the infirmary. The massive stone walls with chalk footings aligned with walls found on an adjacent site (see NEW81 above). The building survived as part of a later structure, the basement of which had destroyed any trace of medieval floors. To the W was found a contemporary stone-lined cesspit. See also CLK86, ENG84 above.

London Archaeol, 5, 1988, 412; *Medieval Archaeol*, 32, 1988, 250
Sloane, B, in prep. *Excavations at the nunnery of St Mary de fonte, Clerkenwell*, MoLAS Monograph series

NEW87

Map site: 37
DGLA(N): Michael
Hutchinson
NGR: TQ 3148 8226

Northampton Buildings, Skinner Street, Corporation Row, Rosoman Street, EC1

Excavation in 1977 revealed no archaeological deposits surviving beneath the 19th-c basements.

London Archaeol, 3, 1978, 161

NTB77

Map site: 38
ILAU: Graham Black
NGR: TQ 314 824

76–78 Old Street, EC1

A testpit survey in 1989 proved inconclusive for the earlier periods. Post-medieval dumping noted in several of the pits may be related to the removal of waste from the City after the Great Fire of 1666. One pit which was dug down to natural revealed medieval stratigraphy above brickearth and below the dumping.

OLD89

Map site: 39
DGLA(N): Gordon Malcolm
NGR: TQ 3226 8227

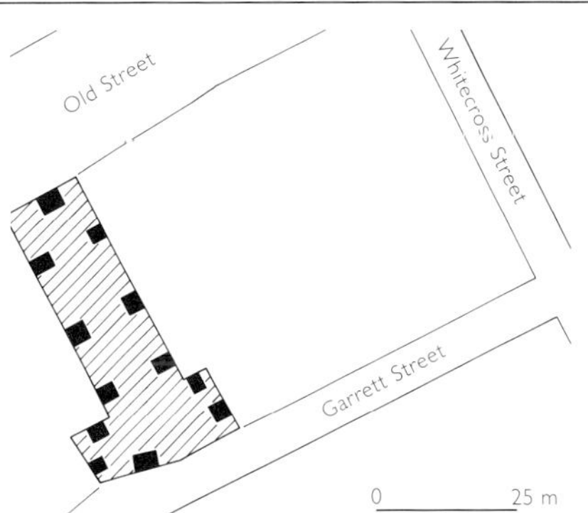

PKF77

Map site: 40
ILAU: Graham Black
NGR: TQ 314 834

Parkfield Street, N1

Excavation in 1977 revealed a length of rubble wall without dating evidence at the S of the site. On its N side were four ditches, possibly for drainage, from one of which was recovered a single sherd of 16th–17th-c pottery. The other ditches were undated.

London Archaeol, 3, 1978, 161

ROS88

Map site: 41

Rosebery Avenue, Topham Street, EC1

Currently there is no further information for this site.

SCT87

Map site: 42
DGLA(N): Stephen Tucker
NGR: TQ 315 822

36–41 Scotswood Street, EC1

Post-holes of a substantial 12th-c timber building, probably an early phase of the nunnery of St Mary Clerkenwell, were cut through an agricultural horizon. A later 12th-c masonry building and associated courtyard overlay this. This building had two doorways, one paved with glazed floor tiles. Further chalk structures were subsequently built in the yard. These were demolished, probably at the Dissolution in 1538. The principal building continued in use to the late 18th c when it was known as the 'Nuns' Hall' (see also NEW81 above).

Medieval Archaeol, 32, 1988, 250

SJL90

Map site: 43
DGLA(W): Mark Atkinson
NGR: TQ 3176 8194
SMR: 080436

6–7 St John's Lane, EC1

Excavation in 1990 within the outer precinct of St John's Priory, Clerkenwell, revealed a large number of 14th–17th-c pits filled with domestic rubbish. Fragments of medieval wall footings from which the stone had been robbed were also recorded.

London Archaeol, 6, 1991, 304; *Medieval Archaeol*, 35, 1991, 154; *Post-Medieval Archaeol*, 25, 1991, 131

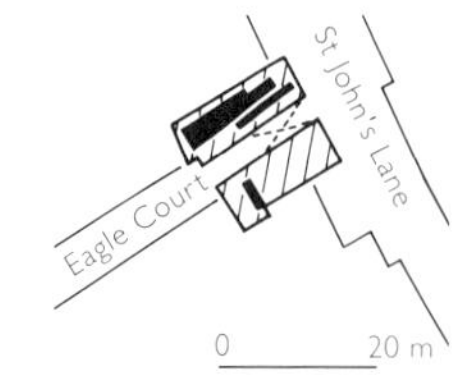

SJS86

Map site: 44
DGLA(N): Kevin Wooldridge
NGR: TQ 317 822
SMR: 080436, 080481

49–52 St John's Square, EC1

Trial trenching in 1986 revealed no medieval surfaces surviving within a standing building thought to have been originally part of the priory of St John Clerkenwell. The floors for the most part overlay natural sands and gravels, but in three of the basement rooms they sealed truncated chalk features of unknown function which probably date from after the Dissolution. In previous investigations chalk and ragstone walls, perhaps part of the conventual buildings, were located, in places surviving to a height of 2.1m above the modern basement floors. Numerous architectural features were observed in the walls, the infill of one of which included two reused Caen stone blocks, suggesting that its construction followed demolition elsewhere in the precinct: conceivably the sacking of the priory during the Peasants' Revolt of 1381. The exact relationship between the walls and the contemporary ground surface could not be established.

London Archaeol, 5, 1987, 275–6; *Medieval Archaeol*, 31, 1987, 130
Wooldridge, K, 1987 '49–52 St John's Square, Clerkenwell, London EC1: excavation and recording of the standing building', *Trans London Middlesex Archaeol Soc*, 38, 131–50

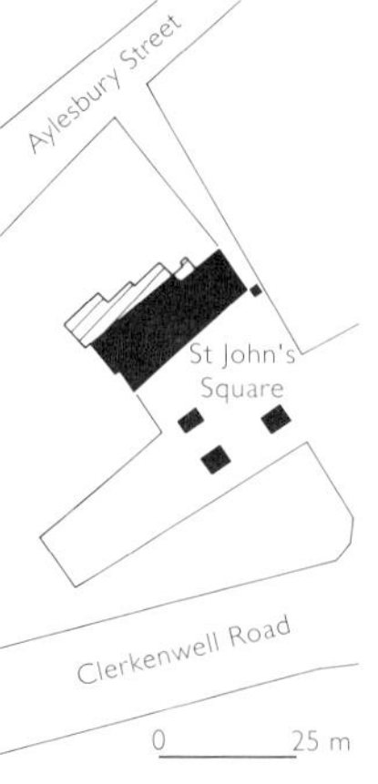

National Car Park, Sans Walk, St James's Row, EC1

Excavations in 1986–7 revealed early buildings, apparently of timber, which were demolished when the ground beneath them was dug for gravel. Thereafter a pipe trench was cut, perhaps related to the main water supply from Sadler's Wells, established c 1430. The next phase was represented by the chalk, ragstone and Reigate stone foundations of two undated masonry buildings.

London Archaeol, 5, 1988, 412; Medieval Archaeol, 32, 1988, 250

SNS86, SNS87

Map site: 45, 46
DLGA(N): Michael Hutchinson
NGR: TQ 3150 8228
SMR: 082122, 082145–7

South Place, EC2

Excavation in 1977 revealed undated finds from a dark organic layer exposed in a sewer trench.

SOP77

Map site: 47
ILAU: J Siegel
NGR: TQ 328 817
SMR: 080499

94–100 St John Street, EC1

An archaeological survey in 1988 revealed, in addition to natural deposits beneath the basement slab, a truncated mortared chalk wall datable by pottery, tile and brick fragments to the 16th c, although a large part of the fabric was probably reused medieval building material. It is likely that the remains represent part of a Tudor rebuilding of the Charterhouse boundary wall. Further excavation in 1989 located a section of wall comprising unworked blocks of chalk and flint laid in irregular courses.

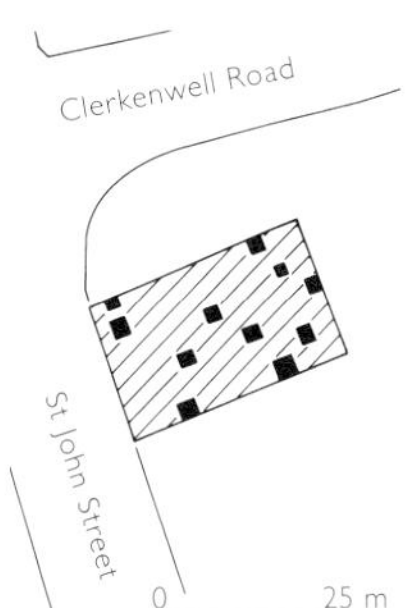

STJ88, STJ89

Map site: 48, 49
DLGA(N): Kevin Williams, Mark Barratt
NGR: TQ 3179 8207
SMR: 082309

Teziac House, 110–115 Aldersgate Street, EC1

A trial excavation in 1988 revealed chalk walls probably belonging to the medieval Charterhouse, as well as chalk, rubble and mortar deposits.

TEZ88

Map site: 50
DLGA(N): C Williams, K Williams
NGR: TQ 3208 8198

Veritas House, 119–125 Finsbury Pavement, EC2

Excavations in 1990 revealed the adaptation of a tributary of the Walbrook as the E arm of the moat of Finsbury Court during the medieval and Tudor periods. Two features of early 17th-c date cut into the infill of the moat.

London Archaeol, 6, 1991, 303; Medieval Archaeol, 35, 1991, 154; Post-Medieval Archaeol, 25, 1991, 147

VER90

Map site: 51
DLGA(N): Vaughan Birbeck
NGR: TQ 3275 8185
SMR: 080399

31–35 Wilson Street, EC2

Excavation in 1989 showed that no archaeological features survived.

WIL89

Map site: 52
DLGA(N): Trevor Cox
NGR: TQ 329 818

WOP88

Map site: 53
DGLA(N): David Bowsher
NGR: TQ 3290 8211
SMR: 082093

19–23 Worship Street, EC2

A watching brief in 1988 revealed a presumed watercourse, backfilled in the 16th c; probably the stream shown bordering Worship Street on the 'Copperplate Map'.

London Archaeol, 6, 1989, 74; Post-Medieval Archaeol, 23, 1989, 39

WTC76

Map site: 54
ILAU: Graham Black
NGR: TQ 324 821
SMR: 080370, 080500–3

Whitbread's Brewery, Whitecross Street, EC1

An exploratory excavation in 1976 demonstrated that the area lay within the Moorfields marsh; most of the reclamation dumping was of 15th-c date, earlier than at Bonhill Street (see BON76 above). The line of Whitecross Street was also seen to have shifted eastwards since the 18th c.

London Archaeol, 3, 1977, 38

KENSINGTON AND CHELSEA

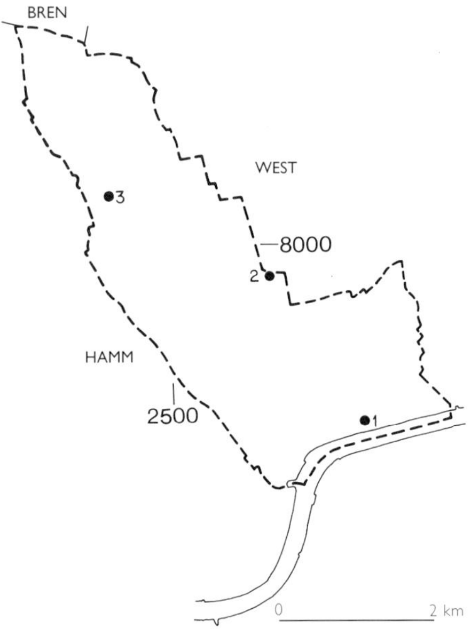

Royal Borough of Kensington and Chelsea

KENS 1   OAK90   25 Oakley Gardens, SW3
KENS 2   THO76   11–15 Thorney Court, Kensington Rd, Palace Gate, W8
KENS 3   WAR78   Walmer Rd (Corporation Yard), W11

See borough map in Introduction for key

OAK90

Map site: 1
DGLA(N): Ian Grainger
NGR: TQ 2737 7775
SMR: 081645

25 Oakley Gardens, SW3

A watching brief in 1990 observed two fragments of foundations, perhaps part of a boundary wall of the Tudor manor house to the S built by Henry VIII in 1536–7 and demolished in the 1750s. One of the fragments was possibly a Georgian rebuild of the original. A layer of brick rubble was also found, perhaps related to the demolition of the manor house.

London Archaeol, 6, 1991, 304; *Post-Medieval Archaeol*, 25, 1991, 148

THO76

Map site: 2
ILAU: Graham Black
NGR: TQ 262 796
SMR: 081686

11–15 Thorney Court, Kensington Road, Palace Gate, W8

Excavation in 1976 failed to locate a minor Roman road which joined the main highway between London and Silchester, most of the site having been destroyed by gravelworking.

London Archaeol, 3, 1977, 38

WAR78

Map site: 3
ILAU: Peter Mills
NGR: TQ 240 805

Corporation Yard, Walmer Road, W11

Observations in 1978 recorded a large, deep pit, dug for clay and possibly Victorian in date.

KINGSTON UPON THAMES

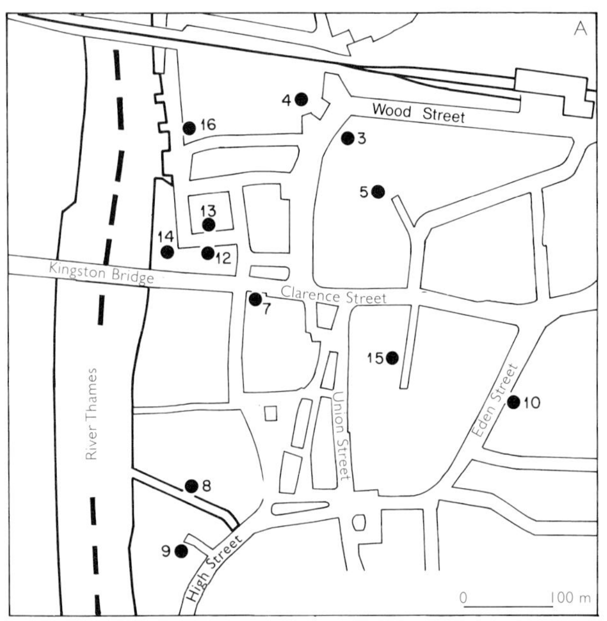

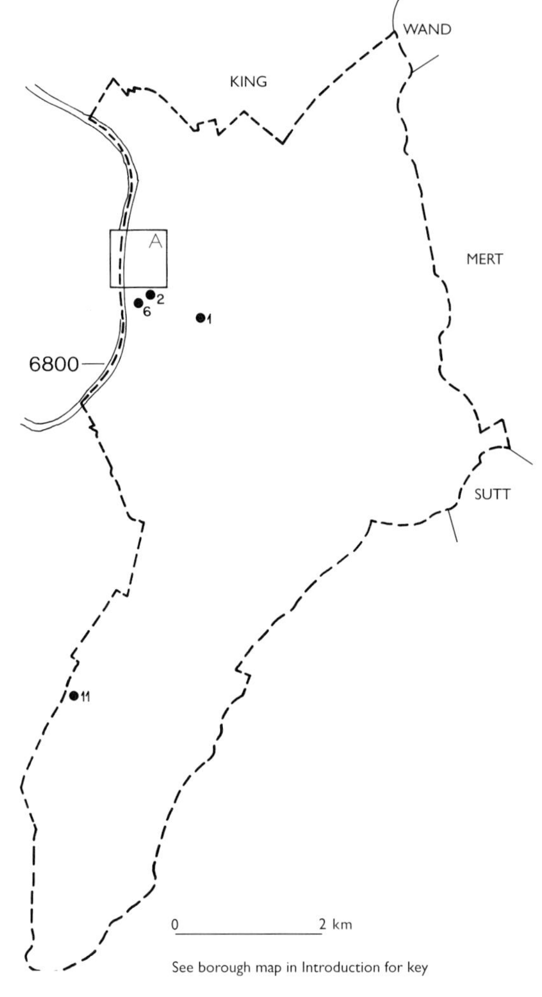

Royal Borough of Kingston upon Thames	KING 6 BIM90	The Bittoms (car park site), Kingston, KT1	KING 12 HOR82 Horse Fair (Old Bridge St), Kingston, KT1
KING 1 AKW90 Athelstan Rd, Kingston, KT1	KING 7 CLA88	2 Clarence St, 34–36 Thames St, Kingston, KT1	KING 13 HOR85 Horse Fair (Old Bridge St, north side), Kingston, KT1
KING 2 BDL89 Bedlesford, 1 Wheatfield Way, Kingston, KT1	KING 8 CQD88	Charter Quay, Market Place, High St, Kingston, KT1	KING 14 HOR86 Horse Fair, Old Bridge St, Thames Side, Kingston, KT1
KING 3 BEN87 Bentall's Redevelopment, Wood St, Kingston, KT1	KING 9 CQD90	Charter Quay (Odeon Cinema site), High St, Kingston, KT1	KING 15 KND82 19 Union St (Knapp-Drewett site), Kingston, KT1
KING 4 BEN88 Bentall's Redevelopment, Wood St, Kingston, KT1	KING 10 EDE89	82 Eden St, 7–17 Lady Booth Rd, Kingston, KT1	KING 16 TUK90 Turk's Boatyard, Thames Side, Kingston, KT1
KING 5 BEN90 Bentall's Department Store, West St, Fife Rd, Clarence St, Kingston, KT1	KING 11 G74	The Grapsome (wood), Hook, KT9	

AKW90

Map site: 1
DGLA(SW): Robert Bazely
NGR: TQ 188 686

Athelstan Road, Kingston, KT1

Excavation in 1990 revealed no structural evidence.

London Archaeol, 6, 1991, 304; *Surrey Archaeol Coll*, 81, 1991–2, 158

Bedlesford, I Wheatfield Way, Kingston, KT I

A watching brief in 1989 to the SE of Kingston town centre and immediately NE of a historic fording point of the Hogsmill river revealed deeply stratified waterlaid deposits, some more than 2m deep. The latest dated to *c* 1600, and possibly represents the infilling of a channel to the E of the town centre; perhaps an earlier or secondary course of the Hogsmill. These deposits were sealed by 17th-c surfaces. N of the present riverbank was a revetment incorporating reused boat timbers and of similar date. Slightly later was a large timber-lined drain, about 1.5m wide, running N–S towards the Hogsmill.

London Archaeol, 6, 1990, 191; Post-Medieval Archaeol, 24, 1990, 178; Surrey Archaeol Coll, 80, 1990, 218

BDL89

Map site: 2
DGLA(SW): Geoffrey Potter
NGR: TQ 1810 6895

Bentall's Redevelopment, Wood Street, Kingston, KT I

A watching brief in 1987–8 recorded a prehistoric river channel adjoining the Thames and previously noted in Eden Walk to the S by Kingston Museum in 1965. The watercourse appears to have been a braided channel of the Thames, present into the post-medieval period as marshy ground, and possibly marking the E limit of early settlement in the town. Roman tile and pottery were located in the upper silting layers.

London Archaeol, 6, 1989, 75; Surrey Archaeol Coll, 79, 1989, 185; 80, 1990, 217

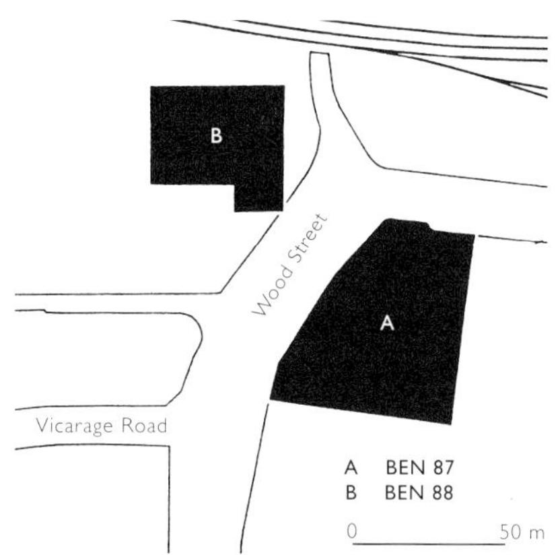

BEN87, BEN88

Map site: 3, 4
DGLA(SW): Geoffrey Potter, Robin Nielsen
NGR: TQ 1800 6950, 1787 6957

Bentall's Department Store, West Street, Fife Road, Clarence Street, Kingston, KT I

A watching brief in 1990 on the site of an ancient river channel (see BEN87, BEN88) cut during the last glacial period and possibly a tributary of the Thames or Hogsmill rivers recorded riverlaid sediments of Roman and earlier date. A fragment of antler, a possible antler pick of Neolithic date, and several pieces of Roman tile and brick were recovered.

London Archaeol, 6, 1991, 304; Surrey Archaeol Coll, 81, 1991–2, 158

BEN90

Map site: 5
DGLA(SW): Pat Miller
NGR: TQ 180 694

The Bittoms (car park site), Kingston, KT I

An evaluation excavation in 1990–1 revealed worked flints and two pits of Saxon date. Post-medieval dumping was also recorded.

London Archaeol, 6, 1991, 304; Surrey Archaeol Coll, 81, 1991–2, 158

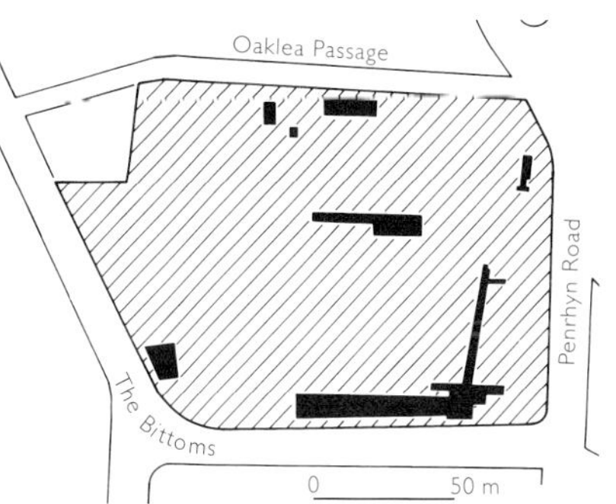

BIM90

Map site: 6
DGLA(SW): John Dillon, Peter Thompson
NGR: TQ 1800 6855
SMR: 021580, 032029–30

CLA88

Map site: 7
DGLA(SW): Philip Emery
NGR: TQ 1787 6935

2 Clarence Street, 34–36 Thames Street, Kingston, KT1

Basement excavations in 1988 revealed the early 18th-c foundations of part of the original Crown and Thistle Inn, on the site of a group of tenements known as The Rookery, first recorded on a 17th-c map and demolished in 1834. The remains consisted of reused Reigate stone blocks, some possibly derived from a Tudor door arch and including a medieval gargoyle. Excavation to the E of the basement after site clearance uncovered the walls and floors of two small tenements, also part of The Rookery. A succession of metalled surfaces was encountered between their frontages and the churchyard to the S. These represented part of an alley, known as 'Birdcage Walk' or 'Washerwomen's Alley', which overlay numerous graves and indicated that the churchyard had once extended further N. Two large pits containing bone and Roman tile were also located.

London Archaeol, 6, 1989, 74–5; *Post-Medieval Archaeol*, 23, 1989, 39; *Surrey Archaeol Coll*, 80, 1990, 217

CQD88

Map site: 8
DGLA(SW): Robin Nielsen
NGR: TQ 1780 6910

Charter Quay, Market Place, High Street, Kingston, KT1

An evaluation excavation in 1988–9 revealed medieval timber waterfront revetments and medieval and post-medieval infill and reclamation, with property boundaries N and S of Hogsmill Creek and 18th-c stables to the S of the creek and N of Emms Passage. They overlay at least two phases of medieval building, the earliest dated to the 13th c. At the S end of the site were found remains of 19th-c and earlier buildings fronting the High Street.

London Archaeol, 6, 1989, 75; 6, 1990, 190; *Medieval Archaeol*, 33, 1989, 184; 34, 1990, 182; *Surrey Archaeol Coll*, 80, 1990, 217

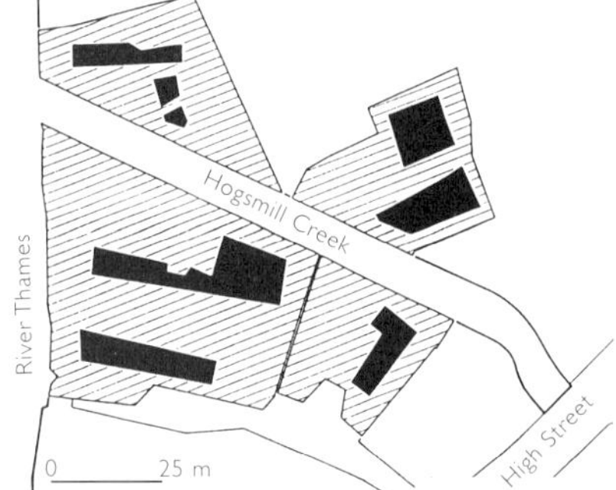

CQD90

Map site: 9
DGLA(SW): Robin Nielsen
NGR: TQ 1780 6910

Charter Quay (Odeon Cinema site), High Street, Kingston, KT1

Further excavation in 1990 along the High Street frontage immediately behind the Thames bank revealed, along the street frontage, occupation layers and remains of structures of 18th- and 19th-c date. Traces of pitch-tile kilns or hearths with large quantities of medieval pottery were also located. Up to three waterfront revetments were recorded, that closest to the Thames being provisionally dated to the late 14th–early 15th c.

London Archaeol, 6, 1991, 304; *Medieval Archaeol*, 35, 1991, 155; *Post-Medieval Archaeol*, 25, 1991, 132; *Surrey Archaeol Coll*, 81, 1991–2, 158

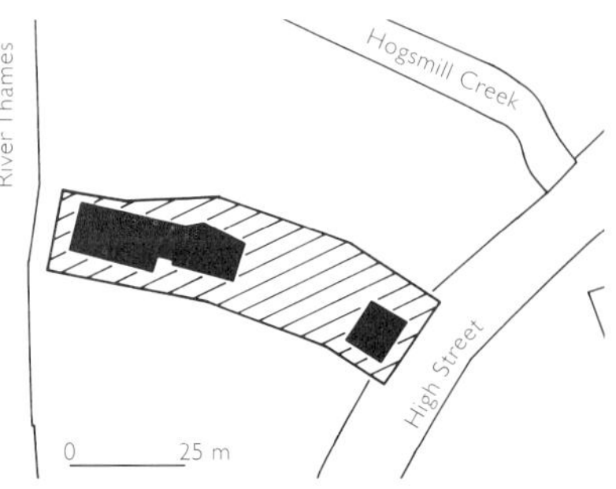

82 Eden Street, 7–17 Lady Booth Road, Kingston, KT1

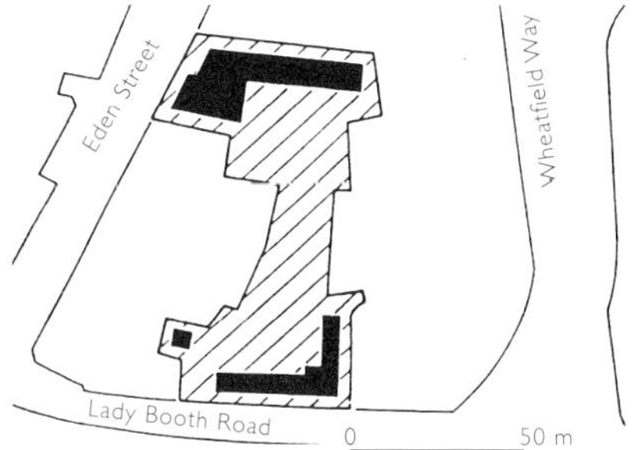

Excavation in 1989 located a river channel infilled by a sequence of waterlaid deposits which included large quantities of pottery, building material, animal bone, metalwork and jewellery as well as more than 350 bronze coins mostly of 4th-c date. The uppermost layer and a V-shaped ditch produced sherds of Early Saxon pottery, probably indicative of continuous activity between the 4th and 6th c. Numerous medieval cut features, including boundary ditches and post-holes, were also excavated. An 18th-c pit yielded a number of Surrey Whiteware sherds, many of them evidently wasters, probably deriving from a medieval kiln behind 70–72 Eden Street, excavated by Kingston Museum in 1968–9.

London Archaeol, 6, 1990, 190; Medieval Archaeol, 34, 1990, 182; Surrey Archaeol Coll, 80, 1990, 218

EDE89

Map site: 10
DGLA(SW): Philip Emery
NGR: TQ 1820 6923
SMR: 021547–53

The Grapsome (wood), Hook, KT9

Excavation in 1974, about 600m W of Leatherhead Road on the line of the Esher by-pass, revealed a medieval ditched enclosure. (Location of records unknown.)

London Archaeol, 2, 1975, 258

G74

Map site: 11
SAS, KUTAS: Martin Dean, I West
NGR: TQ 1705 6360
SMR: 031841

Horse Fair (Old Bridge Street), Kingston, KT1

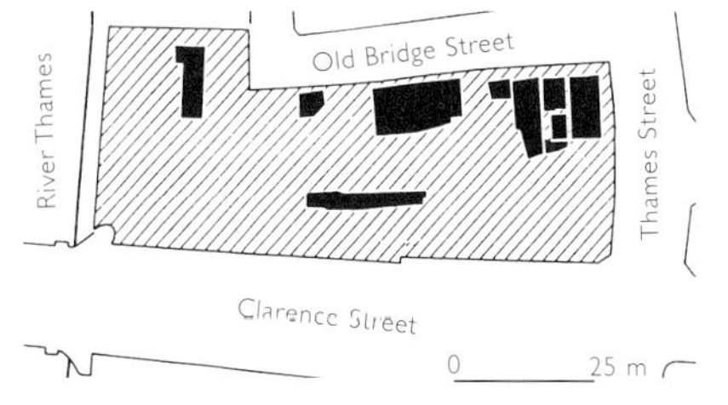

Trial excavation took place in 1982 on two sites on the N side of Old Bridge Street, thought to mark the line of the road leading to the medieval bridgehead. Investigation at the NW end of the street revealed that the ground level had been reduced in the 19th c. No medieval features survived; a chalk-lined well was recorded near the line of the road, as were several 17th- and 18th-c pits which probably represented gravelworkings. A second trench towards the S end of Old Bridge Street revealed the foundations of a 17th-c house in which several floor levels survived, its position suggesting that the contemporary road-line lay further S. The house was built above a 16th-c pit, possibly another gravelworking, and two other pits containing 14th-c pottery were located during excavation.

London Archaeol, 4, 1983, 289; Medieval Archaeol, 27, 1983, 195; Surrey Archaeol Coll, 75, 1984, 270

HOR82

Map site: 12
SWLAU: Scott McCracken
NGR: TQ 178 694

Horse Fair (Old Bridge Street, north side), Kingston, KT1

Excavation in 1985–6 at the junction of Old Bridge Street and Thames Street revealed a well-preserved undercroft constructed of chalk blocks and knapped flints in a chequerboard pattern, which would originally have been situated at the N end of the approach to the medieval bridge. The walls and about 2m of the roof survived intact. Work further along the frontage towards the bridge located two 15th- or 16th-c buildings with stone foundations and clay floors with associated pitched-tile hearths and a tile and flint lined cesspit of c 1500.

London Archaeol, 5, 1986, 162; Medieval Archaeol, 30, 1986, 142; Surrey Archaeol Coll, 78, 1987, 142

HOR85

Map site: 13
DGLA(SW): Scott McCracken
NGR: TQ 1784 6950
SMR: 030516, 031909

HOR86

Map site: 14
DGLA(SW): Geoffrey Potter
NGR: TQ 1778 6942
SMR: 030035

Horse Fair, Old Bridge Street, Thames Side, Kingston, KT1

Excavation of the medieval bridge in 1986–7 revealed the foundations of a landward abutment, and four freestanding piers with a combined span of about 30m, to the E of the present riverbank. The construction was of mortared flint rubble with a dressed Reigate stone facing; three of the piers, protected by timber starlings, originally stood in the river. The bridge is provisionally dated to the later 12th c. Later medieval development included the extension of the landward revetment to form a masonry causeway which enclosed the first and second piers. Two further piers were substantially rebuilt, probably by the mid-14th c, retaining the springing of the arches. The W arch was reconstructed, apparently in the early 16th c. By the 17th c both arches had become 'dry' and were blocked off for storage space. A series of timber waterfronts adjoining the bridge was also examined, one of them constructed from parts of a sizeable boat probably dating to 1250–1300. The other incorporated boat fragments of similar date.

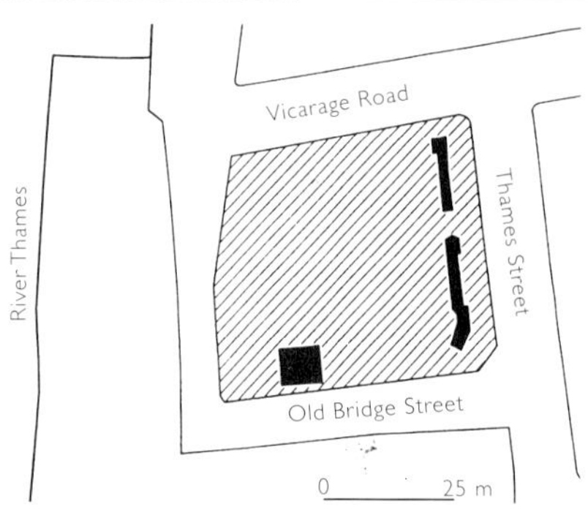

London Archaeol, 5, 1987, 276; 5, 1988, 12; Medieval Archaeol, 31, 1987, 131; 32, 1988, 251; Surrey Archaeol Coll, 78, 1987, 144; 79, 1989, 185

KND82

Map site: 15
SWLAU: Scott McCracken
NGR: TQ 178 694

19 Union Street (Knapp-Drewett site), Kingston, KT1

A trial excavation in 1982, in an area of suspected prehistoric occupation along the bank of a former tributary of the Thames, revealed the point bar deposits to the W of a silted-up channel but no prehistoric features, although a few struck flakes were recovered. The W part of the site comprised a gravel terrace, but no early features survived 19th- and 20th-c disturbance. Pits of 18th- and 19th-c date were found on the E edge of the gravel, at the junction with the point bar deposits. The major discovery was of a part of a Surrey Whiteware kiln at the extreme E limit of the site. Only the stoke-hole, associated flue arch and short segments of the kiln wall N and S of the flue arch survived, and the kiln apparently featured a central core of clay with a channel between it and each side wall. A considerable quantity of wasters was found, including some decorated sherds.

London Archaeol, 4, 1983, 289; Surrey Archaeol Coll, 75, 1984, 270; 78, 1987, 144
McCracken, J S, 1984 'Knapp-Drewett White ware kiln: archaeomagnetic
    date', *Kingston upon Thames Archaeol Soc Newsletter, 19*, 12–13
McCracken, J S, 1985 'Knapp-Drewett White ware kiln, Union Street, Kingston', *Surrey Archaeol Soc Bull, 197*, 1–2

TUK90

Map site: 16
DGLA(SW): Jonathan Nowell
NGR: TQ 178 695

Turk's Boatyard, Thames Side, Kingston, KT1

An evaluation excavation in 1990 revealed evidence of activity on the medieval waterfront near to the contemporary bridge (see HOR86 above). The remains of a timber revetment aligned N–S, parallel with the river and similar to those found in 1986, were sealed by late and post-medieval ground surfaces in which was recorded an E–W ditch of 15th–16th-c date.

London Archaeol, 6, 1991, 304; Medieval Archaeol, 35, 1991, 155; Surrey Archaeol Coll, 81, 1991–2, 158

LAMBETH

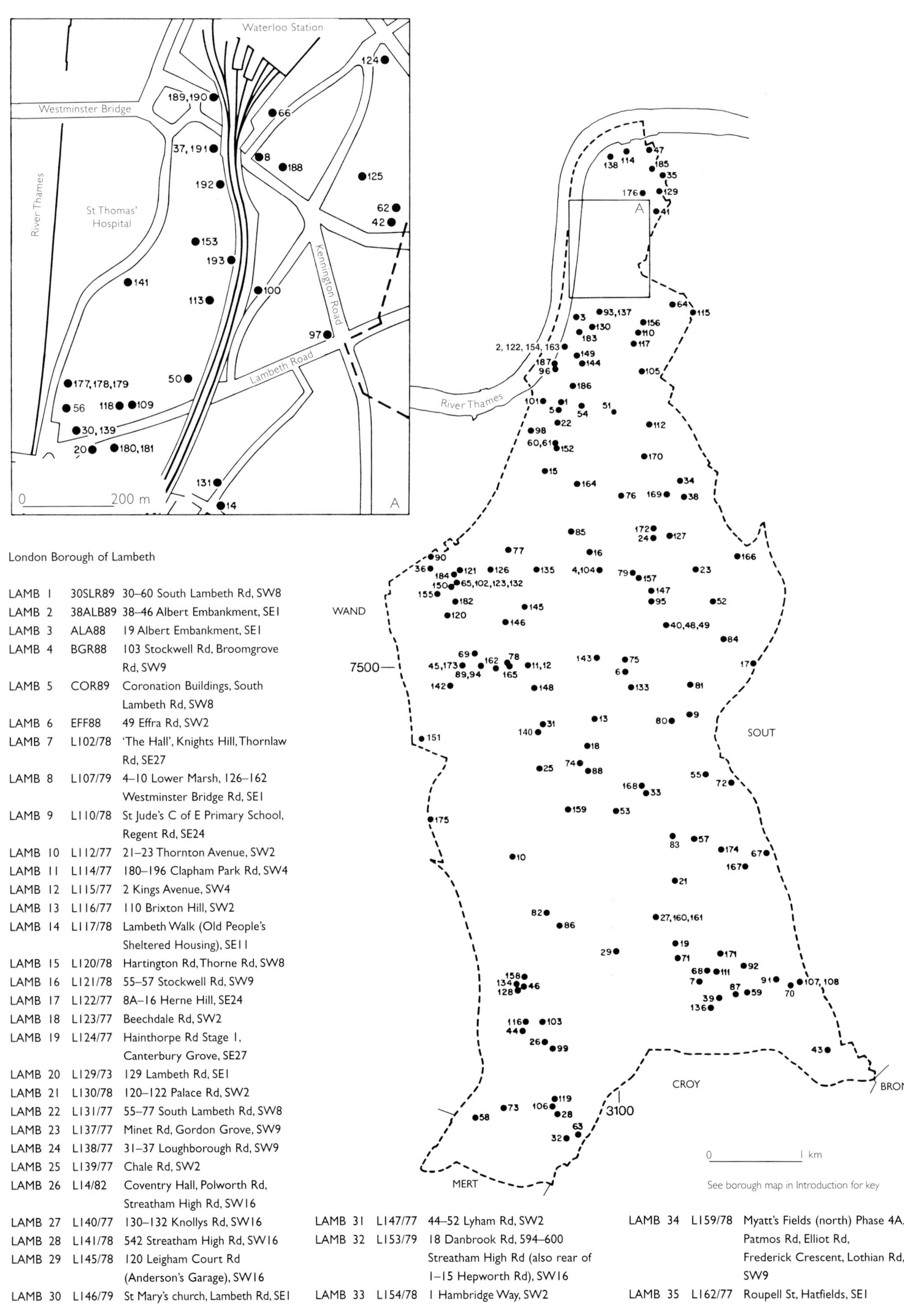

London Borough of Lambeth

LAMB 1	30SLR89	30–60 South Lambeth Rd, SW8
LAMB 2	38ALB89	38–46 Albert Embankment, SE1
LAMB 3	ALA88	19 Albert Embankment, SE1
LAMB 4	BGR88	103 Stockwell Rd, Broomgrove Rd, SW9
LAMB 5	COR89	Coronation Buildings, South Lambeth Rd, SW8
LAMB 6	EFF88	49 Effra Rd, SW2
LAMB 7	L102/78	'The Hall', Knights Hill, Thornlaw Rd, SE27
LAMB 8	L107/79	4–10 Lower Marsh, 126–162 Westminster Bridge Rd, SE1
LAMB 9	L110/78	St Jude's C of E Primary School, Regent Rd, SE24
LAMB 10	L112/77	21–23 Thornton Avenue, SW2
LAMB 11	L114/77	180–196 Clapham Park Rd, SW4
LAMB 12	L115/77	2 Kings Avenue, SW4
LAMB 13	L116/77	110 Brixton Hill, SW2
LAMB 14	L117/78	Lambeth Walk (Old People's Sheltered Housing), SE11
LAMB 15	L120/78	Hartington Rd, Thorne Rd, SW8
LAMB 16	L121/78	55–57 Stockwell Rd, SW9
LAMB 17	L122/77	8A–16 Herne Hill, SE24
LAMB 18	L123/77	Beechdale Rd, SW2
LAMB 19	L124/77	Hainthorpe Rd Stage 1, Canterbury Grove, SE27
LAMB 20	L129/73	129 Lambeth Rd, SE1
LAMB 21	L130/78	120–122 Palace Rd, SW2
LAMB 22	L131/77	55–77 South Lambeth Rd, SW8
LAMB 23	L137/77	Minet Rd, Gordon Grove, SW9
LAMB 24	L138/77	31–37 Loughborough Rd, SW9
LAMB 25	L139/77	Chale Rd, SW2
LAMB 26	L14/82	Coventry Hall, Polworth Rd, Streatham High Rd, SW16
LAMB 27	L140/77	130–132 Knollys Rd, SW16
LAMB 28	L141/78	542 Streatham High Rd, SW16
LAMB 29	L145/78	120 Leigham Court Rd (Anderson's Garage), SW16
LAMB 30	L146/79	St Mary's church, Lambeth Rd, SE1
LAMB 31	L147/77	44–52 Lyham Rd, SW2
LAMB 32	L153/79	18 Danbrook Rd, 594–600 Streatham High Rd (also rear of 1–15 Hepworth Rd), SW16
LAMB 33	L154/78	1 Hambridge Way, SW2
LAMB 34	L159/78	Myatt's Fields (north) Phase 4A, Patmos Rd, Elliot Rd, Frederick Crescent, Lothian Rd, SW9
LAMB 35	L162/77	Roupell St, Hatfields, SE1

LAMB 36	L165/78	Heath Rd Phase II, 150–210 Robertson St, Silverstone Rd, 490–512 Wandsworth St, St Rule St, SW8
LAMB 37	L167/78	Finck St, SE1
LAMB 38	L168/78	St Gabriel's College, Cormont Rd, SE5
LAMB 39	L170/78	31–51 Chapel Rd, SE27
LAMB 40	L171/79	129–131 Coldharbour Lane, SE5
LAMB 41	L174/80	133–155 Waterloo Rd, 4–26 Webber St, 23–77 Gray St, SE1
LAMB 42	L177/78	The Tower public house, 2–5 Morley St, 78–82 Westminster Bridge Rd, 2–16 Pearman St, 5A Emery St, SE1
LAMB 43	L180/78	Becondale Rd, Victoria Crescent, SE19
LAMB 44	L181/78	Station Approach, Streatham High Rd, SW16
LAMB 45	L185/81	Crescent Lane (adjacent to UPW House), SW4
LAMB 46	L186/77	St Leonard's church, Tooting Bec Gardens, SW16
LAMB 47	L188/86	Coin St (site D), SE1
LAMB 48	L190/78	Loughborough Park Development, Coldharbour Lane, Somerleyton Rd, Moorland Rd, SW9
LAMB 49	L191/78	321–331 Coldharbour Lane (Chevron service station), SW9
LAMB 50	L192/78	Archbishop Temple School, Lambeth Rd, SE1
LAMB 51	L199/78	Wisden House, Ashmole Estate, Ashmole St, SW8
LAMB 52	L20/78	1 Hardess St, SE24
LAMB 53	L200/78	Tulse Hill Secondary School, Upper Tulse Hill, SW2
LAMB 54	L201/78	Vauxhall Manor School, Lawn Lane, SW8
LAMB 55	L203/78	Brockwell Park, Norwood Rd (storm sewer), SE24
LAMB 56	L204/80	Lambeth Palace (Great Hall), Lambeth Palace Rd, SE1
LAMB 57	L205/80	321 Norwood Rd, SE24
LAMB 58	L209/78	Streatham Vale Sports and Social Club, Canmore Gardens, SW16
LAMB 59	L211/78	Norwood Park School, Gipsy Rd, SE27
LAMB 60	L212/78	Mawbey-Brough Phase IIA, South Lambeth Rd, Rosetta St, Wilcox Rd, SW8
LAMB 61	L213/79	Mawbey-Brough Phase IIB, South Lambeth Rd, SW8
LAMB 62	L218/83	7–12 Morley St, SE1
LAMB 63	L228/78	328–330 Green Lane, SW16
LAMB 64	L23/78	Renfrew Rd, Gilbert Rd, SE11
LAMB 65	L234/78	45–47A Rectory Grove, SW4
LAMB 66	L235/78	20 Lower Marsh, SE1
LAMB 67	L238/78	Oakfield School, 125–127 Thurlow Park Rd, SE21
LAMB 68	L239/78	Beadman St (factory sites A & B), SE27
LAMB 69	L244/78	St Mary's RC School, 15–31 St Alphonsus Rd, SW4
LAMB 70	L245/79	Clive Rd Phase IA, Hamilton Rd, SE21
LAMB 71	L247/79	Hainthorpe Rd (Jewish Orphanage), SE27
LAMB 72	L249/78	Knights Hill Coal Depot, Rosendale Rd, SE21
LAMB 73	L25/79	Estreham Rd, SW16
LAMB 74	L251/78	Brixton Hill (north of Upper Tulse Hill), SW2
LAMB 75	L252/78	9–17 Effra Rd, SW2
LAMB 76	L254/78	67–73 Hackford Rd, SW9
LAMB 77	L260/80	157 Larkhall Lane, SW4
LAMB 78	L261/78	Bowland Rd Phase II, Haselrigge Rd, SW4
LAMB 79	L262/78	309–313 Brixton Rd, SW9
LAMB 80	L277/78	42 Dulwich Rd, SE24
LAMB 81	L28/76	Shakespeare Rd (Herne Hill railway sidings), SE24
LAMB 82	L280/78	70 Streatham High Rd, SW16
LAMB 83	L29/77	St Martin's in the Field School, 155 Tulse Hill, SW2
LAMB 84	L292/78	41–53 Heron Rd, SE24
LAMB 85	L298/78	219–225 Clapham Rd, SW9
LAMB 86	L30/77	15–17 Leigham Avenue, SW16
LAMB 87	L31/78	11–13 Gipsy Rd, SE27
LAMB 88	L323/79	3–5 Somers Place, 1–19 Upper Tulse Hill, 2–12 Somers Rd, SW2
LAMB 89	L33/78	Carfax Square Phase I, St Alphonsus Rd, SW4
LAMB 90	L34/77	Heath Rd, Robertson St, SW8
LAMB 91	L342/79	Clive Rd Phase IC, Rommany Rd, SE21
LAMB 92	L35/77	Auckland Hill, SE27
LAMB 93	L370/78	206–208 Lambeth Walk, Black Prince Rd, Newport St, SE11
LAMB 94	L389/79	Carfax Square, SW4
LAMB 95	L4/76	33 Gresham Rd, SW9
LAMB 96	L40/77	Vauxhall Bridge Foot, Albert Embankment, SE1
LAMB 97	L42/78	Surrey Lodge, Lambeth Rd, Kennington Rd, Morton Place, Cosser St, SE1
LAMB 98	L436/81	Wandsworth Rd (Eastern Triangle site), SW8
LAMB 99	L437/79	9–11 Streatham Common (north), SW16
LAMB 100	L440/79	38B Hercules Rd (rear of), SE1
LAMB 101	L446/80	87–111 Wandsworth Rd, 10–32 Miles St, 62–84 Bond Way, Parry St, SW8
LAMB 102	L448/80	9–57 Rectory Grove, SW4
LAMB 103	L456/79	2 Rutford Rd, SW16
LAMB 104	L459/79	103 Stockwell Rd, SW9
LAMB 105	L462/79	Milverton St (outside Old Town Hall), SE11
LAMB 106	L464/79	512–522 Streatham High Rd, SW16
LAMB 107	L472/79	Clive Rd Phase IB1, Clive Rd, Hamilton Rd, SE21
LAMB 108	L473/79	Clive Rd Phase IB2, Clive Rd, Hamilton Rd, SE21
LAMB 109	L478/80	Holy Trinity School, 220 Lambeth Rd, SE1
LAMB 110	L491/80	212–214 Kennington Rd, SE11
LAMB 111	L497/81	42–44 Norwood High St, SE27
LAMB 112	L5/77	Kennington Lido, Kennington Park, Brixton Rd, Camberwell New Rd, SE11
LAMB 113	L501/81	Archbishop's Park, Lambeth Palace Rd, SE1
LAMB 114	L502/80	74–78 Upper Ground, SE1
LAMB 115	L515/87	120–124 Newington Butts, SE1
LAMB 116	L518/83	350–372 Streatham High Rd (rear of), SW16
LAMB 117	L519/81	Sancroft St (former LEB substation), SE11
LAMB 118	L525/85	Lambeth Palace (kitchen garden), Lambeth Palace Rd, SE1
LAMB 119	L53/77	2 Baldry Gardens, 285 Streatham High Rd, SW16
LAMB 120	L537/81	34 Old Town (rear of), SW4
LAMB 121	L539/86	Ingleton House, 4 Rectory Grove, SW4
LAMB 122	L54/80	34–46 Albert Embankment, SE1
LAMB 123	L541/84	64–68 Rectory Grove, SW4
LAMB 124	L543/82	Waterloo Rd, Baylis Rd, SE1
LAMB	L544/82	Brashier's and Wallace's Cottages (rear of), New Park Rd, SW2
LAMB 125	L545/83	Campbell Buildings, Baylis Rd, Frazier St, Burdet St, SE1
LAMB 126	L546/83	41 Larkhall Rise (rear of), SW4
LAMB 127	L547/83	Akerman Rd, Evandale Rd, Loughborough Rd, SW9
LAMB 128	L551/83	St Mary's Convent, 3 Tooting Bec Gardens, SW16
LAMB 129	L552/84	50–78 The Cut, SE1
LAMB 130	L554/83	Lambeth Walk, Black Prince Rd, Newport St, SE11
LAMB 131	L555/83	Lambeth Walk, Juxon St, Lollard St, SE11
LAMB 132	L560/83	55–57 Rectory Grove, SW4
LAMB 133	L565/86	59–63 Effra Rd, SW2
LAMB 134	L566/84	Tooting Bec Gardens, SW16
LAMB 135	L567/84	372–376 Clapham Rd, SW9
LAMB 136	L57/77	Knights Hill, Chapel Rd, SE27
LAMB 137	L571/85	9 Newport St (site adjoining), SE11
LAMB 138	L576/85	Museum of the Moving Image, South Bank, SE1
LAMB 139	L577/87	St Mary's church, Lambeth Rd, SE1
LAMB 140	L58/80	Lyham Rd Phase I, 82–118 Lyham Rd, 89 Kings Avenue, SW2
LAMB 141	L582/86	Lambeth Palace (north garden), Lambeth Palace Rd, SE1
LAMB 142	L585/87	1 Elms Rd (site adjoining 53–54 Clapham Common South Side), SW4
LAMB 143	L587/85	7–37 Acre Lane, 30 Baytree Rd, SW2
LAMB 144	L59/77	Auckland St, Burnett St, Leopold Walk, SE11
LAMB 145	L593/86	424 Clapham Rd, SW4
LAMB 146	L594/86	65–79 Clapham High St, SW4
LAMB 147	L596/86	51–81 Wiltshire Rd, 5–25A Western Rd, SW9
LAMB 148	L6/76	Lyham Rd (opposite 35 Lyham Rd), SW2
LAMB 149	L60/77	Vauxhall Walk, SE11
LAMB 150	L602/86	Thurston House, 52 Rectory Grove, SW4
LAMB 151	L608/86	South London Hospital for Women, Clapham Common South Side, SW4
LAMB 152	L61/77	South Lambeth Rd, Thorne Rd, Mawbey St, Brough St, Wilcox Rd, SW8
LAMB 153	L610/87	Holy Trinity Centre, Carlisle Lane, SE1
LAMB 154	L611/87	38–46 Albert Embankment, SE1
LAMB 155	L615/87	11 Lillieshall Rd, SW4
LAMB 156	L62/77	Reedworth St, Kennington Rd, SE11
LAMB 157	L63/78	Villa Rd, Wiltshire Rd, SW9
LAMB 158	L65/77	Prentis Rd, SW16
LAMB 159	L67/79	286–292 Brixton Rd, SW9
LAMB 160	L73/77	150 Knollys Rd, SW16
LAMB 161	L74/77	6 Knollys Close, SW16
LAMB 162	L75/77	St Alphonsus Rd, SW4
LAMB 163	L76/78	Bridge House, Albert Embankment, 9–14 Lambeth High St, SE1

LAMB 164 L77/77	Mursell Estate, Portland Grove, SW9	LAMB 174 L96/79	76 Thurlow Hill, SE21
LAMB 165 L80/77	Bowland Rd Phase I, Bowland Rd, SW4	LAMB 175 L98/77	Zennor Rd, SW12
		LAMB 176 LOO90	99–101 Waterloo Rd, SE1
LAMB 166 L83/77	123 Coldharbour Lane, SE5	LAMB 177 LP88	Lambeth Palace Library, Lambeth Palace Rd, SE1
LAMB 167 L86/79	105–107 Thurlow Park Rd, SE21		
LAMB 168 L90/77	117 Tulse Hill, SW2	LAMB 178 LPC88	Lambeth Palace (Chapel), Lambeth Palace Rd, SE1
LAMB 169 L91/77	Myatt's Fields North (housing scheme), Cowley Rd, Cancell Rd, Patmos Rd, Lothian Rd, Mostyn Rd, SW9	LAMB 179 LPC90	Lambeth Palace (Chapel), Lambeth Palace Rd, SE1
		LAMB 180 NOR88	Norfolk House, 113–125 Lambeth Rd, SE1
LAMB 170 L92/78	91–115 Brixton Rd, SW9	LAMB 181 NOR90	Norfolk House, 113–129 Lambeth Rd, SE1
LAMB 171 L93/77	Dunbar St, SE27		
LAMB 172 L94/77	Myatt's Fields South (housing scheme), Brixton Rd, Mostyn Rd, Akerman Rd, Loughborough Rd, SW9	LAMB 182 OTC88	7 Old Town, SW4
		LAMB 183 RAN88	Randall Row, Tinworth St, Vauxhall Walk, SE11
LAMB 173 L95/77	Crescent Lane (The Studio), SW4	LAMB 184 RGO88	8 Rectory Grove, SW4

LAMB 185 THD89	10–11A Theed St, SE1
LAMB 186 UDL88	5 South Lambeth Rd (Unigate Dairy), SW8
LAMB 187 VBN89	Vauxhall Bridge Foot (north), Albert Embankment, SE1
LAMB 188 WBR88	125–156 Westminster Bridge Rd, Lower Marsh, SE1
LAMB 189 WSB90	29 Addington St (Waterloo Station site B), SE1
LAMB 190 WSC90	Addington St (Waterloo Station site C), SE1
LAMB 191 WSD89	Upper Marsh, Finck St (Waterloo Station site D), SE1
LAMB 192 WSE90	Upper Marsh (Waterloo Station site E), SE1
LAMB 193 WSF90	Carlisle Lane (Waterloo Station site F), SE1

ALA88

Map site: 3
DGLA(S&L): Patricia Price
NGR: TQ 3054 7862
SMR: 091101–3

19 Albert Embankment, SE1

Excavation in 1988 recovered prehistoric flint tools, including small blades and flint cores. Field boundaries of medieval date were recorded, and quantities of dumped wasters and kiln furniture from nearby delftware kilns and a later stoneware factory were found, together with a 19th-c kiln probably involved in pottery manufacture. See also L54/80 below.

London Archaeol, 6, 1989, 75; *Post-Medieval Archaeol,* 23, 1989, 60

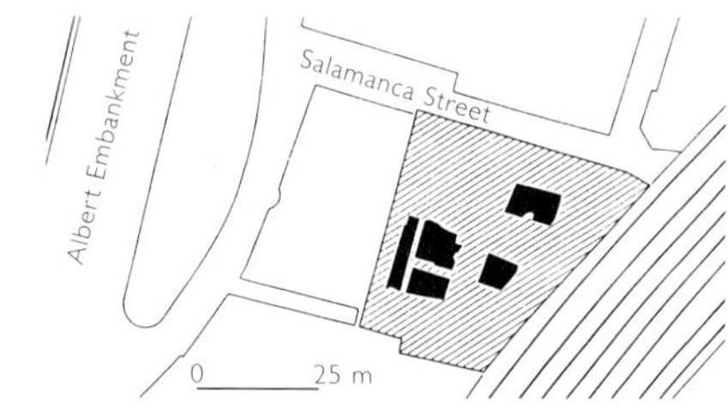

38ALB89

Map site: 2
DGLA(N): Noel Scott
NGR: TQ 3043 7836

38–46 Albert Embankment, SE1

An excavation in 1989–90 revealed the partial remains of at least four kilns, one of them evidently involved in porcelain firing *c* 1750, as indicated also by documentary evidence. The area was seen to have been subject to constant reworking and modification during its 200-year industrial phase. There was little evidence of sustained human activity in earlier periods, when the area was recorded as open and fallow. See also L54/80, L76/78, L611/87 below.

London Archaeol, 6, 1990, 191; 6, 1990, 191; *Post-Medieval Archaeol,* 24, 1990, 201; *Surrey Archaeol Coll,* 80, 1990, 219; 81, 1991–2, 158
Seeley, D, 1989 'Description of excavations on Vauxhall site (38–46 Albert Embankment, SE1)', *Trans English Ceramic Circle,* 13 (3), 223
Stephenson, R, 1989 'Description of ceramic material found on the Vauxhall site', *Trans English Ceramic Circle,* 13 (3), 224–9

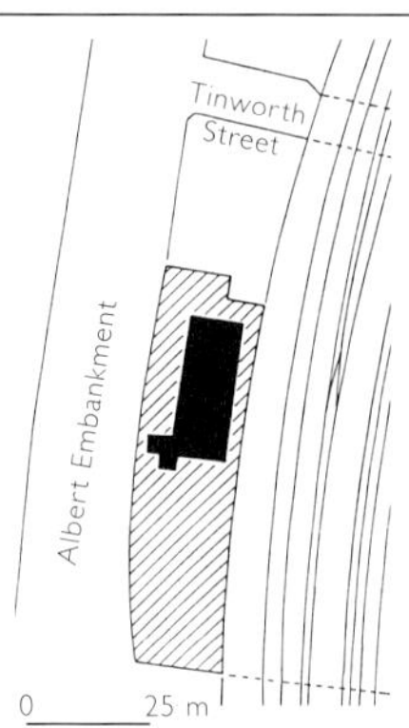

BGR88

Map site: 4
DGLA(S&L): Alison Hawkins
NGR: TQ 3083 7604

103 Stockwell Road, Broomgrove Road, SW9

Excavation in 1988 located 19th-c garden soil overlying natural sand and gravel.

Coronation Buildings, South Lambeth Road, SW8

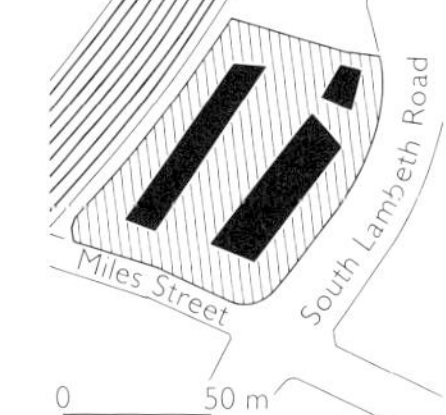

COR89

Map site: 5
DGLA(S&L): Tom McDonald
NGR: TQ 3033 7769
SMR: 091252–4

Excavation in 1989 located a number of pits containing prehistoric flints and pottery, provisionally dated to the Late Neolithic, Bronze and Iron Ages (see also 30SLR89 below). The remains were also found of a large stone structure built of massive ragstone blocks of varying size and dated provisionally to the 13th–14th c.

London Archaeol, 6, 1990, 191; Medieval Archaeol, 34, 1990, 183; Surrey Archaeol Coll, 80, 1990, 218

49 Effra Road, SW2

EFF88

Map site: 6
DGLA(S&L): Wendy Rogers
NGR: TQ 3112 7497
SMR: 091104–6

A trial excavation in 1988 revealed the surface of the natural clay, in which an unworked flint was found. Above was a ploughsoil containing pottery of medieval–19th-c date, including 17th-c sherds and several pieces of 18th-c biscuit delftware. Most of the pottery was 19th c, as were drains and pits cutting the ploughsoil.

London Archaeol, 6, 1989, 75; Post-Medieval Archaeol, 23, 1989, 61; Surrey Archaeol Coll, 80, 1990, 219

99–101 Waterloo Road, SE1

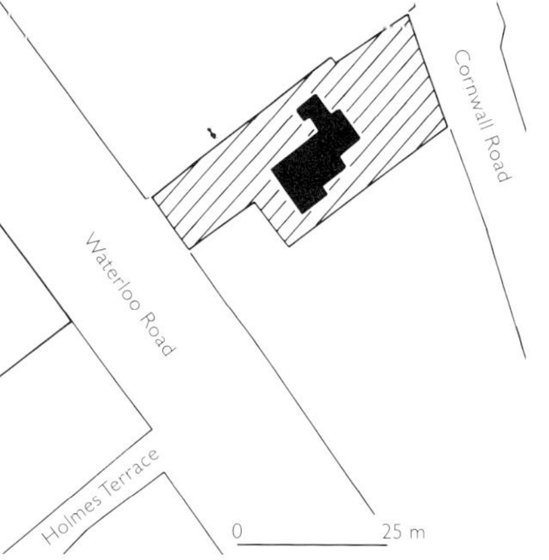

LOO90

Map site: 176
DGLA(S&L): Tom McDonald
NGR: TQ 3126 7995

Excavation in 1990 exposed a straight ditch, containing a fragment of bone, flint flakes and a scraper, cut into the surfaces of a layer of waterlaid clay. These deposits were sealed by a thick band of peat, within which remains of trees could represent part of a trackway. The peat was probably laid down during the Tilbury IV regression, in the Bronze Age. Evidence of medieval activity took the form of a wide shallow drainage ditch running NE–SW and cut into a layer of peat; the feature was backfilled during the late post-medieval period.

London Archaeol, 6, 1991, 307; Surrey Archaeol Coll, 81, 1991–2, 162

Lambeth Palace Library, Lambeth Palace Road, SE1

LP88

Map site: 177
DGLA(S&L): Derek Seeley
NGR: TQ 3059 7908

Excavation in 1988 at the N end of Juxon Hall (built c 1663) revealed earlier medieval structures. Details of the construction phase of the Hall and elements of the Hall itself were also located.

LPC88

Map site: 178
DGLA(S&L): Derek Seeley,
Susan Degnan
NGR: TQ 3060 7910

Lambeth Palace (Chapel), Lambeth Palace Road, SE1

Excavation in 1988 examined large areas of floor previously hidden from view and including the original chapel floor, laid in the second quarter of the 13th c with decorated glazed tiles. Other areas of the floor had been relaid with medieval tiles of similar description.

London Archaeol, 6, 1989, 75; *Medieval Archaeol,* 33, 1989, 184
Degnan, S, & Seeley, D, 1988 'Medieval and later floor tiles in Lambeth Palace Chapel', *London Archaeol,* 6, 116–18

LPC90

Map site: 179
DGLA(S&L): Derek Seeley,
Mark Samuel
NGR: TQ 3060 7910

Lambeth Palace (Chapel), Lambeth Palace Road, SE1

A watching brief in 1990 in the SE part of the early 13th-c chapel recorded a doorway of probably 15th-c date that had been blocked during the remodelling of the palace in the early 19th c. The moulded stones once forming the arch and fragments of a Purbeck marble sill were used as infill. See also L204/80, L525/85 below.

London Archaeol, 6, 1991, 304; *Medieval Archaeol,* 35, 1991, 155; *Surrey Archaeol Coll,* 81, 1991–2, 158

NOR88

Map site: 180
DGLA(S&L): Sophie Jackson
NGR: TQ 3070 7895
SMR: 090016, 091297

Norfolk House, 113–125 Lambeth Road, SE1

An evaluation excavation in 1988–9 revealed substantial foundations of the medieval residence of the dukes of Norfolk. Up to 1m wide, they took the form of a core of chalk blocks interspersed with ragstone and Reigate stone; blocks on the internal face of the wall had been squared off. A large buttressed ragstone wall was also identified, and architectural mouldings recovered. The foundations were reused during the Tudor period to support substantial brick walls. A Tudor brick cellar was also exposed, containing large quantities of potters' clay from the 17th- and 18th-c delftware factory which subsequently occupied the site. The layers predating Norfolk House were left largely intact for future investigation (see NOR90 below), but a fragment of Roman pottery was recovered, and a drainage ditch and ploughsoils containing 10th-c pottery located.

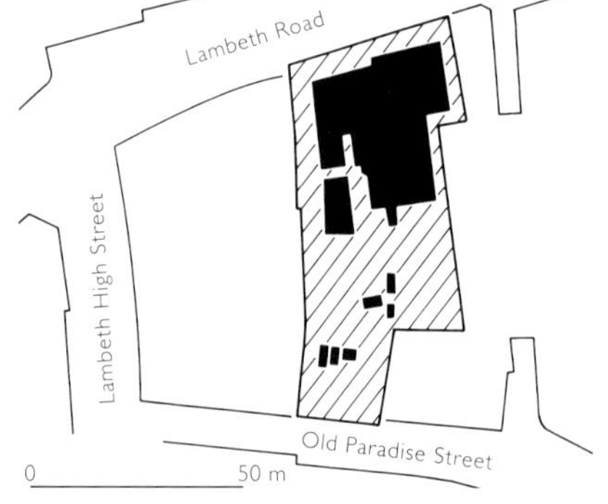

London Archaeol, 6, 1990, 191; *Medieval Archaeol,* 34, 1990, 183; *Post-Medieval Archaeol,* 24, 1990, 189

NOR90

Map site: 181
DGLA(S&L): Michael Webber
NGR: TQ 3070 7897
SMR: 091324–7

Norfolk House, 113–129 Lambeth Road, SE1

Further excavation in 1990 in the same area as NOR88 revealed a number of prehistoric flint tools and a small quantity of Roman pottery as the only evidence of pre-medieval occupation. A group of pits containing much pottery, and a pond and hearth date from the mid-12th to 14th c. The earliest building was a stone structure of late 14th-c date. The remains of five buildings of Tudor date were also uncovered, some with floors surviving. Many alterations were in evidence from the late 16th c, following the sale of the property by the duke of Norfolk and its later conversion as industrial premises. By the mid-18th c the site was occupied by a row of tenements; quantities of household goods, including kitchen, bathroom and dining-room items, were recovered from three brick-lined pits at the rear.

London Archaeol, 6, 1991, 304; *Medieval Archaeol,* 35, 1991, 155; *Post-Medieval Archaeol,* 25, 1991, 148; *Surrey Archaeol Coll,* 81, 1991–2, 158
Webber, M, 1991 'Excavations on the site of Norfolk House, Lambeth Road, SE1', *London Archaeol,* 6, 343–50

7 Old Town, SW4

Excavation in 1988 revealed traces of prehistoric activity in the form of struck flint flakes, but no trace of the Saxon occupation revealed at the nearby Rectory Grove site (see L448/80 below). A ploughsoil horizon was noted, and features included a recut boundary or drainage ditch and a number of refuse pits of medieval or later date.

London Archaeol, 6, 1989, 75; Surrey Archaeol Coll, 80, 1990, 218

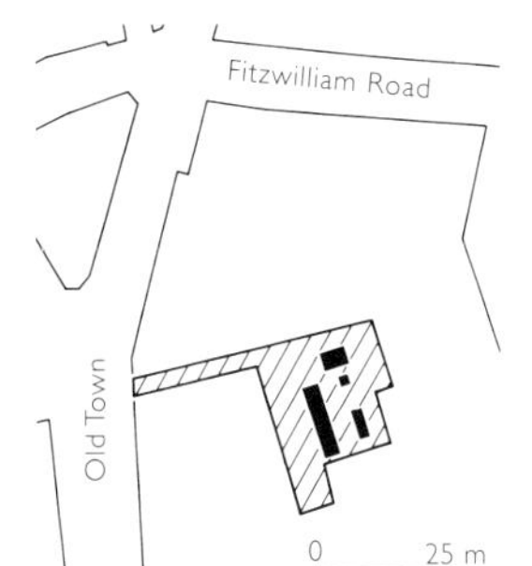

OTC88

Map site: 182
DGLA(S&L): Tom McDonald
NGR: TQ 2926 7569
SMR: 091111–12

Randall Row, Tinworth Street, Vauxhall Walk, SE11

Excavation in 1988 located prehistoric flint flakes and burnt flint. Layers of ploughsoil suggested that the area remained open, perhaps for agricultural use, from the 14th c to the 16th or 17th c.

London Archaeol, 6, 1989, 75; Post-Medieval Archaeol, 23, 1989, 61

RAN88

Map site: 183
DGLA(S&L): Mary Alexander
NGR: TQ 3057 7850
SMR: 091113–14

8 Rectory Grove, SW4

A watching brief in 1988 recorded natural clays overlain by soils and redeposited gravels yielding post-medieval pottery. See also L448/80, L539/86, L602/86 below.

London Archaeol, 6, 1989, 75; Surrey Archaeol Coll, 80, 1990, 218

RGO88

Map site: 184
DGLA(S&L): Kieron Heard
NGR: TQ 2925 7599
SMR: 091115

30–60 South Lambeth Road, SW8

An evaluation excavation in 1989 next to Coronation Buildings (see COR 89 above) and close to the source of the River Effra revealed evidence of prehistoric activity, in the form of a flint flake, which could not be dated more closely and of local topography, including high natural gravels.

London Archaeol, 6, 1990, 191; Post-Medieval Archaeol, 24, 1990, 189; Surrey Archaeol Coll, 80, 1990, 219

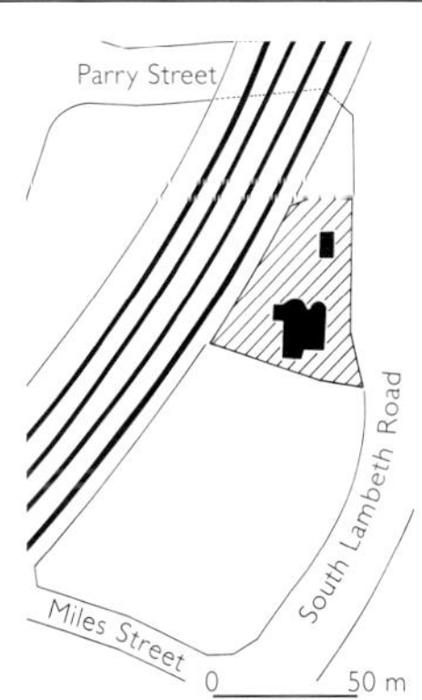

30SLR89

Map site: 1
DGLA(N): Noel Scott
NGR: TQ 3038 7777
SMR: 091253, 091678–85

THD89

Map site: 185
DGLA(S&L): Deborah
Mattocks
NGR: TQ 3135 8018
SMR: 091298–9

10–11A Theed Street, SE1

An evaluation excavation in 1989 indicated that the site had
gone through a series of wet and dry phases, and contained
peats of both Bronze Age (Tilbury IV regression) and
medieval date. Two drainage ditches and associated rows of
timber stakes of probably early post-medieval date were
examined.

London Archaeol, 6, 1990, 191; *Surrey Archaeol Coll,* 80, 1990, 219

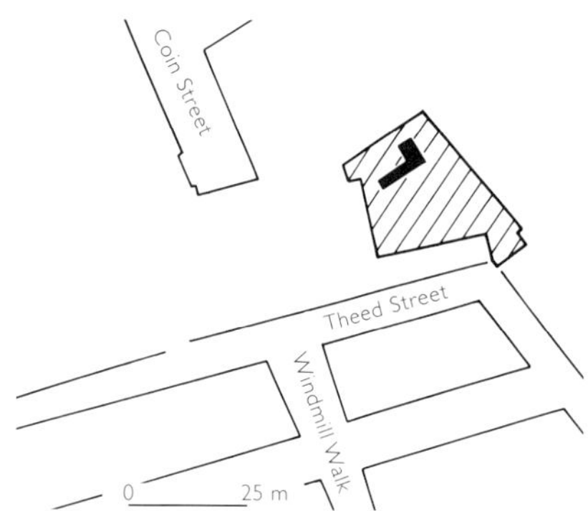

UDL88

Map site: 186
DGLA(S&L): Tom McDonald
NGR: TQ 3054 7795
SMR: 091117–19

Unigate Dairy, 5 South Lambeth Road, SW8

Excavation in 1988 produced, in the S part of the site, flint
implements and pottery mainly of Late Neolithic type, and
a fragment of a loom weight, provisionally dated to the
Early Bronze Age. Further excavation on the N part of the
site revealed flint tools, including a notched flake, blades and
scrapers. No evidence of further activity was noted until
the early medieval period, when the area was farmland,
indicated by a ploughsoil horizon which apparently
persisted until the 16th c. A complex post-medieval
drainage system crossed the site, and later occupation was
represented by post-holes, refuse pits and the foundations
of a 19th-c house.

London Archaeol, 6, 1989, 75; 6, 1990, 191; *Medieval Archaeol,* 34, 1990, 183

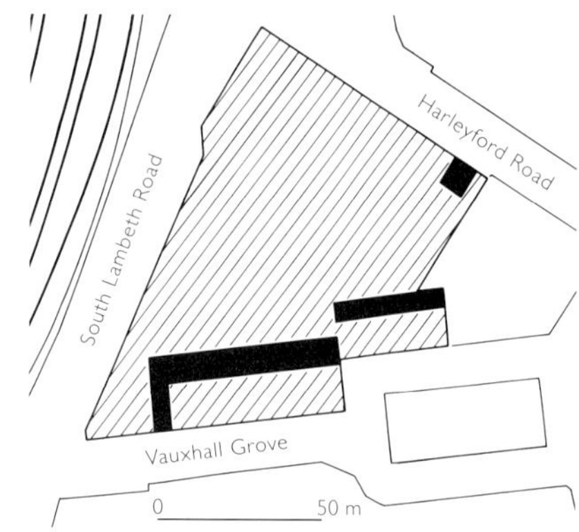

VBN89

Map site: 187
DGLA(S&L): Patricia Price
NGR: TQ 3033 7815
SMR: 090651, 091240–2,
091300

Vauxhall Bridge Foot (north), Albert Embankment, SE1

Excavation in 1989 revealed substantial remains of a 17th-c
glasshouse with much of the kiln intact and large quantities
of waste products. The stone foundations of a medieval or
later structure fronting the Albert Embankment are thought
not to be part of a manor house believed to have existed
in the immediate area. A substantial waterfront complex
was built in the 17th c, and the remains of three brick
boathouses of that date were found, having remained in use
until the 19th c. An inhumation burial of unknown date was
found, dug into the natural gravels.

London Archaeol, 6, 1990, 191; *Medieval Archaeol,* 34, 1990, 183; *Post-Medieval Archaeol,* 24, 1990, 203; *Surrey Archaeol Coll,* 80, 1990, 218

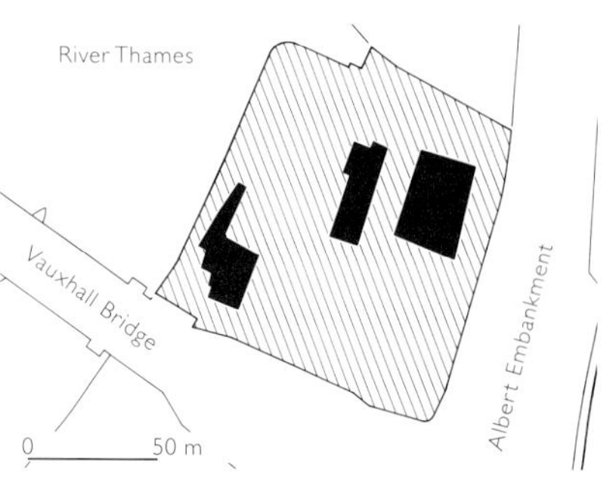

125–156 Westminster Bridge Road, Lower Marsh, SE1

WBR88

Map site: 188
DGLA(S&L): Toby Catchpole
NGR: TQ 3106 7956
SMR: 091107–10

Excavation in 1989 revealed a large quantity of flint tools and pottery of Neolithic, Bronze and Iron Age date. A ditch of Roman date contained medieval as well as Roman pottery. The foundations were located of a large brick building, believed on the basis of documentary sources to have been the mid-16th-c residence of Bishop Bonner but apparently of earlier construction. See also L107/79 below.

London Archaeol, 6, 1989, 75; 6, 1990, 191; Britannia, 21, 1990, 345; Surrey Archaeol Coll, 80, 1990, 219

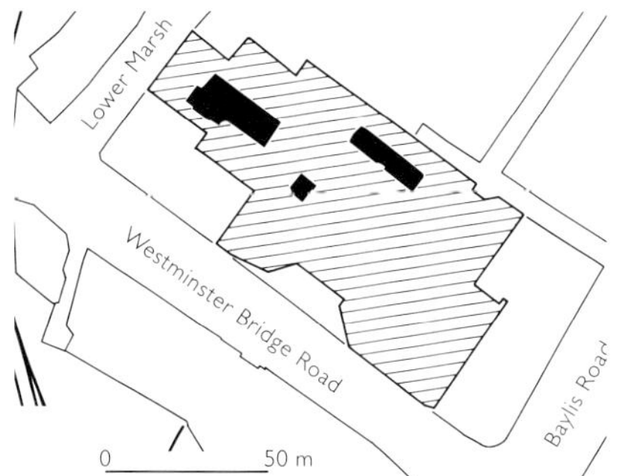

29 Addington Street (Waterloo Station site B), SE1

WSB90

Map site: 189
DGLA(S&L): Tom McDonald
NGR: TQ 3091 7970
SMR: 091308, 091730–1

Excavation in 1990 revealed a sand layer containing a concentration of prehistoric pottery, flint tools and waste flakes, some retrieved from cut features. On the W side of the site was exposed the E bank of a channel, from the bed of which were recovered struck and burnt flint flakes and two animal ribs.

London Archaeol, 6, 1991, 304; Post-Medieval Archaeol, 25, 1991, 132; Surrey Archaeol Coll, 81, 1991–2, 161

Addington Street (Waterloo Station site C), SE1

WSC90

Map site: 190
DGLA(S&L): Tom McDonald
NGR: TQ 3091 7966

Excavation in 1990 revealed numerous prehistoric cut features, pits, post-holes and linear slots at the junction of sands and alluvial silts. These features and the surrounding sands produced many flint tools, flakes and potsherds provisionally attributed to the Late Mesolithic to Early Neolithic periods. A layer sealing the alluvial silts produced pottery dating to the 16th c.

London Archaeol, 6, 1991, 305; Post-Medieval Archaeol, 25, 1991, 132; Surrey Archaeol Coll, 81, 1991–2, 161

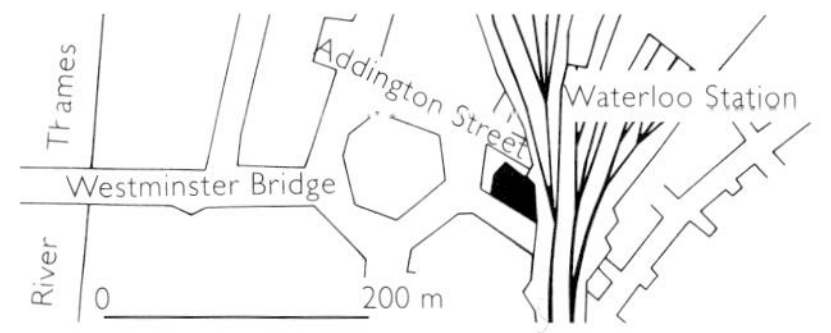

Upper Marsh, Finck Street (Waterloo Station site D), SE1

WSD89

Map site: 191
DGLA(S&L): Toby Catchpole
NGR: TQ 3091 7958

Excavation in 1989 revealed a high sand island with evidence of prehistoric and Roman activity. A late medieval/Tudor chalk building fronting Upper Marsh was also examined.

London Archaeol, 6, 1990, 191; Medieval Archaeol, 34, 1990, 183; Surrey Archaeol Coll, 80, 1990, 219

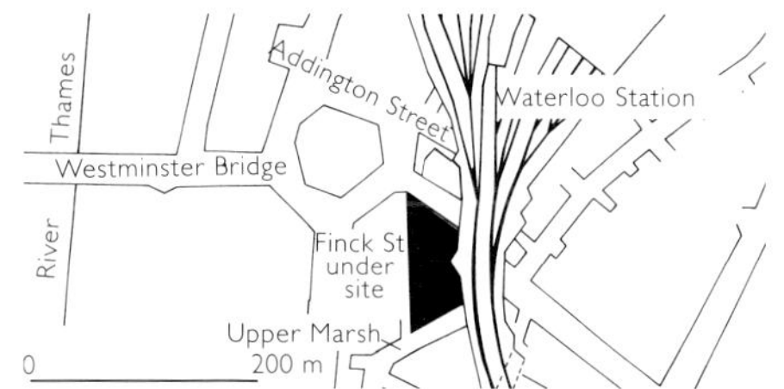

WSE90

Map site: 192
DGLA(S&L): Julian Bowsher
NGR: TQ 3092 7952
SMR: 091312–14

Upper Marsh (Waterloo Station site E), SE1

Excavation in 1990 revealed an area of high sand which produced struck flints and was overlain by ploughsoil rich in 12th-c material; traces of plough furrows were observed in section. Basements of 19th-c date on the street frontage had destroyed evidence of any previous structures, apart from an 18th-c well. A notable feature of the site was the Canterbury Music Hall, built in 1852, rebuilt in 1876 and destroyed by bombing in the Second World War. Many of the cellars survived for examination, as did the foundations of an extension of 1854.

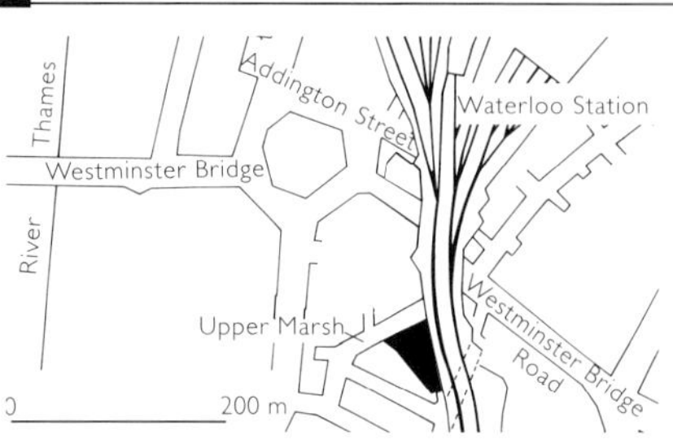

London Archaeol, 6, 1991, 305; Medieval Archaeol, 35, 1991, 155; Post-Medieval Archaeol, 25, 1991, 144; Surrey Archaeol Coll, 81, 1991–2, 161

WSF90

Map site: 193
DGLA(S&L): Lyndon Cooper
NGR: TQ 3095 7936
SMR: 090037, 091352–3

Carlisle Lane (Waterloo Station site F), SE1

Excavation in 1990 within the grounds of medieval Carlisle House located no earlier features than pits containing post-medieval pottery, including quantities of kiln furniture and wasters, probably from the Carlisle House delftware and salt-glazed stoneware kilns. Large 17th- or 18th-c foundations are probably to be identified with a boundary shown on a map of 1799.

London Archaeol, 6, 1991, 305; Post-Medieval Archaeol, 25, 1991, 160; Surrey Archaeol Coll, 81, 1991–2, 161

L4/76

Map site: 95
SLAEC: Robin Densem
NGR: TQ 3135 7570

33 Gresham Road, SW9

Evidence of natural topography only.

L5/77

Map site: 112
SLAEC: Robin Densem
NGR: TQ 3134 7758

Kennington Lido, Kennington Park, Brixton Road, Camberwell New Road, SE11

Evidence of natural topography only.

L6/76

Map site: 148
SLAEC: Robin Densem
NGR: TQ 3012 7480

Lyham Road (opposite 35 Lyham Road), SW2

Observation in 1976 recorded no archaeological features.

Coventry Hall, Polworth Road, Streatham High Road, SW16

L14/82

Map site: 26
SLAEC: Robin Densem,
Derek Seeley
NGR: TQ 3019 7116

Trial excavation in 1982 failed to recover evidence of the Tudor manor house or its successor recorded in this vicinity, but located structures of *c* 1800 forming part of Coventry Hall.

London Archaeol, 4, 1993, 289; Surrey Archaeol Coll, 75, 1984, 271

1 Hardess Street, SE24

L20/78

Map site: 52
SLAEC: Robin Densem
NGR: TQ 3200 7570

Evidence of natural topography only.

Renfrew Road, Gilbert Road, SE11

L23/78

Map site: 64
SLAEC: Robin Densem
NGR: TQ 3157 7879

Evidence of natural topography only.

Estreham Road, SW16

L25/79

Map site: 73
SLAEC: Robin Densem
NGR: TQ 2976 7046

Evidence of natural topography only.

Herne Hill railway sidings, Shakespeare Road, SE24

L28/76

Map site: 81
SLAEC: Robin Densem
NGR: TQ 3178 7485

No excavation.

St Martin's in the Field School, 155 Tulse Hill, SW2

L29/77

Map site: 83
SLAEC: Robin Densem
NGR: TQ 3148 7341

Evidence of natural topography only.

L30/77

Map site: 86
SLAEC: Robin Densem
NGR: TQ 3039 7234

15–17 Leigham Avenue, SW16

Evidence of natural topography only.

L31/78

Map site: 87
SLAEC: Robin Densem
NGR: TQ 3223 7163

11–13 Gipsy Road, SE27

Evidence of natural topography only.

L33/78

Map site: 89
SLAEC: Robin Densem
NGR: TQ 2956 7506

Carfax Square Phase I, St Alphonsus Road, SW4

Evidence of natural topography only. See also L389/79 below.

L34/77

Map site: 90
NGR: TQ 2900 7618
SLAEC: Robin Densem

Heath Road, Robertson Street, SW8

Evidence of natural topography only.

L35/77

Map site: 92
SLAEC: Robin Densem
NGR: TQ 3233 7192

Auckland Hill, SE27

Evidence of natural topography only.

L40/77

Map site: 96
SLAEC: Robin Densem
NGR: TQ 3033 7815
SMR: 091230

Vauxhall Bridge Foot, Albert Embankment, SE1

A trial excavation in 1977 revealed no archaeological features.

London Archaeol, 3, 1978, 161; Surrey Archaeol Coll, 72, 1980, 246

Surrey Lodge, Lambeth Road, Kennington Road, Morton Place, Cosser Street, SE1

Evidence of natural topography only.

L42/78

Map site: 97
SLAEC: Robin Densem
NGR: TQ 3114 7921

2 Baldry Gardens, 285 Streatham High Road, SW16

Evidence of natural topography only.

L53/77

Map site: 119
SLAEC: Robin Densem
NGR: TQ 3033 7055

34–46 Albert Embankment, SE1

Excavation in 1980 revealed that natural was cut by a gully beneath sandy soil which was itself cut by several features, some of which produced pottery of *c* 1480–1620. Above these were the earliest buildings and structures, dated *c* 1620–1720 and succeeded by others dated to *c* 1720–1900. See also ALA88, 38ALB89 above, L76/78, L611/87 below.

London Archaeol, 4, 1981, 48; Post-Medieval Archaeol, 15, 1981, 230

L54/80

Map site: 122
SLAEC: Robin Densem
NGR: TQ 3043 7836

Knights Hill, Chapel Road, SE27

Evidence of natural topography only.

L57/77

Map site: 136
SLAEC: Robin Densem
NGR: TQ 3198 7148

Lyham Road Phase 1, 82–118 Lyham Road, 89 Kings Avenue, SW2

Evidence of natural topography only.

L58/80

Map site: 140
SLAEC: Robin Densem
NGR: TQ 3015 7435

Auckland Street, Burnett Street, Leopold Walk, SE11

Evidence of natural topography only.

L59/77

Map site: 144
SLAEC: Robin Densem
NGR: TQ 3060 7818

L60/77

Map site: 149
SLAEC: Robin Densem
NGR: TQ 3055 7825

Vauxhall Walk, SE11

Evidence of natural topography only.

L61/77

Map site: 152
SLAEC: Robin Densem
NGR: TQ 3033 7730

South Lambeth Road, Thorne Road, Mawbey Street, Brough Street, Wilcox Road, SW8

Evidence of natural topography only.

L62/77

Map site: 156
NGR: TQ 3126 7860
SLAEC: Robin Densem

Reedworth Street, Kennington Road, SE11

Evidence of natural topography only.

L63/78

Map site: 157
SLAEC: Robin Densem
NGR: TQ 3120 7594

Villa Road, Wiltshire Road, SW9

Evidence of natural topography only.

L65/77

Map site: 158
SLAEC: Robin Densem
NGR: TQ 3000 7178

Prentis Road, SW16

Evidence of natural topography only.

L67/79

Map site: 159
SLAEC: Robin Densem
NGR: TQ 310 755

286–292 Brixton Road, SW9

Observation in 1979 recorded a brick-lined well of post-medieval date.

150 Knollys Road, SW16

Evidence of natural topography only.

L73/77

Map site: 160
SLAEC: Robin Densem
NGR: TQ 3146 7244

6 Knollys Close, SW16

Evidence of natural topography only.

L74/77

Map site: 161
SLAEC: Robin Densem
NGR: TQ 3148 7240

St Alphonsus Road, SW4

Evidence of natural topography only.

L75/77

Map site: 162
SLAEC: Robin Densem
NGR: TQ 2970 7500

Bridge House, Albert Embankment, 9–14 Lambeth High Street, SE1

A watching brief in 1978 recorded medieval pottery and a post-medieval kiln flue. See also ALA88, 38ALB89, L54/80 above, L611/87 below.

L76/78

Map site: 163
SLAEC: Robin Densem
NGR: TQ 3060 7885

Mursell Estate, Portland Grove, SW8

Evidence of natural topography only.

L77/77

Map site: 164
SLAEC: Robin Densem
NGR: TQ 3056 7691

Bowland Road Phase I, Bowland Road, SW4

Evidence of natural topography only.

L80/77

Map site: 165
SLAEC: Robin Densem
NGR: TQ 2983 7506

123 Coldharbour Lane, SE5

Evidence of natural topography only.

L83/77

Map site: 166
SLAEC: Robin Densem
NGR: TQ 3226 7618

L86/79

Map site: 167
SLAEC: Robin Densem
NGR: TQ 3232 7295

105–107 Thurlow Park Road, SE21

Evidence of natural topography only.

L90/77

Map site: 168
SLAEC: Robin Densem
NGR: TQ 3125 7378

117 Tulse Hill, SW2

A watching brief in 1977 recorded a number of sections which revealed a general sequence of grey or black earth above natural. A possible post-medieval pit or ditch was observed in a S-facing section.

L91/77

Map site: 169
SLAEC: Robin Densem
NGR: TQ 3150 7680

Myatt's Fields North (housing scheme), Cowley Road, Cancell Road, Patmos Road, Lothian Road, Mostyn Road, SW9

Evidence of natural topography only.

L92/78

Map site: 170
SLAEC: Robin Densem
NGR: TQ 3138 7720

91–115 Brixton Road, SW9

Evidence of natural topography only.

L93/77

Map site: 171
SLAEC: Robin Densem
NGR: TQ 3208 7205

Dunbar Street, SE27

Evidence of natural topography only.

L94/77

Map site: 172
SLAEC: Robin Densem
NGR: TQ 3135 7642

Myatt's Fields South (housing scheme), Brixton Road, Mostyn Road, Akerman Road, Loughborough Road, SW9

Evidence of natural topography only.

The Studio, Crescent Lane, SW4

Evidence of natural topography only.

L 95/77

Map site: 173
SLAEC: Robin Densem
NGR: TQ 2935 7503

76 Thurlow Hill, SE21

Evidence of natural topography only.

L 96/79

Map site: 174
SLAEC: Robin Densem
NGR: TQ 3208 7311

Zennor Road, SW12

Evidence of natural topography only.

L 98/77

Map site: 175
SLAEC: Robin Densem
NGR: TQ 2900 7345

'The Hall', Knights Hill, Thornlaw Road, SE27

Observation in 1978 recorded modern backfill covering dark soils and brown clay. Sections indicated alternate layers of yellow sandy gravel and clinker, suggesting a path or metalled area.

L 102/78

Map site: 7
SLAEC: T Dain
NGR: TQ 3186 7176

4–10 Lower Marsh, 126–162 Westminster Bridge Road, SE1

Excavation in 1979–80 recovered prehistoric pottery and flints, as well as medieval pottery. See also WBR88 above, L235/78 below.

London Archaeol, 3, 1980, 387; 4, 1981, 48; *Britannia*, 11, 1980, 381; 12, 1981, 353

L 107/79

Map site: 8
SLAEC: Robin Densem
NGR: TQ 3105 7955

St Jude's C of E Primary School, Regent Road, SE24

Evidence of natural topography only.

L 110/78

Map site: 9
SLAEC: Robin Densem
NGR: TQ 3175 7452

L112/77

Map site: 10
SLAEC: Robin Densem
NGR: TQ 2988 7307

21–23 Thornton Avenue, SW2

Evidence of natural topography only.

L114/77

Map site: 11
SLAEC: Robin Densem
NGR: TQ 3003 7505

180–196 Clapham Park Road, SW4

Evidence of natural topography only.

L115/77

Map site: 12
SLAEC: Robin Densem
NGR: TQ 3005 7503

2 Kings Avenue, SW4

Evidence of natural topography only.

L116/77

Map site: 13
SLAEC: Robin Densem
NGR: TQ 3069 7447

110 Brixton Hill, SW2

Evidence of natural topography only.

L117/78

Map site: 14
SLAEC: Robin Densem
NGR: TQ 3091 7885

Old People's Sheltered Housing, Lambeth Walk, SE11

A watching brief in 1978 recorded mainly topographical evidence, though two possible features cut into the gravel were noted, and the remnants of a chalk and brick wall were examined in section.

L120/78

Map site: 15
SLAEC: Robin Densem
NGR: TQ 3021 7704

Hartington Road, Thorne Road, SW8

Evidence of natural topography only.

55–57 Stockwell Road, SW9

Evidence of natural topography only.

L121/78

Map site: 16
SLAEC: Robin Densem
NGR: TQ 3070 7623
SMR: 091229

8A–16 Herne Hill, SE24

Evidence of natural topography only.

L122/77

Map site: 17
SLAEC: Robin Densem
NGR: TQ 3245 7508

Beechdale Road, SW2

Evidence of natural topography only.

L123/77

Map site: 18
SLAEC: Robin Densem
NGR: TQ 3068 7429

Hainthorpe Road Stage 1, Canterbury Grove, SE27

Evidence of natural topography only.

L124/77

Map site: 19
SLAEC: Robin Densem
NGR: TQ 3163 7215

129 Lambeth Road, SE1

Excavation in 1973 revealed 13th-c pits in the N and W parts of the site, and more generally drains and cesspits of 17th–19th-c date.

London Archaeol, 2, 1974, 134; *Post-Medieval Archaeol, 8,* 1974, 125
Anon, 1973 'Lambeth Road', Mosaic, *London Archaeol, 2,* 124
Hinton, P, 1988 'Excavations at 129 Lambeth Road', in Hinton, P (ed), *Excavations in Southwark 1973–76, Lambeth 1973–79,* 159–74
Kelly, C G, 1974 'A study of post-medieval pottery from a site at 129 Lambeth Road/1 Lambeth High Street' (unpublished report)

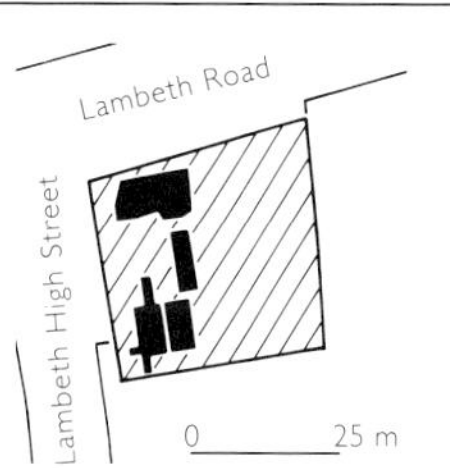

L129/73

Map site: 20
SLAEC: Eric Ferretti
NGR: TQ 3065 7896

120–122 Palace Road, SW2

Evidence of natural topography only.

L130/78

Map site: 21
SLAEC: Robin Densem
NGR: TQ 3159 7277

L131/77

Map site: 22
SLAEC: Robin Densem
NGR: TQ 3038 7755

55–77 South Lambeth Road, SW8

Observation in 1977 revealed modern disturbance only.

L137/77

Map site: 23
SLAEC: Robin Densem
NGR: TQ 3183 7605

Minet Road, Gordon Grove, SW9

Evidence of natural topography only.

L138/77

Map site: 24
SLAEC: Robin Densem
NGR: TQ 3138 7635

31–37 Loughborough Road, SW9

Observation in 1977 recorded modern disturbance only.

L139/77

Map site: 25
SLAEC: Robin Densem
NGR: TQ 3016 7398

Chale Road, SW2

Evidence of natural topography only.

L140/77

Map site: 27
SLAEC: Robin Densem
NGR: TQ 3140 7241

130–132 Knollys Road, SW16

Evidence of natural topography only.

L141/78

Map site: 28
SLAEC: Robin Densem
NGR: TQ 3033 7038

542 Streatham High Road, SW16

Evidence of natural topography only.

L145/78

Map site: 29
SLAEC: Robin Densem
NGR: TQ 3098 7209

120 Leigham Court Road (Anderson's Garage), SW16

Observation in 1978 noted modern disturbance only.

St Mary's church, Lambeth Road, SE1

Excavation in 1979 located only recent material in a small trench dug between the N wall of the chancel and the E wall of the N aisle, but recorded information about the relationship of chancel and aisle. See also L577/87 below.

London Archaeol, 3, 1980, 387

L146/79

Map site: 30
SLAEC: Robin Densem
NGR: TQ 3062 7902

44–52 Lyham Road, SW2

Evidence of natural topography only.

L147/77

Map site: 31
SLAEC: Robin Densem
NGR: TQ 3020 7443

18 Danbrook Road, 594–600 Streatham High Road (also rear of 1–15 Hepworth Road), SW16

Excavation at the rear of the property revealed no trace of the Roman road from London to the Brighton area, conjectured as having crossed this site, and established that natural sands and gravel were overlain by topsoil.

London Archaeol, 3, 1980, 387

L153/79

Map site: 32
SLAEC: Robin Densem
NGR: TQ 3044 7015
SMR: 090206

1 Hambridge Way, SW2

Evidence of natural topography only.

L154/78

Map site: 33
SLAEC: Robin Densem
NGR: TQ 3130 7370

Myatt's Fields (north) Phase 4A, Patmos Road, Elliot Road, Frederick Crescent, Lothian Road, SW9

Evidence of natural topography only.

L159/78

Map site: 34
SLAEC: Robin Densem
NGR: TQ 3166 7692

Roupell Street, Hatfields, SE1

Excavation in 1977 revealed no evidence of early activity; post-medieval hearths were possibly part of the former Halfpenny Hatch, occupied by the late 18th-c botanist William Curtis.

London Archaeol, 3, 1978, 161; *Surrey Archaeol Coll,* 72, 1980, 246

L162/77

Map site: 35
SLAEC: Robin Densem
NGR: TQ 3149 8012
SMR: 090202

L165/78

Map site: 36
SLAEC: Robin Densem
NGR: TQ 2900 7610

Heath Road Phase II, 150–210 Robertson Street, Silverstone Road, 490–512 Wandsworth Road, St Rule Street, SW8

Evidence of natural topography only.

L167/78

Map site: 37
SLAEC: Robin Densem
NGR: TQ 3090 7957
SMR: 090214

Finck Street, SE1

Trial trenching in 1978 recovered no evidence of a continuation to the W of Watling Street, nor of other Roman activity. Two shallow gullies and a ditch, all possibly of late medieval date, were examined and, at the S end of the site, the heavily robbed foundations of the NE corner of a building, which pottery suggests was of Tudor date.

London Archaeol, 3, 1979, 263; *Surrey Archaeol Coll*, 72, 1980, 246
Densem, R, 1988 'Excavations at Finck Street', in Hinton, P (ed), *Excavations in Southwark 1973–76, Lambeth 1973–79*, 175–82

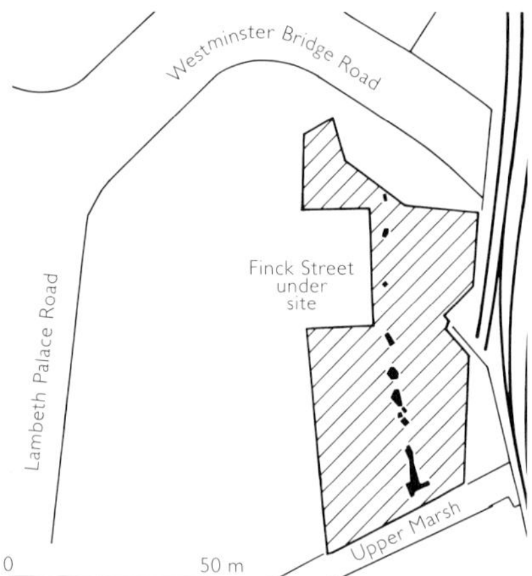

L168/78

Map site: 38
SLAEC: Robin Densem
NGR: TQ 3170 7678

St Gabriel's College, Cormont Road, SE5

Evidence of natural topography only.

L170/78

Map site: 39
SLAEC: Robin Densem
NGR: TQ 3208 7160

31–51 Chapel Road, SE27

Evidence of natural topography only.

L171/79

Map site: 40
SLAEC: Robin Densem
NGR: TQ 3150 7545

129–131 Coldharbour Lane, SE5

Evidence of natural topography only.

133–155 Waterloo Road, 4–26 Webber Street, 23–77 Gray Street, SE1

L174/80

Map site: 41
SLAEC: Robin Densem
NGR: TQ 3143 7972

Evidence of natural topography only.

The Tower public house, 2–5 Morley Street, 78–82 Westminster Bridge Road, 2–16 Pearman Street, 5A Emery Street, SE1

L177/78

Map site: 42
SLAEC: Robin Densem
NGR: TQ 3132 7946

Excavation in 1978 on a site on the line of a possible Roman road from London Bridge to Westminster revealed a ditch with a primary fill of kiln debris dating to *c* 1670 and including broken unglazed delft biscuit ware. The ditch cut into the natural clay over the flood-plain gravels and had apparently removed any earlier features.

London Archaeol, 3, 1979, 264; Surrey Archaeol Coll, 72, 1980, 246

Becondale Road, Victoria Crescent, SE19

L180/78

Map site: 43
SLAEC: Robin Densem
NGR: TQ 3323 7105

Evidence of natural topography only.

Station Approach, Streatham High Road, SW16

L181/78

Map site: 44
SLAEC: Robin Densem
NGR: TQ 2994 7129

Observation in 1978 recorded modern disturbance only.

Adjacent to UPW House, Crescent Lane, SW4

L185/81

Map site: 45
SLAEC: Robin Densem
NGR: TQ 2935 7503

Evidence of natural topography only.

St Leonard's church, Tooting Bec Gardens, SW16

L186/77

Map site: 46
SLAEC: Kenneth Dark
NGR: TQ 3000 7170
SMR: 091060

A trial excavation in 1977 revealed archaeological levels disturbed by vaults.

London Archaeol, 3, 1978, 161; Surrey Archaeol Coll, 72, 1980, 245

L188/86

Map site: 47
DGLA(S&L): Derek Seeley
NGR: TQ 3134 8038

Coin Street (site D), SE1

A watching brief in 1986 revealed no archaeological features.

L190/78

Map site: 48
SLAEC: Robin Densem
NGR: TQ 3150 7540

Loughborough Park Development, Coldharbour Lane, Somerleyton Road, Moorland Road, SW9

Evidence of natural topography only.

L191/78

Map site: 49
SLAEC: Robin Densem
NGR: TQ 3150 7545

Chevron service station, 321–331 Coldharbour Lane, SW9

Evidence of natural topography only.

L192/78

Map site: 50
SLAEC: Robin Densem
NGR: TQ 3085 7914

Archbishop Temple School, Lambeth Road, SE1

Evidence of natural topography only.

L199/78

Map site: 51
SLAEC: Robin Densem
NGR: TQ 3075 7772

Wisden House, Ashmole Estate, Ashmole Street, SW8

Evidence of natural topography only.

L200/78

Map site: 53
SLAEC: Robin Densem
NGR: TQ 3095 7354

Tulse Hill Secondary School, Upper Tulse Hill, SW2

Observation in 1978 recorded modern disturbance only.

L201/78

Map site: 54
SLAEC: Brian Yule
NGR: TQ 3060 7773

Vauxhall Manor School, Lawn Lane, SW8

Evidence of natural topography only.

Brockwell Park, Norwood Road (storm sewer), SE24

L203/78

Map site: 55
SLAEC: Robin Densem
NGR: TQ 3190 7390

Evidence of natural topography only.

Lambeth Palace (Great Hall), Lambeth Palace Road, SE1

L204/80

Map site: 56
SLAEC: Robin Densem
NGR: TQ 3057 7906

Excavation and observation in 1980 on the line of a contractor's trench between Lollards' Tower and the Great Hall and Morton's Gateway revealed Saxo-Norman deposits overlain by a sequence of dumps and layers containing building materials, perhaps associated with towers incorporated into Morton's Gateway in 1490. The deposits were cut by a brick-built drain over which the E tower of the gate was built. To the N, between the gateway and Lollards' Tower, were found the badly damaged and robbed remains of three limestone walls; the construction trench for the Great Hall, constructed by 1663, and a brick foundation against the W face of the hall were also located. See also LPC88 above.

London Archaeol, 4, 1981, 48; *Medieval Archaeol,* 25, 1981, 195
Densem, R, 1981 'Excavations at Lambeth Palace 1980', *London Archaeol,* 4, 39–43

321 Norwood Road, SE24

L205/80

Map site: 57
SLAEC: Robin Densem
NGR: TQ 3180 7322

Evidence of natural topography only.

Streatham Vale Sports and Social Club, Canmore Gardens, SW16

L209/78

Map site: 58
SLAEC: Robin Densem
NGR: TQ 2947 7037

Evidence of natural topography only.

Norwood Park School, Gipsy Road, SE27

L211/78

Map site: 59
SLAEC: Robin Densem
NGR: TQ 3238 7163

Evidence of natural topography only.

Mawbey-Brough Phases IIA & B, South Lambeth Road, Rosetta Street, Wilcox Road, SW8

L212/78, L213/79

Map site: 60, 61
SLAEC: Robin Densem
NGR: TQ 3031 7735

Observation in 1978 noted a cut feature probably of post-medieval date, as well as evidence for natural topography.

L218/83

Map site: 62
SLAEC: Robin Densem
NGR: TQ 3133 7949
SMR: 091237

7–12 Morley Street, SE1

Evidence of natural topography only.

L228/79

Map site: 63
SLAEC: Robin Densem
NGR: TQ 3055 7018

328–330 Green Lane, SW16

Evidence of natural topography only.

L234/79

Map site: 65
SLAEC: Robin Densem
NGR: TQ 2927 7588

45–47A Rectory Grove, SW4

See L448/80 below.

L235/78

Map site: 66
SLAEC: Robin Densem,
Eric Ferretti
NGR: TQ 3108 7965
SMR: 090203

20 Lower Marsh, SE1

Excavation in 1978 investigated a heavily truncated brick structure with a domed roof, apparently the remains of a 19th-c bread oven. The site is known to have been occupied by a baker in that period.

London Archaeol, 3, 1979, 264; Surrey Archaeol Coll, 72, 1980, 246

L238/78

Map site: 67
SLAEC: Robin Densem
NGR: TQ 3258 7308

Oakfield School, 125–127 Thurlow Park Road, SE21

Evidence of natural topography only.

L239/78

Map site: 68
SLAEC: Robin Densem
NGR: TQ 3194 7186

Factory sites A & B, Beadman Street, SE27

Evidence of natural topography only.

L244/78

Map site: 69
SLAEC: Robin Densem
NGR: TQ 2948 7517

St Mary's RC School, 15–31 St Alphonsus Road, SW4

Evidence of natural topography only.

Clive Road Phase IA, Hamilton Road, SE21

Evidence of natural topography only.

L245/79

Map site: 70
SLAEC: Robin Densem
NGR: TQ 3280 7170

Jewish Orphanage, Hainthorpe Road, SE27

Evidence of natural topography only.

L247/79

Map site: 71
SLAEC: Robin Densem
NGR: TQ 3163 7200

Knights Hill Coal Depot, Rosendale Road, SE21

Evidence of natural topography only.

L249/78

Map site: 72
SLAEC: Robin Densem
NGR: TQ 3217 7381

Brixton Hill (north of Upper Tulse Hill), SW2

Evidence of natural topography only.

L251/78

Map site: 74
SLAEC: Robin Densem
NGR: TQ 3058 7404

9–17 Effra Road, SW2

Evidence of natural topography only.

L252/78

Map site: 75
SLAEC: Robin Densem
NGR: TQ 3106 7511

67–73 Hackford Road, SW9

Evidence of natural topography only.

L254/78

Map site: 76
SLAEC: Robin Densem
NGR: TQ 3101 7679

157 Larkhall Lane, SW4

Evidence of natural topography only.

L260/80

Map site: 77
SLAEC: Robin Densem
NGR: TQ 2983 7625

L 2 6 1 / 7 8

Map site: 78
SLAEC: Robin Densem
NGR: TQ 2983 7508

Bowland Road Phase II, Haselrigge Road, SW4

Observation in 1978 recorded post-medieval activity above natural clay.

L 2 6 2 / 7 8

Map site: 79
SLAEC: Robin Densem
NGR: TQ 3124 7600

309–313 Brixton Road, SW9

Evidence of natural topography only.

L 2 7 7 / 7 8

Map site: 80
SLAEC: T Dain
NGR: TQ 3157 7448

42 Dulwich Road, SE24

Evidence of natural topography only.

L 2 8 0 / 7 8

Map site: 82
SLAEC: Robin Densem
NGR: TQ 3020 7248

70 Streatham High Road, SW16

Evidence of natural topography only.

L 2 9 2 / 7 8

Map site: 84
SLAEC: Robin Densem
NGR: TQ 3210 7530

41–53 Heron Road, SE24

Evidence of natural topography only.

L 2 9 8 / 7 8

Map site: 85
SLAEC: Robin Densem
NGR: TQ 3049 7645

219–225 Clapham Road, SW9

Evidence of natural topography only.

L 3 2 3 / 7 9

Map site: 88
SLAEC: Robin Densem
NGR: TQ 3068 7395

3–5 Somers Place, 1–19 Upper Tulse Hill, 2–12 Somers Road, SW2

Evidence of natural topography only.

Clive Road Phase IC, Rommany Road, SE21

Evidence of natural topography only.

L 3 4 2 / 7 9

Map site: 91
SLAEC: Robin Densem
NGR: TQ 3268 7178

206–208 Lambeth Walk, Black Prince Road, Newport Street, SE11

Evidence of natural topography only.

London Archaeol, 3, 1979, 264; Surrey Archaeol Coll, 72, 1980, 246

L 3 7 0 / 7 8

Map site: 93
SLAEC: T Dain
NGR: TQ 3078 7870

Carfax Square, SW4

Evidence of natural topography only. See L33/78 above.

L 3 8 9 / 7 9

Map site: 94
SLAEC: Robin Densem
NGR: TQ 2959 7515

Eastern Triangle site, Wandsworth Road, SW8

Observation in 1981 noted a shallow trench of apparently 17th- or 18th-c date.

L 4 3 6 / 8 1

Map site: 98
SLAEC: Derek Seeley
NGR: TQ 3007 7748

9–11 Streatham Common (north), SW16

Excavation in 1979 examined a chalk-filled feature, probably a foundation of post-medieval date. There was no indication of any connection with the manor house of Colbrands, probably some 100m to the NW.

London Archaeol, 3, 1980, 387

L 4 3 7 / 7 9

Map site: 99
SLAEC: Robin Densem
NGR: TQ 3030 7170
SMR: 090208

Rear of 38B Hercules Road, SE1

Observation in 1979 recorded topographical evidence and indications of post-medieval occupation.

L 4 4 0 / 7 9

Map site: 100
SLAEC: Robin Densem
NGR: TQ 3103 7931

87–111 Wandsworth Road, 10–32 Miles Street, 62–84 Bond Way, Parry Street, SW8

Evidence of natural topography only.

L 4 4 6 / 8 0

Map site: 101
SLAEC: Robin Densem
NGR: TQ 3024 7780

L448/80

Map site: 102
SLAEC: Robin Densem
NGR: TQ 2927 7588
SMR: 090833–7

9–57 Rectory Grove, SW4

Excavation in 1980 and 1982 close to the sites of Clapham manor house and the 12th-c church recovered struck flint flakes and pottery of possible Neolithic date. No Roman features were encountered, though abraded pieces of tile and a few fragments of glass, perhaps from a Roman building near Stane Street some 800m to the SE, were found in Saxon pits. Five of these, some intersecting, were recorded, and contained handmade, coarse and grass-tempered pottery; the largest pit contained a spindle-whorl in the same fabric. Medieval glazed sherds were also recovered. In one area a deposit of gravel was laid over the agricultural soil, apparently in the 17th or early 18th c, perhaps part of a yard associated with the house whose brick-built cellar was exposed. See also RGO88 above, L539/86, L602/86 below.

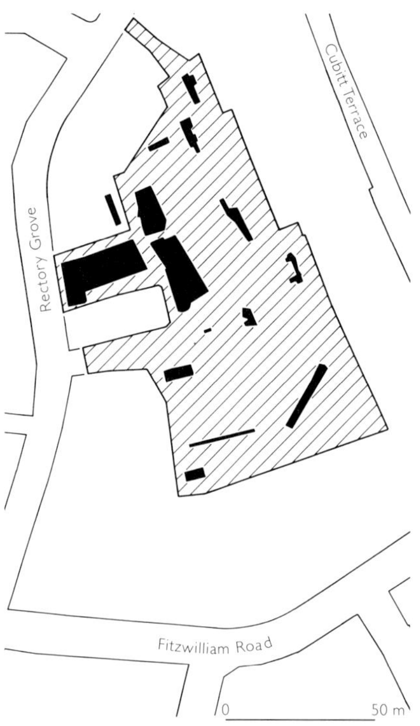

London Archaeol, 4, 1981, 48; 4, 1983, 289; Britannia, 12, 1981, 353; Medieval
Archaeol, 25, 1981, 173; Post-Medieval Archaeol, 15, 1981, 229; Surrey Archaeol
Coll, 74, 1983, 193; 75, 1984, 271
Anon, 1981 'Excavation in Clapham', Mosaic, London Archaeol, 4, 84
Densem, R, & Seeley, D, 1982 'Excavations at Rectory Grove, Clapham,
1980–81', London Archaeol, 4, 177–84

L456/79

Map site: 103
SLAEC: Robin Densem
NGR: TQ 3019 7133

2 Rutford Road, SW16

Evidence of natural topography only.

L459/79

Map site: 104
SLAEC: Robin Densem
NGR: TQ 3081 7602

103 Stockwell Road, SW9

Excavation in 1979 located a 19th-c smithy building which had replaced Sir John Leigh's chapel of c 1523.

London Archaeol, 3, 1980, 387

L462/79

Map site: 105
SLAEC: Robin Densem
NGR: TQ 3125 7811

Outside Old Town Hall, Milverton Street, SE11

Evidence of natural topography only.

L464/79

Map site: 106
SLAEC: Robin Densem
NGR: TQ 3028 7049

512–522 Streatham High Road, SW16

Observation in 1979 recorded modern disturbance only.

Clive Road Phases IB1 & IB2, Clive Road, Hamilton Road, SE21

Evidence of natural topography only.

**L472/79,
L473/79**

Map site: 107, 108
SLAEC: Robin Densem
NGR: TQ 3292 7173

Holy Trinity School, 220 Lambeth Road, SE1

Observations at the former Archbishop Tait's School in 1979 recorded several cut features of post-medieval date as well as topographical data.

L478/80

Map site: 109
SLAEC: Robin Densem
NGR: TQ 3075 7904

212–214 Kennington Road, SE11

Evidence of natural topography only.

L491/80

Map site: 110
SLAEC: Robin Densem
NGR: TQ 3120 7850

42–44 Norwood High Street, SE27

Evidence of natural topography only.

L497/81

Map site: 111
SLAEC: Robin Densem
NGR: TQ 3205 7187

Archbishop's Park, Lambeth Palace Road, SE1

Excavation in 1981 revealed medieval pits and a ditch containing Roman and medieval finds.

Britannia, 12, 1981, 353

L501/81

Map site: 113
SLAEC: Robin Densem
NGR: TQ 3090 7927

74–78 Upper Ground, SE1

Evidence of natural topography only.

L502/80

Map site: 114
SLAEC: Robin Densem
NGR: TQ 3110 8040

L515/87

Map site: 115
SLAEC: Mike Hutchinson
NGR: TQ 3179 7867

120–124 Newington Butts, SE1

Observation in 1987 recorded Roman deposits.

L518/83

Map site: 116
SLAEC: Robin Densem
NGR: TQ 3001 7135

Rear of 350–372 Streatham High Road, SW16

Evidence of natural topography only.

L519/81

Map site: 117
SLAEC: Robin Densem
NGR: TQ 3115 7838

Former LEB substation, Sancroft Street, SE11

Observation in 1981 recorded four trenches, one of them revealing a post-medieval wall.

L525/85

Map site: 118
DGLA(S&L): Derek Seeley
NGR: TQ 3074 7906

Lambeth Palace (kitchen garden), Lambeth Palace Road, SE1

Excavation in 1985 of the SE corner of the palace gardens, about 175m ENE of Morton's Gate Tower (see L204/80 above) and 200m E of the Thames, revealed a prehistoric pit and one other possible feature containing small unabraded sherds of pottery and worked flints. Others were recovered from post-prehistoric contexts. A small medieval ditch was excavated in an area that revealed no other features except for a deposit of garden soil or ploughsoil. Numerous post-medieval pits and post-holes were found, including a large rectangular pit of late 17th- or early 18th-c date which contained kitchen refuse deposits and a large iron key. On the N side of the site the fills of a large pond of post-1750 date were recorded. See also LPC88, LPC90 above, L582/86 below.

London Archaeol, 5, 1986, 162–3; Medieval Archaeol, 30, 1986, 142; Surrey Archaeol Coll, 78, 1987, 144

L537/81

Map site: 120
SLAEC: Robin Densem
NGR: TQ 2918 7553

Rear of 34 Old Town, SW4

Evidence of natural topography only.

L539/86

Map site: 121
DGLA(S&L): Derek Seeley
NGR: TQ 2932 7604
SMR: 090802–3

Ingleton House, 4 Rectory Grove, SW4

A watching brief in 1986 recorded several worked flints from deposits directly overlying natural, and from later features. A fragment of Roman tile was found in the fill of a ditch about 35m long and 1.5m wide, and joined at right angles by a second ditch. See also RGO88, L234/79, L448/80 above, L602/86 below.

London Archaeol, 5, 1987, 276; Surrey Archaeol Coll, 78, 1987, 144

64–68 Rectory Grove, SW4

Evidence of natural topography only.

London Archaeol, 5, 1985, 64; *Medieval Archaeol,* 29, 1985, 177; *Surrey Archaeol Coll,* 77, 1986, 224

L541/84

Map site: 123
DGLA(S&L): Robin Densem
NGR: TQ 2923 7581
SMR: 090670

Waterloo Road, Baylis Road, SE1

Evidence of natural topography only.

L543/82

Map site: 124
SLAEC: Derek Seeley
NGR: TQ 3126 7978

Rear of Brashier's and Wallace's Cottages, New Park Road, SW2

Evidence of natural topography only.

L544/82

Map site: not shown
SLAEC: Robin Densem
NGR: TQ 299 732

Campbell Buildings, Baylis Road, Frazier Street, Burdett Street, SE1

Excavation in 1983 revealed no trace of the Roman road thought to link London Bridge and Westminster or of any other Roman activity. The site was low lying and liable to flooding; a number of streams were traced, some of them having silted up in the medieval period or later. The site remained open ground until the 19th c when it was developed for housing and industrial use.

London Archaeol, 4, 1984, 388; 5, 1985, 64; *Surrey Archaeol Coll,* 76, 1985, 128; 77, 1986, 224

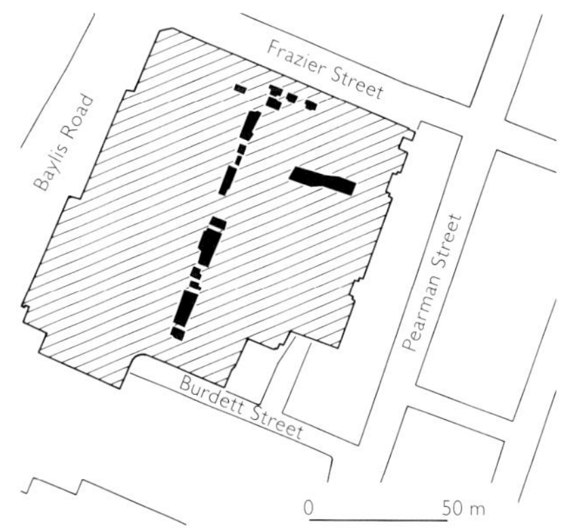

L545/83

Map site: 125
DGLA(S&L): Robin Densem,
John Dillon, Michael
Hutchinson
NGR: TQ 3124 7954
SMR: 090669

Rear of 41 Larkhall Rise, SW4

Observation in 1983 recorded no archaeological features.

L546/83

Map site: 126
SLAEC: Robin Densem
NGR: TQ 2964 7602

L547/83

Map site: 127
SLAEC: Robin Densem
NGR: TQ 3153 7638
SMR: 090667

Akerman Road, Evandale Road, Loughborough Road, SW9

Excavation in 1983 produced no evidence of the nearby medieval manor house recorded as 'le Wyk' and its post-medieval successor Loughborough House, but revealed post-medieval brick walls probably relating to the outbuildings of Loughborough House.

London Archaeol, 4, 1984, 388; Surrey Archaeol Coll, 76, 1985, 128

L551/83

Map site: 128
SLAEC: Robin Densem
NGR: TQ 2993 7167
SMR: 090668

St Mary's Convent, 3 Tooting Bec Gardens, SW16

Excavation in 1983 revealed a rectangular stone-lined cellar, 5.5m x 5.3m, of probable late medieval or Tudor date, its glazed tile floor almost entirely robbed out. Any other evidence of floor surfaces had been removed by modern disturbance.

London Archaeol, 4, 1984, 388; Medieval Archaeol, 28, 1984, 230; Surrey Archaeol Coll, 76, 1985, 128; 80, 1990, 218
Densem, R, 1984 'A late medieval cellar and the archaeology of Streatham', *London Archaeol*, 4, 423–5

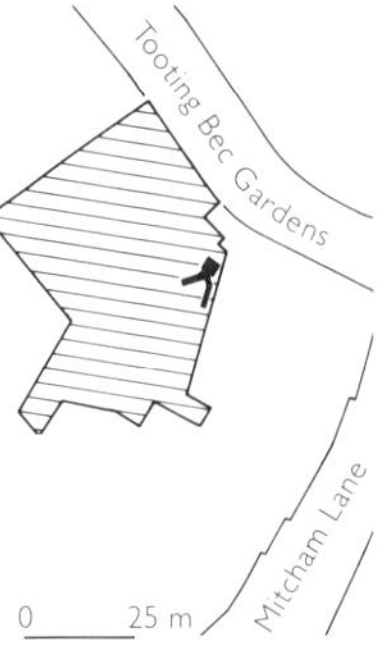

L552/84

Map site: 129
DGLA(S&L): Michael Hutchinson
NGR: TQ 3145 7995

50–78 The Cut, SE1

Observation in 1984 noted modern disturbance only.

L554/83

Map site: 130
SLAEC: Robin Densem
NGR: TQ 3073 7865

Lambeth Walk, Black Prince Road, Newport Street, SE11

Evidence of natural topography only.

L555/83

Map site: 131
SLAEC: Robin Densem
NGR: TQ 3088 7890

Lambeth Walk, Juxon Street, Lollard Street, SE11

Evidence of natural topography only.

55–57 Rectory Grove, SW4

Evidence of natural topography only.

Surrey Archaeol Coll, 76, 1985, 128

L560/83

Map site: 132
SLAEC: Robin Densem
NGR: TQ 2928 7582

59–63 Effra Road, SW2

Evidence of natural topography only.

L565/86

Map site: 133
DGLA(S&L): Derek Seeley
NGR: TQ 3114 7479

Tooting Bec Gardens, SW16

Evidence of natural topography only.

L566/84

Map site: 134
DGLA(S&L): Michael
Hutchinson
NGR: TQ 2993 7172

372–376 Clapham Road, SW9

Evidence of natural topography only.

L567/84

Map site: 135
DGLA(S&L): Derek Seeley
NGR: TQ 3013 7603

Site adjoining 9 Newport Street, SE11

A watching brief in 1985 observed medieval deposits cut into natural sands and gravels.

L571/85

Map site: 137
DGLA(S&L): Derek Seeley
NGR: TQ 3078 7879

Museum of the Moving Image, South Bank, SE1

Observation in 1985 recorded evidence of post-medieval deposition.

L576/85

Map site: 138
DGLA(S&L): Derek Seeley
NGR: TQ 3092 8030

L577/87

Map site: 139
DGLA(S&L): Derek Seeley
NGR: TQ 3059 7901

St Mary's church, Lambeth Road, SE1

Observation in 1987 undertook limited recording of two wall foundations and an arch support, possibly of 19th-c date. See also L146/79 above.

L582/86

Map site: 141
DGLA(S&L): Derek Seeley
NGR: TQ 3074 7931
SMR: 090808–9

Lambeth Palace (north garden), Lambeth Palace Road, SE1

Excavation in 1986 revealed prehistoric features containing pottery and flints, more of which were recovered from deposits directly overlying natural and from later features, ranging in date from Mesolithic to Late Iron Age. Two phases of a large drainage ditch, several pits and a well, all of Roman date, were examined and the backfill of the ditch found to contain two inhumations. A small linear medieval feature was recorded, and evidence of 17th-c horticulture provided by 12 long, parallel growing beds. See also L525/85 above.

London Archaeol, 5, 1987, 276; Medieval Archaeol, 31, 1987, 131; Surrey Archaeol Coll, 78, 1987, 144

L585/87

Map site: 142
DGLA(S&L): Derek Seeley
NGR: TQ 2922 7482

1 Elms Road (site adjoining 53–54 Clapham Common South Side), SW4

Observation in 1987 recorded a possible field ditch containing sherds of 14th–16th-c green-glazed pottery.

L587/85

Map site: 143
DGLA(S&L): Derek Seeley
NGR: TQ 3075 7510

7–37 Acre Lane, 30 Baytree Road, SW2

Evidence of natural topography only.

L593/86

Map site: 145
DGLA(S&L): Derek Seeley
NGR: TQ 2999 7569

424 Clapham Road, SW4

Evidence of natural topography only.

L594/86

Map site: 146
DGLA(S&L): Derek Seeley
NGR: TQ 2978 7548

65–79 Clapham High Street, SW4

Evidence of natural topography only.

51–81 Wiltshire Road, 5–25A Western Road, SW9

L596/86

Map site: 147
DGLA(S&L): Derek Seeley
NGR: TQ 3135 7580

Evidence of natural topography only.

Thurston House, 52 Rectory Grove, SW4

L602/86

Map site: 150
DGLA(S&L): Derek Seeley
NGR: TQ 2920 7585
SMR: 090804–7

Excavation in 1986 recovered a prehistoric flint and an Early Saxon sherd from a deposit directly overlying natural. Short lengths of two medieval ditches were examined. A brick wall foundation and a small brick and tile arched drain of the late 17th c were found, and are believed to be part of the building which preceded the late 18th-c house. See also RGO88, L448/80, L539/86 above.

London Archaeol, 5, 1987, 276; Medieval Archaeol, 31, 1987, 131; Surrey Archaeol Coll, 78, 1987, 144

South London Hospital for Women, Clapham Common South Side, SW4

L608/86

Map site: 151
DGLA(S&L): Derek Seeley
NGR: TQ 2888 7429

Evidence of natural topography only.

Holy Trinity Centre, Carlisle Lane, SE1

L610/87

Map site: 153
DGLA(S&L): Derek Seeley
NGR: TQ 3085 7940

Evidence of natural topography only.

38–46 Albert Embankment, SE1

L611/87

Map site: 154
DGLA(S&L): Derek Seeley
NGR: TQ 3043 7836

A trial excavation in 1987 in the vicinity of a pottery recorded on a map of 1746 revealed a major construction in the 17th–18th c, possibly related to the pottery. Large quantities of discarded kiln furniture and wasters were found: delftware in the earlier levels and stoneware in the later ones. Fragments of porcelain indicate its early manufacture on the site. See also ALA88, 38ALB89, L54/80, L76/78 above.

London Archaeol, 5, 1988, 413; Post-Medieval Archaeol, 22, 1988, 226; Surrey Archaeol Coll, 79, 1989, 185

11 Lillieshall Road, SW4

L615/87

Map site: 155
DGLA(S&L): Derek Seeley
NGR: TQ 2908 7577

Observations in 1987 noted a post-medieval domed brick-lined pit, interpreted as a well.

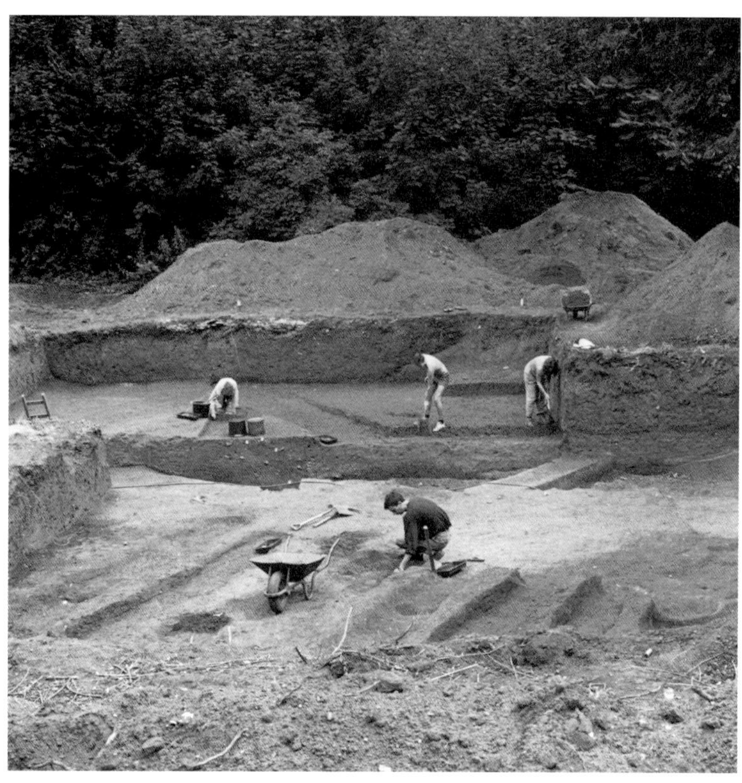

Lambeth L525/85 Lambeth Palace, kitchen garden site, Lambeth Palace Road, SE1. Work in progress within the kitchen garden.

LEWISHAM

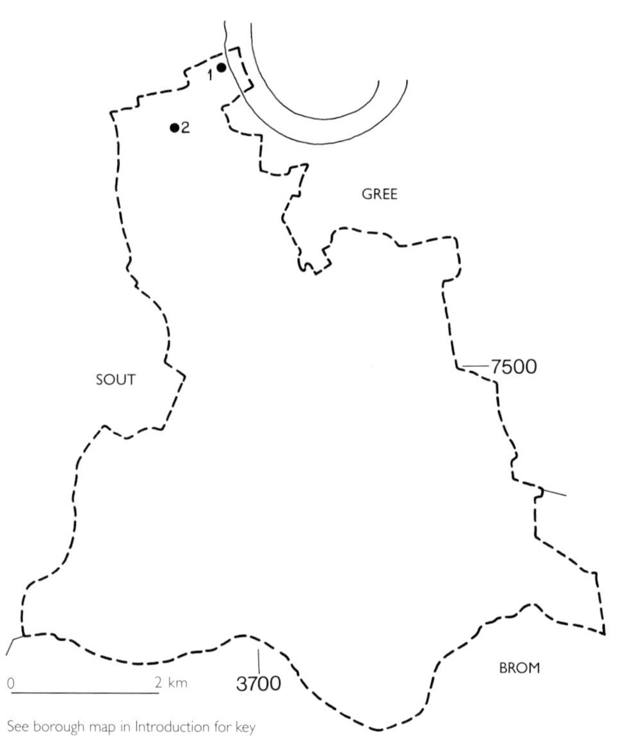

DW87

Map site: 1
MoL Environmental: Ian Tyers
NGR: TQ 3670 7894

Deptford Wharf, Grove Street, SE8

A watching brief in 1987 examined a structure that appeared to be a boat slipway, uncovered during construction works. Parts survived *in situ* and as recognisable fragments on spoil heaps. The structure consisted of two main elements: a platform of large planks pegged and nailed together, set on a bed of clay and other material, sloping down to the river; and to either side of this, a revetment-like structure of piles and bracing elements. Preliminary dating for the structure falls within the range 1665–85.

London Archaeol, 5, 1988, 413; *Post-Medieval Archaeol*, 22, 1988, 207

SCTRL81

Map site: 2
SLAEC: Brian Yule
NGR: TQ 3602 7800

Surrey Canal, Trundley's Road, SE8

A one-day watching brief in July 1981 examined remains of a ragstone wall, within a trench for electric cables.

LONDON BOROUGH OF

MERTON

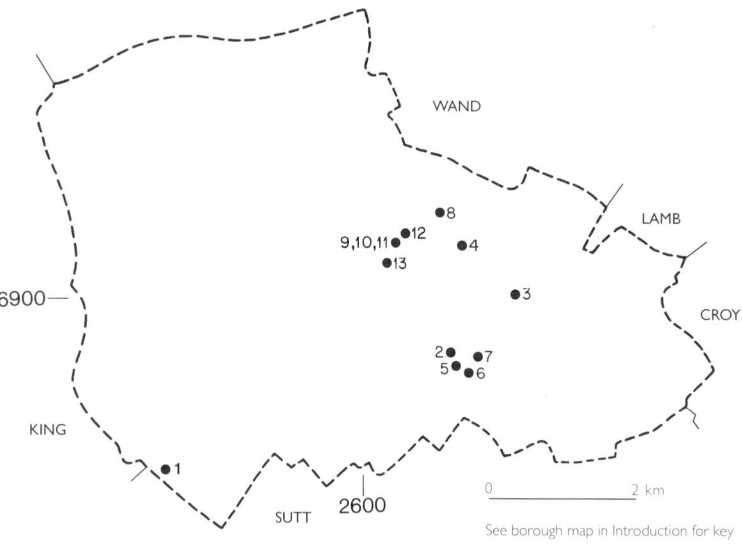

London Borough of Merton

MERT	1	BEV90	Bradbank Sports Ground, Beverley Way, New Malden, KT3
MERT	2	CRL89	Church Rd Link, Benedict Rd, Mitcham, CR4
MERT	3	EGL90	Eagle House, London Rd, Mitcham, CR4
MERT	4	KCG89	King's College Sports Ground, Western Rd, Mitcham, CR4
MERT	5	LMM90	Morden Rd, London Rd (south-west junction), Mitcham, CR4
MERT	6	LRD90	470–472 London Rd, Mitcham, CR4
MERT	7	LRM90	352–356 London Rd (rear of), Mitcham, CR4
MERT	8	MOG89	Merton Bus Garage, Merton High St, SW19
MERT	9	MPY76	Merton Priory (Station Rd), SW19
MERT	10	MPY83	Merton Priory (Station Rd), SW19
MERT	11	MPY86	Merton Priory (Station Rd), SW19
MERT	12	MPY88	Merton Priory, Merantun Way, SW19
MERT	13	SHM89	Streatham House, Windsor Avenue, SW19
MERT		WHS79	28–31 Wimbledon High St, SW19

BEV90

Map site: 1
DGLA(SW): Gill Batchelor
NGR: TQ 2230 6877
SMR: 021258

Bradbank Sports Ground, Beverley Way, New Malden, KT3

Excavation in 1990 revealed areas of truncated natural and post-medieval land drains.

London Archaeol, 6, 1991, 305; Post-Medieval Archaeol, 25, 1991, 158; Surrey Archaeol Coll, 81, 1991–2, 161

CRL89

Map site: 2
DGLA: Tim Hailley
NGR: TQ 2700 6868
SMR: 021176–8

Church Road Link, Benedict Road, Mitcham, CR4

Excavation in 1989 examined an area of ditches and pits containing Romano-British pottery, and early medieval pottery from secondary fills, perhaps the result of slumping from an overlying layer. A second area contained features of medieval date cut into the natural, and evidence of post-medieval activity near the line of Church Road.

London Archaeol, 6, 1990, 191; Medieval Archaeol, 34, 1990, 183; Surrey Archaeol Coll, 80, 1990, 220

EGL90

Map site: 3
DGLA: Philip Emery
NGR: TQ 2777 6826
SMR: 021256

Eagle House, London Road, Mitcham, CR4

Trial trenching in 1990 revealed no archaeological features.

London Archaeol, 6, 1991, 305; Surrey Archaeol Coll, 81, 1991–2, 162

King's College Sports Ground, Western Road, Mitcham, CR4

KCG89

Map site: 4
DGLA(SW): Robert Bazely
NGR: TQ 2720 6980
SMR: 021171–4

Excavation in 1989 on a 30 acre (about 12ha) gravel terrace site revealed a number of prehistoric features with pottery ranging in date from Neolithic (Mortlake ware) to Bronze Age (Deverel-Rimbury ware). Phases of activity were suggested by the cutting of ditches followed by silting and subsequent recutting. The ditches may indicate Bronze Age agriculture and husbandry.

London Archaeol, 6, 1990, 191; *Surrey Archaeol Coll,* 80, 1990, 220

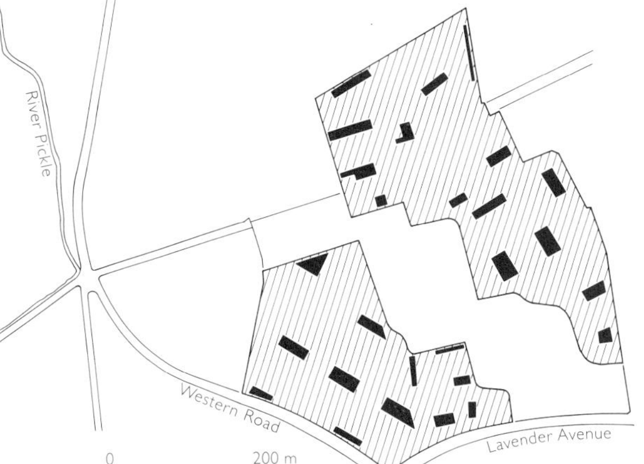

Morden Road, London Road (south-west junction), Mitcham, CR4

LMM90

Map site: 5
DGLA: Bruno Barber
NGR: TQ 2715 6808
SMR: 021257

Trial trenching in 1990 revealed evidence of post-medieval quarrying.

London Archaeol, 6, 1991, 305; *Post-Medieval Archaeol,* 25, 1991, 158; *Surrey Archaeol Coll,* 81, 1991–2, 161

470–472 London Road, Mitcham, CR4

LRD90

Map site: 6
DGLA: David Saxby
NGR: TQ 2720 6820
SMR: 021255

Trial trenching in 1990 located an 18th–19th-c red-brick wall.

London Archaeol, 6, 1991, 305; *Surrey Archaeol Coll,* 81, 1991–2, 162

Rear of 352–356 London Road, Mitcham, CR4

LRM90

Map site: 7
DGLA(SW): Pat Miller
NGR: TQ 2743 6849
SMR: 021168–70

Excavation in 1990 revealed a small pit or post-hole cutting the natural gravel and provisionally dated to the 15th c. Evidence of possible domestic occupation in the 17th c or earlier was encountered in the form of exterior surfaces of either domestic or, because of their robust construction, commercial character.

London Archaeol, 6, 1991, 305

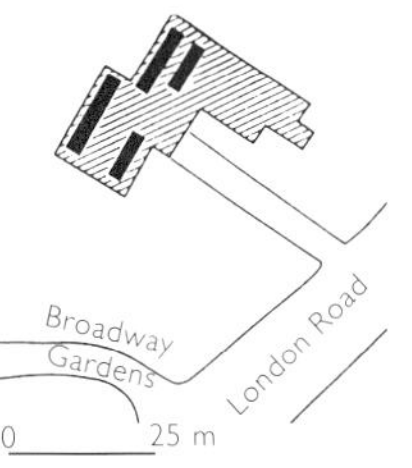

Merton Bus Garage, Merton High Street, SW19

MOG89

Map site: 8
DGLA(SW): Robin Nielsen
NGR: TQ 2680 7030
SMR: 021179–81

Excavation in 1989 revealed a 14th-c ditch to the W of the River Wandle. Medieval post-holes and stake-holes were also examined, and evidence of late medieval/early post-medieval flooding recorded.

London Archaeol, 6, 1990, 191; *Medieval Archaeol,* 34, 1990, 183, *Surrey Archaeol Coll,* 80, 1990, 220

MPY76

Map site: 9
DGLA(SW), SAS, SWLT:
Scott McCracken
NGR: TQ 2650 6990
SMR: 021182, 030376

Merton Priory (Station Road), SW19

Trial excavations in 1976 uncovered the apsidal E end and associated floor levels of the chapter house (c 12th c) of the Augustinian priory of St Mary. Of three burials located there, two had been robbed at the time of demolition (c 1538–40). Excavation of the entire chapter house in 1977–8 showed that the building, originally rectangular with flint foundations on a gravel base, was later enlarged with an apsidal end; 25 burials were recovered. Portions of the cloister, infirmary passage and slype were also investigated, as was the canons' cemetery (ten graves). Two sections of flint and chalk walls were located in a trial trench some 15m E of the apse, and these are thought to be part of the infirmary. Excavations in 1982 of a shallow service trench across the W end of the S transept and along the cloister walk (excavated 1978) W of the chapter house revealed walling at the junction of the S transept and the passage along the N side of the chapter house. (For plan, see MPY88.)

London Archaeol, 3, 1977, 38; 3, 1978, 161; 3, 1979, 264; 4, 1983, 290; Medieval Archaeol, 22, 1978, 159; 23, 1979, 252; Surrey Archaeol Coll, 72, 1980, 246
Anon, 1976 'Merton Priory', Mosaic, London Archaeol, 3, 28
McCracken, J S, 1984 'Archaeological excavations at Merton Priory: the infirmary', Bull of the Wandle Group, Dec, 5–8
McCracken, J S, 1984 'Excavations at Merton Priory: the infirmary', Surrey Archaeol Soc Bull, 196, 3
McCracken, J S, 1977 'Merton Priory excavations', Surrey Archaeol Soc Bull, 135

MPY83

Map site: 10
DGLA: Scott McCracken
NGR: TQ 2650 6990
SMR: 030376

Merton Priory (Station Road), SW19

Trial excavation in 1983 on the presumed site of the priory infirmary revealed a passageway defined by flint walls linked to the chapter house (see MPY76 above). A 'hall' with floors of roof tile and aligned N–S lay immediately E of the passage, and itself opened E into a larger room of unknown extent and with floor tiles of late 15th-c date. Beneath these were found at least three plaster floors as well as a pitched-tile hearth dated to the mid-13th c. The 'hall' and large room indicate a substantial building located SW of the chapter house. (For plan, see MPY88.)

London Archaeol, 4, 1984, 388; Medieval Archaeol, 28, 1984, 230; Surrey Archaeol Coll, 75, 1984, 271; 76, 1985, 128

MPY86

Map site: 11
DGLA: Scott McCracken
NGR: TQ 2650 6990
SMR: 030376

Merton Priory (Station Road), SW19

Excavation in 1986 involved the clearing of a large area in the N half of the priory site to the levels of c 1540 and the excavation of the S transept. The entire N half of the priory church was revealed in 1987, and most of the N transept, Lady Chapel and choir was excavated. Some 160 burials were found within or close to the church. A number of construction phases were distinguished in the N nave wall, and the transept-end chapels were defined. The major periods of building appear to have been the early 12th c for much of the nave, and the mid-13th c for the choir and Lady Chapel extension. N of the choir large spreads of Reigate stone chippings and stone footings suggested that this was an area of temporary buildings used during the construction of the priory. (For plan, see MPY88.)

London Archaeol, 5, 1987, 276; 5, 1988, 413; Medieval Archaeol, 31, 1987, 131; 32, 1988, 251; Surrey Archaeol Coll, 78, 1987, 145; 79, 1989, 186

Merton Priory, Merantun Way, SW19

MPY88

Map site: 12
DGLA: Simon Mason,
Penny Bruce, Jon Nowell
NGR: TQ 2670 7020
SMR: 030376

Excavation in 1988 on the N half of the church revealed
substantial foundations along its entire 100m length. Four
distinct phases of construction have been identified: the
widening of the nave to form N and S aisles; the moving of
the transepts further E; and the addition of a large quire
and Lady Chapel. Also revealed was a later strengthening
phase with large extension buttresses mainly constructed
of reused architectural fragments of Reigate stone or
Purbeck marble. To the N of the church an extensive lay
cemetery of several hundred inhumations was excavated.
Work was also carried out on areas affected by the

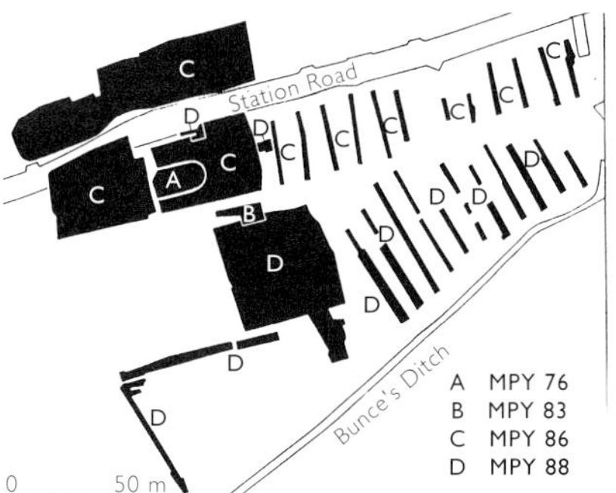

construction of the Merton relief road (Merantun Way), bridging the already exposed chapter house,
S aisle, cloister, canons' cemetery and NW corner of the infirmary building. Investigation of the S area
of the site uncovered large areas of the infirmary and domestic buildings, set around a possible
infirmary cloister. A continuation of the excavations in 1990 concentrated on the site of the infirmary
and domestic ranges, and on the outlying areas to the S and E of the main monastic complex. A large
Reigate stone drainage system was excavated to the SE of the infirmary, and a wharf or slipway,
associated with a channel to the S of the site, was also uncovered. Roman activity was demonstrated
by the presence of a ditch in the infirmary cloister.

London Archaeol, 3, 1989, 75–6; 6, 1990, 191–2; 6, 1991, 305; *Britannia*, 22, 1991, 273; *Medieval Archaeol*, 33, 1989, 185; 34, 1990, 183;
  Surrey Archaeol Coll, 80, 1990, 219
Bruce, P, & Mason, S, 1993 *Merton Priory*, MoLAS & London Borough of Merton

Streatham House, Windsor Avenue, SW19

SHM89

Map site: 13
DGLA(SW): David Saxby
NGR: TQ 2630 6950
SMR: 021175

Excavation in 1989 on the flood plain of the River Wandle some 350m SW of the site of Merton Priory
recovered no traces of occupation, but recorded a sequence of peat deposits which were sampled for
environmental evidence.

London Archaeol, 6, 1990, 192; *Surrey Archaeol Coll*, 80, 1990, 219

28–31 Wimbledon High Street, SW19

WHS79

Map site: not shown
SWLAU: R Adkins, L Adkins
NGR: TQ 2390 7100
SMR: 030728–30

Trial excavation in 1979 on a site within the medieval village of Wimbledon revealed no features earlier
than 1865, and none was recorded by a watching brief on a gravel terrace site to the rear. Pottery
recovered ranged from 16th c to modern.

London Archaeol, 3, 1980, 387
Adkins, L, & Adkins, R, 1987 'Excavations at 28–31 Wimbledon High Street', *Surrey Archaeol Coll*, 78, 178–284

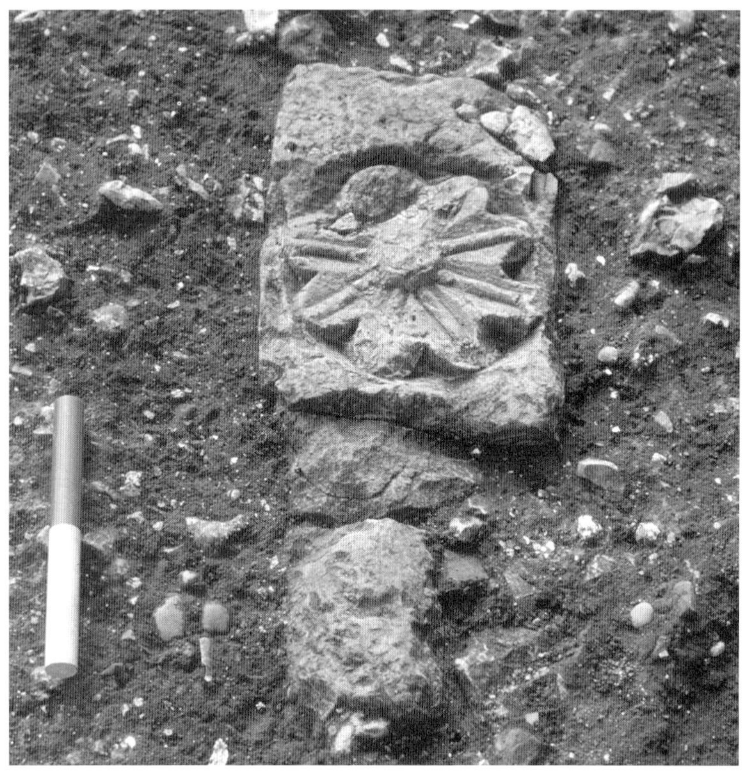

Merton MPY88 Merton Priory, Merantun Way, SW19 Architectural fragment found during excavation

RICHMOND UPON THAMES

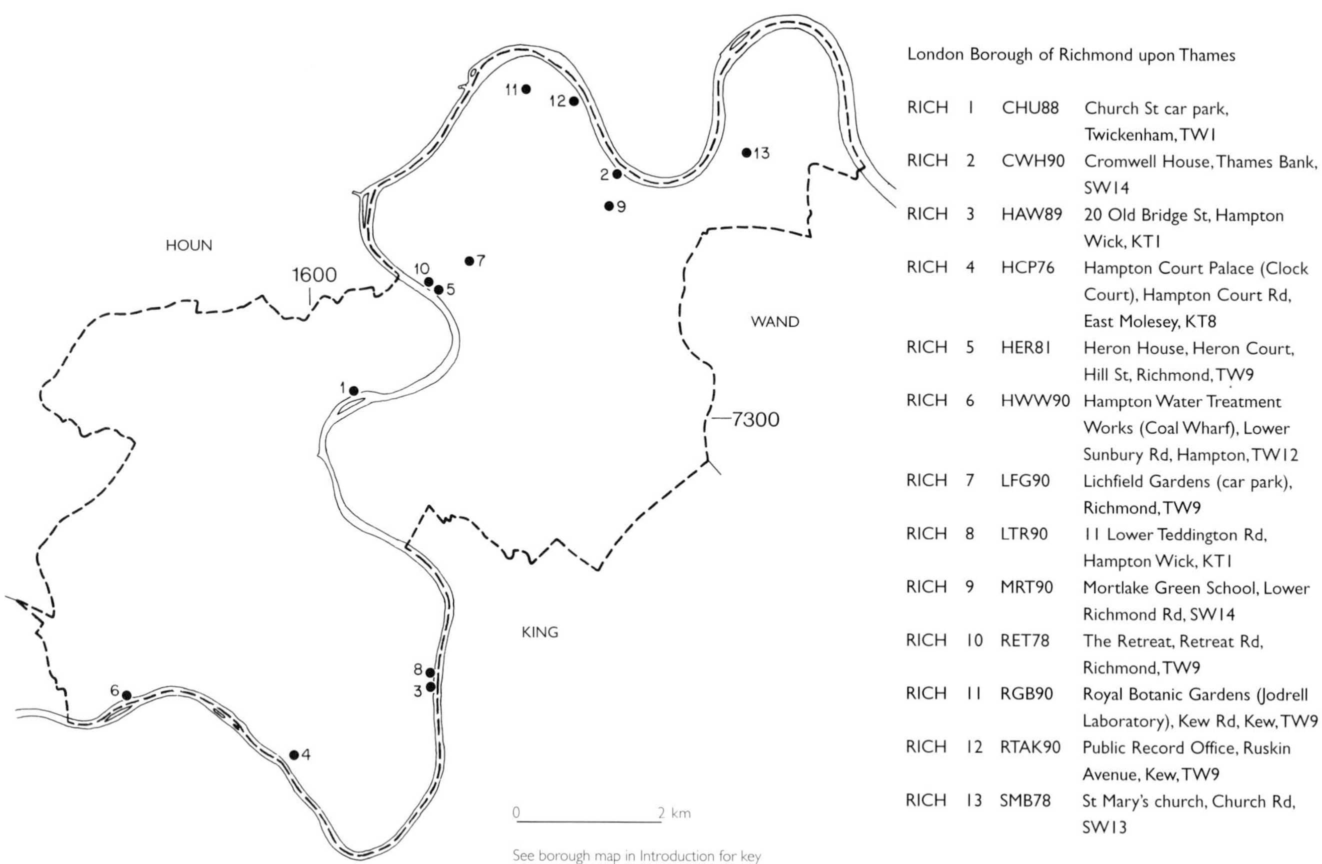

CHU88

Map site: 1
DGLA(SW): Jonathan Nowell
NGR: TQ 165 733
SMR: 021152–3

Church Street car park, Twickenham, TW1

Excavation in 1988, in an area where traces of Mesolithic and Neolithic activity had been recorded in 1966, revealed a length of ditch aligned N–S across the site. On the evidence of several phases of recutting, it apparently served to drain water into the Thames between the early 14th and mid-16th c, predating the late 16th–early 17th-c street frontage. A late 18th-c cesspit contained a large assemblage of pottery of that date. Little prehistoric evidence was found.

London Archaeol, 6, 1989, 76; Medieval Archaeol, 33, 1989, 185; Surrey Archaeol Coll, 80, 1990, 220

CWH90

Map site: 2
DGLA: Mark Barratt
NGR: TQ 2023 7620
SMR: 021273

Cromwell House, Thames Bank, SW14

An evaluation excavation in 1990 on a site immediately adjacent to the Thames foreshore revealed only extensive recent disturbance and no trace of prehistoric or medieval occupation.

London Archaeol, 6, 1991, 305; Surrey Archaeol Coll, 81, 1991–2, 162

20 Old Bridge Street, Hampton Wick, KT1

HAW89

Map site: 3
DGLA(SW): Geoffrey Potter,
Philip Emery
NGR: TQ 1767 6943
SMR: 030035

Excavation in 1989 on the site of Kingston Old Bridge, which was in existence by 1193 and survived until 1828, exposed a number of features including sections of riverwall and parts of the causeway which adjoined the end of the bridge in its final form. The inside face of the upstream causeway wall, observed in section, was probably of medieval date and about 1m thick. Nearly 2m of the downstream wall was exposed, indicating three construction phases: a probable medieval core, and two slightly offset sections of post-medieval refacing. The width of the causeway was about 6m, while its length exceeded 9.5m. Its alignment was noticeably at variance with that of the modern bank and of the Kingston approach opposite (see HOR86 above).

London Archaeol, 6, 1990, 192; Medieval Archaeol, 34, 1990, 184; Surrey Archaeol Coll, 80, 1990, 220

Hampton Court Palace (Clock Court), Hampton Court Road, East Molesey, KT8

HCP76

Map site: 4
ILAU: David Whipp
NGR: TQ 1572 6847
SMR: 021137

Excavation on the S side of Clock Court in 1976 failed to locate the position of a known Tudor moat. Early Tudor dumping in a natural depression had been cut by the construction trenches for two brick walls on chalk footings.

London Archaeol, 3, 1977, 38; Post-Medieval Archaeol, 13, 1979, 279

Heron House, Heron Court, Hill Street, Richmond, TW9

HER81

Map site: 5
ILAU: Scott McCracken
NGR: TQ 177 746
SMR: 020922

A trial excavation in 1981 in the rear garden of Heron House (1694) revealed the flood-plain terrace and original bank of the Thames before infilling to create the present series of garden terraces. Struck flints and Iron Age, medieval and post-medieval sherds were recovered, but no definite features identified.

London Archaeol, 4, 1982, 165; Surrey Archaeol Coll, 74, 1983, 193

Hampton Water Treatment Works (Coal Wharf), Lower Sunbury Road, Hampton, TW12

HWW90

Map site: 6
DGLA: Robert Cowie
NGR: TQ 1340 6925
SMR: 021263–4

An evaluation excavation in 1990 revealed various post-medieval dump layers above the alluvium. A large flat-bottomed feature in the trench was provisionally identified as a coal bunker.

London Archaeol, 6, 1991, 305; Post-Medieval Archaeol, 25, 1991, 132; Surrey Archaeol Coll, 81, 1991–2, 162

Lichfield Gardens (car park), Richmond, TW9

IFG90

Map site: 7
DGLA: Gill Batchelor
NGR: TQ 1820 7510
SMR: 021267

Excavation in 1990 revealed no archaeological features.

London Archaeol, 6, 1991, 305; Surrey Archaeol Coll, 81, 1991–2, 162

LTR90

Map site: 8
DGLA: Jonathan Nowell
NGR: TQ 1760 6960
SMR: 021265–6

11 Lower Teddington Road, Hampton Wick, KT1

Excavation in 1990 revealed three truncated features cutting natural river gravel and containing mixed Roman pottery. Features consisting mainly of small pits associated with domestic activity in a garden area, and a small ditch running N–S across the site, are dated to the post-medieval period.

London Archaeol, 6, 1991, 305; Post-Medieval Archaeol, 25, 1991, 132; Surrey Archaeol Coll, 81, 1991–2, 162

MRT90

Map site: 9
DGLA: David Saxby
NGR: TQ 2010 7580
SMR: 021271–2

Mortlake Green School, Lower Richmond Road, SW14

An evaluation excavation in 1990 revealed sand and clay layers of 17th–19th-c date, deposited naturally and possibly associated with an early watercourse of which only the S edge lay within the excavated area. The depth of the layers (more than 3m) shows the watercourse to have been of substantial size.

London Archaeol, 6, 1991, 305; Surrey Archaeol Coll, 81, 1991–2, 162

RET78

Map site: 10
SWLT, SAS: Annie Robinson
NGR: TQ 1765 7474

The Retreat, Retreat Road, Richmond, TW9

Excavation in 1978 near the supposed site of a late 15th–early 16th-c friary associated with Richmond Palace failed to locate any relevant features. Post-medieval pits were encountered, along with a quantity of Tudor demolition rubble which included two well-preserved wooden barrels.

London Archaeol, 3, 1979, 264; Surrey Archaeol Coll, 72, 1980, 247

RGB90

Map site: 11
DGLA: David Beard
NGR: TQ 1900 7730
SMR: 021268–9

Royal Botanic Gardens (Jodrell Laboratory), Kew Road, Kew, TW9

An evaluation excavation in 1990 produced struck flints on the natural waterlaid sands. Also located was a 19th-c structure, probably a greenhouse forming part of the earlier Jodrell Laboratory.

London Archaeol, 6, 1991, 305; Surrey Archaeol Coll, 81, 1991–2, 162

RTAK90

Map site: 12
DGLA: David Beard
NGR: TQ 1960 7720
SMR: 021270

Public Record Office, Ruskin Avenue, Kew, TW9

An evaluation excavation in 1990 revealed clay and sand soils, including evidence of plough furrows.

London Archaeol, 6, 1991, 305; Surrey Archaeol Coll, 81, 1991–2, 162

St Mary's church, Church Road, SW13

SMB78

Map site: 13
SAS, DGLA(SW): Scott
McCracken
NGR: TQ 220 765
SMR: 021116, 200955

Excavation and observation of the fire-gutted church between 1978 and 1983 revealed fragments of wall painting adhering to the S and E walls of the church and mostly consisting of red lines on white plaster to create the impression of masonry. A Norman arch was uncovered in the S wall, and the roof of the S aisle was found to date to c 1500. In 1979 measured drawings were made of the surviving medieval walls of the original nave and chancel. A study of the fabric suggested several building phases: an original rectangular structure with flint walls and the Norman door; an E extension early in the 13th c; and a W extension, perhaps of the same date in view of structural similarities. A brick tower was added to the W end c 1500. Investigations in 1980 suggested an original flint-built structure of c 1100 with E and W additions of c 1200. Post-medieval burials had removed all traces of medieval floor levels. The original cemetery of the church was found to lie at the W end, below the W extension and the Tudor brick tower. Excavations in 1981 and 1983 continued the work of recording the remains of the church.

London Archaeol, 3, 1979, 264; 3, 1980, 387–8; 4, 1981, 48; 4, 1982, 165; 4, 1984, 390; *Medieval Archaeol,* 23, 1979, 257; 24, 1980, 245; 25, 1981, 198; 26, 1982, 194; 27, 1983, 196; *Surrey Archaeol Coll,* 72, 1980, 247; 74, 1983, 193; 76, 1985, 129

McCracken, J S, 1980 'Barnes: St Mary's parish church', *Surrey Archaeol Soc Bull,* 167

McCracken, J S, 1983 'Barnes: St Mary's parish church', *Surrey Archaeol Soc Bull,* 184

McCracken, J S, 1983 'Further medieval wall paintings from Barnes church', Mosaic, *London Archaeol,* 4, 308

McCracken, J S, 1981 'St Mary's Barnes', *Bull Counc Brit Archaeol Churches Comm,* 14, 9

McCracken, J S, 1983 'Wall paintings at St Mary's Barnes', *Surrey Archaeol Soc Bull,* 184, 3

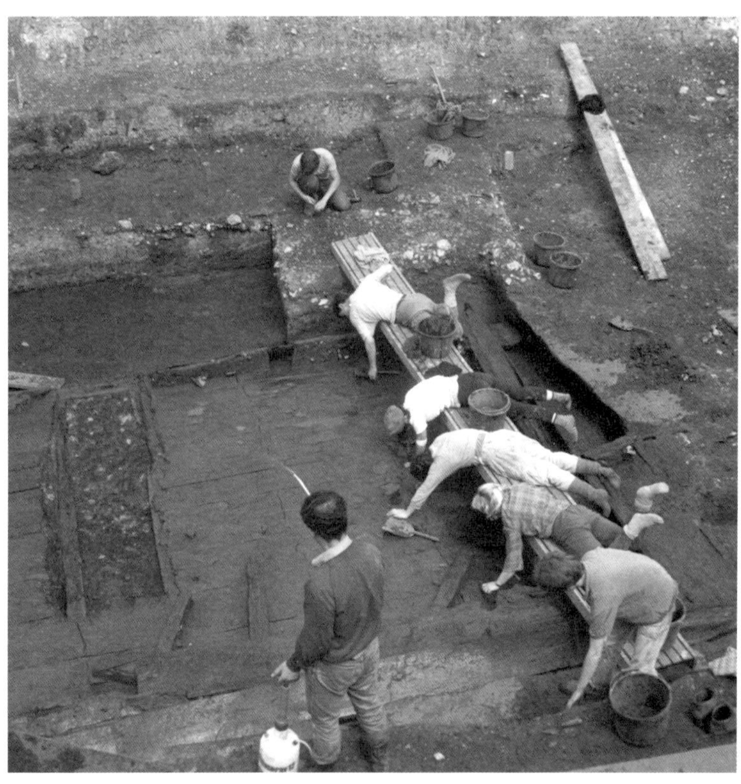

Southwark CO88 Former Courage Brewery, Park Street, SE1. Cleaning the oak-planked floor of a large timber building, dated to the early 2nd c.

SOUTHWARK

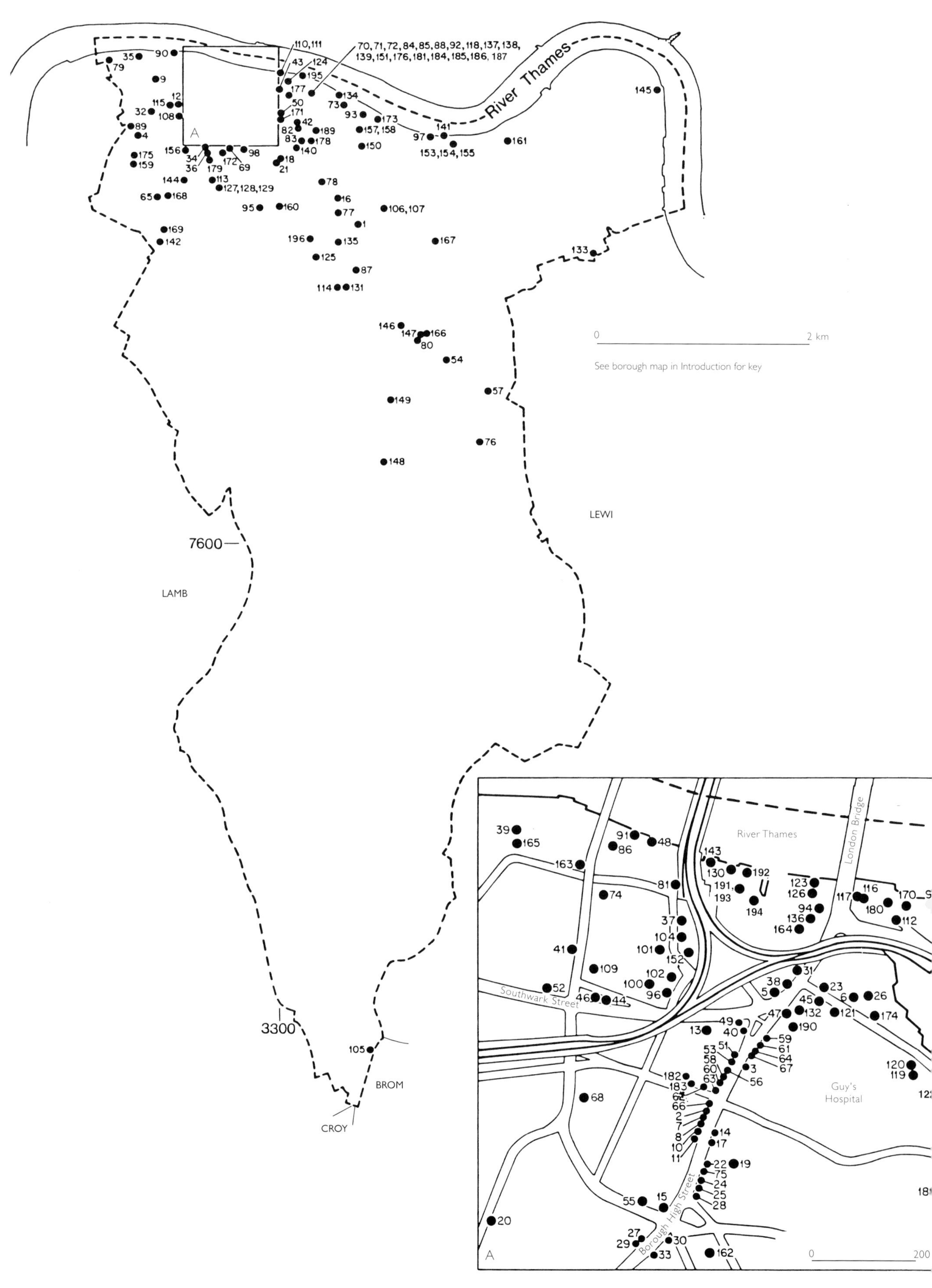
River Thames
110,111
70, 71, 72, 84, 85, 88, 92, 118, 137, 138,
139, 151, 176, 181, 184, 185, 186, 187
35
90
79
9
43
124
195
177
134
145
115
12
32
108
73
93
50
171
42
189
82
83
178
140
97
141
157, 158
173
89
4
156
34
98
18
150
153, 154, 155
161
175
159
36
179
172
69
21
144
113
127, 128, 129
78
65
168
95
160
16
77
106, 107
169
142
196
135
1
167
125
133
87
114
131
146
147
166
80
54
57
149
76
148
LEWI
7600
LAMB
0
2 km
See borough map in Introduction for key
3300
105
BROM
CROY
39
165
91
86
48
River Thames
London Bridge
143
163
130
192
81
191
193
123
126
116
170
180
117
112
74
194
136
94
37
164
104
101
152
41
109
100
102
96
52
46
44
38
31
5
23
6
26
49
47
45
132
121
174
13
40
190
59
61
53
51
64
58
60
67
182
3
56
183
63
120
119
66
65
2
7
8
14
10
17
11
22
75
19
24
25
55
15
28
20
27
29
30
33
162
A
Southwark Street
Borough High Street
Guy's
Hospital
0
200

London Borough of Southwark

SOUT	1	105GRA77	105–106 Grange Rd, SE1
SOUT	2	106BHS73	106–114 Borough High St, SE1
SOUT	3	107BHS81	107–115 Borough High St, SE1
SOUT	4	109BR87	109–115 Blackfriars Rd, SE1
SOUT	5	10SS81	10–16 Southwark St, SE1
SOUT	6	11STS77	11–19 St Thomas St, SE1
SOUT	7	120BHS89	120–124 Borough High St, SE1
SOUT	8	124BHS77	124–126 Borough High St, SE1
SOUT	9	128SS76	128–130 Southwark St, SE1
SOUT	10	128BHS74	128–132 Borough High St, SE1
SOUT	11	134BHS72	134–138 Borough High St, SE1
SOUT	12	154US82	154 Union St (railway arch), SE1
SOUT	13	15SKS80	15–23 Southwark St (Calverts Buildings), SE1
SOUT	14	169BHS74	169B Borough High St, SE1
SOUT	15	170BHS79	170–194 Borough High St, SE1
SOUT	16	170GRA89	170–176 Grange Rd, SE1
SOUT	17	175BHS76	175–177 Borough High St, SE1
SOUT	18	175LL81	175–177 Long Lane, Weston St, SE1
SOUT	19	179BHS89	179–191 Borough High St, SE1
SOUT	20	179SBR80	179 Southwark Bridge Rd, SE1
SOUT	21	180LL80	180–196 Long Lane, SE1
SOUT	22	199BHS74	199 Borough High St, SE1
SOUT	23	1STS74	1–7 St Thomas St, SE1
SOUT	24	201BHS75	201–205 Borough High St, SE1
SOUT	25	207BHS72	207–211 Borough High St, SE1
SOUT	26	20LBS75	20–26 London Bridge St, SE1
SOUT	27	210BHS90	210–212 Borough High St, SE1
SOUT	28	213BHS77	213 Borough High St, SE1
SOUT	29	218BHS79	218–224 Borough High St, SE1
SOUT	30	223BHS81	223–237 Borough High St, SE1
SOUT	31	22BHS88	22 Borough High St, SE1
SOUT	32	235US80	235–241 Union St, SE1
SOUT	33	239BHS87	239 Borough High St, SE1
SOUT	34	244BHS65	244–246 Borough High St, SE1
SOUT	35	245BR87	245 Blackfriars Rd, SE1
SOUT	36	289BHS90	289–299 Borough High St, SE1
SOUT	37	28PS84	28 Park St, SE1
SOUT	38	2SSBS85	2 Southwark St, 1A Bedale St, SE1
SOUT	39	37BS87	37–46 Bankside, SE1
SOUT	40	38BHS79	38 Borough High St, SE1
SOUT	41	38SBR79	38–42 Southwark Bridge Rd, SE1
SOUT	42	42BS86	42–44 Bermondsey St, SE1
SOUT	43	44TS86	44–46 Tooley St, SE1
SOUT	44	48SS89	48 Southwark St, SE1
SOUT	45	4STS82	4–26 St Thomas St, SE1
SOUT	46	52SOS89	52–54 Southwark St, SE1
SOUT	47	57BHS82	57 Borough High St (shaft outside), SE1
SOUT	48	5BS87	5–15 Bankside, SE1
SOUT	49	5SS73	5–7 Southwark St, SE1
SOUT	50	60STS82	60–68 St Thomas St, SE1
SOUT	51	64BHS74	64–70 Borough High St, SE1
SOUT	52	64SS74	64 Southwark St, SE1
SOUT	53	66BHS75	66 Borough High St, SE1
SOUT	54	684OKR86	684–698 Old Kent Rd, SE15
SOUT	55	6MSRD88	6–8 Marshalsea Rd, SE1
SOUT	56	78BHS73	78–80 Borough High St, SE1
SOUT	57	806OKR82	806–814 Old Kent Rd, SE15
SOUT	58	84BHS74	84–86 Borough High St, SE1
SOUT	59	85BHS90	85–87 Borough High St, SE1
SOUT	60	88BHS74	88 Borough High St, SE1
SOUT	61	89BHS75	89 Borough High St, SE1
SOUT	62	8US74	8–10 Union St, SE1
SOUT	63	92BHS74	92–104 Borough High St, SE1
SOUT	64	93BHS74	93–95 Borough High St, SE1
SOUT	65	93LR84	87–100 London Rd, SE1
SOUT	66	96BHS74	96–104 Borough High St, SE1
SOUT	67	97BHS74	97–99 Borough High St, SE1
SOUT	68	99SBR78	99–103 Southwark Bridge Rd, SE1
SOUT	69	AB78	Arcadia Buildings, Silvester St, Great Dover St, SE1
SOUT	70	ABB86	Abbots Lane, Tooley St, SE1
SOUT	71	ABB87	Abbots Lane, Tooley St, SE1
SOUT	72	ABB88	Abbots Lane, Tooley St, SE1
SOUT	73	ABST85	Anchor Brewhouse, Shad Thames (Mill House), SE1
SOUT	74	ACT89	Park St (Anchor Terrace car park), SE1
SOUT	75	AP72	Angel Place, 207 Borough High St, SE1
SOUT	76	ASY75	Asylum Rd, SE15
SOUT	77	AW89	Alaska Works, Grange Rd, SE1
SOUT	78	BA84	Bermondsey Abbey, Abbey Buildings, Long Walk, SE1
SOUT	79	BAG89	1–6 Barge House St, SE1
SOUT	80	BAQ90	Old Kent Rd, Bowles Rd (B and Q Depot), SE1
SOUT	81	BDPS84	Bank End, Park St, SE1
SOUT	82	BER88	39–45 Bermondsey St, SE1
SOUT	83	BER90	100–104 Bermondsey St, SE1
SOUT	84	BFN88	Butter Factory (north), Tooley St, SE1
SOUT	85	BFS88	Butter Factory (south), Tooley St, SE1
SOUT	86	BKS81	5–15 Bankside, SE1
SOUT	87	BLA87	Bricklayers' Arms Railway Depot, Rolls Rd, SE1
SOUT	88	BRA88	Braidwood St, Tooley St, SE1
SOUT	89	BRN88	Boundary Row (north side), SE1
SOUT	90	BS78	Royal George Wharf, Bankside, SE1 (see BKS81)
SOUT	91	BS81	5–15 Bankside, SE1
SOUT	92	BTH88	Bethel Estate, Vine Lane, SE1
SOUT	93	BUT88	Butlers Court, Curlew St, SE1
SOUT	94	BWMC74	Bonded Warehouse, Montague Close, SE1
SOUT		CB80	Calverts Buildings, 15–23 Southwark St, SE1
SOUT	95	CBS77	Cardinal Bourne St, SE1
SOUT	96	CFRW85	Cromwell Flats, Redcross Way, SE1
SOUT	97	CG87	Cherry Garden Pier, Bermondsey Wall East, SE16
SOUT	98	CH75	Chaucer House, Tabard St, SE1
SOUT	99	CHWH83	Chamberlain's Wharf, Tooley St, SE1
SOUT	100	CO87	Courage Brewery, Park St, SE1
SOUT	101	CO88	Courage Brewery, Park St, SE1
SOUT	102	CO89	Courage Brewery, 3 Redcross Way, SE1
SOUT	103	COGA84	Courage, Globe Alley, SE1 (deleted site code, not shown on borough map)
SOUT	104	COSE84	Courage Brewery (south-east), Park St, SE1
SOUT	105	CPPCR85	Crystal Palace Parade, College Rd, SE19
SOUT	106	CRODA86	Croda Gelatine Works (1), Southwark Park Rd, SE1
SOUT	107	CRODA87	Croda Gelatine Works (2), Southwark Park Rd, SE1
SOUT	108	CSSS75	Copperfield St, Suffolk St, SE1
SOUT	109	CSW85	Courage Brewery (south-west), Park St, Thrale St, SE1
SOUT	110	CW83	Cotton's Wharf, Tooley St, SE1
SOUT	111	CWO84	Cotton's Wharf, Tooley St, SE1
SOUT	112	DHS75	District Heating Scheme, Montague Close, Borough High St, Tooley St, SE1
SOUT	113	DIC89	Dickens Square, Harper Rd, SE1
SOUT	114	EAR90	281–333 Old Kent Rd, Earl Rd, SE1
SOUT	115	EWERST87	Ewer St (railway arches), SE1
SOUT	116	FW83	Fenning's Wharf, 1 London Bridge, SE1
SOUT	117	FW84	Fenning's Wharf, 1 London Bridge, SE1
SOUT	118	GAS88	Gun and Shot Wharf, Tooley St, SE1
SOUT	119	GHD90	Guy's Hospital Development (area D), St Thomas St, SE1
SOUT	120	GHL89	Guy's Hospital Development, St Thomas St, SE1
SOUT	121	GHR82	Guy's Hospital Development (area 7), St Thomas St, SE1
SOUT	122	GHSC77	Guy's Hospital (squash courts), St Thomas St, SE1
SOUT	123	HC74	Hibernia Chambers, Montague Close, SE1
SOUT	124	HDA85	Hay's Dock (block A), Tooley St, SE1
SOUT	125	HEN78	Hendre Rd, SE1
SOUT	126	HIB79	Hibernia Wharf, Montague Close, SE1
SOUT	127	HR77	Harper Rd, SE1
SOUT	128	HR78	Harper Rd, SE1
SOUT	129	HR79	Harper Rd, SE1
SOUT	130	HSW90	Horseshoe Wharf, Clink St, SE1
SOUT	131	HUM90	Old Kent Rd, Dunton Rd, Humphrey St (Road Widening Scheme), SE1
SOUT	132	KHYST82	King's Head Yard (sewer trench), SE1
SOUT	133	LR88	305–319 Lower Rd, SE8
SOUT	134	MBW73	Mark Brown's Wharf, Tooley St, SE1
SOUT	135	MDW88	Bricklayers' Arms, Page's Walk, Mandela Way, SE1
SOUT	136	MON90	Montague Chambers, Montague Close, SE1
SOUT	137	MOR86	Morgan's Lane, Tooley St, SE1
SOUT	138	MOR87	Morgan's Lane, Tooley St, SE1
SOUT	139	MOR88	Morgan's Lane, Tooley St, SE1
SOUT	140	MRC90	6–8 Morocco St, SE1
SOUT	141	NAT90	National Wharf, Bermondsey Wall East, SE16
SOUT	142	NB76	Newington Butts, SE11
SOUT	143	NBW90	New British Wharf and Clink Wharf, Clink St, SE1
SOUT	144	NC81	63–67 Newington Causeway, SE1
SOUT	145	NDRS87	Nelson Dock, Rotherhithe St, SE16
SOUT	146	OKR82	Old Kent Rd (SEGB various trenches), SE1
SOUT	147	OKR90	Old Kent Rd (Canal Bridge Highway Improvement Scheme), SE1
SOUT	148	PEC90	1–83 Peckham High St (rear of), SE15

SOUT	149	PHSCW83	Peckham Hill St, Commercial Way, SE15
SOUT	150	PHW88	Phoenix Wharf, 4 Jamaica Rd, SE1
SOUT	151	PIT88	Pitt's Court, Tooley St, SE1
SOUT	152	PRK90	18 Park St (rear of), SE1
SOUT	153	PW86	Platform Wharf, Cathay St, SE16
SOUT	154	PW89	Platform Wharf, Cathay St, SE16
SOUT	155	PW90	Platform Wharf, Cathay St, SE16
SOUT	156	QBCS75	Queen's Buildings, Collinson St, SE1
SOUT	157	QEN88	Queen Elizabeth St (north), SE1
SOUT	158	QESS88	Queen Elizabeth St (south), SE1
SOUT	159	REH88	Royal Eye Hospital, St George's Circus, SE1
SOUT	160	RS76	Rephidim St, SE1
SOUT	161	RUP88	Rupack St, SE16
SOUT	162	SB76	Silvester Buildings, Silvester St, SE1
SOUT	163	SBH88	Southbridge House, 2–10 Southwark Bridge Rd, SE1
SOUT	164	SCC77	Southwark Cathedral (crypt), Cathedral St, SE1
SOUT	165	SIP88	Skinmarket Place, Bankside, SE1
SOUT	166	SJR90	St James's Estate, St James's Rd, SE16
SOUT	167	SJSPR76	St James (area 1), Southwark Park Rd, SE16
SOUT	168	SKS88	Skipton St, SE1
SOUT	169	SLC76	Southwark Leisure Centre, Elephant and Castle, SE1
SOUT	170	SOH84	St Olaf House (west of), Tooley St, SE1
SOUT	171	SRWS73	Sparrick's Row, Weston St, SE1
SOUT	172	SS73	Swan St, Great Dover St (junction of), SE1
SOUT	173	SSD88	St Saviour's Dock, 24 Shad Thames, SE1
SOUT	174	STS88	21–27 St Thomas St, SE1
SOUT	175	SUR90	The Surrey Theatre, 124 Blackfriars Rd, SE1
SOUT	176	SYM88	Symond's Wharf, Tooley St, SE1
SOUT	177	SYTS75	Shipwright Yard, Tooley St, SE1
SOUT	178	TAN87	9 Tanner St, SE1
SOUT	179	TSGPO76	Trinity St (GPO tunnel), SE1
SOUT	180	TW70	Toppings and Sun Wharves, Tooley St, SE1
SOUT	181	UPP88	Unicorn Passage, Tooley St, SE1
SOUT	182	USA88	16–18 Union St, SE1
SOUT	183	USB88	10–14 Union St, SE1
SOUT	184	VIL88	3 Vine Lane, Tooley St, SE1
SOUT	185	VIN86	Vine Lane, Tooley St, SE1
SOUT	186	VIN87	Vine Lane, Tooley St, SE1
SOUT	187	VIN88	Vine Lane, Tooley St, SE1
SOUT	188	WET89	74–90 Weston St, SE1
SOUT	189	WG87	22–28 White's Grounds, SE1
SOUT	190	WHY85	White Hart Yard, SE1
SOUT		WIN85	Winchester Palace, Clink St, SE1
SOUT	191	WP83	Winchester Palace (Pickford's Wharf D), Winchester Square, SE1
SOUT	192	WP84	Winchester Palace (Pickford's Wharf B), Clink St, SE1
SOUT	193	WP83	Winchester Palace (Pickford's Wharf D), Winchester Square, SE1
SOUT	194	WP83	Winchester Palace (Stave and Rosing's Wharves), Clink St, SE1
SOUT		WP83	Winchester Palace (St Mary Overy Wharf and Dock), Clink St, SE1
SOUT	195	WW78	Willsons Wharf, Battle Bridge Lane, SE1
SOUT	196	WWK87	Willow Walk, Page's Walk, Mandela Way, SE1

22BHS88

Map site: 31
DGLA(S&L): Brian Yule
NGR: TQ 3269 8023
SMR: 091124–6

22 Borough High Street, SE1

Excavation in 1988 in the basement of a standing building revealed Roman deposits sealing late prehistoric flood clays and truncated by pits filled with dark earth. Five Roman building horizons were identified, of clay and timber construction and set back about 2.5m from the NW edge of the Roman road (Roman Road 1) running S from London Bridge. Cutting through the dark earth was a chalk and ragstone wall footing, aligned NE–SW and probably of medieval date.

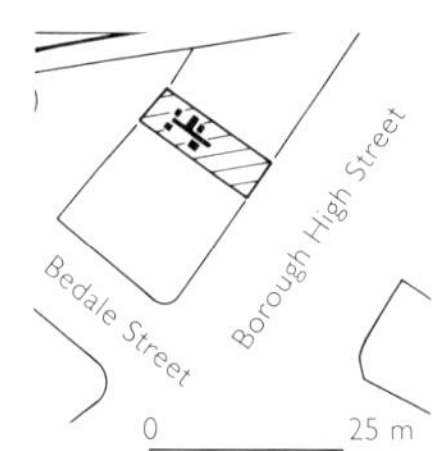

London Archaeol, 6, 1989, 76; *Britannia*, 20, 1989, 309; *Surrey Archaeol Coll*, 80, 1990, 223

38BHS79

Map site: 40
SLAEC: Brian Yule
NGR: TQ 3259 8013

38 Borough High Street, SE1

A watching brief in 1979 revealed late Roman pottery and evidence of dark earth.

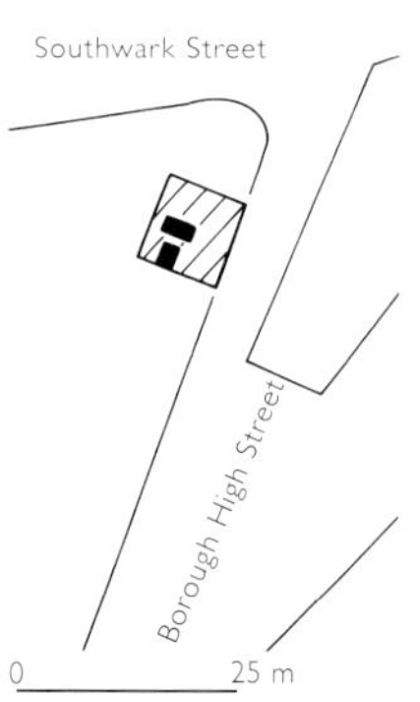

Swain, H, 1988 'Gazetteer of sites', in Hinton, P (ed), *Excavations in Southwark 1973–76, Lambeth 1973–79*, 480 (24)

Shaft outside 57 Borough High Street, SE1

A watching brief in 1982 recorded in section a possible silted-up channel or ditch, floors or surfaces and a major fire horizon.

Swain, H, 1988 'Gazetteer of sites', in Hinton, P (ed), *Excavations in Southwark 1973–76, Lambeth 1973–79*, 480 (25)

57BHS82

Map site: 47
DGLA(S&L): Brian Yule
NGR: TQ 3267 8015

64–70 Borough High Street, SE1

Excavation in 1974, followed by occasional observation in 1975, revealed the W edge of a Roman road (Roman Road 1) leading to London Bridge. A large Roman channel with several phases of revetment and backfilled in the 2nd c was also located.

Britannia, 7, 1976, 351
Graham, A H, 1988 'Excavations at 64–70 Borough High Street', in Hinton, P (ed), *Excavations in Southwark 1973–76, Lambeth 1973–79*, 55–66
SAEC, 1975 'Roman channel at 66 Borough High Street', *London Archaeol*, 2, 277
Swain, H, 1988 'Gazetteer of sites', in Hinton, P (ed), *Excavations in Southwark 1973–76, Lambeth 1973–79*, 480 (26)

64BHS74

Map site: 51
SLAEC: Alan Graham
NGR: TQ 3256 8006
SMR: 090347

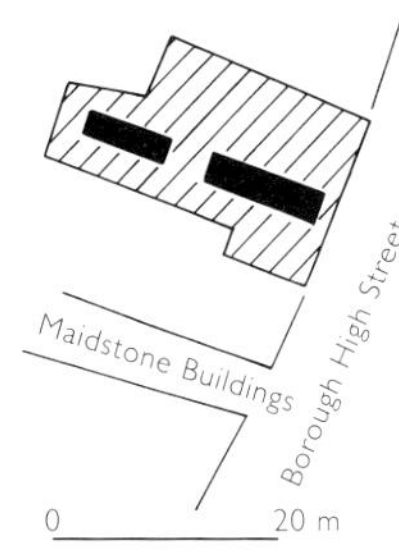

66 Borough High Street, SE1

Excavation in 1975 revealed the SE side of a large Roman channel, aligned NE–SW. Its bank was protected from erosion by a brushwood screen, and was later revetted by wattles supported on large posts; when this collapsed the wattles were replaced by planks. The channel was finally backfilled, probably early in the 2nd c.

London Archaeol, 2, 1976, 372; *Britannia*, 7, 1976, 351
SAEC, 1975 'Roman channel at 66 Borough High Street', *London Archaeol*, 2, 277
Swain, H, 1988 'Gazetteer of sites', in Hinton, P (ed), *Excavations in Southwark 1973–76, Lambeth 1973–79*, 480 (26)

66BHS75

Map site: 53
SLAEC: George Dennis,
Alan Graham
NGR: TQ 3256 8005

78–80 Borough High Street, SE1

A watching brief in 1973 recorded Roman and later deposits.

Swain, H, 1988 'Gazetteer of sites', in Hinton, P (ed), *Excavations in Southwark 1973–76, Lambeth 1973–79*, 480 (27)

78BHS73

Map site: 56
SLAEC: Harvey Sheldon
NGR: TQ 3255 8003
SMR: 090357

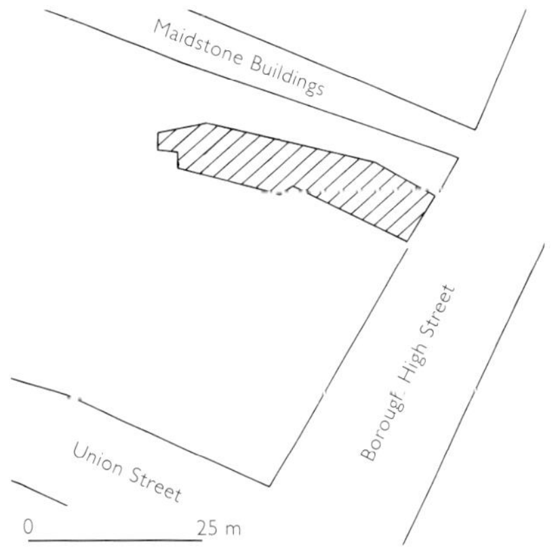

84BHS74

Map site: 58
SLAEC: Alan Graham,
Peter Townsend
NGR: TQ 3255 8002
SMR: 090396

84–86 Borough High Street, SE1

Excavation in 1974 revealed evidence of a Roman road
(Roman Road 1) leading to London Bridge and supported
on a timber corduroy. The road was flanked to the E by an
early Roman building dated to the early–mid-2nd c.

London Archaeol, 2, 1975, 258; *Britannia,* 6, 1975, 270
Graham, A H, & Hinton, P, 1988 '84–6 Borough High Street', in Hinton, P
(ed), *Excavations in Southwark 1973–76, Lambeth 1973–79,* 67–70
Swain, H, 1988 'Gazetteer of sites', in Hinton, P (ed), *Excavations in
Southwark 1973–76, Lambeth 1973–79,* 480 (28)

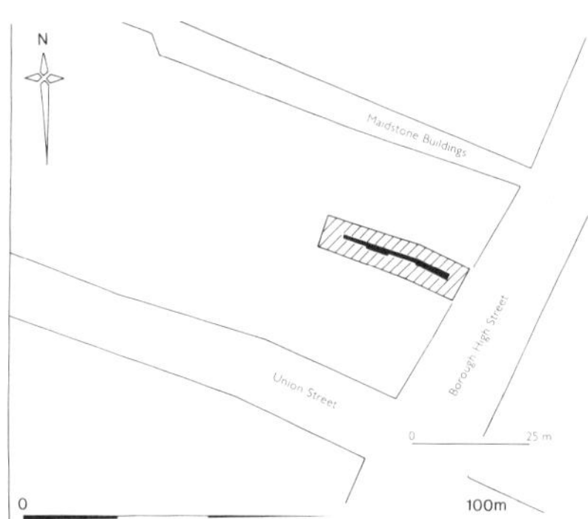

85BHS90

Map site: 59
DGLA(S&L): James Hunter
NGR: TQ 3263 8009
SMR: 090447, 091365–7

85–87 Borough High Street, SE1

Excavation within a lift-shaft and drain trenches in 1990
revealed sands cut by a Roman ditch and sealed by Roman
dumped deposits and a brickearth floor. No evidence was
found of the medieval Tabard Inn, though part of its 17th-c
floor was uncovered.

London Archaeol, 6, 1991, 306; *Post-Medieval Archaeol,* 25, 1991, 132; *Surrey
Archaeol Coll,* 81, 1991–2, 164

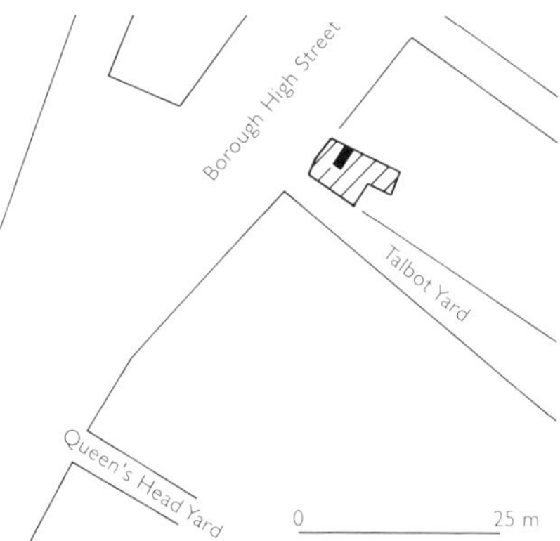

88BHS74

Map site: 60
SLAEC: Brian Yule
NGR: TQ 3254 8002
SMR: 090330

88 Borough High Street, SE1

Excavation in 1975 revealed two phases of Roman building,
the first Flavian and the second perhaps 2nd c. From the
late Roman period to the post-medieval the area may have
been agricultural in character.

London Archaeol, 2, 1975, 258
Swain, H, 1988 'Gazetteer of sites', in Hinton, P (ed), *Excavations in
Southwark 1973–76, Lambeth 1973–79,* 480 (29)
Yule, B, & Hinton, P, 1988 '88 Borough High Street', in Hinton, P (ed),
Excavations in Southwark 1973–76, Lambeth 1973–79, 71–81

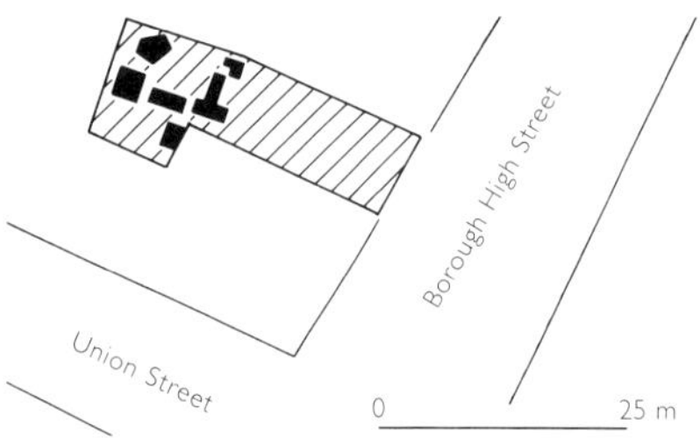

89BHS75

Map site: 61
SLAEC: George Dennis
NGR: TQ 3262 8009
SMR: 090224

89 Borough High Street, SE1

Excavation in 1975 revealed part of a Roman channel with timber revetting, aligned E–W.

London Archaeol, 2, 1976, 372; *Britannia,* 7, 1976, 352
Swain, H, 1988 'Gazetteer of sites', in Hinton, P (ed), *Excavations in Southwark 1973–76, Lambeth 1973–79,* 480 (30)

92–104 Borough High Street, SE1

A watching brief in 1974 revealed topographical evidence only.

Swain, H, 1988 'Gazetteer of sites', in Hinton, P (ed), *Excavations in Southwark 1973–76, Lambeth 1973–79*, 480 (31)

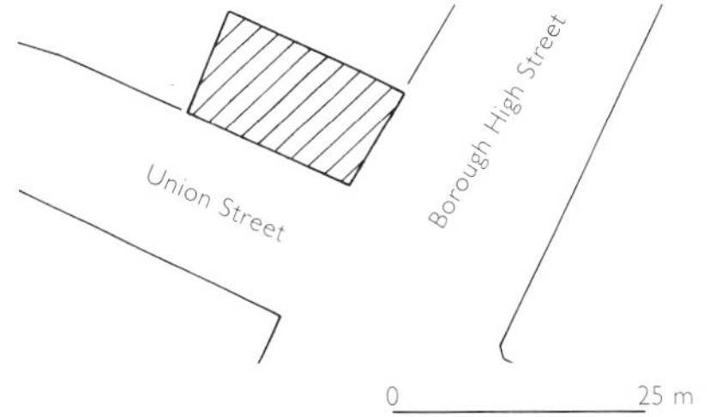

92BHS74

Map site: 63
SLAEC: Harvey Sheldon
NGR: TQ 3252 8000

93–95 Borough High Street, SE1

Excavation in 1974 revealed a stream flowing N–S to the E of the main Roman bridge approach road (Roman Road 1), probably a natural channel with its banks revetted early in the Roman period. Its bed was filled by various layers containing much domestic refuse, some of which had accumulated between c AD70 and 150.

London Archaeol, 2, 1975, 258; *Britannia*, 6, 1975, 270
Bird, H, & Marsh, G, 1978 'Decorated samian', in Sheldon, H, 437–42
Dean, M, 1978 'Organic data', in Sheldon, H, 465–7
Hammerson, M, & Murray, C, 1978 'Other Roman pottery', in Sheldon, H, 440–59
Hartley, K F, 1978 'Stamped mortaria', in Sheldon, H, 459–60
Orton, C, 1978 'Statistical dating of the sequence from trench 2', in Sheldon, H, 460–1
Rixson, D, 1978 'Animal bones', in Sheldon, H, 467–8
Sheldon, H, 1978 'Excavations at 93–95 Borough High Street', in Bird, J, Graham, A H, Sheldon, H, & Townend, P (eds), *Southwark excavations 1972–74*, 423–72
Swain, H, 1988 'Gazetteer of sites', in Hinton, P (ed), *Excavations in Southwark 1973–76, Lambeth 1973–79*, 480 (32)
Townend, P, & Hinton, P, 1978 'Glass', in Sheldon, H, 462
Townend, P, & Hinton, P, 1978 'Small finds', in Sheldon, H, 462–5

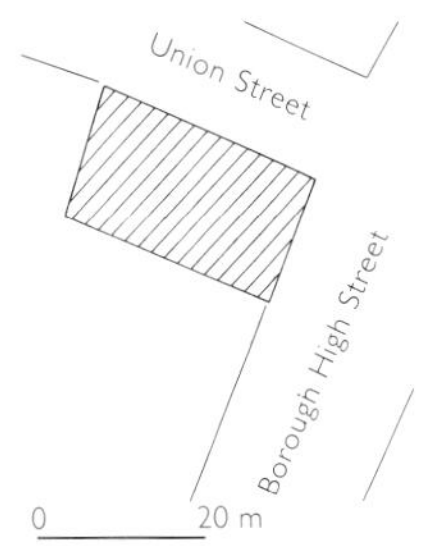

93BHS74

Map site: 64
SLAEC: Harvey Sheldon
NGR: TQ 3261 8008
SMR: 090344

96–104 Borough High Street, SE1

A watching brief in 1974 revealed topographical evidence, and Roman layers including a possible floor and dark earth.

Hammerson, M, & Murray, C, 1978 'Other Roman pottery', in Marsh, G, & Tyers, P, 235
Marsh, G, & Tyers, P, 1978 'Observations at 96–104 Borough High Street', in Bird, J, Graham, A H, Sheldon, H, & Townend, P (eds), *Southwark excavations 1972–74*, 233–5
Swain, H, 1988 'Gazetteer of sites', in Hinton, P (ed), *Excavations in Southwark 1973–76, Lambeth 1973–79*, 480 (33)

96BHS74

Map site: 66
SLAEC: Geoffrey Marsh
NGR: TQ 3253 7998

97–99 Borough High Street, SE1

A watching brief in 1974 recorded a timber revetment and Roman material in waterlaid deposits.

Sheldon, H, 1978 '97–99 Borough High Street', in Bird, J, Graham, A H, Sheldon, H, & Townend, P (eds), *Southwark excavations 1972–74*, 468–72
Swain, H, 1988 'Gazetteer of sites', in Hinton, P (ed), *Excavations in Southwark 1973–76, Lambeth 1973–79*, 480 (34)

97BHS74

Map site: 67
SLAEC: Harvey Sheldon
NGR: TQ 3261 8007

106BHS73

Map site: 2
SLAEC: Irene Schwab
NGR: TQ 3252 7996
SMR: 090334, 090841–3

106–114 Borough High Street, SE1

Excavation in 1973–4 revealed evidence of an early major
Roman road (Roman Road 1), about 7.5m wide, aligned
N–S and built over marshy ground where it was supported
on a raft of timbers in places consisting of two layers, both
lying E–W. Two phases of clay and timber buildings, probably
of mid-2nd-c date, were located on either side of the road,
and the truncated remains of a large pit were revealed,
probably of 11th- or 12th-c date. An early 17th-c chalk
well contained an assemblage of closely datable pottery and
clay pipes.

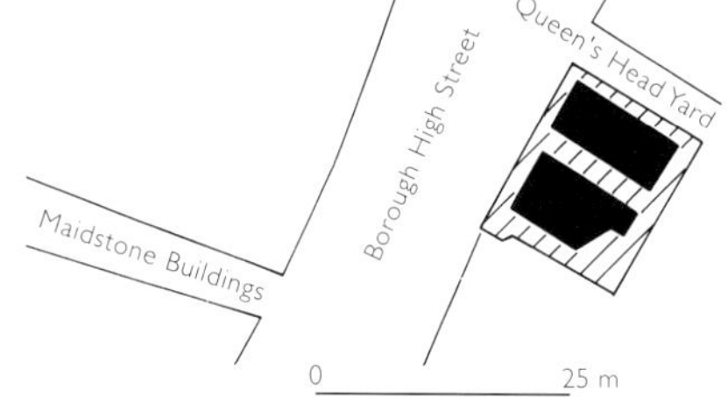

London Archaeol, 2, 1975, 258; *Britannia*, 6, 1975, 270
Barrett, J, 1978 'The prehistoric pottery', in Schwab, I, 197–9
Bird, J, 1978 'Stamped amphorae', in Schwab, I, 211–12
Bird, J, & Marsh, G, 1978 'Decorated samian', in Schwab, I, 199–200
Cresswell, J, 1978 'The flintwork', in Schwab, I, 197
Dean, M, 1978 'Organic data', in Schwab, I, 219–20
Hammerson, M, 1978 'Coins', in Schwab, I, 216
Hammerson, M, & Murray, C, 1978 'Other Roman pottery', in Schwab, I, 201–11
Orton, C, 1978 'Medieval and post-medieval pottery', in Schwab, I, 212–15
Schwab, I, 1978 'Excavations at 106–114 Borough High Street', in Bird, J, Graham, A H, Sheldon, H, & Townend, P (eds), *Southwark excavations 1972–74*, 177–220
Swain, H, 1988 'Gazetteer of sites', in Hinton, P (ed), *Excavations in Southwark 1973–76, Lambeth 1973–79*, 480 (35)
Townend, P, & Hinton, P, 1978 'Glass', in Schwab, I, 215–16
Townend, P, & Hinton, P, 1978 'Small finds', in Schwab, I, 216–19
Walker, S, 1978 'Clay pipes', in Schwab, I, 215

107BHS81

Map site: 3
SLAEC: Brian Yule
NGR: TQ 3259 8005
SMR: 090532, 090860–2

107–115 Borough High Street, SE1

Excavation in 1981–2 close to the Roman bridge approach
road (Roman Road 1) revealed clean alluvial sand crossed
by an early Roman ditch, at right angles to the road, which
drained into a natural channel traversing the site from NE
to SW. Cutting the ditchfills were more than 70 stake-holes
thought to be of Roman date and probably related to
timber buildings which fronted onto the Roman road. In a
small area where the Roman levels had not been truncated,
were found the remains of a 2nd-c clay wall and associated
floors, as well as several cut features including a deep timber-lined well whose fill contained building
material of apparently late 3rd-c date. Medieval cut features were also excavated, and the modern cellar
floors overlay sequences dating back to c 1600.

London Archaeol, 4, 1982, 165; *Britannia*, 13, 1982, 376; *Surrey Archaeol Coll*, 74, 1983, 193
Swain, H, 1988 'Gazetteer of sites' in Hinton, P (ed), *Excavations in Southwark 1973–76, Lambeth 1973–79*, 480 (36)
Yule, B, 1982 'A third-century well group, and the later Roman settlement in Southwark', *London Archaeol*, 4, 243–9

120BHS89

Map site: 7
DGLA(S&L): Mary Alexander
NGR: TQ 3251 7994
SMR: 091277–83

120–124 Borough High Street, SE1

Excavation in 1989 revealed prehistoric features including post-pits and a large ditch aligned E–W.
A complete profile was obtained through the Roman road from London Bridge (Roman Road 1),
represented by a gravel agger surface with small cobbles. On the E side of the road were the remains
of a 1st-c clay and timber building destroyed by fire, which had been used for an industrial purpose,

perhaps smithing, for which there was evidence on the W side of the road. A timber drain cut the W shoulder of the road, and a further timber feature, possibly a large conduit of late or post-Roman date, cut its E side. Fragments of medieval stone foundations were recorded, and a large quantity of pottery vessels of Late Saxon date was recovered, as were medieval and Tudor pots.

London Archaeol, 6, 1990, 192; *Britannia*, 21, 1990, 344; *Medieval Archaeol*, 34, 1990, 184; *Surrey Archaeol Coll*, 80, 1990, 223

124–126 Borough High Street, SE1

124BHS77

Map site: 8
SLAEC: Michael Hammerson
NGR: TQ 3251 7993
SMR: 090846–9

Excavation in 1977 revealed, within natural sands, charcoal and a calcined bone, perhaps the remains of a hearth, and three stake-holes with flint blades of possible Neolithic/Bronze Age date. Cut into the sands was an inhumation burial with legs crossed, perhaps of Iron Age date. The sands were sealed by a soil level containing pottery dating from the Roman conquest period; this was cut by substantial post-holes, probably post-conquest but sealed by a 1st-c Roman road (Roman Road 1). At least two phases of metalling survived, and the S shoulder was cut by a double row of stake-holes parallel to the road and containing large quantities of burnt daub, perhaps from a hearth or kiln. A medieval pit of c 14th-c date and several 18th-c pits were examined.

London Archaeol, 3, 1978, 162; *Britannia*, 9, 1978, 453; *Surrey Archaeol Coll*, 72, 1980, 247
Dean, M, & Hammerson, M, 1980 'Three inhumation burials from Southwark', *London Archaeol*, 4, 17–22
Swain, H, 1988 'Gazetteer of sites', in Hinton, P (ed), *Excavations in Southwark 1973–76, Lambeth 1973–79*, 480 (37)

128–132 Borough High Street, SE1

128BHS74

Map site: 10
SLAEC: Irene Schwab
NGR: TQ 3250 7992
SMR: 090360

A watching brief in 1974 recorded Roman occupation layers including two possible clay floors and a gravel layer covered with charcoal. A second section revealed traces of gravel, possibly the W edge of the road noted nearby (Roman Road 1, see 106BHS73 above), and cut by a pit of unknown date.

Swain, H, 1988 'Gazetteer of sites', in Hinton, P (ed), *Excavations in Southwark 1973–76, Lambeth 1973–79*, 480 (38)

134–138 Borough High Street, SE1

134BHS72

Map site: 11
SLAEC: Harvey Sheldon
NGR: TQ 3248 7992
SMR: 090361, 090844

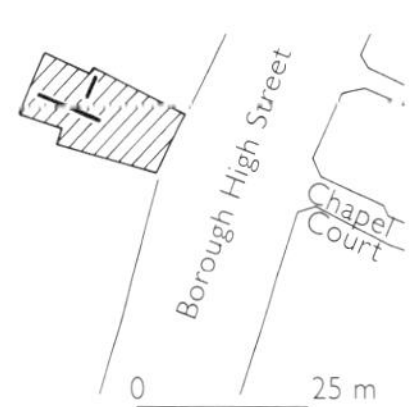

A watching brief in 1972 recorded layers of green and brown earth in section, possibly representing early floors, at which level two ditch-like features were also noted. Above was a flat mortar layer which may have been a floor and which was succeeded by a fine layer of burnt wood, thick at the N end and perhaps representing a collapsed wall timber. Over this in turn was a level of burnt clay, followed by levels of gravels and earth and at least one red clay floor. These levels were cut by a pit containing late Roman pottery. Two large medieval pits were also seen in section.

Swain, H, 1988 'Gazetteer of sites', in Hinton, P (ed), *Excavations in Southwark 1973–76, Lambeth 1973–79*, 480 (39)

169BHS74

Map site: 14
SLAEC: Harvey Sheldon
NGR: TQ 3253 7991
SMR: 090362

169B Borough High Street, SE1

A watching brief in 1974 recorded an undated chalk wall, beneath which was a deposit of dark earth.

Swain, H, 1988 'Gazetteer of sites', in Hinton, P (ed), *Excavations in Southwark 1973–76, Lambeth 1973–79*, 480 (40)

170BHS79

Map site: 15
SLAEC: Laura Schaaf
NGR: TQ 3244 7982
SMR: 090522–4

170–194 Borough High Street, SE1

Excavation in 1979 revealed natural gravel in the NE corner of the site, cut by a wide channel which had eventually silted up, the area becoming marshy in the late 1st c AD. Fifty-two timber stake-holes were located, possibly foundations for a building or jetty, driven into the marsh in the late 1st c and overlaid by layers of dumped earth and domestic refuse of early–mid-2nd-c date. The latter included building material and may have been spread to prepare the ground for building. The dumped deposits were truncated here by a modern cellar floor, but elsewhere were overlaid by dark earth. One of the trenches

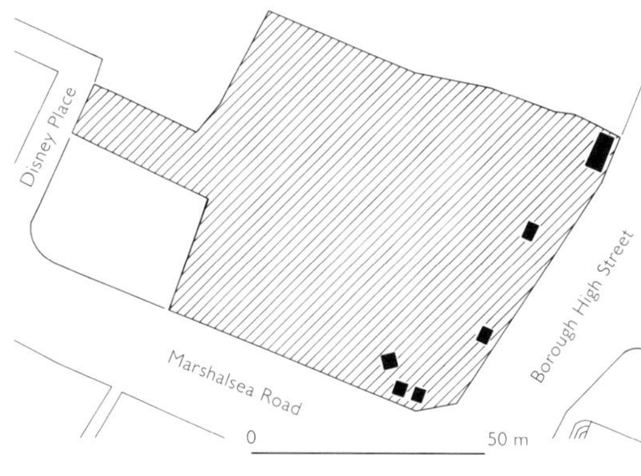

cut through a substantial brick foundation, possibly of Tudor date, which may have formed part of Suffolk Place, a residence of the medieval dukes of Suffolk. A number of post-medieval features were found, including a barrel-lined pit of 18th-c date.

London Archaeol, 3, 1980, 388; Britannia, 11, 1980, 382; Post-Medieval Archaeol, 14, 1980, 208
Swain, H, 1988 'Gazetteer of sites', in Hinton, P (ed), *Excavations in Southwark 1973–76, Lambeth 1973–79*, 480 (41)

175BHS76

Map site: 17
SLAEC: Laura Schaaf
NGR: TQ 3253 7990
SMR: 090345

175–177 Borough High Street, SE1

Excavation in 1976 revealed three Roman channels, two of them revetted and all backfilled in the 1st or 2nd c. Above them was part of a 2nd-c house sealed by late 3rd- or 4th-c deposits. Three 2nd-c wells were also examined.

London Archaeol, 3, 1977, 38; Britannia, 8, 1977, 409; Surrey Archaeol Coll, 72, 1980, 248
Anon, 1976 'Borough High Street Site', Mosaic, London Archaeol, 2, 432
Schaaf, L H, 1976 'Excavations at 175–7 Borough High Street, Southwark', London Archaeol, 3, 3–7
Swain, H, 1988 'Gazetteer of sites', in Hinton, P (ed), *Excavations in Southwark 1973–76, Lambeth 1973–79*, 480 (42)

179BHS89

Map site: 19
DGLA(S&L): Peter Thompson
NGR: TQ 3255 7985
SMR: 091243–5

179–191 Borough High Street, SE1

Excavation in 1989 revealed remains of early Roman clay and timber buildings close to the main Roman road from London Bridge (Roman Road 1), constructed partly over a backfilled revetted channel previously noted in adjacent excavations (see 175BHS76 above). A timber ramp or jetty, consisting of a planked walkway with transverse footholds, projected into the channel, which had been backfilled with domestic rubbish during the 1st–2nd c. Remains of medieval stone buildings were also located.

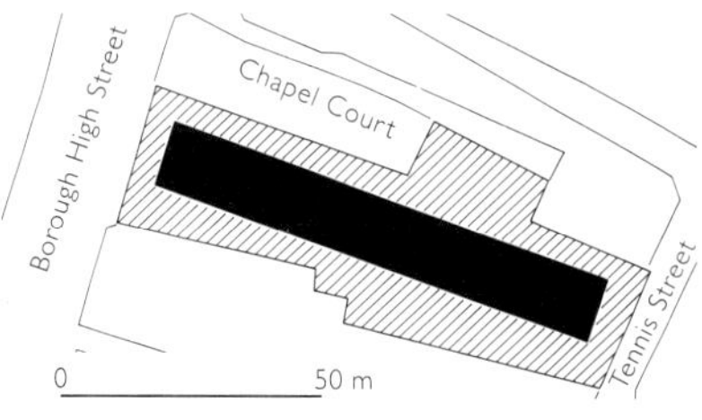

London Archaeol, 6, 1990, 192–3; Britannia, 21, 1990, 344; Medieval Archaeol, 34, 1990, 184; Surrey Archaeol Coll, 80, 1990, 223

199 Borough High Street, SE1

Excavations in 1974–6 revealed, in the W part of the site, four 1st-c ditches perhaps aligned with the N–S Roman road leading to London Bridge (Roman Road 1), and a square wood-lined well which had been burnt in the later 1st c. These were overlaid by later 1st-c floors. To the E, a second complex of late 1st–early 2nd-c ditches was located, into one of which a wooden conduit had been inserted. Several 2nd-c pits and a deposit of 4th-c agricultural soil were recorded at the E limit of the site. A 13th-c tile and chalk structure, probably a cesspit, four 14th–15th-c pits, possibly associated with tanning, two complete 15th-c barrels set into pits, and a brick-lined feature of 17th-c date were also found.

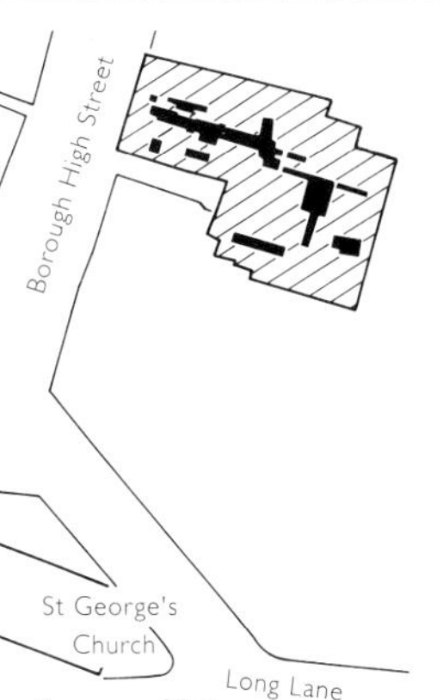

London Archaeol, 2, 1975, 258; 2, 1976, 372; 3, 1977, 38–9; Britannia, 6, 1975, 270; 7, 1976, 352; Surrey Archaeol Coll, 72, 1980, 248

Barrett, J, 1988 'The prehistoric pottery', in Hinton, P, 191

Hassall, M, 1988 'The Roman graffiti', in Hinton, P, 365

Hinton, P (ed), 1988 Excavations in Southwark 1973–76, Lambeth 1973–79

Locker, A, 1988 'The animal bone', in Hinton, P, 427–31

Schaaf, L, 1988 '199 Borough High Street', in Hinton, P, 82–132

Seeley, D, Walker, S, & Orton, C, 1988 'Clay tobacco pipes', in Hinton, P, 366–9

Swain, H, 1988 'Gazetteer of sites', in Hinton, P (ed), Excavations in Southwark 1973–76, Lambeth 1973–79, 480–1 (43)

Turner, D, 1971 'A late medieval and post medieval pottery sequence from 199 Borough High Street, Southwark', Surrey Archaeol Coll, 68, 97–108

Tyers, I, 1988 'Environmental evidence from Southwark and Lambeth', in Hinton, P, 461–71

199BHS74

Map site: 22
SLAEC: Laura Schaaf, Charles Murray
NGR: TQ 3252 7984
SMR: 091015–21

201–205 Borough High Street, SE1

A watching brief in 1975 recorded standing sections during the removal by contractors of all deposits above the flood-plain gravels. Conclusions were consequently limited. Published with 207BHS72.

Swain, H, 1988 'Gazetteer of sites', in Hinton, P (ed), Excavations in Southwark 1973–76, Lambeth 1973–79, 481 (44)

201BHS75

Map site: 24
SLAEC: Eric Ferretti
NGR: TQ 3251 7983

207–211 Borough High Street, SE1

Excavation in 1972 revealed part of a Roman road (Roman Road 1) laid on a timber corduroy and positioned partly across a silted-up channel. Also examined were early Roman drainage ditches and a clay and timber building with possibly associated later stone walls. A 4th-c well, sealed by dark earth, was also recorded. Excavation on the W part of the site revealed a Roman road (Roman Road 1), probably Watling Street, running N–S and presumably joining Stane Street. Marshy ground E of the road was consolidated and settled, probably during the latter part of the 1st c. Published with 201BHS75.

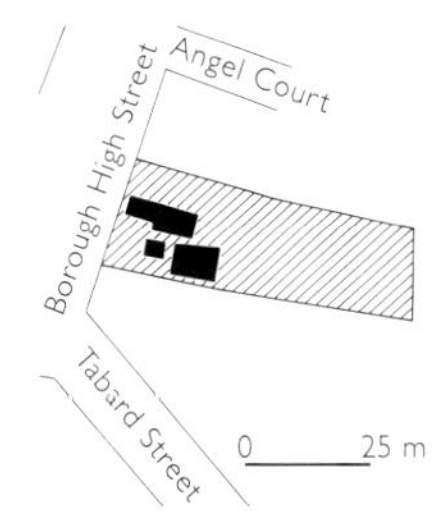

London Archaeol, 2, 1973, 41–2; Britannia, 4, 1973, 307

Bird, J, 1978 'Stamped amphorae', in Ferretti, E, & Graham, A H, 128

Bird, J, & Marsh, G, 1978 'Decorated samian', in Ferretti, E, & Graham, A H, 96–102

Dean, M, 1978 'Organic data', in Ferretti, E, & Graham, A H, 168–70

Ferretti, E, & Graham, A H, 1978 'Excavations at 201–211 Borough High Street', in Bird, J, Graham, A H, Sheldon, H, & Townend, P (eds), Southwark excavations 1972–74, 53–176

Fulford, M G, 1978 'Late colour-coated wares', in Ferretti, E, & Graham, A H, 125–7

207BHS72

Map site: 25
SLAEC: Harvey Sheldon
NGR: TQ 3251 7983
SMR: 090333

Girling, M, 1978 'The insects', in Ferretti, E, & Graham, A H, 170
Hammerson, M, 1978 'Coins', in Ferretti, E, & Graham, A H, 154–6
Hammerson, M, & Murray, C, 1978 'Other Roman pottery', in Ferretti, E, & Graham, A H, 102–25
Jones, A K G, 1978 'The fish', in Ferretti, E, & Graham, A H, 171–2
Orton, C, 1978 'Sequence of medieval and post-medieval pottery', in Ferretti, E, & Graham, A H, 140–6
Rixson, D, 1978 'Animal bones', in Ferretti, E, & Graham, A H, 173–5
Swain, H, 1988 'Gazetteer of sites', in Hinton, P (ed), *Excavations in Southwark 1973–76, Lambeth 1973–79*, 481 (44)
Thorn, J C, 1978 'Medieval and later pottery/Pottery from the medieval pit and well', in Ferretti, E, & Graham, A H, 128–40
Thorn, J, & Thorn, D, 1972 'Heraldic jug', *London Archaeol*, 2, 23
Townend, P, & Hinton, P, 1978 'Glass', in Ferretti, E, & Graham, A H, 151–4
Townend, P, & Hinton, P, 1978 'Small finds', in Ferretti, E, & Graham, A H, 156–68
Watt, R J, 1978 'The human bones', in Ferretti, E, & Graham, A H, 175–6

210BHS90

Map site: 27
DGLA(S&L): Aidan Allen
NGR: TQ 3239 7973
SMR: 091328

210–212 Borough High Street, SE1

A watching brief in 1990 recorded two sections exposed by the construction cut of a modern lift-shaft.

London Archaeol, 6, 1991, 306; Surrey Archaeol Coll, 81, 1991–2, 163

213BHS77

Map site: 28
SLAEC: Robin Densem
NGR: TQ 3249 7981
SMR: 090514–15

213 Borough High Street, SE1

Excavation in 1977, followed by occasional watching briefs, revealed horizontally laid timbers for a causeway, sealed in the fill of a large, deep channel, aligned NW–SE. The make-up and metalling for the Roman bridge approach road (Roman Road 1) lay over the clay and timbers, and traces of Roman activity survived on either side. The Roman levels and a later chalk-lined cesspit were cut by post-medieval cellaring.

London Archaeol, 3, 1978, 162; Britannia, 9, 1978, 453; Surrey Archaeol Coll, 72, 1980, 248
Swain, H, 1988 'Gazetteer of sites', in Hinton, P (ed), *Excavations in Southwark 1973–76, Lambeth 1973–79*, 481 (45)

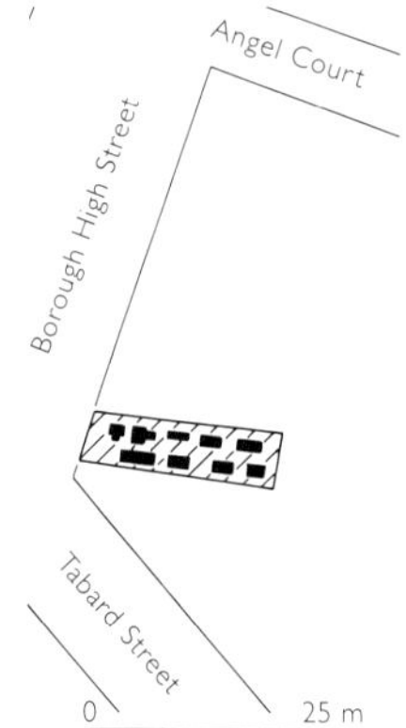

218BHS79

Map site: 29
SLAEC: Eric Ferretti
NGR: TQ 3238 7971
SMR: 090526

218–224 Borough High Street, SE1

A trial excavation in 1979 revealed a possible late medieval ditch at the W end of the site, much disturbed by post-medieval cellaring. A red-tiled cellar floor of probable 18th-c date was overlain by dumped deposits cut by 19th-c pits. One of these, a circular brick-lined structure, contained the personalised crockery of Hinton's Eating House, known to have been established on the site by 1832.

London Archaeol, 3, 1980, 388; Post-Medieval Archaeol, 14, 1980, 208
Swain, H, 1988 'Gazetteer of sites', in Hinton, P (ed), *Excavations in Southwark 1973–76, Lambeth 1973–79*, 481 (46)

223–237 Borough High Street, SE1

Excavation in 1981 and 1982 revealed widespread evidence of quarrying for sand and gravel in the mid–late 1st c, possibly for road building. Subsequently a ditch of late 1st- or early 2nd-c date was dug at right angles to the road (Roman Road 1) leading to Roman London Bridge. This was succeeded by a clay and timber building with a gravelled yard, which appears to have been demolished in the 2nd c. The area was apparently used for agriculture in the later Roman period. Despite the destruction of medieval and later levels by 19th-c cellaring, a number of 13th–14th-c pits and a well were recorded.

London Archaeol, 4, 1982, 165; Britannia, 13, 1982, 376; Surrey Archaeol Coll, 74, 1983, 193
Goffin, R, 1991 'A group of pottery from a medieval pit at 223–227 Borough High Street, Southwark', *London Archaeol, 6*, 315–18
Swain, H, 1988 'Gazetteer of sites', in Hinton, P (ed), *Excavations in Southwark 1973–76, Lambeth 1973–79*, 481 (47)

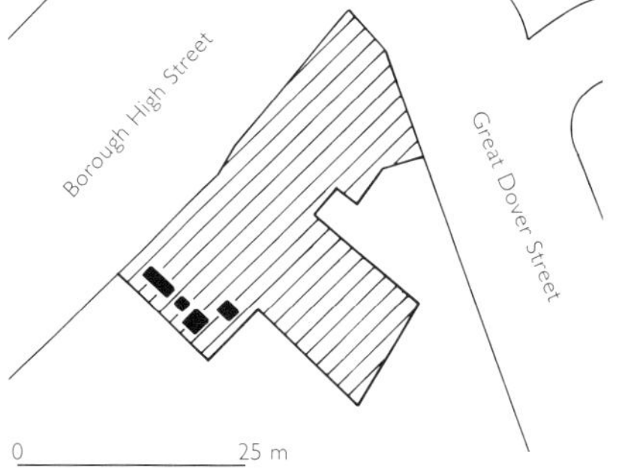

223BHS81

Map site: 30
SLAEC: Peter Hinton, Harvey Sheldon
NGR: TQ 3245 7973
SMR: 090533, 090863

239 Borough High Street, SE1

A watching brief in 1987 recorded a sequence of Roman features cut into natural, at least one of which was probably a quarry pit or ditch associated with the nearby Stane Street (Roman Road 2). One layer consisted of weathered natural sand containing two human bones, perhaps a disturbed burial.

London Archaeol, 5, 1988, 414; Surrey Archaeol Coll, 79, 1989, 185

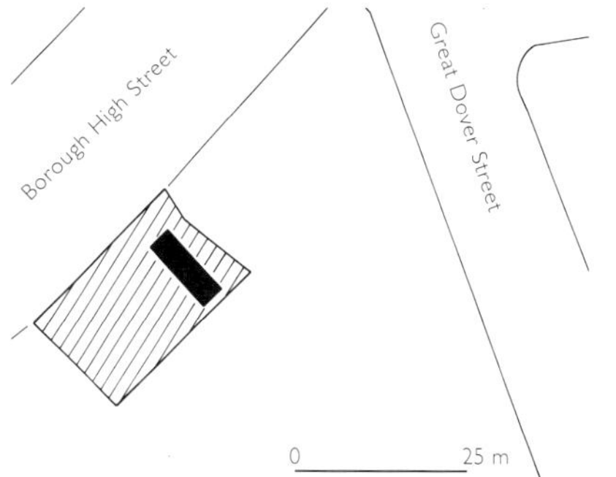

239BHS87

Map site: 33
DGLA(S&L): Carrie Cowan, Hedley Swain
NGR: TQ 3244 7970

244–246 Borough High Street, SE1

Excavation of two areas in 1965 revealed, in one, a silt-filled pit or ditch cut into natural and containing medieval deposits; the sides of the feature coincided with the sides of an alley which superseded it in the 18th c.

Celoria, F S C, & Thorn, J C, 1974 'A medieval deposit from 244–246 Borough High Street, Southwark', *Trans London Middlesex Archaeol Soc, 25*, 264–72

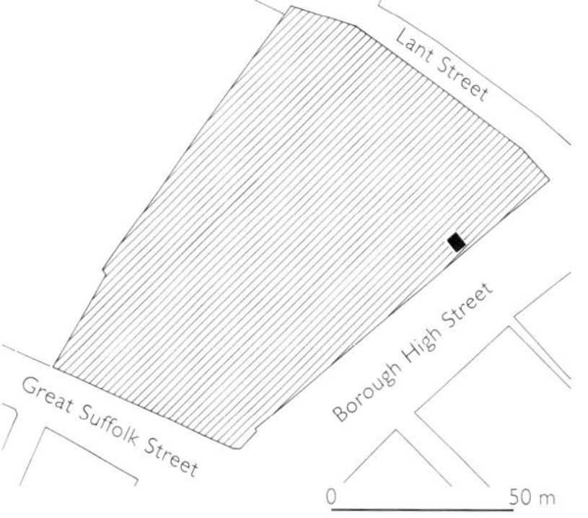

244BHS65

Map site: 34
SLAEC: Francis Celoria
NGR: TQ 3234 7967
SMR: 090342–3

289–299 Borough High Street, SE1

An evaluation excavation in 1990 revealed ploughsoil overlying natural gravel and including a Neolithic/Bronze Age arrowhead. A compacted gravel surface with fragments of limestone and roof tile indicated Roman activity of probable 3rd- and 4th-c date. Post-medieval features included two barrel-lined pits dated to the mid-17th c and a rectangular brick-lined pit containing a large group of mid-18th-c pottery.

London Archaeol, 6, 1991, 306; Britannia, 22, 1991, 273; Post-Medieval Archaeol, 25, 1991, 132; Surrey Archaeol Coll, 81, 1991–2, 163

289BHS90

Map site: 36
DGLA(S&L): Alison Steele
NGR: TQ 3234 7959
SMR: 091358–60

109BR87

Map site: 4
DGLA(S&L): John Roche
NGR: TQ 3136 7974

109–115 Blackfriars Road, SE1

Excavation in 1987 revealed a square-sectioned pit containing late medieval pottery but possibly post-medieval in date. A second pit contained medieval pottery. The earliest find was an unstratified sherd of Early Saxon chaff-tempered pottery. Three parallel linear cut features, approximately on the alignment of the strip field-system recorded on 17th- and 18th-c maps, were also probably medieval. Large pits cutting all earlier features may represent gravel quarries worked in connection with the suburban development of the area after the construction of Blackfriars Bridge in the 1760s. A cast-iron wall plaque was found, bearing the emblem of the Bridge House Trust, former owners of the land.

London Archaeol, 6, 1989, 76; Surrey Archaeol Coll, 80, 1990, 221

245BR87

Map site: 35
DGLA(S&L):
Nicholas Shepherd
NGR: TQ 3168 8042
SMR: 091149–51

245 Blackfriars Road, SE1

Excavation in 1987 revealed the edge of a gravel island, overlain by an agricultural soil containing burnt flints and fragments of Iron Age and Roman pottery. A large N–S channel or ditch was cut through the soil in the late 16th c, and preserved in the silts were two timber base-plates for the support of a small trestle bridge. Two similar base-plates overlay them, showing that the bridge had been replaced at least once. A simple timber revetment was inserted along the W side of the channel, its construction including the reused planking of a 16th–17th-c boat. By the mid-18th c the channel had become blocked, and the bridge was replaced by a road carried on a pile platform. In the late 18th c the road went out of use following a major reorganisation of local property boundaries and the construction of warehouses facing the new approach road to Blackfriars Bridge.

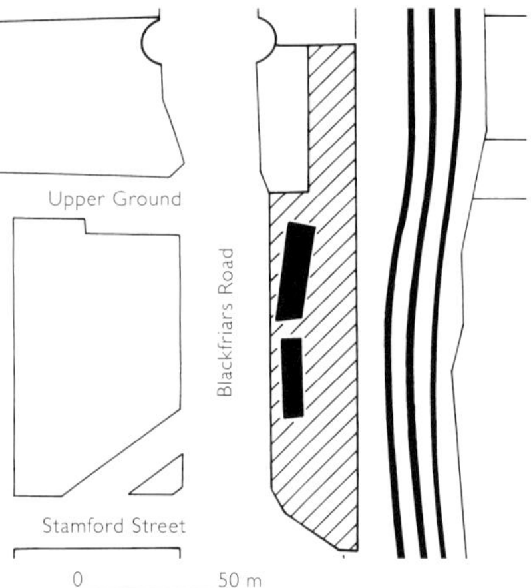

London Archaeol, 5, 1988, 414; Post-Medieval Archaeol, 22, 1988, 207; Surrey Archaeol Coll, 79, 1989, 186

5BS87

Map site: 48
DGLA(S&L): Julian Bowsher
NGR: TQ 3240 8045
SMR: 091144–7

5–15 Bankside, SE1

Excavation in 1987 revealed flooded and reclaimed marshland, and drainage channels of medieval date. Parts of the 14th-c and later rear wall of a property on Bankside were recorded, as was the general development of the riverbank in the 14th c. A timber revetment incorporating reused planking from a medieval clinker-built boat was located some 10m S of the modern bank. This had been subject to erosion by flooding, which had left a series of silt deposits on which chalk rubble had been dumped to form the foundations for a 14th-c stone riverwall, 4m to the N of its predecessor. Part of what was probably a 17th-c road surface was also recorded.

London Archaeol, 5, 1988, 414; Medieval Archaeol, 32, 1988, 251; Surrey Archaeol Coll, 79, 1989, 187

37–46 Bankside, SE1

Excavation in 1987 exposed the tops of at least three parallel E–W revetments of possible late medieval and post-medieval date. Incorporated into the timberwork were reused parts of Tudor wheelbarrows.

London Archaeol, 5, 1988, 414; 5, 1987, 277; *Medieval Archaeol,* 31, 1987, 132; 32, 1988, 252; *Post-Medieval Archaeol,* 22, 1988, 207; *Surrey Archaeol Coll,* 78, 1987, 145; 79, 1989, 187

37BS87

Map site: 39
DGLA(S&L): Peter Thompson
NGR: TQ 3218 8051
SMR: 090678, 091148

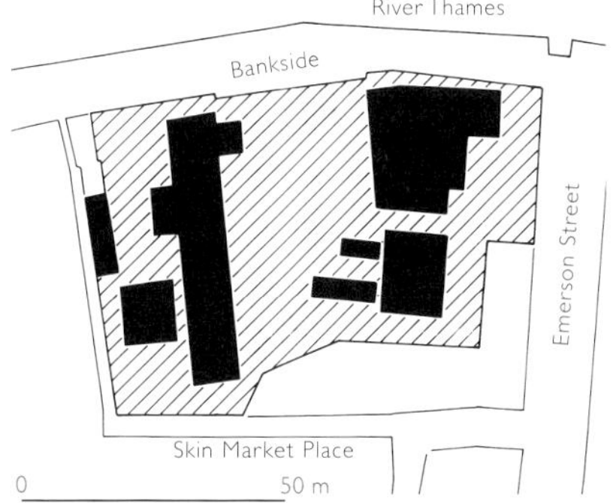

42–44 Bermondsey Street, SE1

A watching brief in 1986 revealed evidence of natural topography only.

Swain, H, 1988 'Gazetteer of sites', in Hinton, P (ed), *Excavations in Southwark 1973–76, Lambeth 1973–79,* 480 (22)

42BS86

Map site: 42
DGLA(S&L): George Dennis
NGR: TQ 3318 7985

105–106 Grange Road, SE1

A watching brief in 1977 recorded evidence of natural topography only.

Swain, H, 1988 'Gazetteer of sites', in Hinton, P (ed), *Excavations in Southwark 1973–76, Lambeth 1973–79,* 482 (93)

105GRA77

Map site: 1
SLAEC: Michael Hammerson
NGR: TQ 3374 7895

170–176 Grange Road, SE1

An evaluation excavation in 1989 located in the SW corner of the precinct of Bermondsey Abbey revealed a pit containing quantities of Late Iron Age/early Roman material, and a series of linear trenches containing Roman finds. A square pit was located, constructed of horn cores and probably of 18th-c date.

London Archaeol, 6, 1990, 193; *Britannia,* 21, 1990, 345; *Surrey Archaeol Coll,* 80, 1990, 225

170GRA89

Map site: 16
DGLA(S&L): Alison Steele
NGR: TQ 3351 7917
SMR: 091284–6

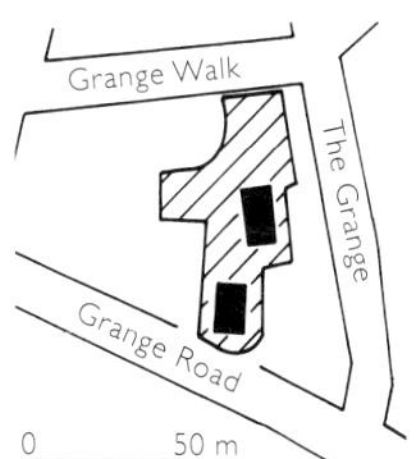

20–26 London Bridge Street, SE1

A watching brief in 1975 recorded no archaeological features, apart from a 'post-Roman' silt sequence.

Swain, H, 1988 'Gazetteer of sites', in Hinton, P (ed), *Excavations in Southwark 1973–76, Lambeth 1973–79,* 483 (137)

20LBS75

Map site: 26
SLAEC: Harvey Sheldon
NGR: TQ 3282 8018

175LL81

Map site: 18
SLAEC: Michael Hammerson
NGR: TQ 3297 7955
SMR: 091232

175–177 Long Lane, Weston Street, SE1

A watching brief in 1981 recorded a wide channel, and Roman and medieval ditches.

Swain, H, 1988 'Gazetteer of sites', in Hinton, P (ed), *Excavations in Southwark 1973–76, Lambeth 1973–79*, 483 (138)

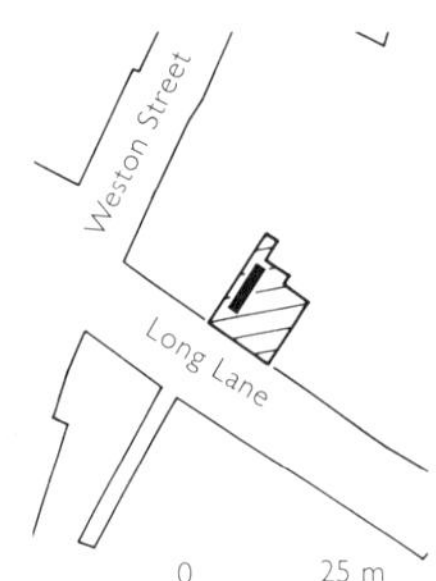

180LL80

Map site: 21
SLAEC: Eric Ferretti
NGR: TQ 3297 7952
SMR: 090527–8

180–196 Long Lane, SE1

An excavation in 1980 located three ditches containing material of early Roman date and cutting natural sand in the SW part of the site. Two were parallel, aligned N–S, and the third crossed them at right angles. A number of pits of medieval and post-medieval date were found, some of them probably gravel quarries.

London Archaeol, 4, 1981, 49; *Britannia*, 12, 1981, 353

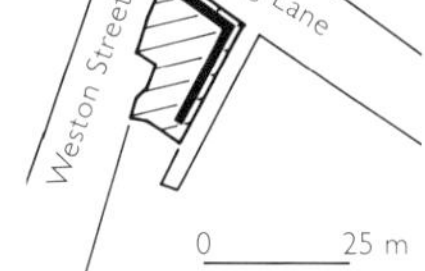

93LR84

Map site: 65
DGLA(S&L): Robin Densem
NGR: TQ 3185 7942

87–100 London Road, SE1

An investigation of 15 testpits in 1984 produced no evidence of the Roman bridge approach road (Roman Road 1), most of the material being post-medieval.

6MSRD88

Map site: 55
DGLA(S&L): Brian Yule
NGR: TQ 3238 7981

6–8 Marshalsea Road, SE1

A watching brief in 1988 recorded natural gravels capped by sand at the SW end of the site and sloping down to the NE. The slope was probably the result of truncation by the late prehistoric channel observed to the E of the site (see 170BHS79, 201BHS75, 213BHS77 above). Evidence of waterlaid deposits and dark earth was noted. Two wall footings were also observed, aligned NE–SW and composed of packed chalk rubble, probably part of the remains of Tudor Suffolk Place.

684OKR86

Map site: 54
DGLA(S&L): Nicholas Shepherd
NGR: TQ 3465 7765

684–698 Old Kent Road, SE15

A trial excavation in 1986 revealed a natural soil profile turned over to agricultural or garden use in the late 18th or early 19th c.

London Archaeol, 5, 1987, 277; *Surrey Archaeol Coll*, 78, 1987, 146
Swain, H, 1988 'Gazetteer of sites', in Hinton, P (ed), *Excavations in Southwark 1973–76, Lambeth 1973–79*, 484 (164)

806–814 Old Kent Road, SE15

A watching brief in 1982 recorded topographical evidence only.

Swain, H, 1988 'Gazetteer of sites', in Hinton, P (ed), *Excavations in Southwark 1973–76, Lambeth 1973–79*, 484 (165)

806OKR82

Map site: 57
SLAEC: Derek Seeley
NGR: TQ 3501 7741

28 Park Street, SE1

Excavation in 1984 exposed the Roman foreshore at the N end of the site, with several phases of erosion and deposition of which the earliest was represented by waterlaid clays. These contained seven timber piles, perhaps part of a jetty or landing-stage, and were overlaid by dumps of building materials covered with deposits of dark earth. At the S end of the site, on higher and drier ground, were recorded several walls and floors of the Roman period, as well as several medieval channels of which the largest ran E–W, its S bank revetted by at least 35 stakes. A number of post-medieval pits were also excavated.

London Archaeol, 5, 1985, 65–6; *Britannia,* 16, 1985, 298; *Medieval Archaeol,* 29, 1985, 178; *Surrey Archaeol Coll,* 77, 1986, 224
Swain, H, 1988 'Gazetteer of sites', in Hinton, P (ed), *Excavations in Southwark 1973–76, Lambeth 1973–79*, 484 (169)
Cowan, C, in prep. *The development of north-west Roman Southwark: excavations at Courage's Brewery 1974–1990*

28PS84

Map site: 37
SLAEC: Robin Densem
NGR: TQ 3248 8031
SMR: 090899–902

38–42 Southwark Bridge Road, SE1

Archaeological salvage work in 1980 recorded a Roman timber revetment consisting of pile-driven oak posts with horizontal planks behind them, set into a marsh deposit. It probably bordered a channel to the W, and formed part of a land reclamation scheme to contain the marsh and drain the ground. Dating evidence from behind the revetment suggests that it was not constructed before the late 3rd c.

London Archaeol, 4, 1981, 49; *Britannia,* 12, 1981, 353
Swain, H, 1988 'Gazetteer of sites', in Hinton, P (ed), *Excavations in Southwark 1973–76, Lambeth 1973–79*, 485 (201)

38SBR79

Map site: 41
DGLA(S&L): George Dennis
NGR: TQ 3227 8023
SMR: 090530

99–103 Southwark Bridge Road, SE1

A watching brief in 1978 revealed evidence of natural topography only.

Swain, H, 1988 'Gazetteer of sites', in Hinton, P (ed), *Excavations in Southwark 1973–76, Lambeth 1973–79*, 484 (202)

99SBR78

Map site: 68
SLAEC: Peter Hinton
NGR: TQ 3227 8001

179SBR80

Map site: 20
SLAEC: Michael Hammerson
NGR: TQ 3209 7973

179 Southwark Bridge Road, SE1

A watching brief in 1980 revealed no archaeological features.

Swain, H, 1988 'Gazetteer of sites', in Hinton, P (ed), *Excavations in Southwark 1973–76, Lambeth 1973–79*, 484 (203)

15SKS80

Map site: 13
DGLA(S&L): Carrie Cowan,
Martin Dean, David Beard,
George Dennis
NGR: TQ 3252 8011
SMR: 090824–7

15–23 Southwark Street (Calverts Buildings), SE1

Excavation in 1980–4 and 1986 revealed features indicative of activity from at least the Beaker period. Use of the area in the later prehistoric period was shown by a number of Iron Age/early Roman gullies. These were succeeded by a substantial Flavian masonry building of official or public character, followed in turn by two phases of clay and timber buildings, perhaps refurbishments, and masonry additions made in the mid-2nd c. Towards the end of the Roman period the area was used as an inhumation cemetery. Dark earth deposits overlay the Roman sequence and were truncated by several medieval and post-medieval pits. A 17th-c masonry building and a clay pipe kiln were also examined. (This site is also known as CB80.)

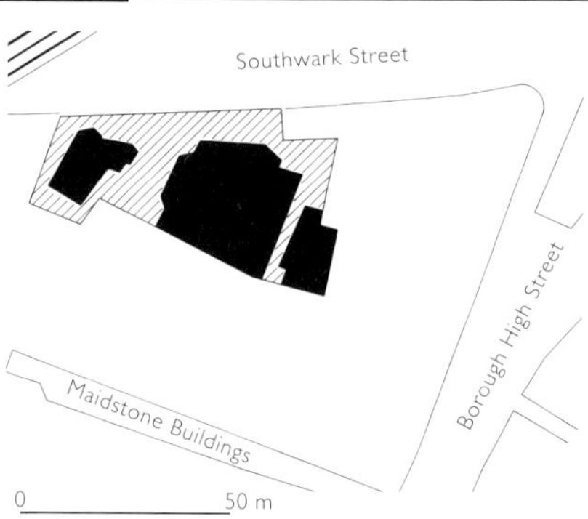

London Archaeol, 4, 1981, 49; 4, 1982, 165; 4, 1984, 290; 4, 1984, 389; 5, 1985, 66; 5, 1987, 276; *Britannia*, 12, 1981, 353; 13, 1982, 377; 14, 1983, 313; 15, 1984, 310; 16, 1985, 298; *Medieval Archaeol*, 25, 1981, 211; 29, 1985, 179; 31, 1987, 132; *Surrey Archaeol Coll*, 74, 1983, 193; 75, 1984, 271; 76, 1985, 129; 77, 1986, 225; 78, 1987, 145

Anon, 1982 'Southwark site continues', Mosaic, *London Archaeol*, 4, 1982, 224

Beard, D, 1982 'Southwark Street excavations', *Rescue News*, 26, 4

Beard, D, & Cowan, C, 1988 'Excavations at 15–23 Southwark Street', *London Archaeol*, 5, 375–81

Bird, J, 1992 'The samian wares', in Cowan, C, 77–80

Burglass, J, 1992 'Shellfish', in Cowan, C, 171

Cotton, J, 1992 'The struck flint', in Cowan, C, 62–7

Cowan, C, 1992 'A possible *mansio* in Roman Southwark: excavations at 15–23 Southwark Street, 1980–86', *Trans London Middlesex Archaeol Soc*, 43, 3–191

Crowley, N, 1992 'Building material', in Cowan, C, 144–57

Dickinson, B, 1992 'Stamped samian', in Cowan, C, 80–1

Goffin, R, 1992 'The wall plaster', in Cowan, C, 157–64

Hammerson, M, 1992 'Coins', in Cowan, C, 137–44

Hammerson, M, 1992 'Roman pottery', in Cowan, C, 70–7

Henig, M, 1992 'Intaglios', in Cowan, C, 119–20

Locker, A, 1992 'Fish bones', in Cowan, C, 170

Pearson, E, & Giorgi, J, 1992 'The plant remains', in Cowan, C, 165–70

Pipe, A, & Rackham, J, 1992 'The mammal and bird bones', in Cowan, C, 171–6

Rackham, J, 1992 'Introduction' to 'Environmental evidence', in Cowan, C, 164–5

Shepherd, J, 1992 'The glass', in Cowan, C, 120–36

Stevenson, J, 1992 'Copper alloy objects', in Cowan, C, 82–97

Stevenson, J, 1992 'Iron objects', in Cowan, C, 97–105

Stevenson, J, 1992 'Lead and lead alloys', in Cowan, C, 105

Stevenson, J, 1992 'Miscellaneous objects', in Cowan, C, 118–19

Stevenson, J, 1992 'Objects of jet and shale', in Cowan, C, 111–13

Stevenson, J, 1992 'Stone and marble', in Cowan, C, 113–15

Stevenson, J, 1992 'The registered finds', in Cowan, C, 81–2

Stevenson, J, 1992 'Worked bone', in Cowan, C, 106–11

Swain, H, 1988 'Gazetteer of sites', in Hinton, P (ed), *Excavations in Southwark 1973–76, Lambeth 1973–79*, 484 (208)

Swain, H, 1992 'Introduction' to 'The finds', in Cowan, C, 61–2

Swain, H, 1992 'Prehistoric pottery', in Cowan, C, 67–70

Tyres, I, 1992 'Dendrochronology: tree-ring analysis of Roman timbers', in Cowan, C, 176–81

Waldron, T, 1992 'Human remains', in Cowan, C, 181–3

Wardle, A, & Groves, J, 1992 'Ceramic objects', in Cowan, C, 115–18

Williams, D, 1992 'Calcite', in Cowan, C, 115

52–54 Southwark Street, SE1

Excavation in 1989 revealed a revetted channel, its bank
sloping to the S. The channel contained Roman demolition
debris including painted wall plaster, and the revetment
appears to have had two phases of construction. Robber
trenches marked the foundations of a Roman building
which postdated the channel and was partly built over it.
A chalk-lined well containing post-medieval pottery was
also recorded.

London Archaeol, 6, 1990, 193; *Britannia*, 21, 1990, 344; *Surrey Archaeol Coll*, 80,
1990, 221

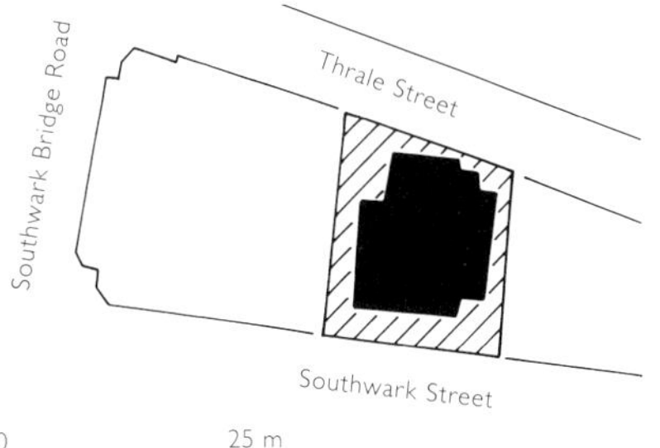

52SOS89

Map site: 46
DGLA(S&L): Kieron Heard
NGR: TQ 3232 8016
SMR: 091246–8

2 Southwark Street, 1A Bedale Street, SE1

Excavation in 1985 revealed evidence of the early phases of the Roman
approach road to London Bridge (Roman Road 1). W of the road and parallel to
it was located a wood-lined drain alongside a robbed stone wall. In the W half of
the site the remains of two superimposed clay and timber buildings of late
1st–2nd-c date survived, the earlier structure having burnt down. All the later
Roman ground surfaces were truncated by post-medieval cellaring. Evidence of
medieval occupation was limited to deep features including a large E–W aligned
ditch and a rectangular chalk cesspit with fill dating to the 15th–16th c, perhaps
the only surviving feature of a medieval tenement fronting Borough High Street.

London Archaeol, 5, 1986, 163; *Britannia*, 17, 1986, 409; *Medieval Archaeol*, 30, 1986, 143; *Surrey Archaeol Coll*, 78, 1987, 145
Swain, H, 1988 'Gazetteer of sites', in Hinton, P (ed), *Excavations in Southwark 1973–76, Lambeth 1973–79*, 480 (20)

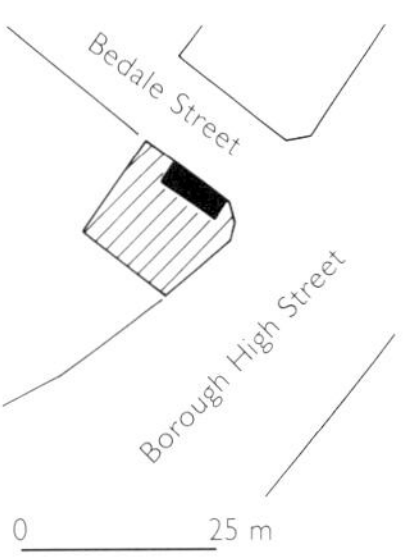

2SSBS85

Map site: 38
DGLA(S&L): George Dennis,
Derek Seeley, Robin Densem
NGR: TQ 3268 8020
SMR: 090701–3

5–7 Southwark Street, SE1

A watching brief in 1973 recorded in section sand cut by Roman and later features.

Swain, H, 1988 'Gazetteer of sites', in Hinton, P (ed), *Excavations in Southwark 1973–76, Lambeth 1973–79*, 485 (206)

5SS73

Map site: 49
SLAEC: Harvey Sheldon
NGR: TQ 3258 8013
SMR: 090369

10–16 Southwark Street, SE1

A watching brief in 1981 recorded possible Roman clay and
timber buildings.

Swain, H, 1988 'Gazetteer of sites', in Hinton, P (ed), *Excavations in
Southwark 1973–76, Lambeth 1973–79*, 485 (207)

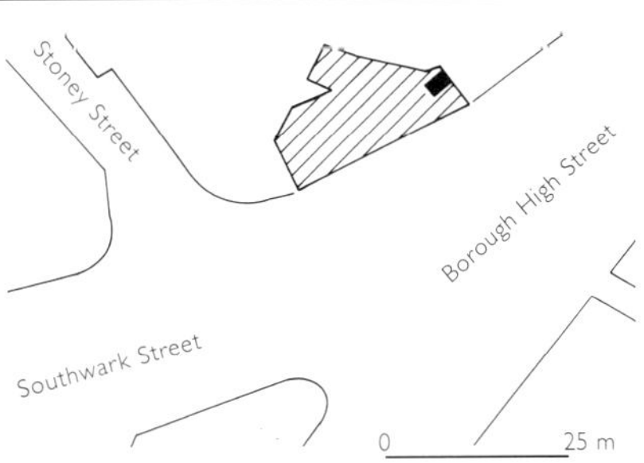

10SS81

Map site: 5
SLAEC: Michael Hammerson
NGR: TQ 3265 8018

48SS89

Map site: 44
DGLA(S&L): Wendy Rogers
NGR: TQ 3234 8017

48 Southwark Street, SE1

A watching brief in 1989 recorded the base of a 19th-c well and some wooden posts.

64SS74

Map site: 52
SLAEC: Harvey Sheldon
NGR: TQ 3222 8019

64 Southwark Street, SE1

A watching brief in 1974 recorded Roman deposits in section; those observed at the N limit of the site, if also Roman, suggest that the waterlevel had risen in the later Roman c, covering the site until well into the post-Roman period.

Swain, H, 1988 'Gazetteer of sites', in Hinton, P (ed), *Excavations in Southwark 1973–76, Lambeth 1973–79*, 485–6 (209)

128SS76

Map site: 9
SLAEC: Michael Hammerson
NGR: TQ 3183 8031

128–130 Southwark Street, SE1

A watching brief in 1976 recorded a channel running S across the site and perhaps aligned SW. Also noted was post-medieval dumping, which produced pottery.

Swain, H, 1988 'Gazetteer of sites', in Hinton, P (ed), *Excavations in Southwark 1973–76, Lambeth 1973–79*, 486 (210)

1STS74

Map site: 23
SLAEC: George Dennis,
Laura Schaaf
NGR: TQ 3273 8019

1–7 St Thomas Street, SE1

Excavation in 1974 revealed a 2nd-c building and a number of pits, finds from which included shoes, textiles, writing tablets and a gemstone. Remains of a substantial building of a later date were also found.

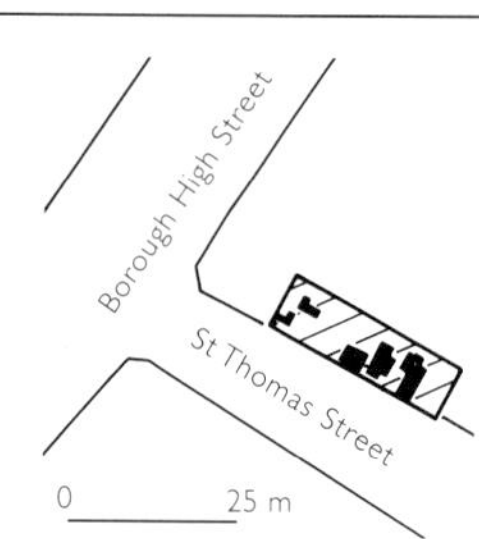

London Archaeol, 2, 1975, 258; *Britannia,* 6, 1975, 270
Bailey, J, & Watson, J, 1978 'The Roman pigments', in Dennis, G, 407
Bird, J, 1978 'Stamped amphorae', in Dennis, G, 376–8
Bird, J, & Marsh, G, 1978 'Decorated samian', in Dennis, G, 333–7
Dean, M, 1978 'Organic data', in Dennis, G, 410
Dennis, G, 1978 'Excavations at 1–7 St Thomas Street', in Bird, J, Graham, A H, Sheldon, H, &
    Townend, P (eds), *Southwark excavations 1972–74,* 291–422
Dennis, G, & Schaaf, L, 1975 'A Roman building at St Thomas Street, Southwark', *London Archaeol,* 2, 270–2
Eames, E, 1978 'Medieval floor tiles', in Dennis, G, 386–7
Girling, M, 1978 'Insects from pits F28 and F29', in Dennis, G, 414
Hammerson, M, 1978 'Coins', in Dennis, G, 390
Hammerson, M, & Murray, C, 1978 'Other Roman pottery', in Dennis, G, 337–75
Henig, M, 1975 '"Eagle and standards" intaglio from St Thomas's St Southwark', *London Archaeol,* 2, 243
Jones, A K G, 1978 'The fish remains', in Dennis, G, 414–16
Orton, C, 1978 'The medieval and later pottery', in Dennis, G, 378–86
Rixson, D, 1978 'Animal bones', in Dennis, G, 418–22
Spencer, P J, 1975 'St Thomas Street environmental work: interim report', *London Archaeol,* 2, 273–4
Swain, H, 1988 'Gazetteer of sites', in Hinton, P (ed), *Excavations in Southwark 1973–76, Lambeth 1973–79*, 485 (192)
Townend, P, & Hinton, P, 1978 'Glass', in Dennis, G, 387–90
Townend, P, & Hinton, P, 1978 'Small finds', in Dennis, G, 390–405
Wild, J P, 1978 'The textiles', in Dennis, G, 405–7
Willcox, G H, 1978 'Seeds from the late 2nd-century pit F28', in Dennis, G, 411–13

4–26 St Thomas Street, SE1

4 S T S 8 2

Map site: 45
DGLA(S&L): Peter Hinton,
Derek Seeley
NGR: TQ 3274 8016
SMR: 090883–7

Excavation in 1982 close to the Roman London Bridge approach road (Roman Road 1) revealed several prehistoric pits, flint tools and Iron Age pottery, while three early Roman ditches were located running N–S across the site and a timber structure was uncovered at its E end. To the W, nearer the road, was a clay and timber building which had been enlarged in the 2nd c. The N end of the cellar of a large ragstone building on pile foundations was examined, revealing a pillar base and possible evidence of a flight of steps; a contemporaneous well alongside was backfilled in the 3rd c. Two other square, timber-lined wells were also found. Many pits of 13th-c and later date were excavated, and the remains of a medieval or early post-medieval building were recorded, shown in the graveyard of St Thomas's Hospital on Rocque's map (1746) and in an early 19th-c watercolour. A Tudor building with a finely built stone and tile fireplace and a small garderobe were also recorded.

London Archaeol, 4, 1984, 290; Britannia, 14, 1983, 313; Medieval Archaeol, 27, 1983, 196; Surrey Archaeol Coll, 75, 1984, 271

11–19 St Thomas Street, SE1

1 1 S T S 7 7

Map site: 6
SLAEC: George Dennis,
Wendy McIsaac
NGR: TQ 3280 8017
SMR: 090999–1007

Excavation in 1977 revealed sands apparently disturbed by root action and containing sherds of possible Iron Age date. The sands were overlain by silts of probable pre-Roman–Roman date, and the area was probably waterlogged before being levelled with rubble for a later Roman building, of which a ragstone footing and mortar floor survived. Above this were pits, further silt and a possible agricultural soil layer. One of several gullies contained pottery of Pingsdorf type and a halfpenny of Alfred. The substantial stone walls of a stone cellar or undercroft were revealed, probably of later medieval date and almost certainly part of St Thomas's Hospital: at one end were external buttresses and a finely built relieving arch, apparently intended to carry a considerable weight, perhaps the base of a tower. The medieval structure was superseded by a substantial brick building, probably part of the 16th-c rebuilding of the hospital. Subsequent building at the hospital resulted in the progressive levelling of the site.

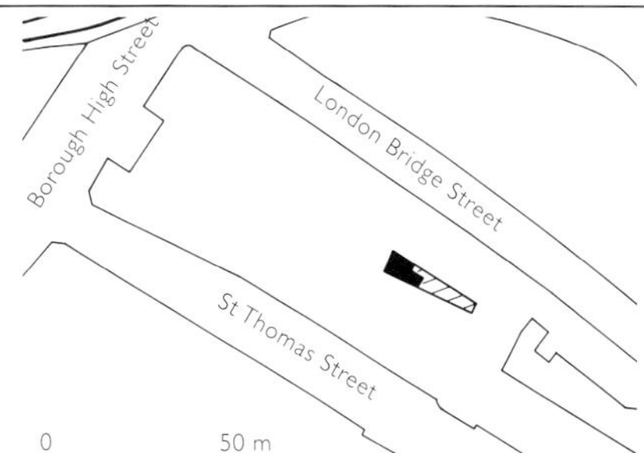

London Archaeol, 3, 1978, 162; Britannia, 9, 1978, 455; Post-Medieval Archaeol, 12, 1978, 113; Surrey Archaeol Coll, 72, 1980, 248

60–68 St Thomas Street, SE1

6 0 S T S 8 2

Map site: 50
SLAEC: Michael Hammerson
NGR: TQ 3306 7996

A watching brief in 1982 recorded thick waterlaid deposits within the top of which was a dump of animal bone, and two sherds of Guy's type ware perhaps indicating a Tudor date.

44–46 Tooley Street, SE1

4 4 T S 8 6

Map site: 43
DGLA(S&L): Brian Yule
NGR: TQ 3300 8023

A watching brief in 1986 recorded a post-medieval brick-lined drain built over a medieval stone-built drain, both aligned E–W. Other undated evidence, including gravel metalling, was also recorded from an exposed section.

8US74

Map site: 62
SLAEC: Geoffrey Marsh
NGR: TQ 3251 8001

8–10 Union Street, SE1

Excavation in 1974 revealed a 1st-c clay and timber building cut by an oak-lined 3rd-c well.

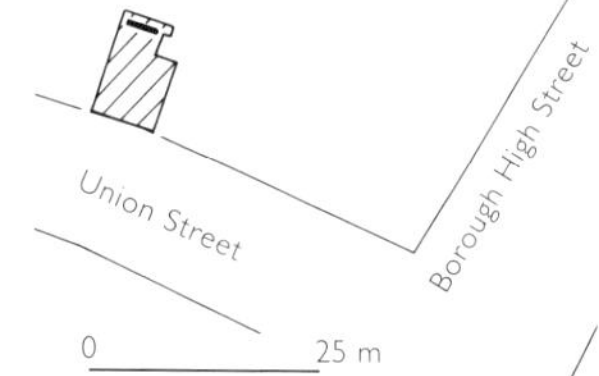

London Archaeol, 2, 1975, 258
Anon, 1974 'Roman well at Southwark', Mosaic, *London Archaeol,* 2, 180
Bird, J, & Marsh, G, 1978 'Decorated samian', in Marsh, G, 225
Dean, M, 1978 'Organic data', in Marsh, G, 231
Hammerson, M, & Murray, C, 1978 'Other Roman pottery', in Marsh, G, 225–30
Marsh, G, 1978 'Excavations at 8 Union Street' in Bird, J, Graham, A H, Sheldon, H,
    & Townend, P (eds), *Southwark excavations 1972–74,* 221–32
Rixson, D, 1978 'Animal bones', in Marsh, G, 231–2
Townend, P, & Hinton, P, 1978 'Small finds', in Marsh, G, 230

154US82

Map site: 12
SLAEC: Peter Hinton
NGR: TQ 3199 8004

154 Union Street (railway arch), SE1

A watching brief in 1982 recovered clay pipes and strips of pipe clay, together with a piece of muffle found on the spoil heap.

235US80

Map site: 32
SLAEC: Brian Yule
NGR: TQ 3181 7999

235–241 Union Street, SE1

A watching brief in 1980 revealed that most of the stratigraphy had been truncated by cellaring, except at the S edge of the site where burnt deposits and a possible thick floor of late post-medieval date were found above the surviving top of the clay.

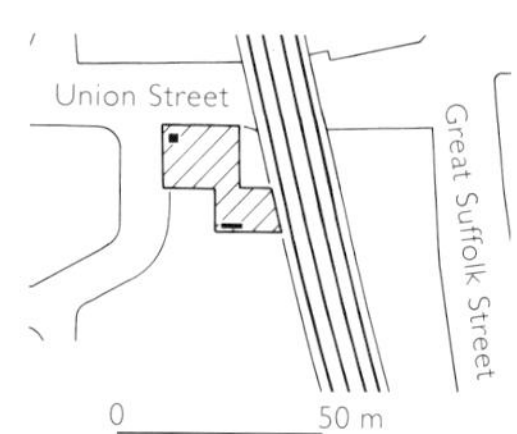

AB78

Map site: 69
SLAEC: Martin Dean
NGR: TQ 3257 7966

Arcadia Buildings, Silvester Street, Great Dover Street, SE1

Excavation in 1978 revealed Roman Watling Street (Roman Road 1) traversing the site from NW to SE with at least five phases of road-metalling overlying a cambered base. A wooden corduroy track beneath the road make-up was either an earlier road, perhaps of military character, or a foundation for the road base. Occupation layers were uncovered on either side of the road, including evidence of a timber building on the NE side and a wood-lined latrine, probably of 2nd-c date. Dark earth overlay the Roman deposits and was cut by numerous post-medieval features. Post-holes for a rectangular building of apparently early medieval date were located on the SW side of the road. Two parallel gullies with pairs of post-holes along their edges have been provisionally identified as medieval cloth-stretching tenter frames. Evidence was found for many post-medieval industries including brushmaking, cloth fulling and clay pipe manufacture (in the form of part of a 17th-c clay pipe kiln complex).

London Archaeol, 3, 1979, 264; 3, 1980, 388; *Britannia,* 10, 1979, 318; 11, 1980, 381; *Surrey Archaeol Coll,* 72, 1980, 247
Dean, M, 1980 'Excavations at Arcadia Buildings, Southwark', *London Archaeol,* 3, 367–73

Abbots Lane, Tooley Street, SE1

A trial excavation in 1986 revealed a post and plank revetment of medieval date, aligned E–W, with waterlaid deposits to the N. The timbers included reused material from a clinker-built boat. The location and date of the revetment suggest that it marks the inner bank of the N arm of the moat enclosing Fastolf's Place.

London Archaeol, 5, 1987, 277; Medieval Archaeol, 31, 1987, 131; Post-Medieval Archaeol, 21, 1987, 289; Surrey Archaeol Coll, 78, 1987, 146

ABB86

Map site: 70
DGLA(S&L): Alan Thompson
NGR: TQ 3334 8020
SMR: 091171

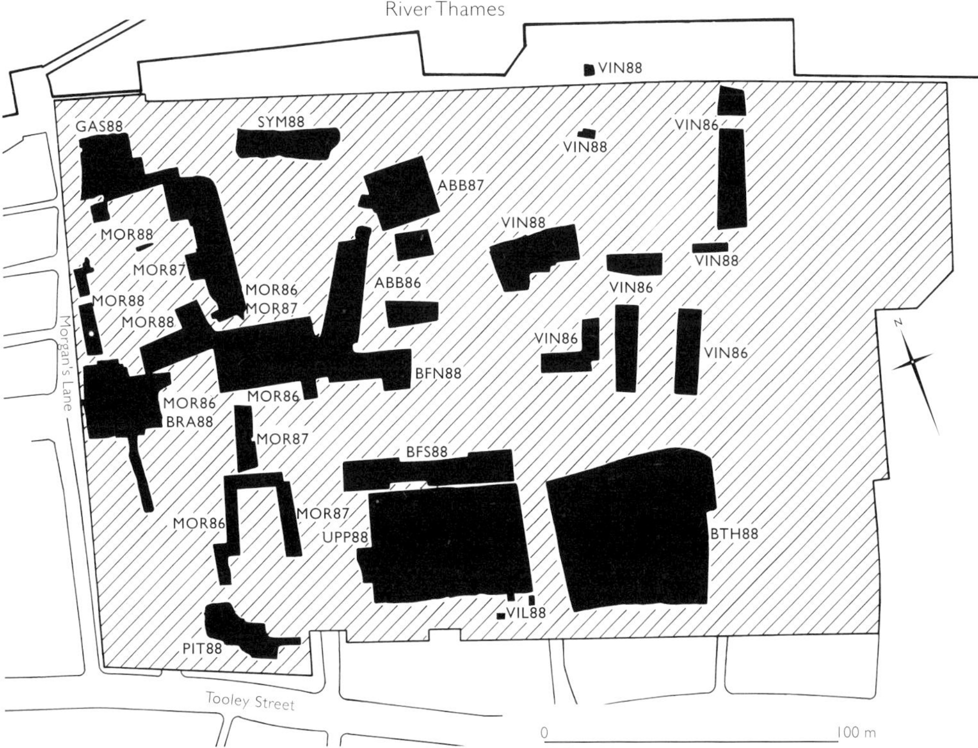

Abbots Lane, Tooley Street, SE1

Excavation in 1987 revealed a medieval channel containing several phases of revetments which incorporated a high proportion of reused timbers with large sections of clinker-built boats. Post-medieval features included a large number of timber and brick lined drains. See also GAS88 below. (For plan see ABB86.)

London Archaeol, 5, 1988, 414; Medieval Archaeol, 32, 1988, 251; Surrey Archaeol Coll, 79, 1989, 188

ABB87

Map site: 71
DGLA(S&L): James Hunter
NGR: TQ 3334 8020
SMR: 091142–3

Abbots Lane, Tooley Street, SE1

A watching brief in 1988 recorded the E side of an 18th-c wood-lined drain running along the W side of Abbots Lane. A length of clinker-built boat was also recovered. (For plan, see ABB86.)

London Archaeol, 6, 1989, 77; Medieval Archaeol, 33, 1989, 185; Post-Medieval Archaeol, 23, 1989, 40; Surrey Archaeol Coll, 80, 1990, 224

ABB88

Map site: 72
DGLA(S&L): James Hunter
NGR: TQ 3320 8020
SMR: 091186

ABST85

Map site: 73
DGLA(S&L): Brian Yule
NGR: TQ 3365 8005

Anchor Brewhouse, Shad Thames (Mill House), SE1

A watching brief in 1985 on a small trial hole in the NW corner of the Mill building recorded a post and plank revetment to the S of the riverwall and aligned roughly E–W: the felling date for the timber was apparently 1570–1615. The space between the revetment and riverwall had been filled with crushed chalk interleaved with flood silt.

Post-Medieval Archaeol, 20, 1986, 340

ACT89

Map site: 74
DGLA(S&L): Simon
McCudden
NGR: TQ 3234 8037
SMR: 090268, 091271–3

Anchor Terrace car park, Park Street, SE1

Excavation in 1989 revealed a chalk foundation, or possibly riverfront ramp, of medieval date. A small section of the NE part of the Globe Theatre (1599–1644) was examined in the extreme NW of the site, as were contemporary levels elsewhere. The remainder of the theatre lies beneath Anchor Terrace, a listed early 19th-c terrace abutting Southwark Bridge Road.

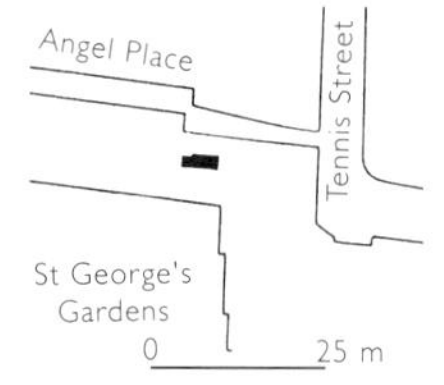

London Archaeol, 6, 1990, 192; *Post-Medieval Archaeol,* 24, 1990, 208; *Surrey Archaeol Coll,* 80, 1990, 221
Blatherwick, S, 1997 'The archaeological evaluation of the Globe playhouse', in Mulryne, J R, & Shewring, M (eds), *Shakespeare's Globe rebuilt,* 66–80
McCudden, S, 1989 'And now the Globe!', Mosaic, *London Archaeol,* 6, 140
McCudden, S, 1990 'The discovery of the Globe Theatre', *London Archaeol,* 6, 143–4

AP72

Map site: 75
SLAEC: Harvey Sheldon
NGR: TQ 3251 7983

Angel Place, 207 Borough High Street, SE1

Excavation in 1972 revealed a shallow gully and a scatter of post-holes sealed by a black soil which contained pottery and coins of late 4th-c date, and whose top survived as the land surface up to the late medieval period. A quantity of 14th-c pottery in the top of the soil suggested manuring and mixing, probably in connection with gardening or agriculture. A large ditch of early 14th-c date which had contained (possibly flowing) water was probably related to an early medieval drainage and embanking system, and had filled up by the end of the c.
The latest structure on the site, apparently of late 17th-c date, was a brick-built cellar. Subsequently a pair of brick walls, possibly of a cellar or sub-basement, were demolished, and the earlier garden soils sealed by brick rubble.

ASY75

Map site: 76
SLAEC: Michael Hammerson
NGR: TQ 3495 7690
SMR: 090506

Asylum Road, SE15

An excavation in 1976 revealed a Roman field or boundary ditch.

Britannia, 8, 1977, 409
Anon, 1977 'Roman Southwark's hinterland', Mosaic, *London Archaeol,* 3, 56

Alaska Works, Grange Road, SE1

An evaluation excavation in 1989 revealed natural sands containing burnt flint and Late Bronze Age pottery. An early Roman ditch was apparently backfilled during the 1st c, along with other early Roman pits.

London Archaeol, 6, 1990, 193; Britannia, 21, 1990, 345; Surrey Archaeol Coll, 80, 1990, 224

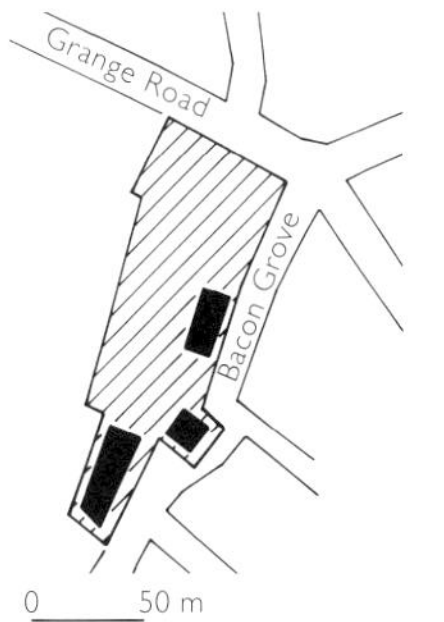

AW89

Map site: 77
DGLA(S&L): Michael Webber
NGR: TQ 3359 7908

Bermondsey Abbey, Abbey Buildings, Long Walk, SE1

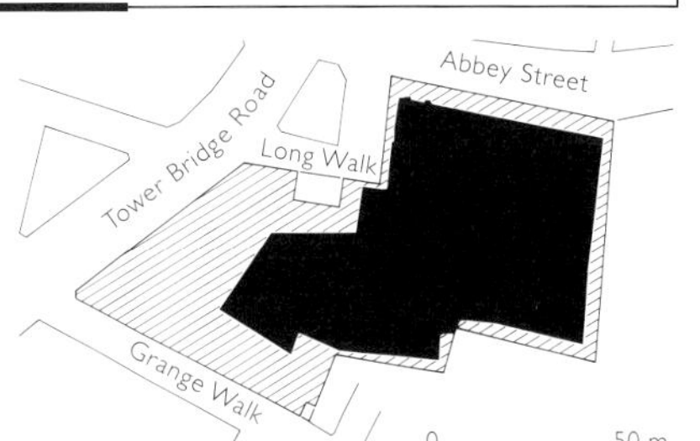

BA84

Map site: 78
DGLA(S&L): David Beard
NGR: TQ 3340 7935
SMR: 091202–4

Excavations between 1984 and 1988 on the SE part of the site of a late 11th-c Cluniac foundation revealed Neolithic struck flints, tools and cores, and a quantity of Bronze Age pottery. Several small, possibly Bronze Age, gullies were cut into natural sand and gravel. No definite Roman features were located, although quantities of Roman pottery and building material were recovered. Several quarry pits predating the earliest Cluniac drain were found and contained chaff-tempered pottery and loom weights, probably of Middle Saxon date; large quantities of Late Saxon to early medieval pottery were also recovered. A large ditch (presumed to be a boundary ditch), a large hurdle- or timber-revetted drain and a fence-line with a related small structure were also recorded. A number of buildings from the claustral range of both the Cluniac priory and succeeding Benedictine abbey were examined. The claustral buildings included two phases of the frater, apparently of later medieval date and possibly relating to the kitchens, the S part of the dorter, the reredorter and the great drain. Further features included the E wall of the chapter house, a small apsidal feature (possibly a vestry), four phases of the infirmary chapel and three phases of the infirmary hall and a second cloister. Two hundred *in situ* burials were excavated, fifteen of them in stone cists. Substantial alterations were recorded to the surviving E wall of the dorter on its incorporation into Sir Thomas Pope's mansion, Bermondsey House. A number of pits were located, several lined with horn cores and associated with the local leather industry. Also revealed were the remains of a 19th-c glass furnace.

London Archaeol, 5, 1985, 65; 5, 1986, 163; 5, 1987, 276; 5, 1988, 413–14; 6, 1989, 76; Medieval Archaeol, 29, 1985, 178; 30, 1986, 142; 31, 1987, 132; 32, 1988, 251; 33, 1989, 186; Post-Medieval Archaeol, 20, 1986, 339; 21, 1987, 275; 22, 1988, 207; 23, 1989, 53; Surrey Archaeol Coll, 77, 1986, 225; 78, 1987, 146; 79, 1989, 187; 80, 1990, 224
Beard, D, 1986 'The infirmary of Bermondsey Priory', *London Archaeol, 5, 186–91*

1–6 Barge House Street, SE1

Excavation in 1989 revealed timber features sealed beneath clays of medieval or later date and associated with Saxo-Norman pottery. Substantial evidence of post-medieval tanning was recovered.

London Archaeol, 6, 1990, 192; Medieval Archaeol, 34, 1990, 184; Post-Medieval Archaeol, 24, 1990, 203; Surrey Archaeol Coll, 80, 1990, 220

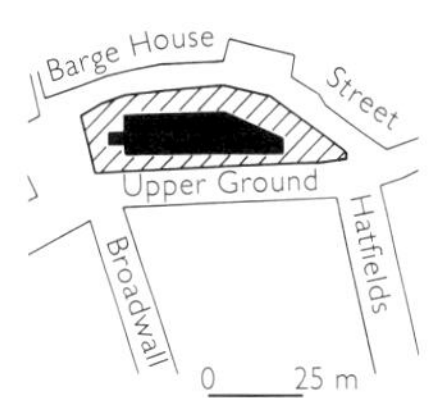

BAG89

Map site: 79
DGLA(S&L): Toby Catchpole
NGR: TQ 3139 8047
SMR: 091275–6

BAQ90

Map site: 80
DGLA(S&L): Wendy Rogers
NGR: TQ 3430 7789
SMR: 091321–3

B and Q Depot, Old Kent Road, Bowles Road, SE1

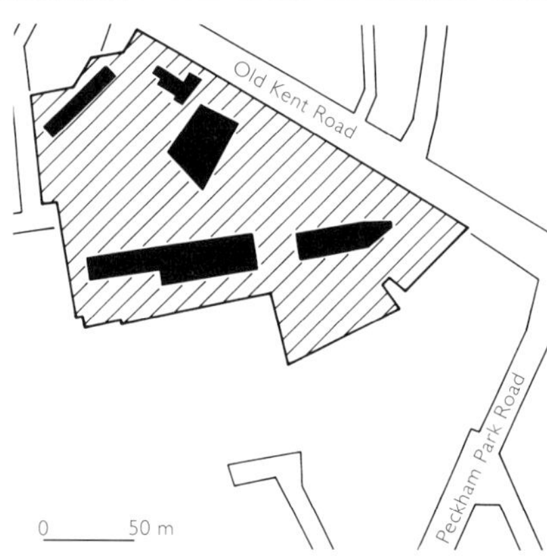

Evaluation and excavation in 1990 revealed, in all areas examined, weathered sand directly overlying natural sands and gravels and containing prehistoric flint tools, burnt daub and bone, and worked sandstone. Two areas produced large concentrations of flint, one of them amounting to about 1780 pieces. Many of the flint fragments could be reassembled, indicating the local manufacture of tools, and the assemblages date to the Early Mesolithic and Early Neolithic periods. A substantial stretch of Watling Street (Roman Road 1) was excavated, parallel to and 20m distant from ditches on either side. A section through the road showed it to consist of several layers, including two distinct upper levels of gravel metalling. The camber of the uppermost road surface had been truncated by later activity on the site. Dating evidence from the road and adjacent areas belongs to the 1st–4th c.

London Archaeol, 6, 1991, 306; Britannia, 22, 1991, 273; Surrey Archaeol Coll, 81, 1991–2, 165
Rogers, W, 1990 'Mesolithic and Neolithic flint-tool manufacturing areas buried beneath Roman Watling Street in Southwark', *London Archaeol, 6, 227–31*

BDPS84

Map site: 81
DGLA(S&L):
Michael Hutchinson
NGR: TQ 3247 8038

Bank End, Park Street, SE1

A watching brief on a sewer trench in 1984 revealed that all materials were redeposited.

BER88

Map site: 82
DGLA(S&L):
Simon Blatherwick
NGR: TQ 3321 7988

39–45 Bermondsey Street, SE1

A watching brief in 1988 recorded in section part of a standing wall of chalk and mortar, possibly part of the outer precinct wall of Bermondsey Abbey, and overlaid by a post-medieval cellar fill.

BER90

Map site: 83
DGLA(S&L): Aidan Allen
NGR: TQ 3323 7970
SMR: 091368

100–104 Bermondsey Street, SE1

An evaluation excavation in 1990 revealed clay deposits containing domestic refuse of 13th–14th-c date, mixed with similar post-medieval material and overlaid by a number of 17th- or 18th-c mortar floors. A stone wall provisionally dated to the mid-13th c, but possibly built at a later date with reused stone, was located next to the street frontage.

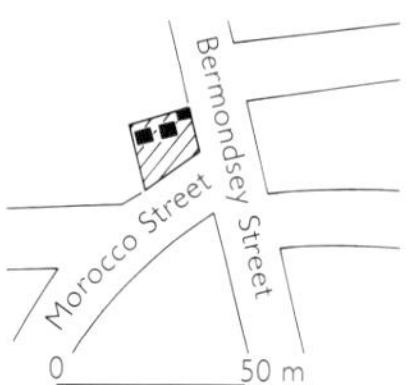

London Archaeol, 6, 1991, 305; Medieval Archaeol, 35, 1991, 155; Post-Medieval Archaeol, 25, 1991, 132; Surrey Archaeol Coll, 81, 1991–2, 164

Butter Factory (north), Tooley Street, SE1

An excavation in 1988 revealed the foundation of medieval and later buildings beside the E bank of a
N–S flowing watercourse, probably the moat of the house of Sir John Fastolf built *c* 1443. The bank was
originally reinforced by the planting of elms (as a 'green revetment'), and then by a tied-back post and
plank revetment before being culverted and reclaimed in the 17th c. (For plan, see ABB86.)

London Archaeol, 6, 1989, 77; *Medieval Archaeol*, 33, 1989, 185; *Post-Medieval Archaeol*, 23, 1989, 40; *Surrey Archaeol Coll*, 80, 1990, 224

BFN88

Map site: 84
DGLA(S&L): James Hunter
NGR: TQ 3320 8020
SMR: 091187–8

Butter Factory (south), Tooley Street, SE1

Excavation in 1988 revealed a large feature, thought to be a pond, dug in the 15th c but backfilled in the
17th. The backfill contained many organic finds including a saddle, saddle wallets and two blankets.
A N–S aligned watercourse was also found, and both features are assumed to have been part of the
house of Sir John Fastolf. Also located was a brick-aisled structure of 18th-c date, possibly related to
Close's Brewery, and a line of brick cesspits. (For plan, see ABB86.)

London Archaeol, 6, 1989, 77; *Medieval Archaeol*, 33, 1989, 185; *Post-Medieval Archaeol*, 23, 1989, 40; *Surrey Archaeol Coll*, 80, 1990, 224

BFS88

Map site: 85
DGLA(S&L): James Hunter
NGR: TQ 3320 8020
SMR: 091189–90

5–15 Bankside, SE1

Excavation in 1981 revealed a deep waterlaid sequence, probably part of a large creek running inland
from the river. The lowest level examined comprised a thick peat deposit found elsewhere in the
Thames Estuary and probably laid down some 3000 years ago. The peat was cut by a medieval ditch,
possibly a drainage dike, which was in turn cut by an erosion plain representing substantial river
flooding. A group of mid-14th-c pottery, including many wasters, was dumped on the newly formed
foreshore, suggesting the existence close to Bankside of a previously unknown kiln producing Surrey
Whitewares. The site did not appear to have been built up until relatively late, the sequence being
overlain by the fragmentary remains of 16th- and 17th-c buildings. A pit containing four oak barrels was
also investigated. (The site is also referred to as BS81.)

London Archaeol, 4, 1982, 165; *Medieval Archaeol*, 26, 1982, 194
Dennis, M, & Hinton, P, 1983 'A medieval kiln group from Bankside SE1', *London Archaeol*, 4, 283–7

BKS81, BS81

Map site: 86, 91
SLAEC: George Dennis
NGR: TQ 3236 8045

Bricklayers' Arms Railway Depot, Rolls Road, SE1

Excavation in 1987 revealed
topographical evidence including
Tilbury IV peat layers. A prehistoric
platform was located, made of
interlacing sections of wood. Flint
flakes and two Neolithic stone axes
were also found.

London Archaeol, 5, 1988, 414; 6, 1989, 76–7;
   Surrey Archaeol Coll, 79, 1989, 187; 80, 1990, 225
Anon, 1988 'Builders sponsor Museum
   excavation', Mosaic, *London Archaeol*, 5, 420

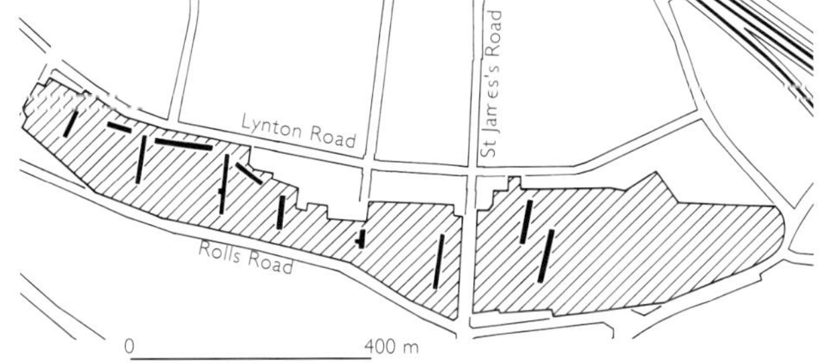

BLA87

Map site: 87
DGLA(S&L): Helen Jones
NGR: TQ 3380 7850
SMR: 091172–5

BRA88

Map site: 88
DGLA(S&L): Alan Thompson
NGR: TQ 3320 8020
SMR: 091183–4

Braidwood Street, Tooley Street, SE1

Excavation in 1988 revealed evidence of a millstream known to have existed in the area from the medieval period. The width of the stream appears to have been gradually reduced, wooden drains being guided into it during the 16th and 17th c. Eventually the millstream was confined within a brick culvert fed by inlets, and the area was reclaimed by timber boxing backfilled with rubble. (For plan, see ABB86.)

London Archaeol, 6, 1989, 77; Medieval Archaeol, 33, 1989, 185; Surrey Archaeol Coll, 80, 1990, 224

BRN88

Map site: 89
DGLA(S&L): Alison Hawkins
NGR: TQ 3160 7985

Boundary Row (north side), SE1

Excavation in 1988 revealed no archaeological features.

BS78

Map site: 90
SLAEC: Michael Hammerson
NGR: TQ 3203 8053

Royal George Wharf, Bankside, SE1

Excavation in 1978 revealed a simple evolution of the riverfront from river deposition in the 14th c and dumping of occupation debris in the second half of the 16th c. This debris was then levelled and spread over the foreshore by tidal action. Late 15th- or early 16th-c timber structures possibly represent boatbuilding or docking facilities, and were associated with large quantities of waste leather probably deriving from the nearby leather market.

London Archaeol, 3, 1979, 264; Medieval Archaeol, 23, 1979, 268; Surrey Archaeol Coll, 72, 1980, 248

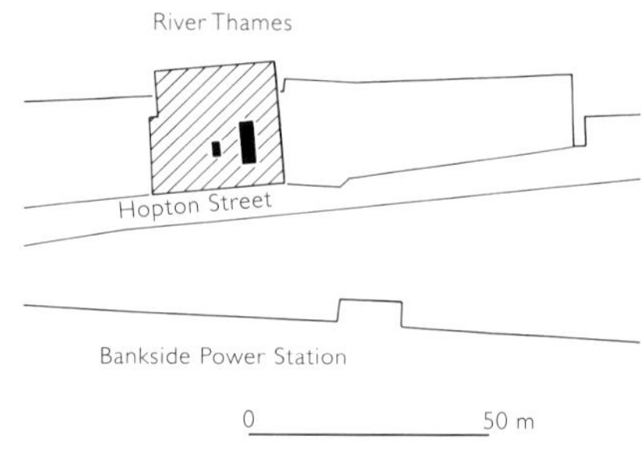

BS81: see BKS81

5–15 Bankside, SE1

BTH88

Map site: 92
DGLA(S&L): Helen Jones
NGR: TQ 3320 8020
SMR: 091176–9

Bethel Estate, Vine Lane, SE1

Excavation in 1988 revealed sands cut by a small linear ditch and other features which contained sherds of abraded Roman pottery. A watercourse flowed E–W across the S part of the site, and is thought to have been the moat of Sir John Fastolf's manor house built *c* 1443. Brick-lined wells, soak-aways and pits lined with horn cores indicated industrial activity on the site. Much pottery of 14th–17th-c date was recovered. (For plan, see ABB86.)

London Archaeol, 6, 1989, 77; Medieval Archaeol, 33, 1989, 185; Post-Medieval Archaeol, 23, 1989, 40; Surrey Archaeol Coll, 80, 1990, 224

BUT88

Map site: 93
DGLA(S&L): Stephen Davis
NGR: TQ 3372 7993

Butlers Court, Curlew Street, SE1

Excavation in 1988 revealed a sequence elsewhere attributed to Tilbury IV peat.

Bonded Warehouse, Montague Close, SE1

BWMC74

Map site: 94
SLAEC: Alan Graham
NGR: TQ 3272 8033

Excavation in 1974 revealed part of a Roman road (Roman Road 2) which ran in a NW–SE direction and had been resurfaced at least five times. It may date from the pre-Flavian period, and occupation close by continued into the late 4th c. A late Roman well and two stone walls were sealed by dark earth. On the E side of the site was found a medieval wall, probably part of the priory of St Mary Overy.

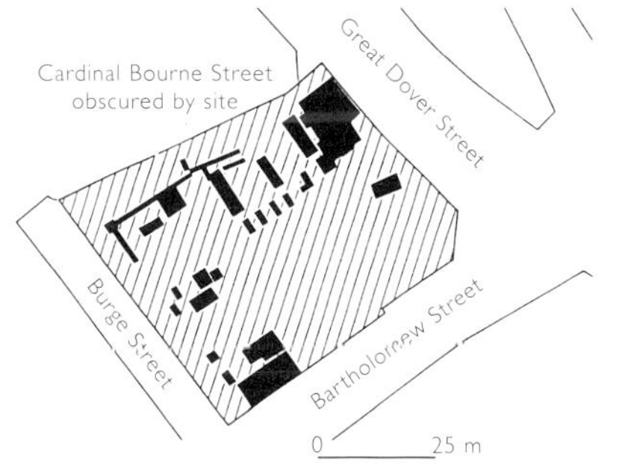

London Archaeol, 2, 1975, 258; Britannia, 7, 1976, 351
Bird, J, 1978 'Stamped amphorae', in Graham, A, 282
Bird, J, & Marsh, G, 1978 'Decorated samian', in Graham, A, 262–5
Dean, M, 1978 'Organic data', in Graham, A, 287
Graham, A, 1978 'The Bonded Warehouse, Montague Close', in Bird, J,
   Graham, A H, Sheldon, H, & Townend, P (eds), Southwark excavations 1972–74, 237–90
Hammerson, M, 1978 'Coins', in Graham, A, 285
Hammerson, M, & Murray, C, 1978 'Other Roman pottery', in Graham, A, 265–80
Orton, C, 1978 'Medieval and post-medieval pottery', in Graham, A, 282–4
Rixson, D, 1978 'Animal bones', in Graham, A, 288–90
Townend, P, & Hinton, P, 1978 'Glass (Roman)', in Graham, A, 285
Townend, P, & Hinton, P, 1978 'Small finds (Roman)', in Graham, A, 285–7
Watt, R J, 1978 'The human bones', in Graham, A, 290

Cardinal Bourne Street, SE1

CBS77

Map site: 95
SLAEC: Michael Hammerson
NGR: TQ 3283 7912

Excavation in 1977 revealed two converging streams on a site that was probably waterlogged during most of the Roman period. A higher gravel spread to the N may have represented the edge of a road or similar feature.

London Archaeol, 3, 1978, 162; Britannia, 9, 1978, 453; Surrey Archaeol Coll, 72, 1980, 248

Cromwell Flats, Redcross Way, SE1

CFRW85

Map site: 96
DGLA(S&L): Robin Densem
NGR: TQ 2468 8016

Observation in 1985 recorded modern disturbance only.

Cherry Garden Pier, Bermondsey Wall East, SE16

CG87

Map site: 97
DGLA(S&L): Roland Flook,
Derek Seeley
NGR: TQ 3450 7968
SMR: 091153–6

Excavation in 1987 revealed several pits and deposits on the surface of the natural and containing Iron Age pottery and flint flakes. Concentrated in a small area of higher ground were a Roman ditch and other features as well as three cremation burials. A clay-filled channel was found to contain a large Saxon timber resting against a wattle structure, possibly the remains of a revetment. Post-medieval features included a number of pits of mostly 18th-c date and containing large groups of domestic pottery.

London Archaeol, 5, 1988, 414; Britannia, 19, 1988, 464; Medieval Archaeol, 32, 1988, 252; Surrey Archaeol Coll, 79, 1989, 188

CH75

Map site: 98
SLAEC: Brian Yule, Laura
Schaaf, Eric Ferretti
NGR: TQ 3266 7962
SMR: 090327, 090424–5

Chaucer House, Tabard Street, SE1

Excavation in 1975–6 revealed a probable road ditch
aligned with Watling Street (Roman Road 1) at the SW end
of the site, and apparently used for drainage or as a source
of road-metalling. To the NE were three more ditches; two,
of 2nd-c date, were probably drains, and the other, of 4th-c
date, probably marked a boundary. Like a fenced gravel
path, also recorded, all these features lay parallel to the
road ditch. Two inhumation burials were found, as were a
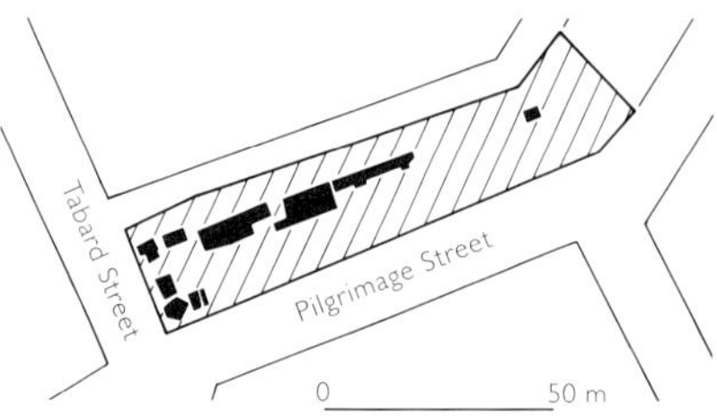

late medieval ditch and agricultural soil, and a series of 17th-c pits related to buildings shown on early
maps of Tabard Street. In 1976 a late medieval building with tile hearths was found, as well as medieval
rubbish pits and drainage ditches, and evidence of land reclamation in the 16th–17th c.

London Archaeol, 2, 1976, 372; 3, 1977, 39; *Britannia,* 7, 1976, 352; 8, 1977, 410; *Post-Medieval Archaeol,* 12, 1978, 91; *Surrey Archaeol Coll,* 72,
1980, 248
Anon, 1977 'Chaucer House continues', Mosaic, *London Archaeol,* 3, 84
Robinson, J, 1989 'A late medieval pilgrim badge from Chaucer House, Southwark', *London Archaeol,* 6, 66–9
Yule, B, 1976 'A Roman burial from Southwark', *London Archaeol,* 2, 359

CHWH83

Map site: 99
DGLA(S&L): Ian Tyers
NGR: TQ 3294 8033
SMR: 090675–7

Chamberlain's Wharf, Tooley Street, SE1

A watching brief in 1983–4 recorded a square timber-lined well dated by dendrochronology to AD231
or later, containing pottery and leather; and a natural channel flowing across the site from S to N,
containing medieval pottery in its upper fills. An 18th- or 19th-c brick-lined cesspit was also recorded.

London Archaeol, 4, 1984, 390; *Britannia,* 15, 1984, 310; *Surrey Archaeol Coll,* 76, 1985, 130

CO87

Map site: 100
DGLA(S&L): John Dillon
NGR: TQ 3241 8020
SMR: 091159–62, 091375–6

Courage Brewery, Park Street, SE1

Excavation in 1987 recovered a number of flint axes
including Late Neolithic tools and part of a polished stone
axe. An arc of six post-holes was located, thought to be
part of a large round-house, and three further post-holes
aligned E–W and containing Iron Age pottery may have
been part of a second structure. Roman levels included
two 1st-c ditches sealed by a narrow road 2m wide and
associated with 1st-c timber buildings. S of the road were
up to three phases of clay and timber buildings cut by six
large cesspits; N of the road industrial dumps were sealed
by a 3rd-c mortar-floored building, which also cut the road.
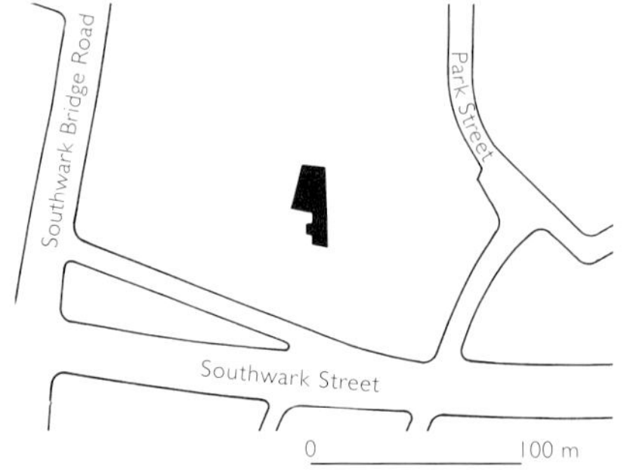

Subsequently the whole site was sealed beneath dark earth. See COSE84, CSW85 below.

London Archaeol, 5, 1988, 414; *Britannia,* 19, 1988, 464; *Surrey Archaeol Coll,* 79, 1989, 187
Hammer, F, in prep. *Industry in north-west Roman Southwark: excavations at Courage's Brewery, 1974–90*

CO88

Map site: 101
DGLA(S&L): John Dillon
NGR: TQ 3244 8026
SMR: 091193–201

Courage Brewery, Park Street, SE1

Excavation in 1988 recovered flint tools and flakes, and a pit containing sherds of Late Bronze Age
pottery. A number of post-holes were found, their fills containing flint flakes, close to the arc of post-
holes discovered in 1987 (see CO87 above) and believed to be part of a round-house of unknown date.

To the N, on the edge of the high ground, was a natural gravel surface thought to represent the prehistoric foreshore of the River Thames. It contained two hearths, animal bone and burnt clay and flint fragments, including a concentration of at least 30 flint flakes and one core. The gravel surface was sealed by a layer of peat, probably of Tilbury Phase IV, and dated to c 1000BC. Two phases of Roman industrial activity were recorded, in the form of blacksmithing and bronze-casting workshops, and a length of stone-lined flue was found next to the remains of a clay and timber building. This activity was succeeded in the later Roman period by a building with three rooms, a mortar and tile floor, and walls covered with painted plaster; and there were also two timber-lined wells. The Roman levels were sealed by dark earth. To the N, the earliest Roman activity took the form of 1st-c dumping over the Thames clays, while a flimsy revetment running approximately N–S was sealed by a gravelled area which may represent a narrow E–W road. Cutting the gravel was a construction trench for a large timber building with oak-planked floors almost intact, and an entrance ramp. This structure is dated by pottery to the early 2nd c, and is interpreted as a dockside warehouse.

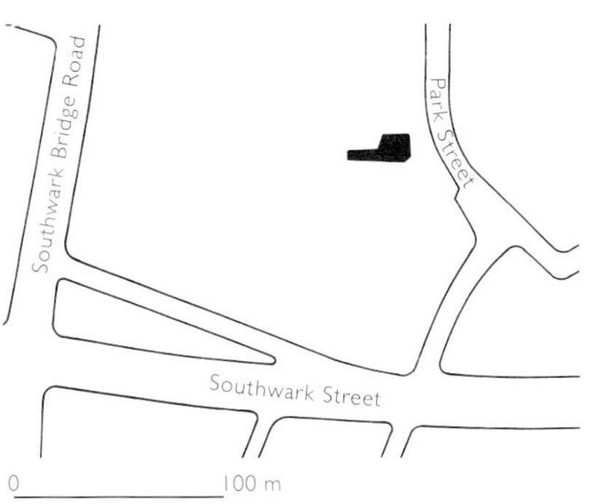

London Archaeol, 6, 1989, 77–8; Britannia, 20, 1989, 309; Surrey Archaeol Coll, 80, 1990, 222

Brigham, T, Goodburn, D, & Tyers, I, 1995 'A Roman timber building on the Southwark waterfront', Archaeol J, 152, 1–72

Cowan, C, in prep. The development of north-west Roman Southwark: excavations at Courage's Brewery, 1974–90

Dillon, J, 1989 'A Roman timber building from Southwark', Britannia, 20, 229–31

Hammer, F, in prep. Industry in north-west Roman Southwark: excavations at Courage's Brewery, 1974–90

Courage Brewery, 3 Redcross Way, SE1

CO89

Map site: 102
DGLA(S&L): Sophie Jackson
NGR: TQ 3245 8020

Excavation in 1989 revealed prehistoric features cutting the high natural sands. Early Roman clay and timber buildings were partly overlaid by a metalled road which had been resurfaced several times. A further series of clay and timber structures, possibly shops fronted by a timber porch, was erected alongside the road. Another building to the S featured walls decorated on both faces with painted plaster. Substantial beam slots on the same alignment may represent later Roman construction.

London Archaeol, 6, 1990, 193; Britannia, 21, 1990, 344; Surrey Archaeol Coll, 80, 1990, 223

Cowan, C, in prep. The development of north-west Roman Southwark: excavations at Courage's Brewery, 1974–90

Courage Brewery (south-east), Park Street, SE1

COSE84

Map site: 104
DGLA(S&L): Robin Densem
NGR: TQ 3247 8031
SMR: 090896–8

Excavation in 1984 revealed parts of clay and timber buildings which were replaced by a large structure with stone foundations. Part of a fallen wall constructed of reused tegulae was also discovered. In the late Roman period the site was used for burials, including two possibly Christian 'plaster' inhumations. Dark earth overlay the Roman deposits. Two medieval or later clay-filled channels crossed the N part of the site, and many pits of 17th–18th-c date were examined, including brick-lined cesspits and a chalk-lined well. See CO87, CO88, CO89 above, CSW85 below.

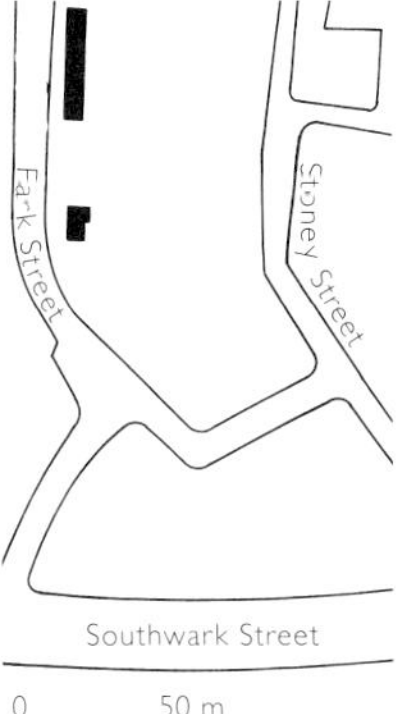

London Archaeol, 5, 1985, 65; 5, 1986, 163; Britannia, 16, 1985, 298; Surrey Archaeol Coll, 77, 1986, 224; 78, 1987, 145

Cowan, C, in prep. The development of north-west Roman Southwark: excavations at Courage's Brewery, 1974–90

CPPCR85

Map site: 105
DGLA(S&L): Peter Hinton
NGR: TQ 3390 7140

Crystal Palace Parade, College Road, SE19

Observation in 1985 revealed evidence of natural topography only.

CRODA86, CRODA87

Map site: 106, 107
DGLA(S&L): Hedley Swain
NGR: TQ 3396 7908

Croda Gelatine Works, Southwark Park Road, SE1

Excavation in 1986 revealed natural sands of 'Bermondsey Island' and two N–S aligned water channels, one of them open from the late medieval to early post-medieval period. An inhumation of Roman date was found in a mortar-lined grave, whose fill contained large iron coffin nails and a bronze finger-ring. A Roman ditch was also examined, as were several shallow field ditches of 17th–19th-c date.

London Archaeol, 5, 1987, 277; Surrey Archaeol Coll, 78, 1987, 146

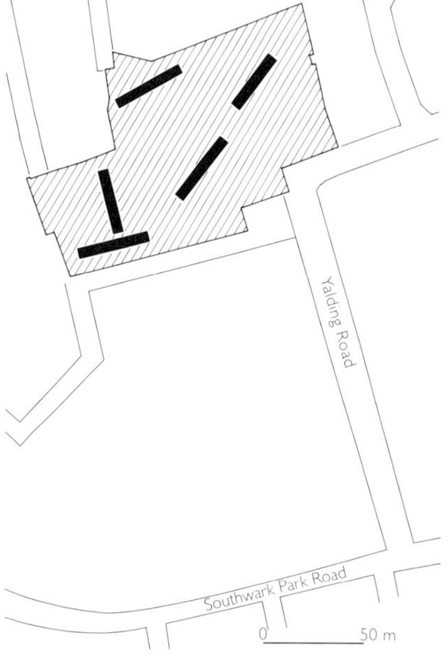

CSSS75

Map site: 108
SLAEC: Alan Graham, Harvey Sheldon
NGR: TQ 3193 7998
SMR: 090350

Copperfield Street, Suffolk Street, SE1

A watching brief in 1975 recovered a flint blade and recorded Roman mudflats.

London Archaeol, 2, 1976, 372; Britannia, 7, 1976, 352

CSW85

Map site: 109
DGLA(S&L): Michael Hammerson, Brian Yule, Bruce Watson
NGR: TQ 3230 8023

Courage Brewery (south-west), Park Street, Thrale Street, SE1

Observation of a series of sections in 1985 recorded evidence of the development of the N edge of a prehistoric island in the Thames and subsequent activity including possible revetting and reclamation of Roman date. See CO87, CO88, CO89, COSE84 above.

CW83

Map site: 110
DGLA(S&L): Derek Seeley
NGR: TQ 3303 8031
SMR: 090892–5

Cotton's Wharf, Tooley Street, SE1

Excavation in 1983 revealed several prehistoric pits sealed by waterlaid clays. The earliest Roman feature was a large circular pit, possibly a gravel quarry, of 2nd-c date. At the N end of the site a number of partially robbed ragstone foundations of 2nd- and 3rd-c date were recorded; the structure had gone out of use by the 4th c. At the S end of the site was located the N edge of a channel aligned E–W which contained Roman material in its waterlaid clays and sands and was completely filled with clay by the medieval period. No medieval ground surface survived, but the period was represented by truncated features including two ditches and several pits. One of the latter was square in plan, wattle lined and dated probably to the 13th c. The remains of a 17th-c circular brick-lined structure were examined in the NW corner of the site. See also CWO84 below.

London Archaeol, 4, 1984, 389; 5, 1985, 65; Britannia, 15, 1984, 310; 16, 1985, 298; Surrey Archaeol Coll, 76, 1985, 130

Cotton's Wharf, Tooley Street, SE1

A watching brief following the previous year's excavation (see CW83 above) enabled the W and S limits of the 'island' to be roughly recorded. Some 75,000sq m in area, the island extended from Cottons Yard to Battlebridge Lane, N of Tooley Street, the high ground being protected to the W by a post and plank revetment. Lines of stakes interlaced with wattles were erected beyond and perpendicular to this W edge, and may have functioned as groynes to prevent river erosion. A hoard of 44 bronze coins, the latest dating to AD378–83, was discovered close to the Roman structure excavated in 1983.

London Archaeol, 5, 1985, 65; *Britannia,* 16, 1985, 298; *Surrey Archaeol Coll,* 77, 1986, 225
Hammerson, M J, 1987 'The Cottons Wharf, Tooley Street, London hoard', in Burnett, A M, & Bland, R F (eds), *Coin hoards from Roman Britain VII,* 201–4, British Museum

CWO84

Map site: 111
DGLA(S&L): Brian Yule
NGR: TQ 3300 8030

District Heating Scheme, Montague Close, Borough High Street, Tooley Street, SE1

A watching brief in 1975 recorded sections of two Roman roads (Roman Roads 1 and 2) at their approach to the river crossing. Also noted were 1st- and 2nd-c clay and timber buildings, a 3rd-c stone hypocausted building in Tooley Street, medieval dumping and the S wall of a watergate.

London Archaeol, 2, 1975, 258; 2, 1976, 372; *Britannia,* 7, 1976, 351
Graham, A H, 1988 'Excavations at the District Heating Scheme', in Hinton, P (ed), *Excavations in Southwark 1973–76, Lambeth 1973–79,* 27–54

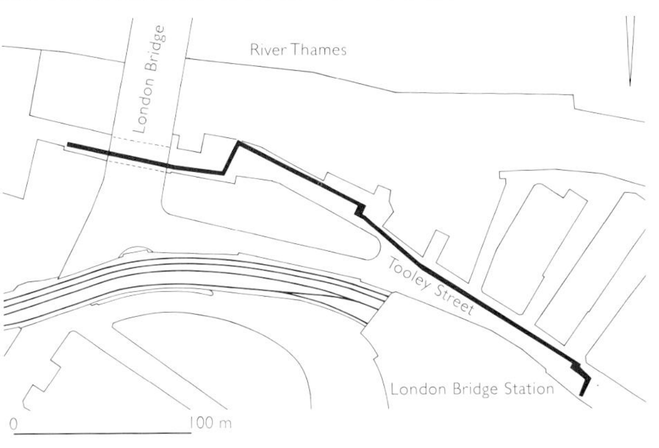

DHS75

Map site: 112
SLAEC: Alan Graham
NGR: TQ 3291 8031

Dickens Square, Harper Road, SE1

Excavation in 1989 revealed high sands bordered by a low peaty area shelving to the S towards a known area of deep peats derived from a glacial scour hollow. Flint flakes indicated prehistoric activity, and two ditches contained quantities of Roman pottery, mainly of 2nd-c date.

London Archaeol, 6, 1990, 193; *Britannia,* 21, 1990, 345; *Surrey Archaeol Coll,* 80, 1990, 221

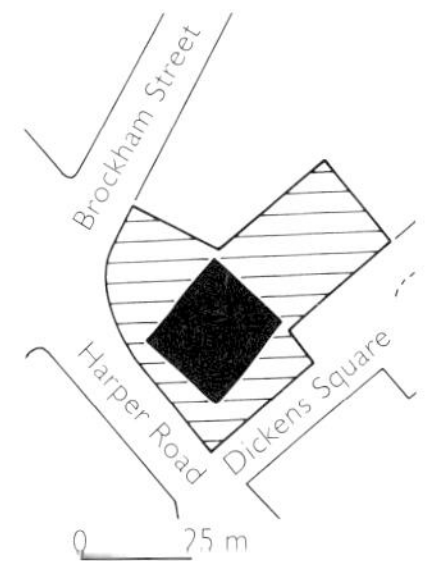

DIC89

Map site: 113
DGLA(S&L): Helen Jones
NGR: TQ 3238 7935
SMR: 091249–51

281–333 Old Kent Road, Earl Road, SE1

A limited evaluation excavation in 1990 revealed post-medieval wall foundations together with deeper, undated stratigraphy, perhaps suggesting the presence of natural channels, among other features.

London Archaeol, 6, 1991, 306; *Post-Medieval Archaeol,* 25, 1991, 133; *Surrey Archaeol Coll,* 81, 1991–2, 164

EAR90

Map site: 114
DGLA(S&L): Peter Thompson
NGR: TQ 3360 7840
SMR: 091316–17

EWERST87

Map site: 115
DGLA(S&L): Michael Hammerson
NGR: TQ 3204 8013

Ewer Street (railway arches), SE1

Observation in 1987 recorded Dissenter burials reinterred when the railway arches were built over a known 17th–18th-c Quaker burial ground in 1864.

FW83

Map site: 116
DGLA(S&L): Robin Densem, John Dillon
NGR: TQ 3286 8037

Fenning's Wharf, 1 London Bridge, SE1

Excavation and observation in 1983 revealed within a testpit the interior of the NW corner of a medieval ragstone foundation consisting of a well-built wall above two roughly built offsets. It had been constructed on a raft of chalk rubble, set in soft brown clay, its top truncated by modern intrusions. The structure was filled with layers of chalk rubble, earth and gravel, and was probably part of one of the piers of London Bridge, built between 1176 and 1209.

London Archaeol, 4, 1984, 390; *Medieval Archaeol*, 28, 1984, 231; *Surrey Archaeol Coll*, 76, 1985, 130
Watson, B, Dyson, T, & Tyers, I, in prep. *London Bridge and its environs: an archaeological history*

FW84

Map site: 117
DGLA(S&L): George Dennis
NGR: TQ 3286 8037
SMR: 090686–9

Fenning's Wharf, 1 London Bridge, SE1

Excavation in 1984 revealed a ring ditch enclosing a shallow central pit which contained sherds provisionally dated to the Late Bronze or Early Iron Age. The ditch contained a cremation and, though not securely dated, is thought to have been a barrow. The entire site was truncated below any Roman land surface, only pits of that date surviving. One of these pits was rectangular with a timber lining, and another contained a group of 1st-c pottery. The massive landward abutment of medieval London Bridge, surviving largely intact up to the base of the arch vaulting, was located behind the modern riverwall. The original 12th-c bastion was built against and into the bank, and the core of ragstone and chalk rubble was contained within a good-quality ashlar facing; this rested upon substantial oak sills and was protected externally by rows of elm piles. Later phases of repair and widening were in evidence. Beneath the stone bridge was a substantial oak box structure with an adjacent foreshore causeway; both perhaps part of a previous timber bridge. A number of brick features were recorded, principally 17th- or 18th-c cellars of buildings fronting the bridge approach ramp.

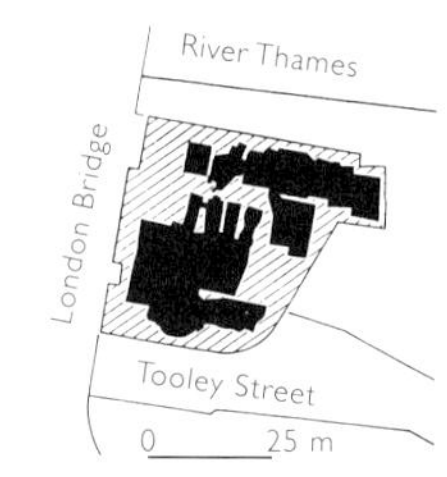

London Archaeol, 5, 1985, 65; *Britannia*, 16, 1985, 298; *Medieval Archaeol*, 29, 1985, 178; *Surrey Archaeol Coll*, 77, 1986, 225
Dennis, M G, 1984 'Medieval London Bridge', *London Archaeol*, 4, 429
Watson, B, Dyson, T, & Tyers, I, in prep. *London Bridge and its environs: an archaeological history*

GAS88

Map site: 118
DGLA(S&L): Alan Thompson
NGR: TQ 3320 8020
SMR: 091180–2

Gun and Shot Wharf, Tooley Street, SE1

Excavation in 1988 revealed further remains of the moated enclosure excavated in 1987 (see ABB87 above), now considered to be part of the house built c 1325, known as 'The Rosary' and owned by King Edward II. A large section of the moat was revealed, turning S at its W end and indicating two phases of revetment construction associated with a stone and timber bridge giving access to the house from the N. N of the moat were the remains of two timbered docks or inlets. (For plan, see ABB86.)

London Archaeol, 6, 1989, 77; *Medieval Archaeol*, 33, 1989, 185; *Surrey Archaeol Coll*, 80, 1990, 224

Guy's Hospital Development (area D), St Thomas Street, SE1

GHD90

Map site: 119
DGLA(S&L): Robin Wilson
NGR: TQ 3292 8003
SMR: 091255–9

Excavation in 1990 revealed the remains of a small building more than 4.6m square and dating to the 17th c, its floor constructed from large blocks of chalk, with four rectangular sill-beams surviving at the base of each wall. The lower plank of each wall was still intact, though they remained undisturbed only in the S and E walls.

London Archaeol, 6, 1991, 306; Post-Medieval Archaeol, 25, 1991, 133; Surrey Archaeol Coll, 81, 1991–2, 164

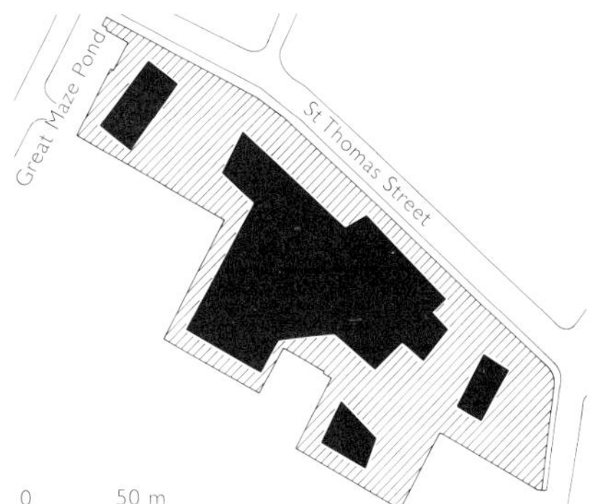

Guy's Hospital Development, St Thomas Street, SE1

GHL89

Map site: 120
DGLA(S&L): Robin Wilson
NGR: TQ 3292 8003
SMR: 091255–9

Excavation in 1989 revealed a series of parallel Roman drainage ditches. A substantial timber structure, probably the revetment of the W side of the Guy's Hospital Roman channel, was located. A timber-revetted channel of early post-medieval date was also found.

London Archaeol, 6, 1990, 193; Britannia, 21, 1990, 344; Surrey Archaeol Coll, 80, 1990, 223

Guy's Hospital Development (area 7), St Thomas Street, SE1

GHR82

Map site: 121
SLAEC: Brian Yule
NGR: TQ 327 801

Excavation in 1982 recovered prehistoric pottery sherds and flints from the top of natural. The sequence of Roman deposits included two gullies, one of them cut by post-pits along its length, and a ditch probably of 1st-c date. The remains of a clay and timber building, possibly contemporaneous with a ditch backfilled in the 2nd c, were also recorded. All these features were aligned NW–SE, at right angles to the Roman bridge approach road (Roman Road 1). Four inhumations of probable Roman date were examined. Dark earth sealed all the Roman strata. Medieval pits and a channel of Tudor date were also uncovered.

London Archaeol, 4, 1984, 290; Britannia, 14, 1983, 314; Surrey Archaeol Coll, 75, 1984, 271

Guy's Hospital (squash courts), St Thomas Street, SE1

GHSC77

Map site: 122
SLAEC: Brian Yule
NGR: TQ 3298 8000

Observation in 1977 revealed an 18th–19th-c revetment.

Hibernia Chambers, Montague Close, SE1

HC74

Map site: 123
SLAEC: Alan Graham
NGR: TQ 3275 8036

Excavation in 1974 revealed the edge of the metalling and other evidence of a Roman road (Roman Road 2) running from London Bridge towards a probable crossing at Westminster. (For plan, see BWMC74.)

London Archaeol, 2, 1976, 372; Britannia, 7, 1976, 351

HDA85

Map site: 124
DGLA(S&L): Brian Yule
NGR: TQ 3313 8032

Hay's Dock (block A), Tooley Street, SE1

A watching brief in 1985 recorded a revetted channel containing 16th-c metalwork. The location of the channel is consistent with that of the medieval millstream which defined the SE boundary of the town house of the abbots of Battle and served mills on the waterfront.

London Archaeol, 5, 1986, 163; Medieval Archaeol, 30, 1986, 143; Post-Medieval Archaeol, 20, 1986, 340; Surrey Archaeol Coll, 78, 1987, 145

HEN78

Map site: 125
SLAEC: George Dennis
NGR: TQ 3336 7865
SMR: 090519–20

Hendre Road, SE1

A trial excavation in 1978 revealed a Roman ditch cut into natural strata at right angles to the nearby Old Kent Road, itself on the presumed line of Roman Watling Street (Roman Road 1). Post-medieval garden soil was also recorded.

London Archaeol, 3, 1979, 264; Britannia, 10, 1979, 318; Surrey Archaeol Coll, 72, 1980, 248

HIB79

Map site: 126
SLAEC: George Dennis
NGR: TQ 3274 8040
SMR: 090584, 090876–82

Hibernia Wharf, Montague Close, SE1

Excavation in 1979–80 in the SW part of the site revealed evidence of quarrying in the later 1st c, possibly to provide metalling for the road from Roman London Bridge to a ford between Lambeth and Westminster. The quarries were eventually filled in, probably in the late 1st or 2nd c. Three rectangular timber-lined pits were located, at least one of which may have been Late Saxon in date. The main feature excavated was a linear channel, apparently manmade, which crossed the site from NW to SE and cut the possible Late Saxon pit; it had partly silted up by the 11th c, and so may have been dug in the 10th. Documentary evidence suggests that St Mary Overy dock dates from the early medieval period, and the channel must therefore either have been part of the dock or have fed into it. A small chalk and brick lined cellar, possibly of the 16th c, was also recorded. Further work on the SE part of the site provided additional evidence of gravel-quarrying in the 1st c, and part of a ditch for the road recorded in 1979. These features indicated that flooding of the area in the 1st c was more extensive than previously thought. The ditch was infilled by the 2nd c, when a clay and timber structure with wooden pile foundations was built partly over it and the ditch itself was recut in the form of a narrow revetted drain. The building fronted onto the road and was probably a workshop. Five wells of 2nd-c date were found elsewhere within the area examined. Several rectangular early medieval pits, probably cesspits, were located, as well as the truncated chalk footings of the cloister of St Mary Overy. The base of one post-medieval pit, containing delftware wasters, was revealed.

London Archaeol, 3, 1980, 388; 4, 1981, 49; Britannia, 11, 1980, 382; 12, 1981, 353; Medieval Archaeol, 24, 1980, 228; 25, 1981, 211
de Rouffignac, C, 1985 'Parasite egg survival and identification from Hibernia Wharf, Southwark', *London Archaeol*, 5, 103–5

HR77, HR78, HR79

Map site: 127, 128, 129
SLAEC: Martin Dean
NGR: TQ 3246 7930
SMR: 090716

Harper Road, SE1

Excavation in 1977 revealed an inhumation burial of 4th-c date, surrounded by iron nails, probably the remains of a coffin. An E–W aligned ditch was located, provisionally of the same date; as there was no slope to its base this probably served as a boundary rather than as a drain. Thirteen gullies of 17th-c date were probably the foundation trenches of tenter frames used in cloth finishing: two 18th-c maps show tenter grounds in this area. Excavation in 1979 revealed a second inhumation with associated iron nails, probably the remains of a wooden coffin. A mid-1st-c date was indicated by a Hofheim-type flagon alongside the head. A short section of a 4th-c ditch, at right angles to one found in 1977, suggested a field-system.

London Archaeol, 3, 1978, 162; 3, 1980, 388; Britannia, 9, 1978, 455; 11, 1980, 382; Surrey Archaeol Coll, 72, 1980, 247
Dean, M, 1977 'SLAEC excavations at Harper Road, Southwark', *London Archaeol*, 3, 122

Horseshoe Wharf, Clink Street, SE1

HSW90

Map site: 130
DGLA(S&L): Luke Fagan
NGR: TQ 3257 8041
SMR: 091354–7

Excavation in 1990, within the site of Winchester Palace and adjacent to 12th- and 14th-c timber waterfronts and a later stone riverwall (see NBW90 below), revealed at the SE corner a finely cobbled road surface with limestone kerbing aligned NW–SE and leading towards the slype at the W end of the Great Hall of the palace. It was sealed by a mid-17th-c floor containing building debris. The S side of a substantial stone-built riverwall of 16th–17th-c date was also recorded. (For plan, see WP83: Pickford's Wharf D.)

London Archaeol, 6, 1991, 306; Post-Medieval Archaeol, 25, 1991, 149; Surrey Archaeol Coll, 81, 1991–2, 163

Road Widening Scheme, Old Kent Road, Dunton Road, Humphrey Street, SE1

HUM90

Map site: 131
DGLA(S&L): Peter Thompson
NGR: TQ 3365 7835
SMR: 091332–4

Excavation in 1990 recovered flint waste flakes concentrated directly above natural strata in the E half of the site and accompanied by pottery sherds. A small gully, probably of prehistoric date, was found to contain a layer of burnt material. Two Roman ditches were examined, probably drains although the larger of them may have been a field or land boundary. Medieval and post-medieval features included a large ditch running N–S and a large channel on the same alignment, perhaps both dating to the 17th c. Two further ditches of similar date were discovered

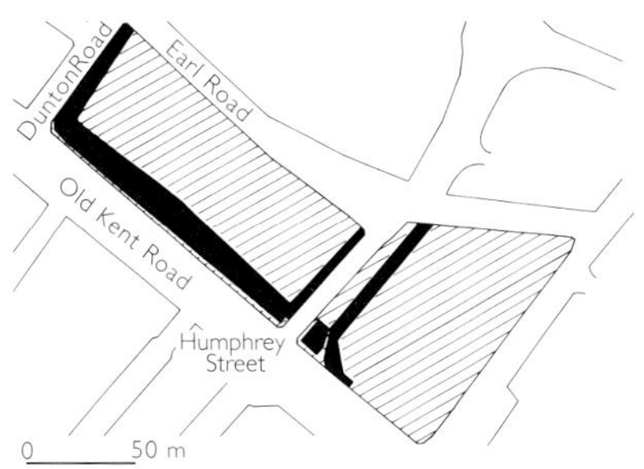

at the W end of the site, and evidence for 18th- and 19th-c bedding trenches and ploughsoil was recorded.

London Archaeol, 6, 1991, 306; 6, 1992, 421; Britannia, 22, 1991, 273; Surrey Archaeol Coll, 81, 1991–2, 164

King's Head Yard (sewer trench), SE1

KHYST82

Map site: 132
SLAEC: Brian Yule
NGR: TQ 3269 8016

A watching brief in 1982 recorded possible evidence of 2nd-c construction.

Swain, H, 1988 'Gazetteer of sites', in Hinton, P (ed), *Excavations in Southwark 1973–76, Lambeth 1973–79*, 483 (120)

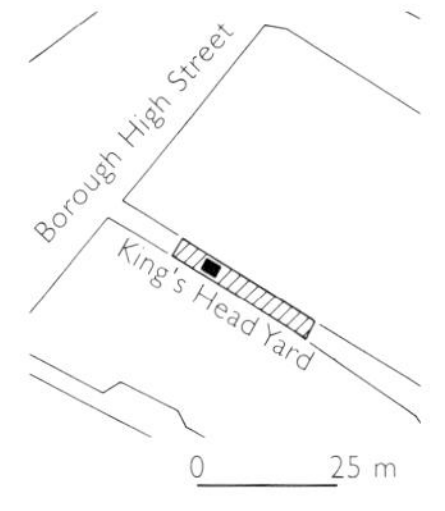

305–319 Lower Road, SE8

LR88

Map site: 133
DGLA(S&L): Peter Thompson
NGR: TQ 3598 7864

A trial excavation in 1988 revealed mainly topographical information, though some struck flints and several undated pits were located in natural sand and may represent limited prehistoric activity on the edge of an undefined sand island.

London Archaeol, 6, 1989, 77; Surrey Archaeol Coll, 80, 1990, 225

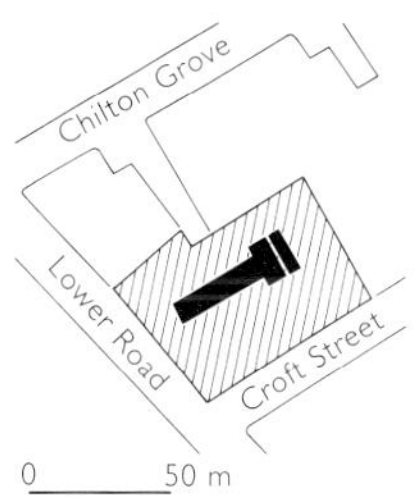

MBW73

Map site: 134
SLAEC: Harvey Sheldon, John Alexander
NGR: TQ 3347 8018
SMR: 090478, 091052–4

Mark Brown's Wharf, Tooley Street, SE1

Excavation in 1973 revealed, in the S area, 17th- and 18th-c building debris and evidence of dumping of delftware manufacture waste. Further traces of this were also recorded in the N area, where the main feature was a band of peat 0.6m thick, thought to represent a regression of the river in the later prehistoric period. If this was combined with the silt deposits above it, the area would have been underwater in the Roman period.

London Archaeol, 2, 1974, 135; *Post-Medieval Archaeol*, 8, 1974, 125
Hinton, P, Orton, C, & Yule, B, 1988 'Excavations at Mark Browns Wharf', in Hinton, P (ed), *Excavations in Southwark 1973–76, Lambeth 1973–79*, 133–56

MDW88

Map site: 135
DGLA(S&L): Alison Steele
NGR: TQ 3340 7880

Bricklayers' Arms, Page's Walk, Mandela Way, SE1

A trial excavation in 1988 revealed peats overlying clays which apparently represented the W edge of an early mere or marshy area subject to flooding, drying and vegetation growth according to the level of the Thames. The peat may be a further instance of the Tilbury IV Late Bronze Age peats found elsewhere in N Southwark. In the E part of the site flood clays and natural strata were cut by 18th- and early 19th-c intrusions.

London Archaeol, 6, 1989, 77; *Surrey Archaeol Coll*, 80, 1990, 224

MON90

Map site: 136
DGLA(S&L): Kieron Heard
NGR: TQ 3271 8032
SMR: 091340–2

Montague Chambers, Montague Close, SE1

Excavation in 1990 revealed the truncation of natural gravels, probably by quarrying during the construction of the nearby Roman roads. A fragmentary sequence of three clay and timber buildings, all aligned on the road to London Bridge (Roman Road 1), was uncovered. The earliest building, probably dating from the 1st c, contained at least two rooms. Medieval rubbish pits and layers of crushed stone and building material were truncated by two post-medieval foundations, one incorporating moulded masonry fragments probably derived from the priory of St Mary Overy.

London Archaeol, 6, 1991, 306; *Britannia*, 22, 1991, 273; *Medieval Archaeol*, 35, 1991, 156; *Post-Medieval Archaeol*, 25, 1991, 133; *Surrey Archaeol Coll*, 81, 1991–2, 164

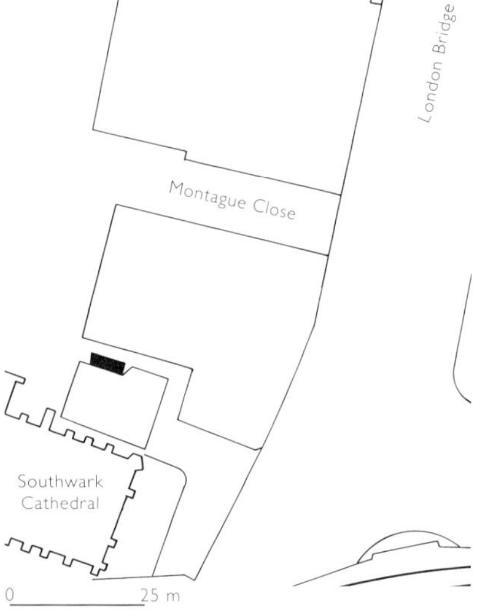

MOR86, MOR87, MOR88

Map site: 137–9
DGLA(S&L): Alan Thompson
NGR: TQ 3324 8020
SMR: 090812–14, 091180

Morgan's Lane, Tooley Street, SE1

A trial excavation in 1986 revealed a sequence of waterlaid clays over a peat horizon thought to represent the Bronze Age Tilbury IV deposit. Also exposed was a medieval waterfront structure of oak, aligned E–W, with raking braces, to the N of which lay parts of a building set behind a later waterfront, both constructed of chalk and stone and of late medieval date. In addition, traces were found of a large ditch or channel which probably fed into the millstream running along the W boundary of the site, and which was replaced by brick culverts, possibly in the 17th c. Excavation in 1987 revealed the remains of a substantial moated building, including external N- and S-facing masonry walls, timber revetments retaining the external moat banks and details of internal buildings.

The moated enclosure is probably to be identified with Fastolf's Place, built by Sir John Fastolf in the mid-15th c. Further work in 1988 revealed at least three wall fragments composed of squared ragstone blocks, from 'The Rosary' (see GAS88 above). Immediately to the E of Morgan's Lane was found a millstream, flowing into the Thames. (For plan, see ABB86.)

London Archaeol, 5, 1987, 277; 5, 1988, 414; 6, 1989, 77; *Medieval Archaeol*, 31, 1987, 132; 32, 1988, 252; 33, 1989, 185; *Post-Medieval Archaeol*, 21, 1987, 289; *Surrey Archaeol Coll*, 78, 1987, 146; 79, 1989, 188; 80, 1990, 224

6–8 Morocco Street, SE1

MRC90

Map site: 140
DGLA(S&L): Aidan Allen
NGR: TQ 3316 7965
SMR: 091343–5

An excavation in 1990 revealed waterlaid clay sealed by a peat layer thought to represent the Bronze Age Tilbury IV horizon. Further layers of clay sealed the peat, and the earliest evidence of development dates to the post-medieval period. This took the form of a drainage ditch, buildings along the street frontage and the digging of pits for use in the tanning industry.

London Archaeol, 6, 1991, 306; *Post-Medieval Archaeol*, 25, 1991, 163; *Surrey Archaeol Coll*, 81, 1991–2, 164

National Wharf, Bermondsey Wall East, SE16

NAT90

Map site: 141
DGLA(S&L): Aidan Allen
NGR: TQ 3472 7974
SMR: 091338–9

An evaluation excavation in 1990 revealed deposits dating from the early 17th c. Two phases of timber waterfronts were exposed, both incorporating reused boat timbers. The waterfront structures were sealed by substantial dumped deposits.

London Archaeol, 6, 1991, 306; *Post-Medieval Archaeol*, 25, 1991, 133; *Surrey Archaeol Coll*, 81, 1991–2, 165

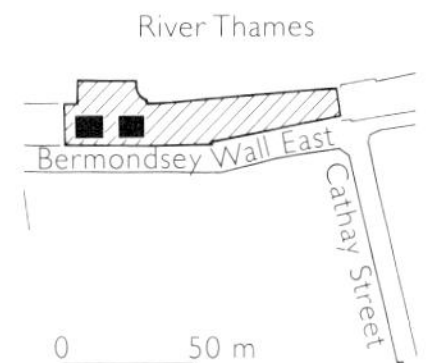

Newington Butts, SE11

NB76

Map site: 142
SLAEC: Robin Densem
NGR: TQ 3186 7870

A watching brief in 1976 revealed a number of ditches or pits of late Roman and medieval date, cutting natural.

Swain, H, 1988 'Gazetteer of sites', in Hinton, P (ed), *Excavations in Southwark 1973–76, Lambeth 1973–79*, 484 (157)

New British Wharf and Clink Wharf, Clink Street, SE1

NBW90

Map site: 143
DGLA(S&L): Sophie Jackson
NGR: TQ 3253 8042
SMR: 091335–7, 091649

An evaluation excavation in 1989 on a site adjoining Winchester Palace revealed a 12th-c timber post at Clink Wharf, sealed by 12th–14th-c dumped deposits containing residual Roman material. A 15th–16th-c stone riverwall with a tidal drain was partly revealed at New British Wharf, and was continued or replaced by a similar wall at Clink Wharf. The foundations of 18th- and 19th-c buildings were constructed on dumped deposits behind the riverwall on both wharves. Beyond the stone riverwall at New British Wharf was late 18th- to early 19th-c dumping, interpreted as infill behind a replacement riverwall that had reclaimed more of the Thames foreshore. (For plan, see WP83: Pickford's Wharf D.)

London Archaeol, 6, 1991, 306; *Medieval Archaeol*, 35, 1991, 155; *Post-Medieval Archaeol*, 25, 1991, 133; *Surrey Archaeol Coll*, 81, 1991–2, 163

NC81

Map site: 144
SLAEC: Brian Yule
NGR: TQ 3212 7937
SMR: 091231

63–67 Newington Causeway, SE1

A watching brief in 1981 recorded evidence of natural topography only.

Britannia, 12, 1981, 353

NDRS87

Map site: 145
DGLA(S&L): Carrie Cowan,
Hedley Swain, Ian Tyers
NGR: TQ 3655 8021

Nelson Dock, Rotherhithe Street, SE16

Observation in 1987, following the reported uncovering of 17th-c dock timbers, revealed numerous timbers *in situ* and in the spoil which were considered to be of recent date and not to warrant further work.

OKR82

Map site: 146
SLAEC: Derek Seeley
NGR: TQ 3420 7800

SEGB trenches (various), Old Kent Road, SE1

A watching brief in 1982 revealed an inhumation burial of probable Roman date.

Swain, H, 1988 'Gazetteer of sites', in Hinton, P (ed), *Excavations in Southwark 1973–76, Lambeth 1973–79,* 484 (166)

OKR90

Map site: 147
DGLA(S&L): Peter Thompson
NGR: TQ 3430 7792
SMR: 091361–4

Canal Bridge Highway Improvement Scheme, Old Kent Road, SE1

Excavation in 1990 revealed natural waterlaid sands, gravels and clays sloping down towards the E and covered by a thin layer of weathered sand containing flint blades, scrapers, cores and waste flakes. Three shallow, undated gullies may be contemporary. Waterlaid clays sealed the prehistoric levels and were cut by a number of Roman drainage ditches containing large quantities of pottery indicative of nearby settlement. Also located was a metalled gravel surface which probably formed part of a small yard and included pottery dating to the 2nd c.

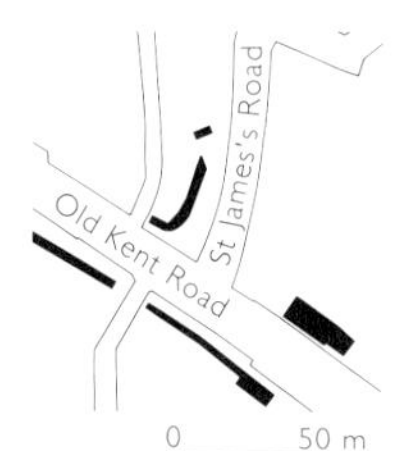

London Archaeol, 6, 1991, 306 ; *Britannia,* 22, 1991, 273; *Surrey Archaeol Coll,* 81, 1991–2, 165

PEC90

Map site: 148
DGLA(S&L): James Hunter
NGR: TQ 3404 7674
SMR: 091318–20

Rear of 1–83 Peckham High Street, SE15

Excavation in 1990 recovered flint flakes and abraded pottery as the only evidence of prehistoric and Roman presence in the area. A pit, ditch and other manmade features contained 12th-c and residual Saxon pottery. A sequence of post-holes was dated by pottery to the 14th c. Most of the features examined, however, related to post-medieval market gardening.

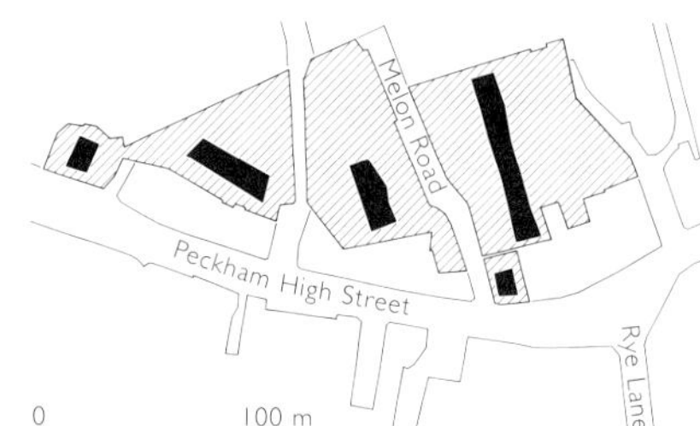

London Archaeol, 6, 1991, 306; *Medieval Archaeol,* 35, 1991, 156; *Post-Medieval Archaeol,* 25, 1991, 133; *Surrey Archaeol Coll,* 81, 1991–2, 164

Peckham Hill Street, Commercial Way, SE15

A watching brief in 1983 recorded evidence of natural topography only.

PHSCW83

Map site: 149
SLAEC: Peter Hinton
NGR: TQ 3414 7725

Phoenix Wharf, 4 Jamaica Road, SE1

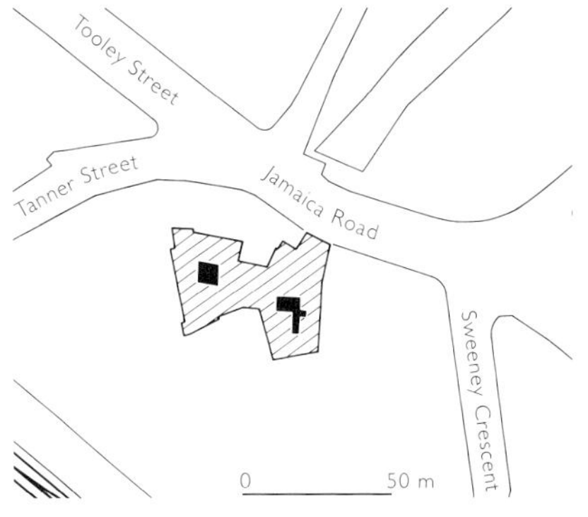

A trial excavation in 1988 revealed in the W trench high
natural sands overlying gravels into which had cut the N
bank of a river flowing from SW to NE and recorded on
17th-c maps: there was evidence of a 17th-c revetment
followed by silting. The E trench produced no evidence of
the S bank of the river, though the riverbed deposits sealed
a buried prehistoric land surface. A ploughsoil containing
flints and pottery sealed the natural sands and was scored
by ard marks of Bronze Age date. Spade marks and
post-holes were also found, and preceding the agricultural
phase was a rectangular cooking pit, fed by a small E–W
stream. Also examined was a deep N–S aligned channel
cutting the prehistoric features, part of the original inlet of St Saviour's before it was formalised as a
dock in the medieval period.

London Archaeol, 6, 1989, 78; *Surrey Archaeol Coll*, 80, 1990, 225
Anon, 1988 'Earliest agricultural activity in London', Mosaic, *London Archaeol*, 6, 28
Bowsher, J M C, 1991 'A burnt mound from Phoenix Wharf, south-east London: a preliminary report', in Hodder, M A, & Barfield, L H
  (eds), *Burnt mounds and hot stone technology: papers from the Second International Burnt Mound Conference, Sandwell*, 11–19

PHW88

Map site: 150
DGLA(S&L): Julian Bowsher
NGR: TQ 3379 7969
SMR: 091128–31

Pitt's Court, Tooley Street, SE1

Excavation in 1988 yielded limited archaeological evidence in the form of garden soils with traces of
tree roots and modern rubbish pits. (For plan, see ABB86.)

London Archaeol, 6, 1989, 77; *Medieval Archaeol*, 33, 1989, 185; *Surrey Archaeol Coll*, 80, 1990, 224

PIT88

Map site: 151
DGLA(S&L). Alan Thompson
NGR: TQ 3320 8020
SMR: 091185

Rear of 18 Park Street, SE1

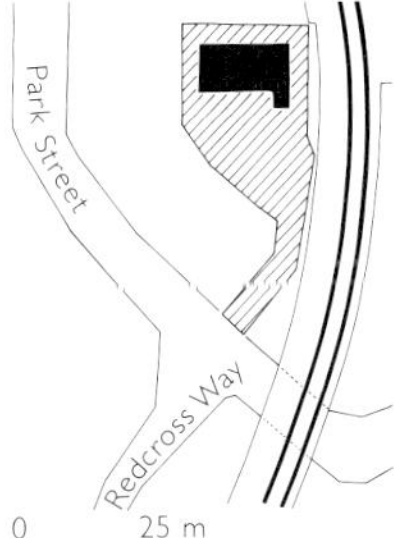

Excavation in 1990 revealed dark earth sealing a series of Roman deposits and a
ditch aligned N–S, which continued beyond the limit of excavation and probably
dated from the mid- to late 1st c. Just to the W several intercutting linear
ditches were also located, all aligned NE–SW and assumed to follow an existing
boundary: one of the ditches featured several post-holes in its base. Two phases
of clay and timber buildings were excavated: the earlier aligned NE–SW and
constructed of upright timbers surrounded by clay, while the later phase was
aligned E–W and constructed with squared timber beams. The sequence
probably reflects a reorganisation of property boundaries. Ditches on the later,
E–W, alignment were also located and contained material which suggested an
early 2nd-c date.

London Archaeol, 6, 1991, 307; *Britannia*, 22, 1991, 273; *Surrey Archaeol Coll*, 81, 1991–2, 163
Cowan, C, in prep. *The development of north-west Roman Southwark: excavations at Courage's Brewery, 1974–90*

PRK90

Map site: 152
DGLA(S&L): Helen Jones
NGR: TQ 3250 8027
SMR: 091346–50, 091378

PW86

Map site: 153
DGLA(S&L): Eric Norton
NGR: TQ 3480 7972
SMR: 090592–3

Platform Wharf, Cathay Street, SE16

Trial work in 1986 succeeded in locating a medieval building first discovered in 1907: the stone walls of a large rectangular structure about 30m x 20m, and a moat about 8m wide, were revealed, probably parts of the royal residence constructed at Rotherhithe for Edward III in the mid-14th c. The external walls survived to a height of more than 3m, and internal walls and floor surfaces were also recorded. A clay wall, which may have enclosed the buildings of an outer court, was also located. In the early 17th c the residence became a delftware factory; the brick base of a kiln was found to cut the walls of the NW tower, and two brick-lined puddling pits were inserted into the E wall and the backfilled moat. The factory appears to have been abandoned by the end of the 17th c, and a layer of kiln waste 1m thick was dumped into the moat. (See also PW89, PW90, below.)

London Archaeol, 5, 1986, 163; 5, 1987, 276–7; *Medieval Archaeol,* 31, 1987, 132; *Post-Medieval Archaeol,* 21, 1987, 288; *Surrey Archaeol Coll,*
   78, 1987, 146
Norman, P, 1908 'Remains of an ancient building at Rotherhithe', *Surrey Archaeol Coll,* 20, 132–42
Norton, E, 1988 'The moated manor house at Platform Wharf, Rotherhithe', *London Archaeol,* 5, 395–401

PW89, PW90

Map site: 154, 155
DGLA(S&L): Simon
Blatherwick
NGR: TQ 3478 7972
SMR: 091238–9, 091369–72

Platform Wharf, Cathay Street, SE16

A trial excavation in 1989 S of the moated manor house of Edward III (see PW86 above) located prehistoric flint tools, waste flakes and a core, together with possible structures and extensive dumps of waste material, both associated with the 17th-c delftware factory. Further excavation in 1990 on the S half of the site recovered a superb Neolithic polished axe and at least one Mesolithic blade, and revealed a linear gully which predated the moat and produced pottery of early medieval date; its S portion contained a line of stake-holes which ran along the W edge and turned E at its S end. A series of medieval post-holes and beam slots, which predated three chalk-lined pits (probably cesspits), was also revealed. No structure was located that could definitely be associated with the 17th-c pottery factory, although large quantities of delftware and kiln material were recovered.

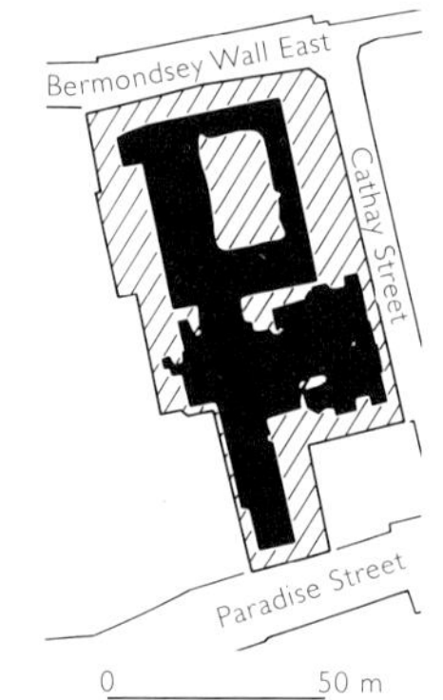

London Archaeol, 6, 1990, 193; 6, 1991, 307; *Medieval Archaeol,* 35, 1991, 156; *Post-Medieval Archaeol,* 24, 1990, 201; 25, 1991, 163;
   Surrey Archaeol Coll, 80, 1990, 225; 81, 1991–2, 165
Blatherwick, S, in prep. *A royal residence at Rotherhithe: Edward III's manor house at Platform Wharf, Rotherhithe, London SE16, 1985–1994*

QBCS75

Map site: 156
SLAEC: Alan Graham,
C Murray
NGR: TQ 3209 7958

Queen's Buildings, Collinson Street, SE1

A watching brief in 1975 recorded Roman and medieval agricultural soils but no occupation levels.

London Archaeol, 2, 1976, 372

QEN88

Map site: 157
DGLA(S&L): Toby Catchpole
NGR: TQ 3376 7985

Queen Elizabeth Street (north), SE1

A trial excavation in 1988 revealed that the site lay N of the sands and gravels of the Horsleydown island. An early N–S aligned channel with gently sloping sides was examined and found to have been recut with a sharp V-profile 4m wide. Into it had been inserted two pegged timbers, one a horizontal beam and the other a pine plank standing on its edge, possibly intended to create a water reservoir for a post-medieval tannery. The channel had silted up and been filled in, to be replaced by a timber drain formed of a bored elm trunk into which was inserted a square-sectioned pipe made of four elm planks nailed together. Four pits, apparently of the same date as the drain, were lined with pine planking and served either as handling or soaking pits for the tannery.

London Archaeol, 6, 1989, 78; Britannia, 21, 1990, 345; Post-Medieval Archaeol, 23, 1989, 40; Surrey Archaeol Coll, 80, 1990, 225

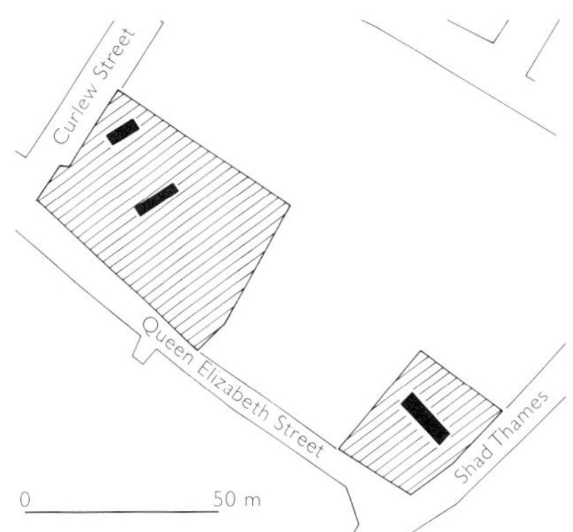

Queen Elizabeth Street (south), SE1

A trial excavation in 1988 revealed a scatter of worked Neolithic flints and some prehistoric pottery sherds in the weathered surface of the natural sands capping Horsleydown island, and indicating early occupation there. A recut drainage ditch of Roman date ran NE–SW across the site. Substantial remains were found of features relating to the extensive post-medieval tanning industry of N Southwark, including a horncore-lined circular pit and channels.

London Archaeol, 6, 1989, 78; Britannia, 21, 1990, 345; Post-Medieval Archaeol, 23, 1989, 40; Surrey Archaeol Coll, 80, 1990, 225

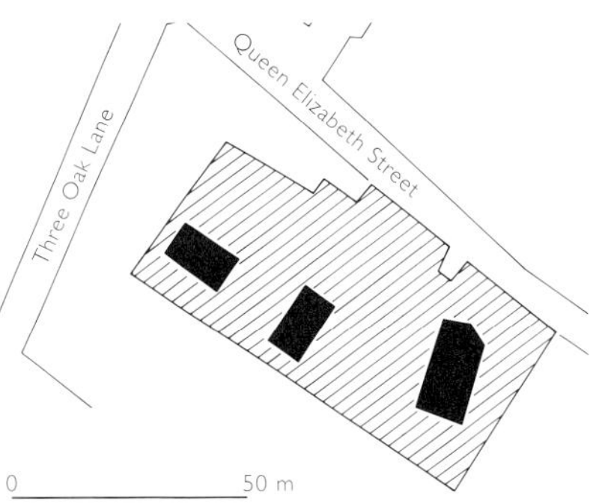

QESS88

Map site: 158
DGLA(S&L): Tom McDonald
NGR: TQ 3376 7985
SMR: 091132–5

Royal Eye Hospital, St George's Circus, SE1

Trial excavation in 1988 revealed ploughsoil overlying natural gravels, and cut features containing tile and pottery of medieval to 18th-c date.

London Archaeol, 6, 1989, 78; Surrey Archaeol Coll, 80, 1990, 221

REH88

Map site: 159
DGLA(S&L): John Roche
NGR: TQ 3160 7947
SMR: 091136

Rephidim Street, SE1

Excavation in 1976 revealed evidence of Roman agricultural activity, close to the presumed line of Watling Street (Roman Road 1).

London Archaeol, 3, 1977, 39; Britannia, 8, 1977, 410; Surrey Archaeol Coll, 72, 1980, 248

RS76

Map site: 160
SLAEC: Michael Hammerson
NGR: TQ 3290 7920

Rupack Street, SE16

A trial excavation in 1988 recovered a flint scraper, blade and several fragments of pottery beneath waterlaid clays. A possible Roman ditch was located, containing a coin of Constantine the Great.

London Archaeol, 5, 1988, 414; Surrey Archaeol Coll, 79, 1989, 188

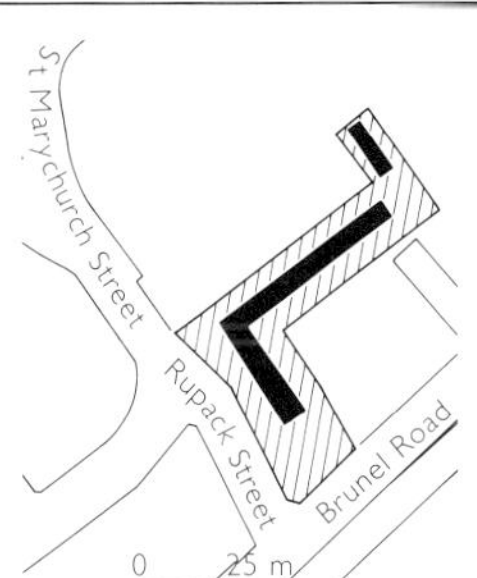

RUP88

Map site: 161
DGLA(S&L): Simon Blatherwick
NGR: TQ 3517 7967
SMR: 091157–8

<table>
<tr><td>

SB76

Map site: 162
SLAEC: Brian Yule
NGR: TQ 3250 7970
SMR: 090720

</td><td>

Silvester Buildings, Silvester Street, SE1

Excavation in 1976 revealed evidence of flooding on low-lying ground in the early Roman period. A 1st-c pit and a late Roman well were located, as well as pits of medieval date, close to the frontage of Kent Street, a medieval thoroughfare.

London Archaeol, 3, 1977, 39; *Britannia*, 8, 1977, 410; *Surrey Archaeol Coll*, 72, 1980, 247

</td></tr>
</table>

<table>
<tr><td>

SBH88

Map site: 163
DGLA(S&L): Julian Bowsher,
Simon Blatherwick; EH(CEU):
John Hinchcliffe,
David Batchelor
NGR: TQ 3228 8042

</td><td>

Southbridge House, 2–10 Southwark Bridge Road, SE1

Excavation in 1988 uncovered remains of the Rose Theatre (*c* 1587–1605), in which two construction phases were identified. The first (*c* 1587–92) consisted of a polygonal building with perhaps 12 or 14 sides, its inner and outer walls some 3.5m apart; an inner yard, with a partly raked mortar floor, some 13m in diameter; and a stage about 5–6m wide. In the second phase the theatre was extended to the N, the yard area increased and the stage moved back some 3m; the yard was refloored with a layer of clinker and crushed hazelnuts. The superstructure was of timber with a lath and plaster infill, and rested on brick sleeper walls set in turn on chalk foundation pads. A humic layer represented thatching from the roof, and wooden shingles may have been part of the stage roof. (Some of the site records are held by EH.)

</td><td>

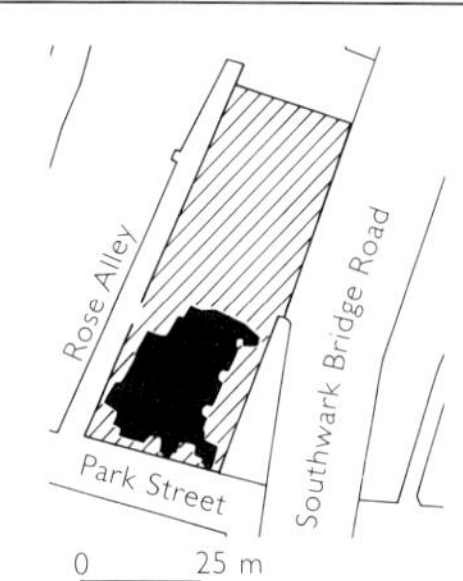

</td></tr>
</table>

London Archaeol, 6, 1990, 193; *Post-Medieval Archaeol*, 24, 1990, 209
Blatherwick, S, & Bowsher, J, 1989 'The Rose Theatre', *Rescue News*, 48, 2
Blatherwick, S, & Bowsher, J, 1989 'The Rose Theatre', *The Shakespeare Newsletter*
Bowsher, J, 1998 *The Rose Theatre: an archaeological discovery*
Museum of London, nd, *The Rose Theatre: past, present & future*

<table>
<tr><td>

SCC77

Map site: 164
SLAEC: Michael Hammerson
NGR: TQ 3270 8030

</td><td>

Southwark Cathedral (crypt), Cathedral Street, SE1

Excavation in 1977 revealed traces of clay and timber buildings of 1st-c date, and a timber-lined well of probably late Roman date. The well contained a group of sculpted stone provisionally dated to the 2nd c and perhaps the furnishings of a mausoleum, with a large quantity of building rubble, much of which was burnt and damaged. A substantial medieval chalk wall was also recorded.

London Archaeol, 3, 1978, 161; *Britannia*, 9, 1978, 453; *Surrey Archaeol Coll*, 72, 1980, 248
Anon, 1977 'Dig under Southwark Cathedral', Mosaic, *London Archaeol*, 3, 112
Hammerson, M, 1978 'Excavations under Southwark Cathedral', *London Archaeol*, 3, 206–12

</td></tr>
</table>

<table>
<tr><td>

SIP88

Map site: 165
DGLA(S&L): Michael Webber
NGR: TQ 3217 8045
SMR: 091289–93

</td><td>

Skinmarket Place, Bankside, SE1

An excavation in 1988–9 located a previously unknown island of high sand which yielded Neolithic pottery and flints and was sealed by flood clays cut by early medieval ditches. These were covered in turn by further flood clays of 14th–15th-c date, cut by a pit of probable Tudor date which contained two bear skeletons, evidently from a known bearbaiting ring on the site. Evidence of timber-revetted 17th-c fishponds was also examined, and the King's Pike Garden located.

</td><td>

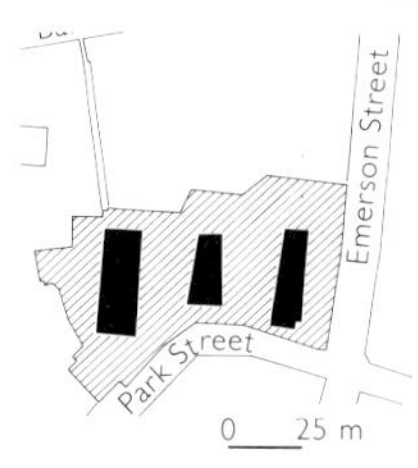

</td></tr>
</table>

London Archaeol, 6, 1990, 193; *Medieval Archaeol*, 34, 1990, 184; *Post-Medieval Archaeol*, 24, 1990, 209; *Surrey Archaeol Coll*, 80, 1990, 221

St James's Estate, St James's Road, SE16

An excavation in 1990 revealed natural waterlaid clays and peats in part destroyed by 19th-c industrial intrusion, and in places sealed by a thick layer of brick rubble and sand which was probably related to the construction of the nearby Surrey Canal.

London Archaeol, 6, 1991, 307; Surrey Archaeol Coll, 81, 1991–2, 165

SJR90

Map site: 166
DGLA(S&L): Wendy Rogers
NGR: TQ 3440 7970
SMR: 091306–7

St James (area 1), Southwark Park Road, SE16

A watching brief in 1976 revealed evidence of natural topography only.

Swain, H, 1988 'Gazetteer of sites', in Hinton, P (ed), *Excavations in Southwark 1973–76, Lambeth 1973–79*, 485 (187)

SJSPR76

Map site: 167
SLAEC: Harvey Sheldon
NGR: TQ 3450 7875

Skipton Street, SE1

Excavation in 1988–9 on the W side of Newington Causeway, presumed to follow the line of Roman Stane Street, revealed a metalled area close to the road, which may have been a yard or track leading to it. Two ditches of Roman date were found, one running parallel to the Roman road, and one at right angles to it. Three large circular pits and a third ditch yielded a quantity of tile, 3rd-c coins and pottery, and fragments of two Roman sculptures provisionally dated to the early 2nd c. A Roman cremation burial in a broken flagon was found in a ditch.

London Archaeol, 6, 1990, 193; Britannia, 21, 1990, 345; 22, 1991, 273; Medieval Archaeol, 34, 1990, 184; Surrey Archaeol Coll, 80, 1990, 221

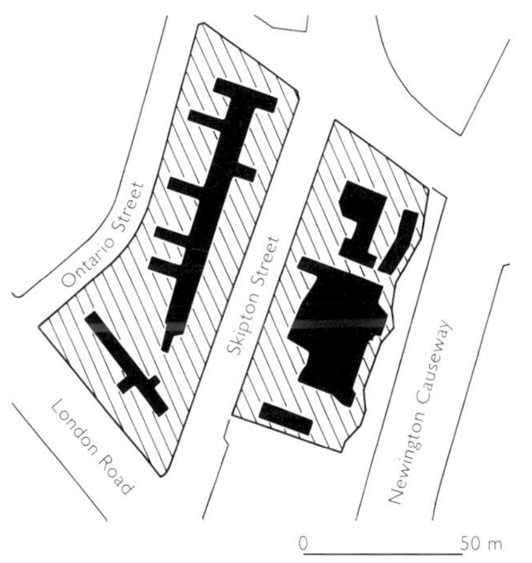

SKS88

Map site: 168
DGLA(S&L): Wendy Rogers
NGR: TQ 3190 7920
SMR: 091260

Southwark Leisure Centre, Elephant and Castle, SE1

A watching brief in 1976 revealed topographical evidence with Tilbury IV deposits.

Swain, H, 1988 'Gazetteer of sites', in Hinton, P (ed), *Excavations in Southwark 1973–76, Lambeth 1973–79*, 485 (205)

SLC76

Map site: 169
SLAEC: Brian Yule
NGR: TQ 3190 7890

St Olaf House (west of), Tooley Street, SE1

Observation in 1984 recorded a sequence of Roman dumped deposits overlying natural clay and cut by truncated medieval foundations. The remains of the 18th-c hexagonal stone and brick built tower of St Olaf's church survived to the modern street level.

London Archaeol, 5, 1986, 163; Britannia, 17, 1986, 409; Medieval Archaeol, 30, 1986, 143; Post-Medieval Archaeol, 20, 1986, 333; Surrey Archaeol Coll, 78, 1987, 145

SOH84

Map site: 170
NGR: TQ 3290 8035
DGLA(S&L): Michael Hammerson, George Dennis, Derek Seeley

SRWS73

Map site: 171
SLAEC
NGR: TQ 3296 7995
SMR: 090406

Sparrick's Row, Weston Street, SE1

Evidence of natural topography only.

SS73

Map site: 172
SLAEC: Alan Graham,
Bernard Johnson, Irene
Schwab, Laura Schaaf
NGR: TQ 2347 7961

Junction of Swan Street, Great Dover Street, SE1

Excavation in 1973–4 revealed two Roman inhumations of 3rd–4th-c date, both cut into the side of a wide shallow ditch aligned NE–SW whose fill was probably of 3rd-c date. Evidence was recovered of the marshy character of the area in the early Roman period.

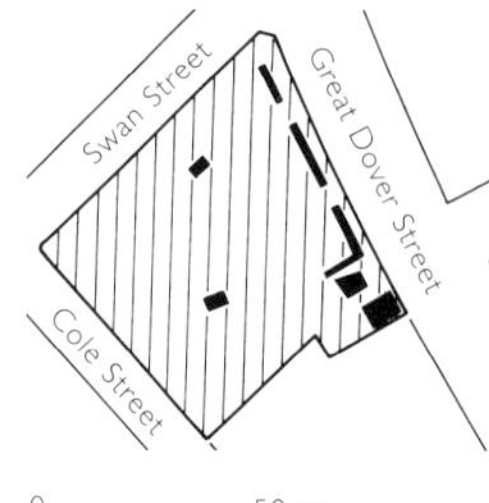

London Archaeol, 2, 1974, 135; 2, 1975, 258
Andrew, N, 1978 'Human bones: burials 1 and 2', in Graham, A, 495–6
Bird, J, & Marsh, G, 1978 'Decorated samian', in Graham, A, 482
Graham, A, 1978 'Excavations at Swan Street/Great Dover Street', in Bird, J, Graham, A H, Sheldon, H, & Townend, P (eds), *Southwark excavations 1972–74,* 473–97
Hammerson, M, 1978 'Coin', in Graham, A, 491
Hammerson, M, & Murray, C, 1978 'Other Roman pottery', in Graham, A, 482–90
Rixson, D, 1978 'Animal bones', in Graham, A, 494–5
Spencer, P J, 1978 'Organic data/mollusca from the Roman ditch', in Graham, A, 493–4
Townend, P, & Hinton, P, 1978 'Glass', in Graham, A, 490–1
Townend, P, & Hinton, P, 1978 'Small finds', in Graham, A, 491–3
Watt, R J, 1978 'Other human bones', in Graham, A, 497

SSD88

Map site: 173
DGLA(S&L): Toby Catchpole
NGR: TQ 3388 7984

St Saviour's Dock, 24 Shad Thames, SE1

Excavation in 1988 revealed evidence of the slow accumulation of waterlaid clays until the 16th c. The presence of imported material, such as Spanish olive jars and German jettons, indicates that much of the earliest activity was related to the dock. A large timber frame was constructed, probably in the 17th c, perhaps to form a dockside wharf. The S half of the site was composed of dumped layers dating from the mid-17th to the late 18th c.

STS88

Map site: 174
DGLA(S&L): Peter Thompson
NGR: TQ 3283 8014
SMR: 091137–8

21–27 St Thomas Street, SE1

An excavation in 1988 of a site at the E limit of Roman and medieval settlement in N Southwark revealed linear Roman ditches and gullies beneath a sequence of Roman dumping and silting. Several lengths of late medieval chalk and flint foundations were located, the best preserved of them in association with a surface of crushed chalk and tile. A continuation of the wall-line was represented by a series of post-holes representing piling for the foundations.

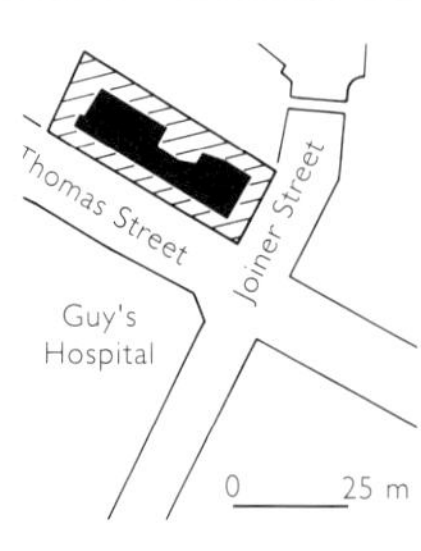

London Archaeol, 6, 1989, 78; *Britannia,* 20, 1989, 309; *Medieval Archaeol,* 33, 1989, 186; *Surrey Archaeol Coll,* 80, 1990, 223

The Surrey Theatre, 124 Blackfriars Road, SE1

Excavation in 1990 to investigate the surviving evidence of the Surrey Theatre revealed substantial remains of the 1865 music hall, including the foyer, pit and stalls area, the orchestral part of the suspended pit floor, and ancillary rooms. The depth of the stage area precluded examination there, but possible traces of the original Circus of 1782 were recorded. There was no evidence of the first theatre of 1808.

London Archaeol, 6, 1991, 307; *Surrey Archaeol Coll*, 81, 1991–2, 163

SUR90

Map site: 175
DGLA(S&L): Aidan Allen
NGR: TQ 3163 7951

Symond's Wharf, Tooley Street, SE1

Excavation in 1988 revealed the NE corner of the moat of 'The Rosary', indicating an enclosure measuring some 50m x 40m. Further E, and directly associated with the river frontage, were the remains of two substantial docks or inlets, the easternmost being of an early phase of construction and dated by pottery to *c* 1298–1350. (For plan, see ABB86.)

London Archaeol, 6, 1989, 77; *Medieval Archaeol*, 33, 1989, 185; *Surrey Archaeol Coll*, 80, 1990, 224

SYM88

Map site: 176
DGLA(S&L): Alan Thompson
NGR: TQ 3320 8020
SMR: 091180–1

Shipwright Yard, Tooley Street, SE1

A watching brief on a small section in 1975 recorded only late dumped material and topographical evidence.

Swain, H, 1988 'Gazetteer of sites', in Hinton, P (ed), *Excavations in Southwark 1973–76, Lambeth 1973–79*, 485 (196)

SYTS75

Map site: 177
SLAEC: George Dennis
NGR: TQ 3310 8016
SMR: 090408

9 Tanner Street, SE1

Excavation in 1987 revealed alluvial clays and peats of unknown date overlaid by further clays containing medieval pottery. Several post-medieval pits and a ditch were located, as well as a small natural channel running E–W and including large quantities of 18th-c material. The channel was cut by a linear pit containing four upright barrels, and by a further pit containing large quantities of horn cores and sheep metapodials. Three large 19th-c tanning pits with linings of pine planking backed with clay were also found.

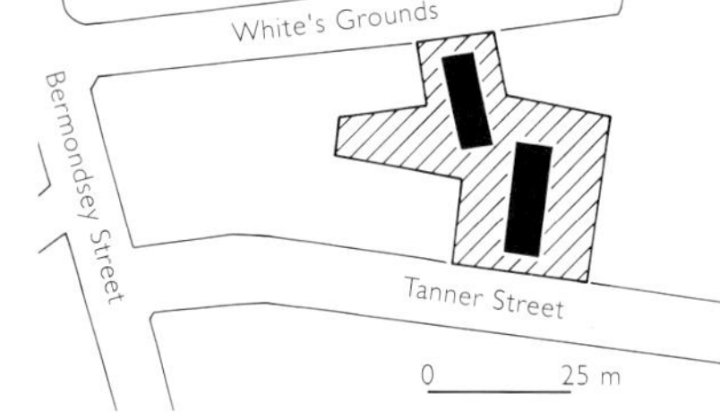

London Archaeol, 5, 1988, 414; *Post-Medieval Archaeol*, 22, 1988, 208; *Surrey Archaeol Coll*, 79, 1989, 187

TAN87

Map site: 178
DGLA(S&L): Kieron Heard
NGR: TQ 3331 7972
SMR: 091163–7

Trinity Street (GPO tunnel), SE1

A watching brief in 1976 recorded evidence of natural topography only.

Swain, H, 1988 'Gazetteer of sites', in Hinton, P (ed), *Excavations in Southwark 1973–76, Lambeth 1973–79*, 486 (232)

TSGPO76

Map site: 179
SLAEC: Michael Hammerson
NGR: TQ 3229 7959

TW70

Map site: 180
SLAEC: Harvey Sheldon
NGR: TQ 3286 8034
SMR: 090872–4

Toppings and Sun Wharves, Tooley Street, SE1

Excavation in 1970 revealed clay and timber buildings dating to the 1st c. A medieval stone building and a medieval and Tudor dock were examined.

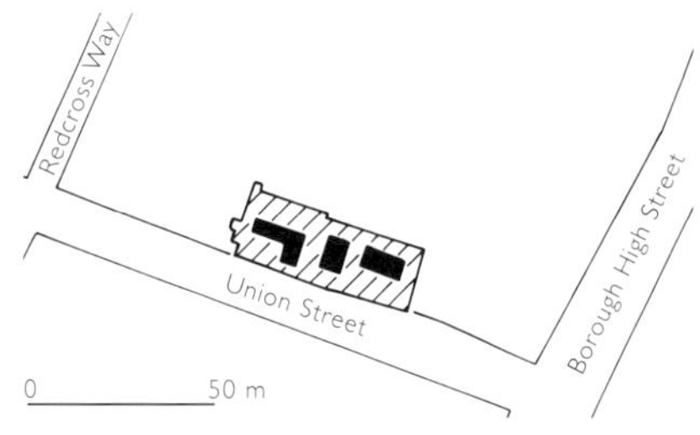

Britannia, 2, 1971, 274; 3, 1972, 337; *Medieval Archaeol*, 15, 1971, 155
Barrett, J, 1974 'Prehistoric pottery', in Sheldon, H L, 32
Bird, J, 1974 'The samian ware', in Sheldon, H L, 34–41
Cresswell, J, 1974 'Flints', in Sheldon, H L, 31–3
Edwards, R, 1974 'Documentary sources in relation to the excavation', in Sheldon, H L, 3–8
Evans, P, 1974 'The other Roman pottery from the early Roman settlement', in Sheldon, H L, 41–63
Hammerson, M J, 1974 'Coins', in Sheldon, H L, 87–90
Orton, C, Orton, J, & Evans, P, 1974 'Medieval and Tudor pottery', in Sheldon, H L, 64–87
Pratt, P, & Pye, E, 1974 'The clay wall from building III and the plaster from building VI', in Sheldon, H L, 112–13
Rixson, D, 1974 'Animal bones', in Sheldon, H L, 108–11
Schwab, I, 1974 'Glass', in Sheldon, H L, 103 & 106–7
Schwab, I, 1974 'Small finds', in Sheldon, H L, 100–3
Sheldon, H, 1971 'Excavations at Toppings Wharf, Tooley Street, Southwark', *London Archaeol*, 1, 252–4
Sheldon, H L, 1974 'Excavations at Toppings and Sun Wharves, Southwark, 1970–72', *Trans London Middlesex Archaeol Soc*, 25, 1–116
Spencer, B W, 1974 'The lead ampulla', in Sheldon, H L, 113–15
Thomas, K D, 1974 'Roman oyster shells from buildings III and IV', in Sheldon, H L, 111
Tribbick, R, 1974 'Metal small finds', in Sheldon, H L, 90–9

UPP88

Map site: 181
DGLA(S&L): Jim Hunter
NGR: TQ 3320 8020

Unicorn Passage, Tooley Street, SE1

Excavation during 1988 uncovered a large feature, interpreted as a pond, dug in the 15th c and backfilled in the 17th c. Its backfill contained many organic finds, including a saddle, saddle wallets and two blankets. This pond, and a N–S watercourse, were presumably associated with the house of Sir John Fastolf, built *c* 1443. To the N was an 18th-c aisled brick structure, possibly associated with Close's Brewery, and to the S was a line of brick cesspits. (For plan, see ABB86.)

London Archaeol, 6, 1989, 77; *Medieval Archaeol*, 33, 1989, 185; *Surrey Archaeol Coll*, 80, 1990, 224

USA88, USB88

Map site: 182, 183
DGLA(S&L): Kieron Heard
NGR: TQ 3245 8002
SMR: 091139–41, 091294–6

10–18 Union Street, SE1

Excavations at 16–18 Union Street in 1988 (USA88) revealed numerous sand and gravel layers overlying natural and containing Roman pottery. The layers were cut by several pits containing 1st–2nd-c Roman pottery and were sealed in turn by dark earth deposits. A large channel or ditch, aligned N–S, was examined in section; a few sherds of Roman and medieval pottery were found in it, its fills indicating that it had silted up over a long period. It was subsequently recut on a much more modest scale and partly revetted, and late medieval pottery was recovered from the fills of this final phase when it is thought to have been part of the E boundary of the manor of the bishops of Winchester, known after the late 15th c as the Clink Manor. Excavations to the SE at 10–14 Union Street in 1988 (USB88) revealed make-up deposits of 1st-c date, followed by two phases of 1st–2nd-c clay and timber buildings, both featuring walls with painted plaster. Roman pits and a timber-lined well containing 3rd-c pottery were examined, as was a 4th-c pit. A continuation was found of the large N–S channel, previously located, containing medieval pottery.

London Archaeol, 6, 1989, 79; 6, 1990, 193–4; *Britannia*, 20, 1989, 309; 21, 1990, 344; *Medieval Archaeol*, 33, 1989, 186; 34, 1990, 184; *Surrey Archaeol Coll*, 80, 1990, 221
Heard, K, 1989 'Excavations at 10–18 Union Street, Southwark', *London Archaeol*, 6, 126–31

3 Vine Lane, Tooley Street, SE1

A watching brief in 1988 recorded a watercourse and a post-medieval structure. (For plan, see ABB86.)

VIL88

Map site: 184
DGLA(S&L): James Hunter
NGR: TQ 3320 8020

Vine Lane, Tooley Street, SE1

A trial excavation in 1986 revealed a layer of peat thought to represent the Tilbury IV deposit of Bronze Age date. Also located were extensive deposits possibly related to the nearby delftware factory, and the remains of two E–W aligned waterfronts as yet undated. (For plan, see ABB86.)

London Archaeol, 5, 1987, 277; Post-Medieval Archaeol, 21, 1987, 289; Surrey Archaeol Coll, 78, 1987, 146

VIN86

Map site: 185
DGLA(S&L): Alan Thompson
NGR: TQ 3340 8015
SMR: 090815–17

Vine Lane, Tooley Street, SE1

A watching brief in 1987 recorded an undated barrel only. (For plan see ABB86.)

VIN87

Map site: 186
DGLA(S&L): James Hunter
NGR: TQ 3340 8020

Vine Lane, Tooley Street, SE1

Excavation in 1988 revealed a watercourse, presumed to be part of the moat of the 15th-c house of Sir John Fastolf, together with its post-medieval revetting and reclamation levels. To the W, next to Vine Lane, were found features apparently associated with the Pickle Herring delftware kiln established by Christian Wilhelm in 1618. (For plan, see ABB86.)

London Archaeol, 6, 1989, 77; Medieval Archaeol, 33, 1989, 185; Post-Medieval Archaeol, 23, 1989, 40; Surrey Archaeol Coll, 80, 1990, 224

VIN88

Map site: 187
DGLA(S&L): James Hunter
NGR: TQ 3320 8020
SMR: 091191–2

74–90 Weston Street, SE1

An evaluation excavation in 1989 revealed a roughly circular pit containing a flint tool and sealed by a layer of clay and Tilbury IV peat. A linear U-profile ditch extended E–W across the site, and contained in its backfill two sherds of Roman pottery, one of them dated to the 2nd c. The ditch was probably manmade, and appears to represent an early attempt at land drainage. Post-medieval features included a brick-lined and a stone-capped drain.

WET89

Map site: 188
DGLA(S&L): Aidan Allen
NGR: TQ 3298 7980

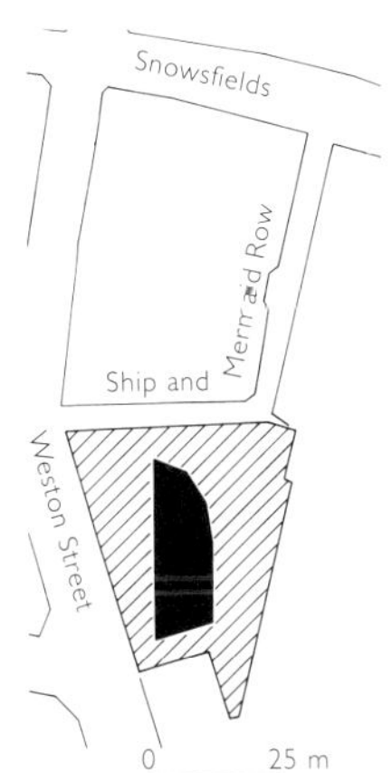

WG87

Map site: 189
DGLA(S&L): Toby Catchpole
NGR: TQ 3335 7980
SMR: 091168–70

22–28 White's Grounds, SE1

Excavation in 1987 revealed Neolithic flint tools and pottery in sandy soil, possibly part of Horsleydown island. Also examined were a Roman ditch and flood levels, and a post-medieval well and drain.

London Archaeol, 5, 1988, 414; Surrey Archaeol Coll, 79, 1989, 187

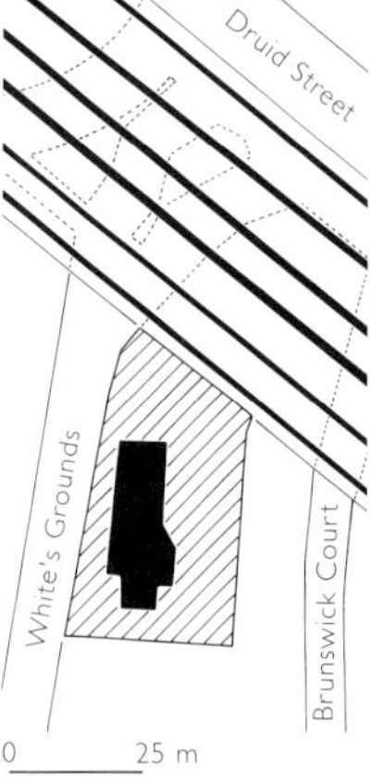

WHY85

Map site: 190
DGLA(S&L): Peter Hinton,
Derek Seeley
NGR: TQ 3268 8013
SMR: 090698–9

White Hart Yard, SE1

Observation in 1985 revealed deposits of early Roman to post-medieval date, including evidence of building activity in the Roman period. Chalk foundations of buildings facing on to White Hart Yard were also recorded.

London Archaeol, 5, 1986, 163–4; Britannia, 17, 1986, 409; Medieval Archaeol, 30, 1986, 143; Surrey Archaeol Coll, 78, 1987, 145

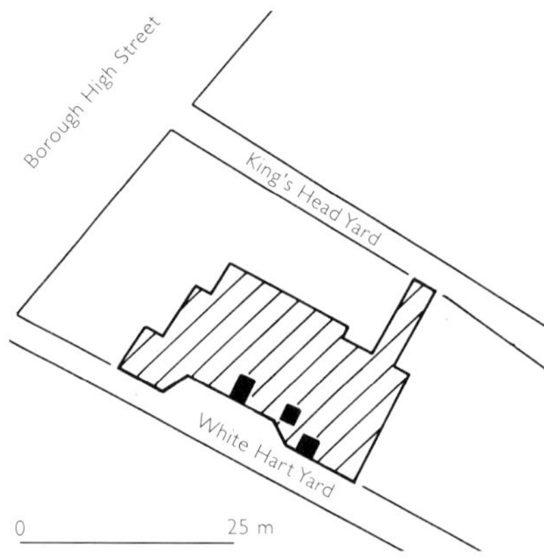

WIN85

Map site: not shown
DUA: Richard Lea,
Mark Samuel
NGR: TQ 3257 8039

Winchester Palace, Clink Street, SE1

A survey was made of the standing remains of the medieval palace of the bishops of Winchester, including a wall containing a large rose window, at the W end of the original Great Hall of the palace. (For plan, see WP83: Pickford's Wharf D. Another site code, WP86, was assigned to records of parts of the Great Hall.)

Seeley, D, in prep. The palace in Southwark of the medieval bishops of Winchester: excavations at Winchester Palace, London, 1983–1990, Part 2

WP83

Map site: 191, 193
DGLA(S&L): Derek Seeley
NGR: TQ 3259 8042

Pickford's Wharf D (Winchester Palace), Winchester Square, SE1

Excavation in 1983 on the site of the medieval Winchester Palace revealed dumped deposits of late 1st- to early 2nd-c date, which probably represented reclamation of marginal ground, and were sealed by a gravel surface. A fragmentary E–W aligned foundation was located, built of ragstone on timber and dated to 1095–1125, which was cut by a chalk foundation also aligned E–W and probably dating to the mid-12th c. This extended beyond the limits of the site and possibly formed part of the palace, built by Henry of Blois, bishop of Winchester. Stone foundations of a 13th-c hall, lying to the E of the partially standing W wall, were exposed, together with a large 13th-c stone drain running E–W across the site. (Another site code, WPPC83, was originally assigned to this site.)

London Archaeol, 4, 1984, 389; Britannia, 15, 1984, 310; Surrey Archaeol Coll, 76, 1985, 129

Seeley, D, in prep. The palace in Southwark of the medieval bishops of Winchester: excavations at Winchester Palace, London, 1983–1990, Part 2

Yule, B, in prep. Roman buildings on the Southwark waterfront: excavations at Winchester Palace, London, 1983–1990, Part 1

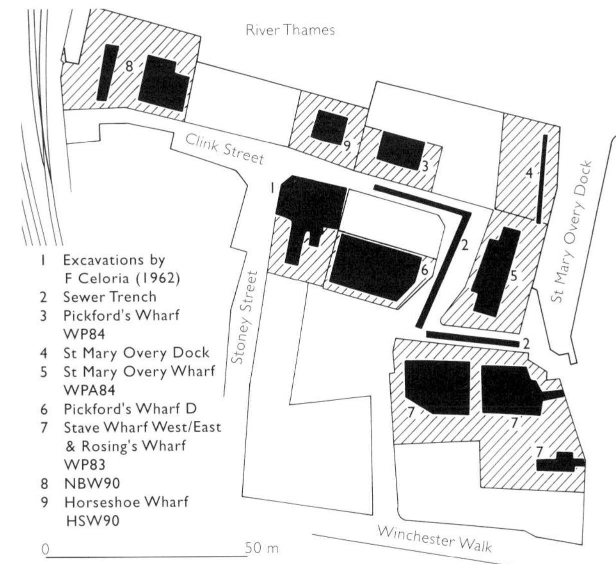

Details of the excavations in the area of Winchester Palace will be found under the site codes WP83, WIN85, WP84, HSW90, NBW90. Other site codes originally assigned to some of these excavations have been changed to WP83.

St Mary Overy Wharf and Dock (Winchester Palace), Clink Street, SE1

WP83

Map site: not shown
DGLA(S&L): Brian Yule
NGR: TQ 3261 8037

Excavation in 1984 on the last of the Winchester Palace sites revealed three heavily robbed stone walls aligned NW–SE and identified as part of a room, as was the Roman building excavated to the S (see below, WP83 Stave and Rosing's Wharves). Contemporaneous ground surfaces were truncated by deep modern warehouses. Two medieval features, probably forming part of the main structural phases of the palace of the bishops of Winchester, were located. These consisted of a heavily robbed E–W aligned stone wall and a parallel line of stake-holes of probable 12th-c date, and, across the N half of the area, the massive stone wall footings of the E end of the Great Hall of the palace, constructed in the early 13th c. The internal dimensions of the hall were 40.8m x 8.7m N–S; and S of the hall was a large stone drain, also found at Pickford's Wharf D to the W (see above, WP83 Pickford's Wharf D). Observations during the widening of St Mary Overy Dock, immediately E of the site, recorded no evidence of the early history of the dock; two medieval timber revetments and a possible Tudor riverwall were recorded in section and were part of the same features investigated more fully at Pickford's B (WP84) 40m to the W. (For plan, see WP83: Pickford's Wharf D. Other site codes, WPA84 and WP84 (SMO), were originally assigned to these sites.)

London Archaeol, 5, 1985, 66

Stave and Rosing's Wharves (Winchester Palace), Clink Street, SE1

WP83

Map site: 194
DGLA(S&L): Brian Yule
NGR: TQ 3260 8035

Excavation in 1983 within the site of the medieval palace of the bishops of Winchester revealed early Roman quarry pits partly filled with waterlaid clay, suggesting continuous inundation of the area in the mid-1st c AD. The Roman sequence in the E part of the site included clay and timber buildings aligned NW–SE and consisting of at least two phases of later 1st-c date. In the late 1st–early 2nd c a N–S timber fence was erected across the line of one of the now demolished clay and timber buildings; to the W was a gravel path and an apsidal-ended building, and to the E the line of the fence was continued to the N by the W wall of a building with an internal mortar floor and a circular tile hearth built into its clay S wall. The fence and structures to the E and W had been demolished by the mid-2nd c, and tips of ironworking waste were over the area. The latest Roman structure discovered had reverted to the NW–SE alignment.

Remains of a single masonry building complex, extending across the area of excavation, suggested a substantial riverfront property. To the SW of the building five rooms were identified, three with hypocaust systems of which one had been provided with a mosaic floor and wall frescoes.

Alterations in the building layout fell into perhaps four major structural phases and would suggest a fairly lengthy period of use, probably from the late 2nd c to the second half of the 4th. Evidence of Late Saxon–medieval occupation was limited by truncation, but several deep pits and dark earth dumps could be dated to the 10th–11th c. The remains of Winchester Palace at the W end of the site comprised three principal phases of chalk and ragstone wall foundations defining the SE corner of the 13th–14th-c courtyard ranges, fronting onto the Great Hall of the palace. The third building phase involved considerable modification of the S end of the E range in the 14th c for the insertion of a garderobe pit, which continued in use until the 17th c. The medieval courtyard buildings probably continued in use into the 19th c; a brick-lined cellar was constructed at the S end of the E range in the 18th c, and at about this time cellared buildings encroached upon the courtyard and the N part of the garderobe area. (For plan, see WP83: Pickford's Wharf D. Another site code, WPSR84, was originally assigned to this site.)

London Archaeol, 4, 1984, 389–90; Surrey Archaeol Coll, 76, 1985, 129
MacKenna, S A, & Ling, R, 1991 'Wall paintings from the Winchester Palace site, Southwark', Britannia, 22, 159–71
Seeley, D, in prep. The palace in Southwark of the medieval bishops of Winchester: excavations at Winchester Palace, London, 1983–1990, Part 2
Yule, B, 1989 'Excavations at Winchester Palace, Southwark', London Archaeol, 6, 31–9
Yule, B, in prep. Roman buildings on the Southwark waterfront: excavations at Winchester Palace, London, 1983–1990, Part 1

WP84

Map site: 192
DGLA(S&L): Derek Seeley
NGR: TQ 3259 8042

Pickford's Wharf B (Winchester Palace), Clink Street, SE1

Excavation in 1984 revealed remains of two substantial E–W aligned medieval timber waterfronts and their associated backfills; the earlier had been cut by the backbraces of the later, situated further N and constructed of timbers with a dendrochronological felling date of 1354. These timber waterfronts were superseded by a stone riverwall that directly overlay the front base-plate of its later predecessor, perhaps in the 15th or 16th c. (For plan, see WP83: Pickford's Wharf D.)

London Archaeol, 5, 1985, 66; Britannia, 16, 1985, 298; Medieval Archaeol, 29, 1985, 179; Surrey Archaeol Coll, 77, 1986, 225
Seeley, D, in prep. The palace in Southwark of the medieval bishops of Winchester: excavations at Winchester Palace, London, 1983–1990, Part 2

WW78

Map site: 195
SLAEC: Brian Yule
NGR: TQ 3314 8023
SMR: 090409, 091061–3

Willsons Wharf, Battle Bridge Lane, SE1

Observations in 1978 recorded dumped post-medieval deposits covering waterlaid clays which sealed flood-plain gravels. During the medieval period deposits in the N part of the site were cut by river erosion and there was subsequent silting up, as at Toppings and Sun Wharves.

London Archaeol, 3, 1979, 264; Surrey Archaeol Coll, 72, 1980, 249

WWK87

Map site: 196
DGLA(S&L): Alison Steele
NGR: TQ 3340 7880

Willow Walk, Page's Walk, Mandela Way, SE1

A trial excavation in 1987 revealed 18th–early 19th-c intrusions cutting flood clays which overlay natural. At the E end of the area examined, apparently at the W edge of a mere or marsh, the clays were overlaid by peats, possibly of the Bronze Age Tilbury IV period.

London Archaeol, 6, 1989, 77

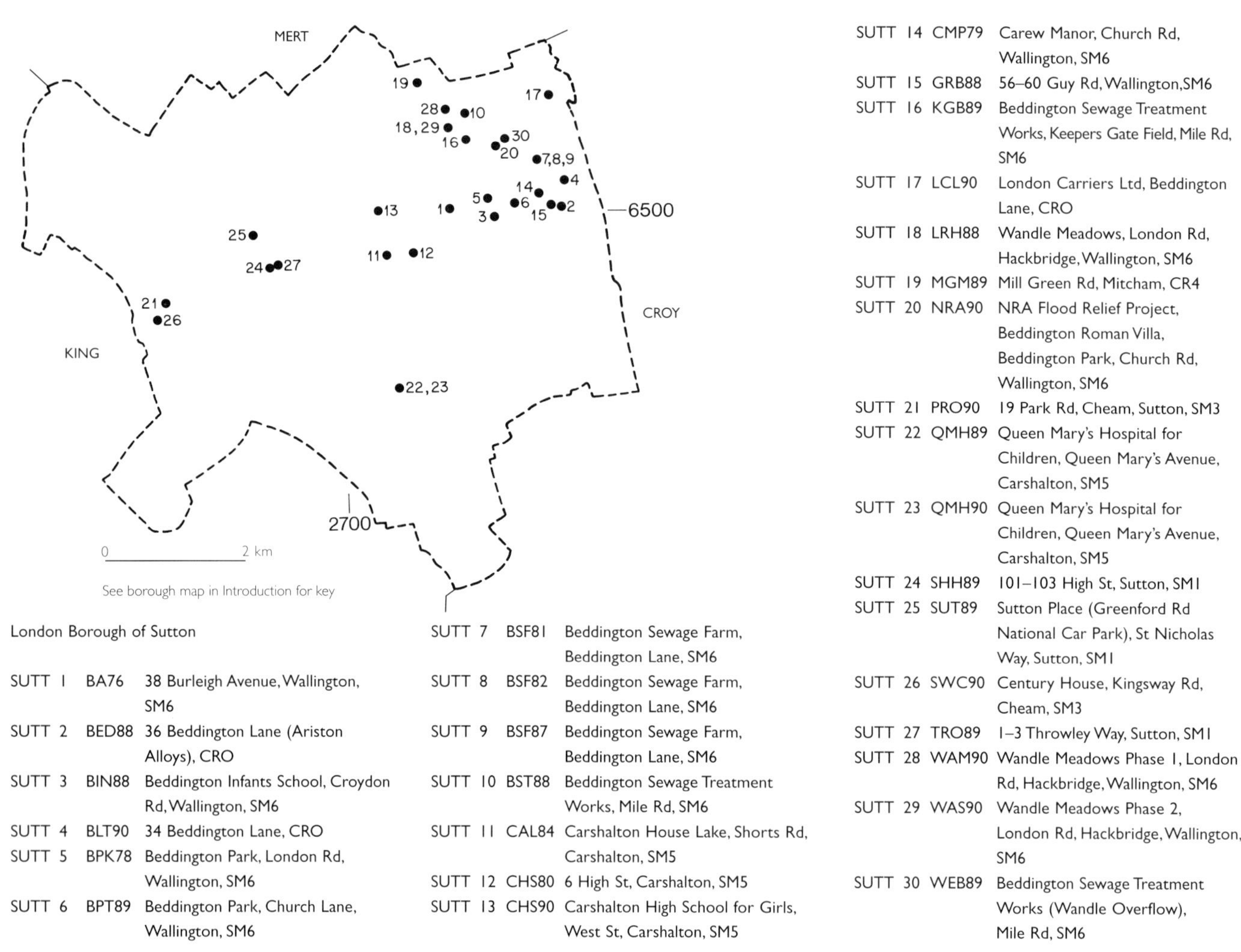

London Borough of Sutton

SUTT 1	BA76	38 Burleigh Avenue, Wallington, SM6
SUTT 2	BED88	36 Beddington Lane (Ariston Alloys), CRO
SUTT 3	BIN88	Beddington Infants School, Croydon Rd, Wallington, SM6
SUTT 4	BLT90	34 Beddington Lane, CRO
SUTT 5	BPK78	Beddington Park, London Rd, Wallington, SM6
SUTT 6	BPT89	Beddington Park, Church Lane, Wallington, SM6
SUTT 7	BSF81	Beddington Sewage Farm, Beddington Lane, SM6
SUTT 8	BSF82	Beddington Sewage Farm, Beddington Lane, SM6
SUTT 9	BSF87	Beddington Sewage Farm, Beddington Lane, SM6
SUTT 10	BST88	Beddington Sewage Treatment Works, Mile Rd, SM6
SUTT 11	CAL84	Carshalton House Lake, Shorts Rd, Carshalton, SM5
SUTT 12	CHS80	6 High St, Carshalton, SM5
SUTT 13	CHS90	Carshalton High School for Girls, West St, Carshalton, SM5
SUTT 14	CMP79	Carew Manor, Church Rd, Wallington, SM6
SUTT 15	GRB88	56–60 Guy Rd, Wallington, SM6
SUTT 16	KGB89	Beddington Sewage Treatment Works, Keepers Gate Field, Mile Rd, SM6
SUTT 17	LCL90	London Carriers Ltd, Beddington Lane, CRO
SUTT 18	LRH88	Wandle Meadows, London Rd, Hackbridge, Wallington, SM6
SUTT 19	MGM89	Mill Green Rd, Mitcham, CR4
SUTT 20	NRA90	NRA Flood Relief Project, Beddington Roman Villa, Beddington Park, Church Rd, Wallington, SM6
SUTT 21	PRO90	19 Park Rd, Cheam, Sutton, SM3
SUTT 22	QMH89	Queen Mary's Hospital for Children, Queen Mary's Avenue, Carshalton, SM5
SUTT 23	QMH90	Queen Mary's Hospital for Children, Queen Mary's Avenue, Carshalton, SM5
SUTT 24	SHH89	101–103 High St, Sutton, SM1
SUTT 25	SUT89	Sutton Place (Greenford Rd National Car Park), St Nicholas Way, Sutton, SM1
SUTT 26	SWC90	Century House, Kingsway Rd, Cheam, SM3
SUTT 27	TRO89	1–3 Throwley Way, Sutton, SM1
SUTT 28	WAM90	Wandle Meadows Phase 1, London Rd, Hackbridge, Wallington, SM6
SUTT 29	WAS90	Wandle Meadows Phase 2, London Rd, Hackbridge, Wallington, SM6
SUTT 30	WEB89	Beddington Sewage Treatment Works (Wandle Overflow), Mile Rd, SM6

BA76

Map site: 1
BC&WAS: Clive Orton
NGR: TQ 2852 6501

38 Burleigh Avenue, Wallington, SM6

Excavation in 1976 revealed two burials about 10m NW of a medieval chapel (excavated in 1921). The S burial cut an Iron Age or Saxon oven and a ditch, probably of the same date, running NE–SW. All features except the N burial were covered by a 17th-c chalk spread.

London Archaeol, 3, 1977, 39; Surrey Archaeol Coll, 72, 1980, 249

BED88

Map site: 2
DGLA(SW): Stephen Tucker
NGR: TQ 3020 6550
SMR: 021184

Ariston Alloys, 36 Beddington Lane, CRO

Excavation in 1988 revealed no archaeological features.

Surrey Archaeol Coll, 80, 1990, 226

Beddington Infants School, Croydon Road, Wallington, SM6

Excavation in 1988 revealed a ditch containing Late Bronze Age pottery and flints.

London Archaeol, 6, 1990, 194; Surrey Archaeol Coll, 80, 1990, 226

BIN88

Map site: 3
DGLA(SW): Simon Mason
NGR: TQ 2920 6494
SMR: 021314

34 Beddington Lane, CR0

An evaluation excavation in 1990 recovered prehistoric fire-cracked flints.

*London Archaeol, 6, 1991, 307; Britannia, 22, 1991, 273; Post-Medieval Archaeol,
25, 1991, 158; Surrey Archaeol Coll, 81, 1991–2, 166*

BLT90

Map site: 4
DGLA(SW): David Saxby
NGR: TQ 3020 6540
SMR: 021284

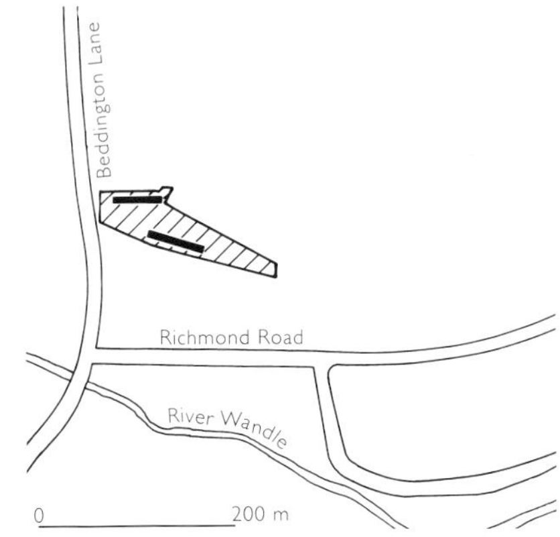

Beddington Park, London Road, Wallington, SM6

Excavation in 1978, prompted by the discovery of three silver pennies and a William I halfpenny by metal-detection, located no further coins but recovered a quantity of shell-tempered pottery and struck flint, probably Mesolithic in date.

London Archaeol, 3, 1979, 264; Surrey Archaeol Coll, 72, 1980, 249

BPK78

Map site: 5
SWLT, SAS: Scott McCracken
NGR: TQ 2910 6520

Beddington Park, Church Lane, Wallington, SM6

Excavation in 1989 revealed possible medieval activity, represented by redeposited sand mixed with roof tile. A spread of chalk rubble, perhaps part of the debris of the Partioner's House demolished in the 19th c, was also found.

Surrey Archaeol Coll, 80, 1990, 226

BPT89

Map site: 6
DGLA(SW): Stephen Tucker
NGR: TQ 2950 6512

Beddington Sewage Farm, Beddington Lane, SM6

Excavation in 1981 revealed the end of the bath-house, to the N of its supposed site. To the S was a series of cobbled and rough yard surfaces, one of them overlain by a spread of Roman plaster fragments, covering an area of more than 20sq m and found *in situ* where it had collapsed from a building, evidence for which suggested a timber-framed cob wall construction. To the W of the building

BSF81, BSF82

Map site: 7, 8
SWLAU: Lesley Adkins,
Roy Adkins
NGR: TQ 2979 6576
SMR: 020575–7

were found traces of a second building, other timber structures and a clay-walled oven. In this area was a large ditch running N–S parallel to a shallow beam slot, and related to a late boundary marked by a ditch and a fence or palisade. To the N of the bath-house was a series of post-holes as evidence of further timber buildings. A wide range of Romano-British pottery (one urn containing a cremation) was recovered, in addition to Neolithic–Late Bronze Age material. Little medieval or post-medieval pottery was found. Further work in 1982–3 examined the remainder of the bath-house site, E of which masonry walls and robber trenches provided evidence of the main domestic buildings of the villa. No floor levels survived, but at least two construction phases were distinguished. Further E, a series of post-holes indicated at least one more timber building, while to the S further cobbled surfaces were located. Underlying the main Romano-British structures were numerous prehistoric and early Roman pits and ditches.

London Archaeol, 4, 1982, 165–6; 4, 1983, 290–1; 5, 1986, 164; *Britannia,* 13, 1982, 375; 14, 1983, 321; 16, 1985, 298; 17, 1986, 409; 18, 1987, 337; *Surrey Archaeol Coll,* 74, 1983, 194; 75, 1984, 272; 76, 1985, 130; 78, 1987, 147
Adkins, L, & Adkins, R, 1982 'Excavations at Beddington, 1981', *London Archaeol,* 4, 199–203
Adkins, L, & Adkins, R, 1983 'Beddington Roman Villa', *Current Archaeol,* 88, 155–7
Adkins, L, & Adkins, R, 1983 'Beddington Roman Villa', *Surrey Archaeol Soc Bull,* 184, 3–4
Adkins, L, & Adkins, R, 1983 'Excavations at Beddington, 1982', *London Archaeol,* 4, 326–9

BSF87

Map site: 9
DGLA(SW): Lesley Adkins, Roy Adkins, J G Perry
NGR: TQ 2979 6576
SMR: 020577–9, 030412

Beddington Sewage Farm, Beddington Lane, SM6

Excavation in 1984–5, to the S of that undertaken in 1981–3 (see BSF81 above), revealed many prehistoric pits, post-holes and ditches, as well as at least 12 round-houses, dating from the Late Bronze to the Late Iron Age. The main focus of prehistoric settlement seems to have been a ditch bounding an enclosure possibly of up to 150m in diameter, which was backfilled in the Late Iron Age. Roman occupation was mainly represented by three large buildings, probably barns of different dates. Several ditches forming field boundaries, and a tufa and chalk lined well, were recorded. In 1987 the final phase of excavation concentrated on completing the work on the three Roman barns; a timber-lined Roman well was revealed to the E of the barns.

London Archaeol, 5, 1986, 164; 5, 1987, 277; 5, 1988, 414; *Britannia,* 19, 1988, 464; *Surrey Archaeol Coll,* 79, 1989, 188
Adkins, L, Adkins, R, & Perry, J G, 1987 'Excavations at Beddington 1984–87', *London Archaeol,* 5, 349–52

BST88

Map site: 10
DGLA(SW): Stephen Tucker
NGR: TQ 2875 6650
SMR: 021200–2

Beddington Sewage Treatment Works, Mile Road, SM6

An evaluation excavation in 1988–9 revealed intercutting ditches which indicated various phases of activity, without good dating evidence.

London Archaeol, 6, 1990, 194; *Surrey Archaeol Coll,* 80, 1990, 226

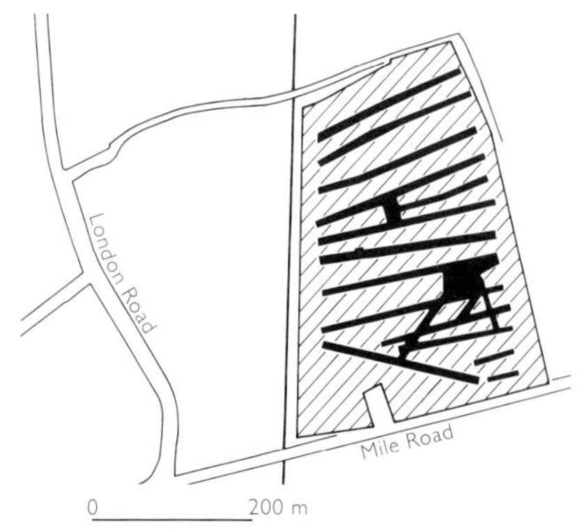

Carshalton House Lake, Shorts Road, Carshalton, SM5

Excavation in 1984 and 1985 in the now dry lake of Carshalton House revealed structures apparently of two phases. The earlier was represented by the chalk block foundation of buildings forming three sides of a square, with wooden features considered to be of early–mid-17th-c date, possibly a stockyard. Of probably later date was a plank-bedded brick base, perhaps of a watercourse, thought to be part of an 18th-c formal garden and lake construction.

London Archaeol, 5, 1985, 66; 5, 1986, 164

CAL84

Map site: 11
BC&WAS: H N Waterhouse,
Clive Orton
NGR: TQ 2760 6440
SMR: 200157

6 High Street, Carshalton, SM5

A trial excavation in 1980 in a yard to the rear of a 16th–17th-c house revealed a flat-bottomed ditch as the only feature earlier than the house. A possibly circular laid stone surface dated to *c* 1700 was located, but had been largely robbed out. Late 18th- and 19th-c rubbish pits and garden features were examined.

London Archaeol, 4, 1981, 49

CHS80

Map site: 12
BC&WAS: Clive Orton
NGR: TQ 2800 6440
SMR: 200077

Carshalton High School for Girls, West Street, Carshalton, SM5

Excavation in 1990 examined two areas, the first of which was eventually abandoned on account of severe truncation. The earliest feature in the second area was a V-shaped ditch which produced struck flints but no dating evidence; covered by medieval ploughsoil, it is assumed to be of possibly Iron Age date. Other features recorded were a post-medieval boundary ditch and a possible Victorian well.

London Archaeol, 6, 1991, 307; Post-Medieval Archaeol, 25, 1991, 159; Surrey Archaeol Coll, 81, 1991–2, 166

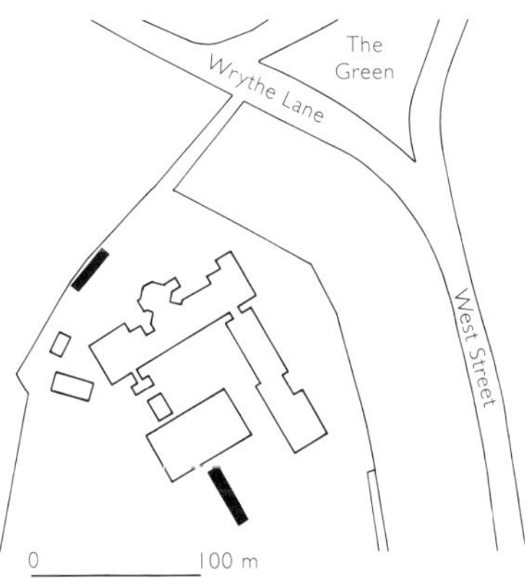

CHS90

Map site: 13
DGLA(SW): Stephen Tucker
NGR: TQ 2750 6505
SMR: 021279–81

Carew Manor, Church Road, Wallington, SM6

Excavation in 1979 revealed stone facing from the inner edge of two arms of a moat, backed by mortared flint foundations. The E arm had been filled in, and the S arm was covered by a brick culvert, probably of *c* 1710. Observations suggest that the moat was approximately square with sides about 65m long, and had enclosed the present hall range (late 15th c) and later wings.

London Archaeol, 3, 1980, 388

CMP79

Map site: 14
BC&WAS: Clive Orton
NGR: TQ 2985 6528

56–60 Guy Road, Wallington, SM6

An evaluation excavation in 1988 revealed evidence of extensive quarrying, probably dating to the 19th c.

Surrey Archaeol Coll, 80, 1990, 226

GRB88

Map site: 15
DGLA(SW): Stephen Tucker
NGR: TQ 3003 6524
SMR: 021183

KGB89

Map site: 16
DGLA: Neil Bugler
NGR: TQ 286 658
SMR: 021329

Beddington Sewage Treatment Works, Keepers Gate Field, Mile Road, SM6

Excavation in 1989 revealed a complex system of field and property boundaries of various dates and possibly different purposes. The rectilinear ditches would appear to have been more suitable for arable farming, while the sub-circular ditch may indicate some sort of enclosure for domestic animals.

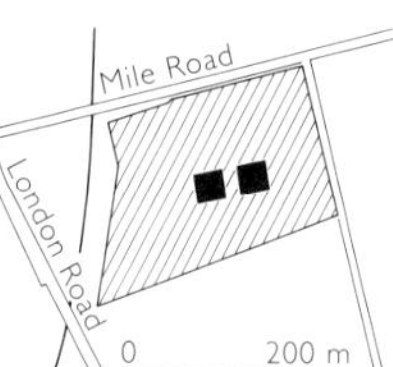

LCL90

Map site: 17
DGLA: Stephen Tucker
NGR: TQ 2996 6665
SMR: 021208–10

London Carriers Ltd, Beddington Lane, CRO

Excavation in 1990 examined three areas, one of which revealed two semicircular features possibly of Late Bronze Age date. A V-shaped ditch was also located in this area, running NW and possibly representing a field ditch of Roman date. The two other areas contained the remains of possibly two parallel drainage ditches.

London Archaeol, 6, 1991, 307; *Surrey Archaeol Coll*, 81, 1991–2, 166

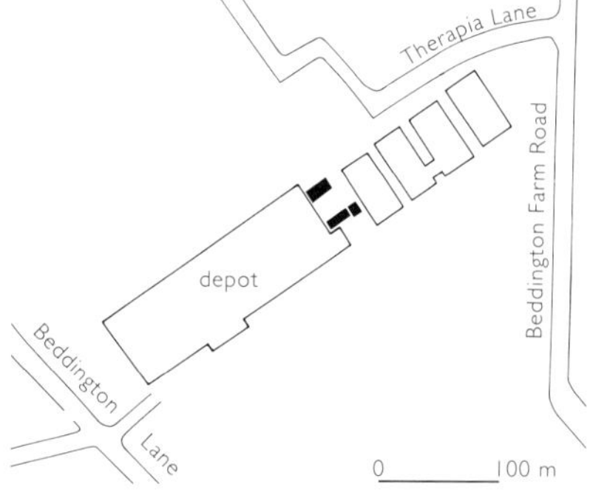

LRH88

Map site: 18
DGLA(SW): Robert Bazely
NGR: TQ 2850 6620
SMR: 021212

Wandle Meadows, London Road, Hackbridge, Wallington, SM6

Excavation in 1988 revealed several Bronze Age pits.

London Archaeol, 6, 1990, 194; *Surrey Archaeol Coll*, 80, 1990, 226

MGM89

Map site: 19
DGLA: Neil Bugler
NGR: TQ 2810 6685
SMR: 021313

Mill Green Road, Mitcham, CR4

Excavation in 1989 revealed evidence of probable late medieval/Tudor occupation in the form of a chalk structure and well.

Medieval Archaeol, 34, 1990, 185; *Surrey Archaeol Coll*, 80, 1990, 220

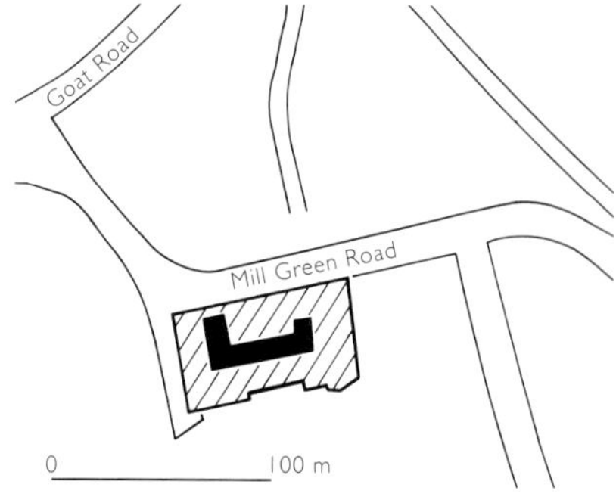

NRA Flood Relief Project, Beddington Roman Villa, Beddington Park, Church Road, Wallington, SM6

NRA90

Map site: 20
DGLA(SW): Robert Bazely
NGR: TQ 296 655

Excavation in 1990 exposed a possible prehistoric or Romano-British trackway of metalled flint nodules. Flint flakes and waste flakes were found in silt sealing layers. Ditches of 17th–18th-c date were also located.

London Archaeol, 6, 1991, 307; Post-Medieval Archaeol, 25, 1991, 159; Surrey Archaeol Coll, 81, 1991–2, 166

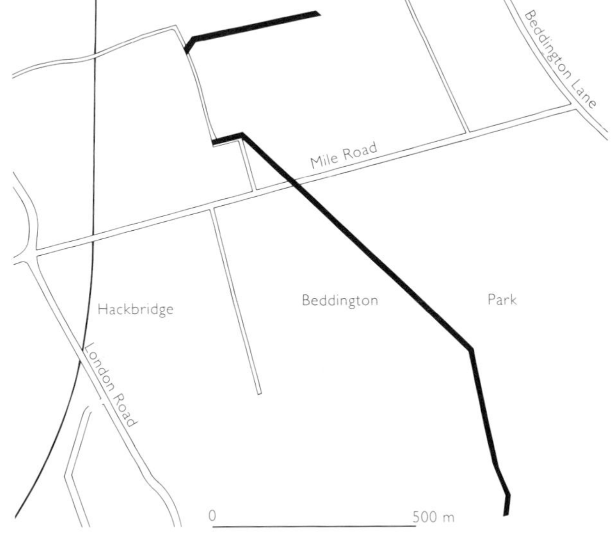

19 Park Road, Cheam, Sutton, SM3

PRO90

Map site: 21
DGLA(SW): Philip Emery
NGR: TQ 2433 6377
SMR: 021185–8

Excavation in 1990 took place in two areas to the W and S of a standing Victorian house. The prehistoric ground surface had been truncated by gardening activity, but quantities of struck and burnt flint were recovered from medieval and later deposits. A V-shaped ditch, aligned E–W, produced 11th–12th-c pottery in its fill and much burnt flint. At the S end of the site a length of ditch was found in each trench on a common E–W alignment; part of this produced Guy's type ware and Cheam ware sherds. Several large cuts found in the W area and dated from 1600 and later are believed to have been sand and brickearth quarries. Two comparatively shallow cuts were recorded, containing large quantities of 18th-c finds.

London Archaeol, 6, 11, 1991, 307–8; Medieval Archaeol, 35, 1991, 156; Surrey Archaeol Coll, 81, 1991–2, 165

Queen Mary's Hospital for Children, Queen Mary's Avenue, Carshalton, SM5

QMH89

Map site: 22
DGLA(SW): Stephen Tucker
NGR: TQ 2780 6248
SMR: 021194–5

An evaluation excavation on a Scheduled Late Bronze Age site in 1989 revealed numerous ditches and pits containing prehistoric pottery, bone and flint fragments. One large pit had been backfilled with a series of burnt deposits containing Iron Age pottery and larger pieces of clay loom weights.

London Archaeol, 6, 1990, 194; Surrey Archaeol Coll, 80, 1990, 226

QMH90

Map site: 23
DGLA(SW): Penny Bruce
NGR: TQ 2770 6250
SMR: 021276

Queen Mary's Hospital for Children, Queen Mary's Avenue, Carshalton, SM5

A watching brief in 1990 recorded prehistoric fire-cracked flints.

London Archaeol, 6, 1991, 308; Surrey Archaeol Coll, 81, 1991–2, 166

SHH89

Map site: 24
DGLA(SW): Jonathan Nowell
NGR: TQ 2587 6423
SMR: 021198

101–103 High Street, Sutton, SM1

Excavation on the W side of the High Street in 1989 revealed the remains of two late medieval buildings. Evidence for the first was in the form of a wall 11.5m long and standing 2.5m high, constructed of alternating blocks of chalk and flint to produce a chequered effect. This apparently represents the S external wall of a substantial building perhaps still surviving beneath 105 High Street. The second building was of two distinct phases, the first consisting of a rectilinear structure with a beaten-earth floor and a large central hearth. The insertion of a wall across the middle of the room and the replacement of the central hearth by a smaller one with an enclosing smoke hood placed in the angle of the dividing wall and the existing W wall marked a second phase. Both buildings are dated to the early 16th c, and for the first time demonstrate medieval settlement at the S extremity of Sutton, remote from the presumed focus of occupation around The Green to the N.

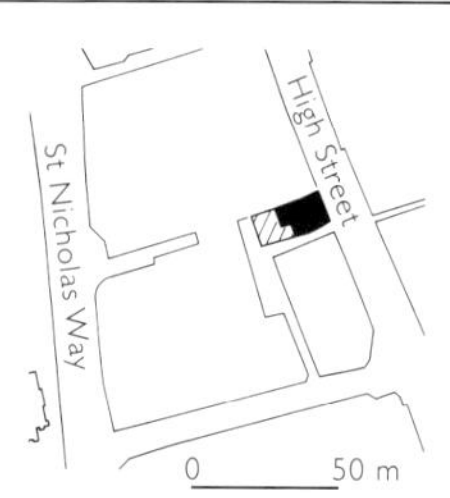

London Archaeol, 6, 1990, 194; Medieval Archaeol, 34, 1990, 184; Post-Medieval Archaeol, 24, 1990, 178; Surrey Archaeol Coll, 80, 1990, 225

SUT89

Map site: 25
DGLA(SW): Tim Haillay,
Pat Miller
NGR: TQ 2560 6470

Sutton Place (Greenford Road National Car Park), St Nicholas Way, Sutton, SM1

Excavation on the W side of Sutton High Street in 1989 revealed medieval features including two boundary ditches, a pond and a wooden structure, all at the rear of the property where local Cheam and possibly Kingston wares of the 12th–13th c were recovered. On the frontage a chalk floor, hearth and cellar were recorded; and post-medieval features included walls, pits and floor layers.

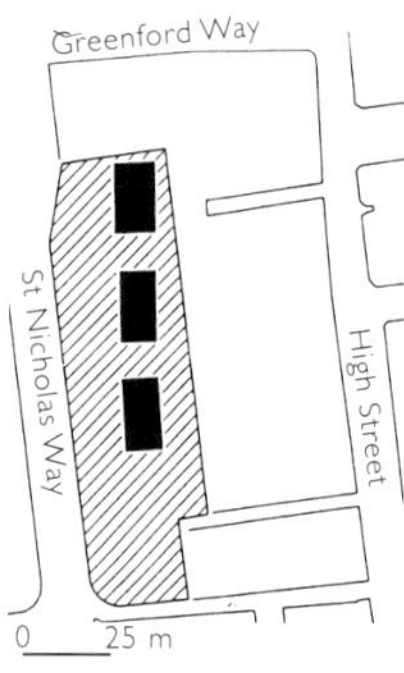

London Archaeol, 6, 1990, 194; Medieval Archaeol, 34, 1990, 185; Surrey Archaeol Coll, 80, 1990, 225

SWC90

Map site: 26
DGLA(SW): Pat Miller
NGR: TQ 2427 6350
SMR: 021277–8

Century House, Kingsway Road, Cheam, SM3

An evaluation excavation of two areas of the site in 1990 disclosed to the SE an undated truncated ditch and three small cut features; running N–S for about 5m was a badly disturbed wall or footing 0.9m wide and constructed of two lines of rough-hewn chalk blocks filled with rubble. The second area revealed a line of boundary post-holes aligned N–S, a small square structure and two large pits. The subsoil occasionally produced pieces of medieval and post-medieval material; beneath it was natural chalk. The whole site appears to have been farmland since the medieval period, and a farm is specifically recorded from the Tudor period when the area was perhaps associated with Nonsuch Palace. The present site was not built upon nor enclosed until the 17th c, and a 17th–18th-c pit and 18th–19th-c boundary fence probably relate to Cheam Court Farm, whose buildings were demolished early in the 20th c.

London Archaeol, 6, 1991, 307; Post-Medieval Archaeol, 25, 1991, 158; Surrey Archaeol Coll, 81, 1991–2, 166

1–3 Throwley Way, Sutton, SM1

Excavation in 1989 revealed two phases of activity of Late Saxon/early medieval date represented by plough marks and domestic occupation. A trench behind the E side of the High Street revealed several pits containing 11th–12th-c material.

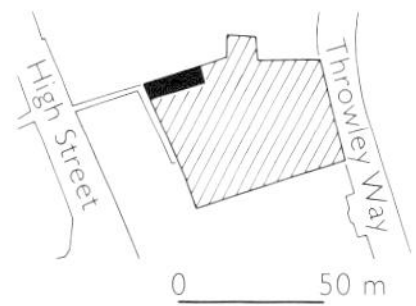

London Archaeol, 6, 1990, 194; *Medieval Archaeol,* 34, 1990, 185; *Surrey Archaeol Coll,* 80, 1990, 225

TRO89

Map site: 27
DGLA(SW): Jonathan Nowell
NGR: TQ 2590 6450

Wandle Meadows Phase 1, London Road, Hackbridge, Wallington, SM6

An evaluation excavation on the flood plain of the River Wandle in 1990 located in one area a ditch running E–W, possibly a field drain or boundary, its fill containing a sherd of Late Bronze Age pottery. To the N was a pit or post-hole, and in the middle of the trench were four more such cuts, some 1m apart and apparently aligned NW–SE, perhaps representing a structure, as also may four smaller post-holes to the S, which were regularly spaced at 1.4m intervals in a semicircular pattern. The purpose of three irregularly shaped isolated pits is unknown; one of them contained a fire-cracked flint and a small sherd of late Roman pottery. In another trench was a ditch running NE and containing many pieces of fire-cracked flint and Late Bronze Age pottery; it cut a small ditch to its S. See WAS90 below.

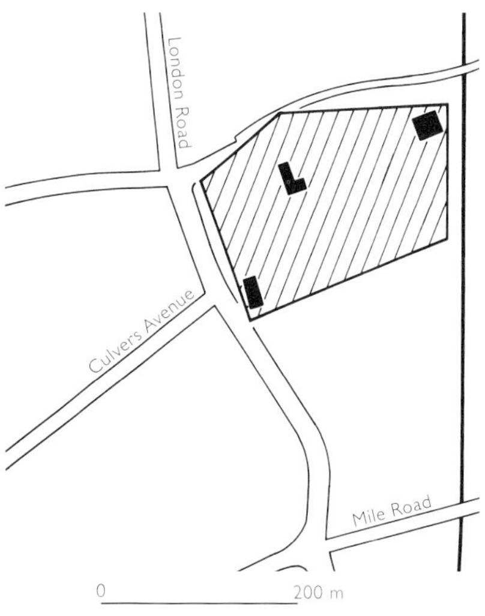

London Archaeol, 6, 1991, 308; *Surrey Archaeol Coll,* 81, 1991–2, 166

WAM90

Map site: 28
DGLA(SW): David Saxby
NGR: TQ 2850 6650
SMR: 021203, 021211

Wandle Meadows Phase 2, London Road, Hackbridge, Wallington, SM6

An evaluation excavation in 1990 revealed a Neolithic pit containing pottery sherds and flints. A ditch provisionally dated to the Bronze Age was also uncovered, possibly part of a field-system. See WAM90 above.

London Archaeol, 6, 1991, 308

WAS90

Map site: 29
DGLA(SW): David Saxby
NGR: TQ 2850 6620
SMR: 021274–5

Beddington Sewage Treatment Works (Wandle Overflow), Mile Road, SM6

Site watching and limited excavation in 1989 revealed field-system features of possible prehistoric date and later. A prehistoric watercourse was also located, as were ditches of Roman date (W of Beddington Roman villa) and post-medieval features.

Surrey Archaeol Coll, 80, 1990, 226

WEB89

Map site: 30
DGLA(SW): Robin Nielsen
NGR: TQ 2938 6600

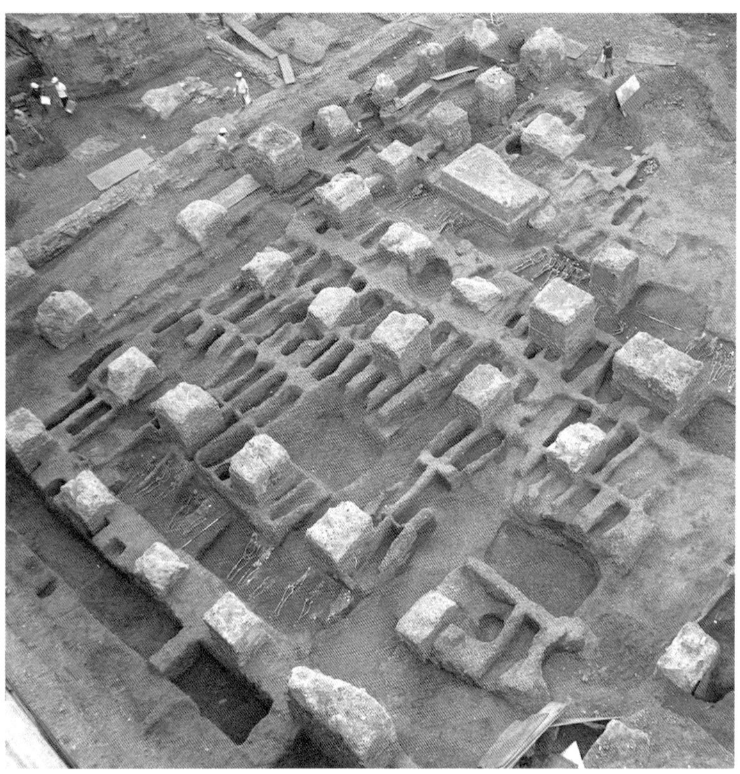

Tower Hamlets   MIN87   Royal Mint, East Smithfield, EC3. Part of the cemetery of the Cistercian abbey of St Mary Graces (founded 1350).

LONDON BOROUGH OF

TOWER HAMLETS

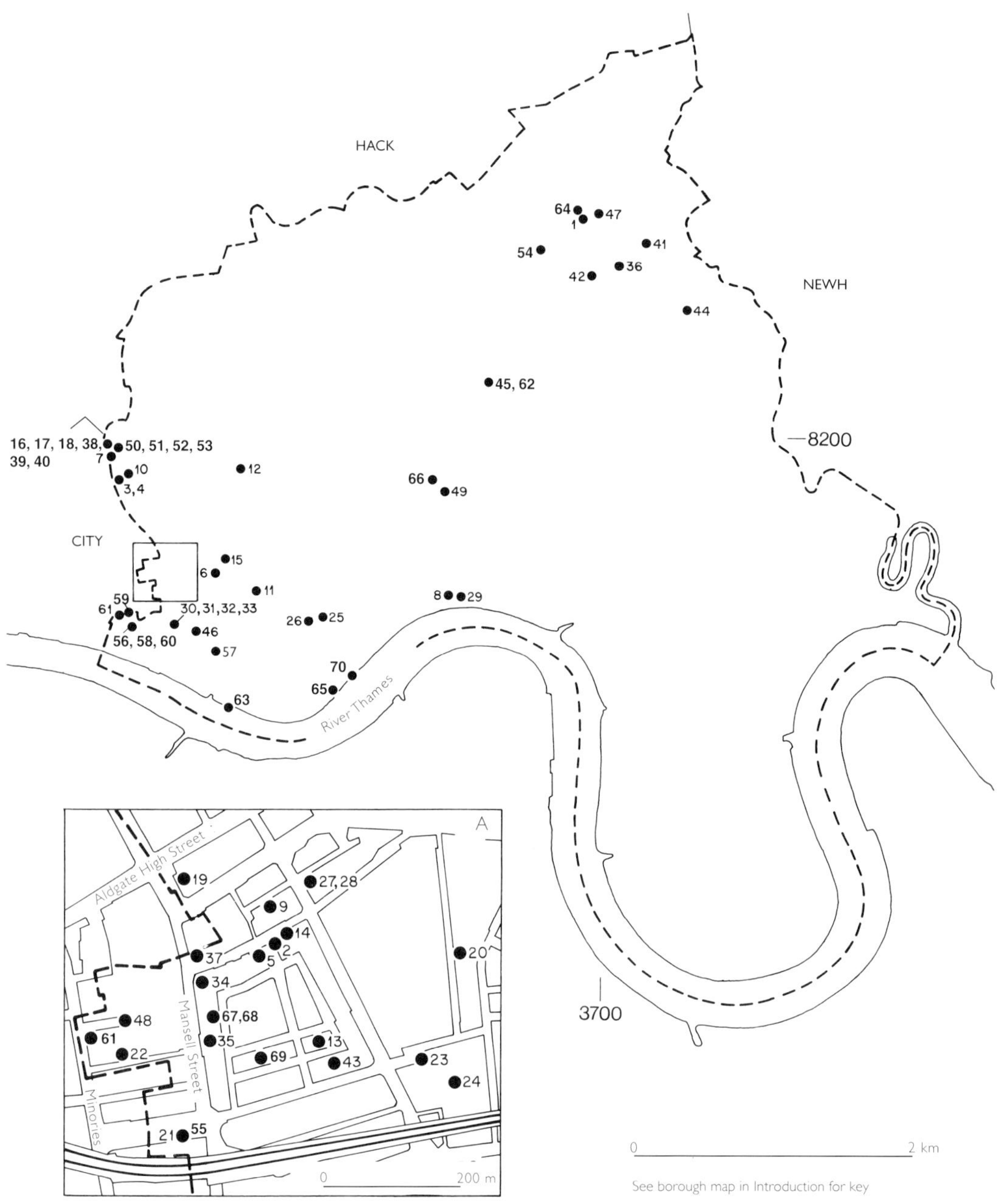

London Borough of Tower Hamlets

TOWE	1	AGH90	72A Armagh Rd, 91–93 Parnell Rd, E3
TOWE	2	ALS88	28 Alie St, E1
TOWE	3	ARL76	37–39 Artillery Lane, E1
TOWE	4	ART76	27–33 Artillery Lane, E1
TOWE	5	ASH87	24 Alie St, E1
TOWE	6	BCL88	95–105 Back Church Lane, E1
TOWE	7	BPH87	St Botolph's Hall, Spital Square, E1
TOWE	8	BTR75	Butcher Row, E14
TOWE	9	CAM81	9–25 Camperdown St, E1
TOWE	10	CRI88	Crispin St, Brushfield St, E1
TOWE	11	CSV85	Cable St, E1
TOWE	12	DAV77	Davenant St, E1
TOWE	13	ETN88	East Tenter St, Scarborough St, E1
TOWE	14	FAB88	36–44 Alie St, E1
TOWE	15	FAG90	2–6 Fairclough St, E1
TOWE	16	FLG77	19–27 Folgate St, 1–4 Blossom St, E1
TOWE	17	FOL76	6–8 Folgate St, E1
TOWE	18	FOL77	29–33 Folgate St, 1–3 Elder St, 9–10 Fleur de Lis St, E1
TOWE	19	GDC80	Gardiner's Corner, Mansell St, Whitechapel High St, E1
TOWE	20	GOW89	36–44 Gowers Walk, E1
TOWE	21	GYD75	Goodman's Yard, E1
TOWE	22	HAY86	13 Haydon St, EC3
TOWE		HIG74	The Highway, E1
TOWE	23	HOO86	Hooper St, E1
TOWE	24	HOO88	Hooper St, E1
TOWE	25	LD74	The Highway, E1
TOWE	26	LD76	London Docks, The Highway, E1
TOWE	27	LEM87	19 Leman St, 24–26 Buckle St, E1
TOWE	28	LEM88	19 Leman St, 24–26 Buckle St, E1
TOWE	29	LLK89	Limehouse Link Rd, The Highway, E14
TOWE	30	MIN83	Royal Mint, East Smithfield, EC3
TOWE	31	MIN84	Royal Mint, East Smithfield, EC3
TOWE	32	MIN86	Royal Mint, East Smithfield, EC3
TOWE	33	MIN87	Royal Mint, East Smithfield, EC3
TOWE	34	MNL87	65–73 Mansell St, E1
TOWE	35	MNL88	65–73 Mansell St, E1
TOWE	36	MS72	Morville St, E3
TOWE	36	MS73	Morville St, E3
TOWE		MSL87	49–55 Mansell St, E1
TOWE	37	MST87	31–43 Mansell St, 1–7 Alie St, E1
TOWE	38	NOF82	38 Norton Folgate, E1
TOWE	39	NRF88	4–12 Norton Folgate, E1
TOWE	40	NRT85	1–3 Norton Folgate, E1
TOWE	41	OFF85	413–417 Wick Lane, E3
TOWE	42	ORD88	2–16 Ordell Rd, E3
TOWE	43	PRE89	63–66 Prescot St, E1
TOWE	44	PRS77	Priscilla Rd, off Bow Rd, E3
TOWE	45	QMC90	Queen Mary and Westfield College, 343–345 Mile End Rd, E1
TOWE	46	RMS75	Royal Mint Square Development, Cartwright St, E1
TOWE	47	ROM80	Roman Rd, Parnell Rd, E3
TOWE	48	SCS83	9 St Clare St, EC3
TOWE	49	SHS79	Stepney High St, E1
TOWE	50	SIN88	15 Spital Square, E1
TOWE	51	SPQ87	4 Spital Square, E1

TOWE 52 SPT82 Central Foundation Girls School, Spital Square, E1

TOWE SPT85 Central Foundation Girls School, Spital Square, E1

TOWE 53 SSQ88 38 Spital Square, E1

TOWE 54 STS75 St Stephen's Rd, E3

TOWE 55 THL78 Goodman's Yard, E1

TOWE 56 THL78 Tower Hill, EC3

TOWE 57 TMS88 Thomas More St, E1

TOWE 58 TOL79 Tower Postern, Tower Hill, EC3

TOWE 59 TRT85 41–42 Trinity Square, EC3

TOWE 60 TSG87 Tower Hill Station, Trinity Square, EC3

TOWE 61 TTL85 The Three Lords public house, 27 Minories, EC3

TOWE 62 UNC90 Queen Mary and Westfield College, 343–345 Mile End Rd, E1

TOWE 63 UNI83 Union Stairs, Wapping High St, E1

TOWE UR74 Usher Rd, E3

TOWE 64 USH76 Usher Rd, Armagh Rd, E3

TOWE 65 WAW84 Wapping Wall, Garnet St, Monza St, E1

TOWE 66 WOR85 Worcester House, Stepney Green, E1

TOWE 67 WTE88 29 West Tenter St, E1

TOWE 68 WTE90 29 West Tenter St, 59 Mansell St, E1

TOWE 69 WTN83 West Tenter St, Scarborough St, St Mark St, South Tenter St, E1

TOWE 69 WTN84 West Tenter St, Scarborough St, St Mark St, South Tenter St, E1

TOWE 70 WWL85 Jubilee Wharf, 76 Wapping Wall, E1

72A Armagh Road, 91–93 Parnell Road, E3

AGH90

Excavation in 1990 revealed early Roman gravelling, presumably for the construction of the London to Colchester road. The quarries were backfilled on the construction of the first structures, represented by a series of post-holes and ditches which may also have been property boundaries. Occupation may have been agricultural, on the evidence of ploughsoil, and a more substantial building was indicated by groundbeams supporting wattle and daub walls. See also ROM80, USH76 below.

London Archaeol, 6, 1991, 308; *Britannia,* 22, 1991, 272

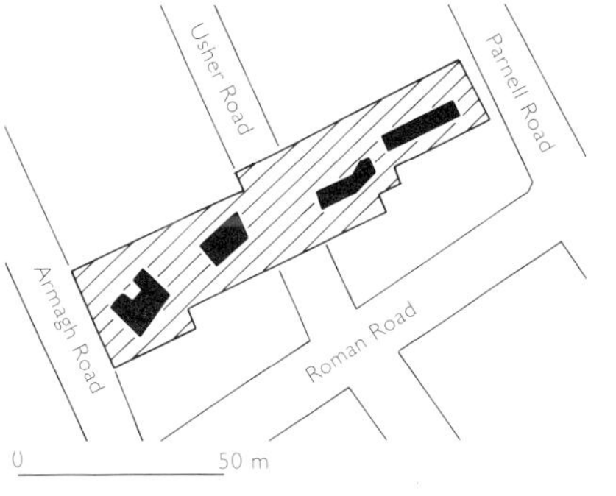

Map site: 1
DGLA(N): Kenneth Pitt
NGR: TQ 3684 8351
SMR: 082335–7

28 Alie Street, E1

ALS88

A testpit survey and watching brief in 1988 revealed several deposits of uncertain character.

Map site: 2
DGLA(N): Stephen Haynes
NGR: TQ 3498 8125

37–39 Artillery Lane, E1

ARL76

Excavation in 1976 revealed the remains of a plague pit.

London Archaeol, 3, 1977, 39; *Post-Medieval Archaeol,* 11, 1977, 91

Map site: 3
ILAU: David Whipp
NGR: TQ 3349 8171
SMR: 080985

ART76

Map site: 4
ILAU: Irene Schwab
NGR: TQ 3346 8172
SMR: 080984, 082213

27–33 Artillery Lane, E1

Excavation in 1976 revealed a number of 2nd-c and 14th–15th-c gravel pits. Any burials in this Roman cemetery area had been removed by 19th-c basements.

London Archaeol, 3, 1977, 39; Britannia, 8, 1977, 409

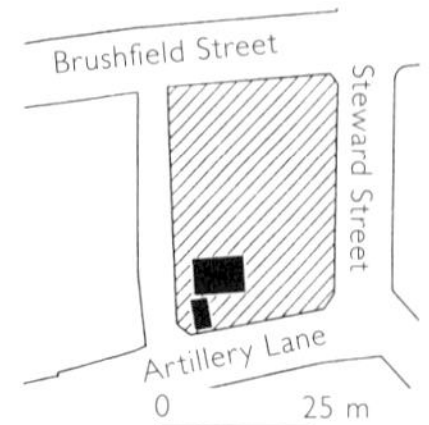

ASH87

Map site: 5
DGLA(N): Chris Thomas
NGR: TQ 3390 8114

24 Alie Street, E1

A watching brief and site assessment in 1987–8 showed that natural strata had been reduced at some date and then this area backfilled with a mixture of domestic waste and demolition rubble. The edges of a linear cut were observed through the clay of a quarry-pit backfill; at the bottom were fragments of leather and late medieval pottery sealed by a peat deposit.

BCL88

Map site: 6
DGLA(N): John Roche
NGR: TQ 3420 8105
SMR: 082095

95–105 Back Church Lane, E1

An evaluation excavation in 1988 revealed traces of Roman features, though the stratigraphy had been extensively damaged by a post-medieval cemetery and standing buildings. The site is crossed by the conjectured line of a Roman road.

London Archaeol, 6, 1989, 79

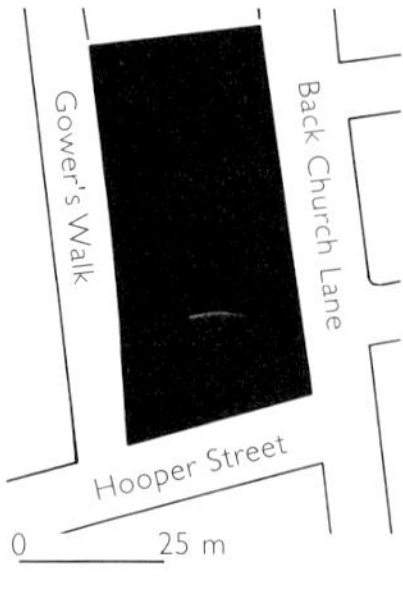

BPH87

Map site: 7
DGLA(N): Gavin Evans
NGR: TQ 3342 8188

St Botolph's Hall, Spital Square, E1

An investigation of three testpits, two inside St Botolph's Hall and one against the outside of the E wall, in 1987 revealed significant remains in only one of the inside pits in the form of a chalk block foundation, aligned E–W and incorporating a possible drain culvert aligned N–S. The drain had apparently been deliberately blocked with dressed Reigate stone fragments, and it is assumed to be either medieval (and part of the priory or hospital of St Mary Spital) or early post-medieval. It was overlain by post-medieval demolition or levelling and cut features. Similar depths of post-medieval features were observed in the other two pits.

Butcher Row, E14

BTR75

Map site: 8
ILAU: Irene Schwab
NGR: TQ 3590 8090
SMR: 080730, 080834,
080923, 081585–9

An excavation in 1975 revealed, in the N of the site, evidence for a creek running NE–SW, which had been filled in towards the end of the medieval period. Above the infill was a chalk and flint boundary wall on the same alignment and overlain by traces of three 17th-c buildings with gravel yards. In the S, only traces of a Tudor garden soil and three 17th-c pits survived beneath the 18th–19th-c warehouses.

London Archaeol, 2, 1976, 372; *Medieval Archaeol,* 20, 1976, 191
Locker, A, 1977 'Animal bone', in Schwab, I, & Nurse, B, 249–50
Locker, A, 1977 'The environmental evidence', in Schwab, I, & Nurse, B, 250
Morley, P, 1977 'The tokens', in Schwab, I, & Nurse, B, 247
Nurse, B, 1977 'The Royal Foundation of St Katherine, Butcher Row, E14', in Schwab, I, & Nurse, B, 231–9
Platts, E, 1977 'The pottery from the excavation', in Schwab, I, & Nurse, B, 239–47
Schwab, I, & Nurse, B, 1977 'Butcher Row, Ratcliff, E14', *Trans London Middlesex Archaeol Soc,* 28, 215–51

9–25 Camperdown Street, E1

CAM81

Map site: 9
DGLA(N): Robert Whytehead
NGR: TQ 3390 8120
SMR: 082222

Excavation in 1981 revealed several undated pits cut into the natural.

Crispin Street, Brushfield Street, E1

CRI88

Map site: 10
DGLA(N): Naomi Hamilton
NGR: TQ 3358 8177

A watching brief in 1988 recorded, from sections, open land built up in the 17th c. Evidence for two pits was also noted.

Cable Street, E1

CSV85

Map site: 11
DGLA(N): Paul Falcini
NGR: TQ 3451 8083

A watching brief in 1985 recorded post-medieval features and dumping.

Post-Medieval Archaeol, 21, 1987, 275

Davenant Street, E1

DAV77

Map site: 12
ILAU: Irene Schwab
NGR: TQ 3440 8180
SMR: 081050–1

Excavation in 1977 of a trench about 100m long, from Old Montague Street to Whitechapel Road, revealed no trace of the Roman road to Colchester, but observations of contractors' trenches in the W part of the site recorded burials to be associated with a known burial ground of 17th–18th-c date.

London Archaeol, 3, 1978, 162

ETN88

Map site: 13
DGLA(N): David Bowsher
NGR: TQ 3399 8102
SMR: 082096–8

East Tenter Street, Scarborough Street, E1

Excavation in 1988 revealed shallow Roman deposits, eight burials (three of them in chalk) and two fragments of a mortared flint structure which may have been part of a mausoleum. Along the E fragment of wall was an inhumation. Also found were many large cut features, perhaps gravel pits.

London Archaeol, 6, 1989, 79; *Britannia*, 20, 1989, 308
Barber, B, & Bowsher, D, in prep. *The eastern cemetery of Roman London: excavations 1983–1990*
Barber, B, Bowsher, D, & Whittaker, K, 1990 'Recent excavations of a cemetery of *Londinium*', *Britannia*, 21, 1–12

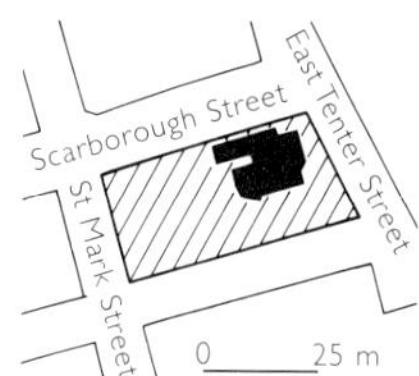

FAB88

Map site: 14
DGLA(N): Bruno Barber,
Kevin Wooldridge
NGR: TQ 3394 8116
SMR: 082094

36–44 Alie Street, E1

The excavation of 22 testpits in 1988 produced extensive evidence of pitting, presumably for brickearth and gravel extraction. The pits were filled with domestic refuse, but their exact purpose and extent were not established. No Roman burials were located in this known burial area.

London Archaeol, 6, 1989, 79

FAG90

Map site: 15
DGLA(N): Bruno Barber
NGR: TQ 3425 8114
SMR: 082332

2–6 Fairclough Street, E1

An evaluation excavation in 1990 revealed extensive truncation of natural gravels by 17th- and 18th-c quarrying. No earlier features survived.

London Archaeol, 6, 1991, 308; *Post-Medieval Archaeol*, 25, 1991, 159

FLG77

Map site: 16
ILAU: Graham Black
NGR: TQ 3340 8200

19–27 Folgate Street, 1–4 Blossom Street, E1

A watching brief in 1977 recorded layers of post-medieval dumping over natural strata.

FOL76

Map site: 17
ILAU: Graham Black
NGR: TQ 3340 8200
SMR: 080380

6–8 Folgate Street, E1

Observation in 1976 recorded the clunch rubble foundations of a wall, probably of medieval date.

London Archaeol, 3, 1978, 162

29–33 Folgate Street, 1–3 Elder Street, 9–10 Fleur de Lis Street, E1

FOL77

Map site: 18
ILAU: Irene Schwab
NGR: TQ 3360 8200
SMR: 082219

A trial excavation in 1977 produced no evidence of use before the 17th c, when dumping occurred.

London Archaeol, 3, 1978, 162

Gardiner's Corner, Mansell Street, Whitechapel High Street, E1

GDC80

Map site: 19
ILAU: Robert Whytehead
NGR: TQ 3380 8125

A watching brief in 1980 established that the Roman cemetery in this area had been completely obliterated by late medieval gravel and sand extraction pits. Residual Roman pottery and cremated bone were found, together with evidence of Tudor industrial processes.

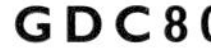

London Archaeol, 4, 1981, 50
Hammerson, M J, 1984 'Coins', in Whytehead, R L, 44
Locker, A, 1984 'The animal bones', in Whytehead, R L, 54–5
McIsaac, W, 1984 'Other small finds', in Whytehead, R L, 44
McIsaac, W, 1984 'Roman pottery', in Whytehead, R L, 42–4
Orton, C, 1984 'Building material', in Whytehead, R L, 49
Orton, C, 1984 'Post-medieval glass', in Whytehead, R L, 49
Orton, C, & Platts, E, 1984 'Saxon, medieval and post-medieval pottery', in Whytehead, R L, 44–9
Stott, P, 1984 'Medieval coin', in Whytehead, R L, 49
Tobert, N, 1984 'Medieval leather', in Whytehead, R L, 49–53
Whytehead, R L, 1984 'Sitewatching at Gardiner's Corner, Aldgate, E1', *Trans London Middlesex Archaeol Soc,* 35, 37–57

36–44 Gower's Walk, E1

GOW89

Map site: 20
DGLA(N): Stewart Hoad
NGR: TQ 3417 8116

Excavation in 1989 investigated two areas of which the first revealed a sandy layer beneath garden soil dated to the 16th c; subsequently the area was used for rubbish disposal with extensive pitting of the garden soil. Structures included a basement, well and cesspit, probably also of 16th-c date. In the second area, a small part of a Dissenters' burial ground apparently remained intact.

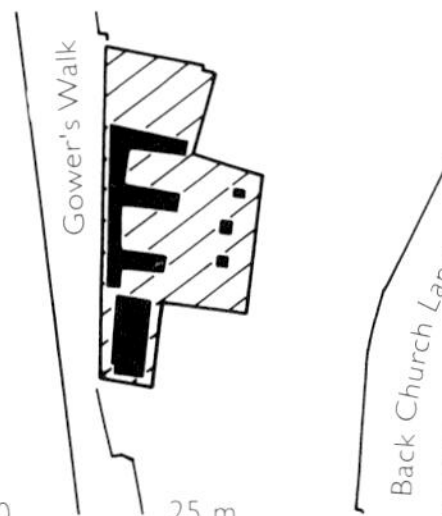

Goodman's Yard, E1

GYD75

Map site: 21
ILAU: Graham Black
NGR: TQ 3380 8090
SMR: 080986

Trial trenching in 1975 revealed 13th-c gravelworking W of Mansell Street. See also THL78 below.

London Archaeol, 2, 1976, 372

HAY86

Map site: 22
DGLA(N): Kevin Wooldridge,
Robert Ellis
NGR: TQ 3370 8105
SMR: 081500

13 Haydon Street, EC3

Excavation in 1986 revealed 17 Roman inhumations of 3rd-c date, accompanied by rich gravegoods. Structural remains at the corner of the cloister of the Franciscan nunnery of St Clare were found, standing to first-floor height and incorporated in the fabric of a Victorian warehouse.

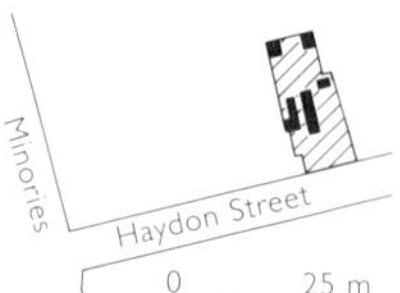

London Archaeol, 5, 1987, 277; *Medieval Archaeol,* 31, 1987, 133
Barber, B, & Bowsher, D, in prep. *The eastern cemetery of Roman London: excavations 1983–1990*
Barber, B, Bowsher, D, & Whittaker, K, 1990 'Recent excavations of a cemetery of *Londinium*', *Britannia,* 21, 1–12

HIG74

Map site: not shown
NGR: TQ 350 807
SMR: 080776, 080935, 081094

The Highway, E1

See LD74 below.

London Archaeol, 2, 1976, 372

HOO86, HOO88

Map site: 23, 24
DGLA(N): Bruno Barber,
David Bowsher
NGR: TQ 3420 8100
SMR: 082099, 082105

Hooper Street, E1

Excavation in 1988, within a ditched area of an extensive Roman cemetery lying alongside a road or trackway, encountered numerous burials including both cremations and inhumations, and adults and children. Gravegoods included hobnailed shoes, shale bracelets, glass beads and a possible jewel casket. The orientation suggested that some interments may have formed distinct groups. Some of the cremations were contained in amphorae, and one was found on top of a coffin. Half of an inscribed tombstone was recovered from a pit.

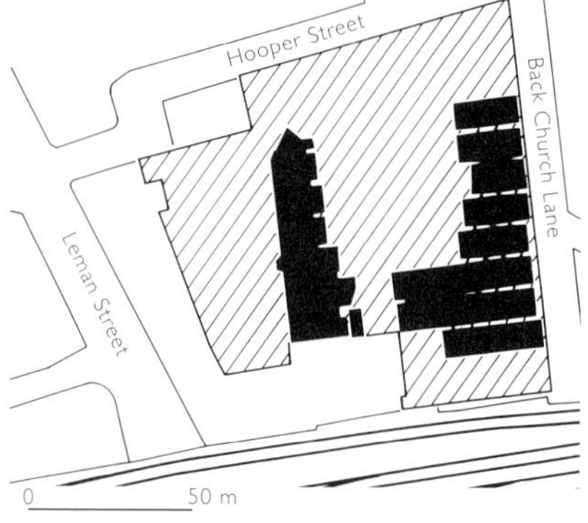

London Archaeol, 6, 1989, 79; *Britannia,* 20, 1989, 309
Barber, B, & Bowsher, D, in prep. *The eastern cemetery of Roman London: excavations 1983–1990*
Barber, B, Bowsher, D, & Whittaker, K, 1990 'Recent excavations of a cemetery of *Londinium*', *Britannia,* 21, 1–12

LD74

Map site: 25
LAMAS: Tony Johnson; ILAU:
Graham Black
NGR: TQ 350 807
SMR: 081623

The Highway, E1

Excavations in 1974 revealed the foundations, mostly robbed out, of a masonry building about 8m square, as well as traces of timber buildings, well-preserved timber-lined drains and a water-storage tank, and ditches to the S. The evidence of coins, a notable assemblage of late samian pottery, and belt-fittings suggests that the building was a military watch tower or signal tower of late 3rd–4th-c date. See also HIG74 above and LD76 below.

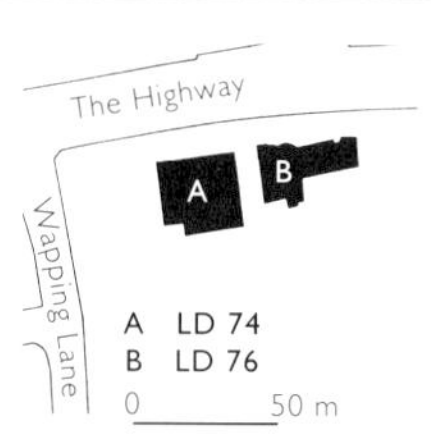

Britannia, 6, 1975, 269; 7, 1976, 351
Johnson, T, 1974 'A late Roman military site at London Docks', *London Archaeol,* 2, 165
Johnson, T, 1975 'A Roman signal tower at Shadwell, E1 (interim note)', *Trans London Middlesex Archaeol Soc,* 26, 278–80

London Docks, The Highway, E1

Excavation in 1976, E of the signal tower (see LD74 above), revealed evidence of a late Roman timber building with an associated ditch system and metalled surface. Five early 2nd-c cremation burials were found to the E of the building. (For plan, see LD74.)

London Archaeol, 3, 1977, 39; 3, 1978, 162; *Britannia,* 10, 1979, 317

LD76

Map site: 26
ILAU: David Whipp
NGR: TQ 3495 8074
SMR: 080752

19 Leman Street, 24–26 Buckle Street, E1

An evaluation excavation in 1987 revealed no positive archaeological features. A trial excavation in 1988 revealed various undated layers and pits above natural. (For plan, see LD74.)

**LEM87,
LEM88**

Map site: 27, 28
DGLA(N): Chris Thomas,
Stephen Haynes
NGR: TQ 3396 8124

Limehouse Link Road, The Highway, E14

Excavation in 1989 recovered many prehistoric worked flints and located the remains of the 18th-c manufactory which produced Limehouse porcelain. Several phases of industrial buildings in brick were recorded, including premises for pickling and lime burning.

Pontin, L, & St John Aubin, J, 1990 'Limehouse uncovered', *Sotheby's Preview* (Sept–Oct) 1009, 22–4

LLK89

Map site: 29
DGLA(N): L Pontin
NGR: TQ 360 809
SMR: 082202–4

Royal Mint, East Smithfield, EC3

An evaluation excavation in 1983 on the site of the Cistercian abbey of St Mary Graces (founded 1350) revealed 76m of abbey walls, the dining hall, hospital block, S chapel, Lady Chapel and chapter house, in addition to other buildings.

London Archaeol, 5, 1985, 67; *Medieval Archaeol,* 29, 1985, 179
Mills, P, 1985 'The Royal Mint: first results', *London Archaeol,* 5, 69–77

**MIN83,
MIN84**

Map site: 30, 31
DGLA(N): Peter Mills
NGR: TQ 3390 8070

Royal Mint, East Smithfield, EC3

Excavation in 1986–7 (see MIN83, MIN84 above) revealed both truncated pits containing Roman pottery and quarry pits, cut into the natural. The S walkway of the abbey cloisters was uncovered, its floor of crushed chalk and mortar replaced by brick in the 17th c. The frater ran S from the cloister at an acute angle, and areas of medieval tile floor were located as well as sections of wall. Along the S side of the cloister lay the warming house with the remains of an external chimney on the S side, and a series of tile and brick floors with a half basement. The reredorter was in the SE corner of the cloister, and although internal details had been destroyed by later intrusions, sockets in the E wall suggested that a

MIN86

Map site: 32
DGLA(N): Peter Mills
NGR: TQ 3390 8070
SMR: 080928, 081501–2

timber floor had covered the drain. Rebuilt twice in the post-medieval period, the drain survived in its original form (chalk and tile vaulting) at its S end. Next to the reredorter was a substantial building which may have been the chapter house: only a small section of floor survived, showing a tile floor replaced by one of clay. Separated from this building by a yard was the infirmary, partly demolished in the 16th c but later repaired. Traces of joists indicated that it had once had a timber floor. After the Dissolution the abbey passed into private hands and c 1560 was purchased by the Crown and converted into a victualling yard for the Royal Navy, which used most of the existing buildings until the mid-17th c. Extension in the late 17th c involved demolition of the warming house and cloister wall.

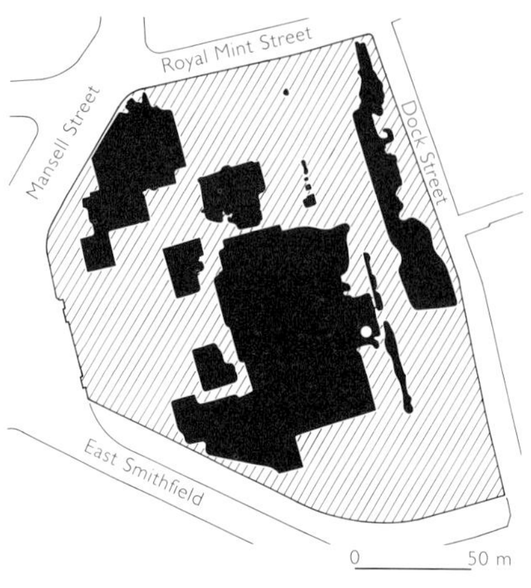

London Archaeol, 5, 1987, 277–8; 5, 1988, 415; 6, 1989, 79; Medieval Archaeol, 31, 1987, 133; Post-Medieval Archaeol, 21, 1987, 268
Anon, 1986 'The Mint with the hole', Mosaic, London Archaeol, 5, 224
Grainger, I, Hawkins, D, with Falcini, P, & Mills, P, 1988 'Excavations at the Royal Mint site 1986–1988', London Archaeol, 5, 429–36
Grainger, I, Falcini, P, & Hawkins, D, in prep. St Mary Graces, London: excavations at the Royal Mint 1986–1988

MIN87

Map site: 33
DGLA(N): Peter Mills
NGR: TQ 3390 8070
SMR: 081097, 082233–4

Royal Mint, East Smithfield, EC3

See MIN86 above. Excavation of the Black Death cemetery in 1987 revealed some 420 trench burials, more than 300 of them from individual graves. Further work on the abbey remains uncovered the E end of the church, a large lay cemetery with 400 graves and further parts of the infirmary and possible chapter house. Areas of tiled floor were recovered from inside the church. Further evidence was recorded of the naval victualling yard, and its rebuilding in the 18th c.

London Archaeol, 5, 1988, 415; Medieval Archaeol, 32, 1988, 252; 33, 1989, 187; Post-Medieval Archaeol, 23, 1989, 27
Grainger, I, Falcini, P, & Hawkins, D, in prep. St Mary Graces, London: excavations at the Royal Mint 1986–1988

MNL87, MNL88

Map site: 34, 35
DGLA(N): Stephen Haynes
NGR: TQ 3383 8002

65–73 Mansell Street, E1

Excavations revealed five inhumations of Roman date, including one 'chalk burial', with associated hobnailed shoes, and animal and bird bones. Contemporary ditches and a metalled surface were also recorded, the latter perhaps a continuation of a road found to the W (see SCS83 below).

Barber, B, & Bowsher, D, in prep. The eastern cemetery of Roman London: excavations 1983–1990
Barber, B, Bowsher, D, & Whittaker, K, 1990 'Recent excavations of a cemetery of Londinium', Britannia, 21, 1–12

Morville Street, E3

Excavation in 1972–3 revealed a ditch, burial pit and shallow gullies containing Roman pottery of the late 1st or early 2nd c.

London Archaeol, 2, 1973, 42; 2, 1974, 135

MS72, MS73

Map site: 36
SLAEC: Irene Schwab
NGR: TQ 3715 8320

49–55 Mansell Street, E1

Excavations recorded about 230 inhumations and 26 cremation burials, many with gravegoods, dated from the late 1st to perhaps the early 5th c. Ditches and traces of the foundations of mausolea were also found.

Barber, B, & Bowsher, D, in prep. *The eastern cemetery of Roman London: excavations 1983–1990*
Barber, B, Bowsher, D, & Whittaker, K, 1990 'Recent excavations of a cemetery of *Londinium*', *Britannia*, 21, 1–12

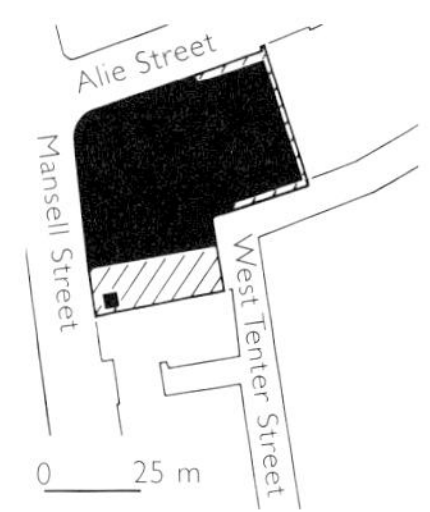

MSL87

Map site: not shown
DGLA(N): Al Mackie, Kevin Wooldridge
NGR: TQ 3380 8110

31–43 Mansell Street, 1–7 Alie Street, E1

Excavation in 1987 revealed a shallow Roman ditch which apparently served as the N boundary of a cemetery or burial plot. To the S, and parallel or at right angles to it, were 85 inhumations including 16 'plaster' burials and one grave lined with tiles. Gravegoods were present in some of the burials, usually personal ornaments or pottery vessels.

London Archaeol, 5, 1988, 415
Barber, B, & Bowsher, D, in prep. *The eastern cemetery of Roman London: excavations 1983–1990*
Barber, B, Bowsher, D, & Whittaker, K, 1990 'Recent excavations of a cemetery of *Londinium*', *Britannia*, 21, 1–12

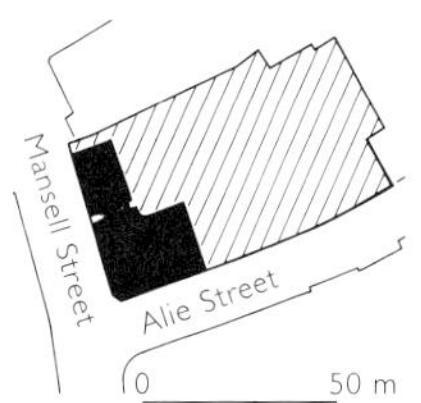

MST87

Map site: 37
DGLA(N): Ken Whittaker
NGR: TQ 3382 8115
SMR: 081811

38 Norton Folgate, E1

Observation in 1982 recorded traces of a possible chalk raft.

NOF82

Map site: 38
ILAU: Robert Whytehead
NGR: TQ 3340 8200

4–12 Norton Folgate, E1

Excavation in 1988 on the site of the W part of the precinct of the priory and hospital of St Mary without Bishopsgate, revealed Roman features, probably boundary ditches. In the SE corner of the site, the earliest medieval structure consisted of two piers forming an arcade aligned N–S and interpreted as part of the N transept of the priory church. To the W lay a later medieval hall, butting onto the W wall of the earlier building; examination of its N end (the S part having already been excavated, see NRT85 below) showed that the roof was supported on four square piers placed centrally along the hall. A number of burials predating the hall suggest that it was previously

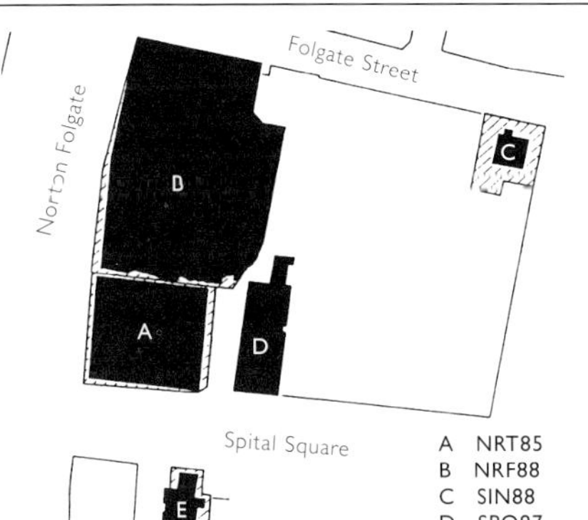

NRF88

Map site: 39
DGLA(N): Chris Thomas, Barney Sloane
NGR: TQ 3341 8196
SMR: 080934, 082271

the site of the original hospital cemetery, which still remained in use further W until the construction of a precinct wall along the W side of the site. A large drain, apparently contemporary with a later hall to the S, was subsequently disused and robbed. Two more drains were built at the W end, and a building with a tiled floor aligned E–W was built over the old drain. At the N end of the site an open garden was revealed, bounded by the 'precinct wall' to the W and another wall to the E. Inside the garden was a well, a drain running across the site, and a possible timber building. After the Dissolution much demolition and rebuilding occurred, some of it utilising the medieval fabric.

London Archaeol, 6, 1989, 79; *Britannia,* 20, 1989, 308; *Medieval Archaeol,* 33, 1989, 187; *Post-Medieval Archaeol,* 23, 1989, 27
Brehm, B, Shepherd, J D, & Thomas, C, 1997 'The glass', in Thomas, C, Sloane, B, & Phillpotts, C, 210–15
Conheeney, J, 1997 'The human bone', in Thomas, C, Sloane, B, & Phillpotts, C, 218–31
Crowley, N, 1997 'Ceramic building material', in Thomas, C, Sloane, B, & Phillpotts, C, 195–201
Davis, A, 1997, 'The plant remains', in Thomas, C, Sloane, B, & Phillpotts, C, 234–45
Egan, G, 1997 'Non-ceramic finds', in Thomas, C, Sloane, B, & Phillpotts, C, 201–10
Goodburn-Brown, D, 1997 'Conservation', in Thomas, C, Sloane, B, & Phillpotts, C, 248–9
Heard, K, 1997 'Clay tobacco pipes', in Thomas, C, Sloane, B, & Phillpotts, C, 217–18
Locker, A, 1997 'The fish bones', in Thomas, C, Sloane, B, & Phillpotts, C, 234
Nailor, A, 1997 'The leather', in Thomas, C, Sloane, B, & Phillpotts, C, 215–17
Pipe, A, 1997 'The animal bone', in Thomas, C, Sloane, B, & Phillpotts, C, 231–4
de Rouffignac, C, 1997 'Parasite remains', in Thomas, C, Sloane, B, & Phillpotts, C, 247–8
Samuel, M, with de Domingo, C, 1997 'Moulded stone', in Thomas, C, Sloane, B, & Phillpotts, C, 186–95
Sidell, J, 1997 'The eggshell', in Thomas, C, Sloane, B, & Phillpotts, C, 248
Smith, D, 1997 'Insect fauna', in Thomas, C, Sloane, B, & Phillpotts, C, 245–7
Stephenson, R, with Spoerry, P, 1997 'The pottery', in Thomas, C, Sloane, B, & Phillpotts, C, 184–6
Thomas, C, Sloane, B, & Phillpotts, C, 1997 *Excavations at the Priory and Hospital of St Mary Spital, London,* MoLAS Monograph 1

NRT85

Map site: 40
DGLA(N): Rob Ellis
NGR: TQ 3340 8192
SMR: 081095–6

1–3 Norton Folgate, E1

Excavation in 1985 within the site of a Roman cemetery area and of the medieval precinct of St Mary without Bishopsgate located Roman quarry pits backfilled with domestic and building debris. Medieval drainage ditches and gullies were exposed, predating the hospital and its cemetery, where 52 inhumations were recovered. The foundations of a substantial medieval building were partially examined, and a N–S aligned wall on the W side of the site may represent part of the precinct boundary. (For plan, see NRF88.)

London Archaeol, 5, 1986, 164; *Britannia,* 17, 1986, 409; *Medieval Archaeol,* 30, 1986, 143
Brehm, B, Shepherd, J D, & Thomas, C, 1997 'The glass', in Thomas, C, Sloane, B, & Phillpotts, C, 210–15
Conheeney, J, 1997 'The human bone', in Thomas, C, Sloane, B, & Phillpotts, C, 218–31
Crowley, N, 1997 'Ceramic building material', in Thomas, C, Sloane, B, & Phillpotts, C, 195–201
Davis, A, 1997, 'The plant remains', in Thomas, C, Sloane, B, & Phillpotts, C, 234–45
Egan, G, 1997 'Non-ceramic finds', in Thomas, C, Sloane, B, & Phillpotts, C, 201–10
Goodburn-Brown, D, 1997 'Conservation', in Thomas, C, Sloane, B, & Phillpotts, C, 248–9
Heard, K, 1997 'Clay tobacco pipes', in Thomas, C, Sloane, B, & Phillpotts, C, 217–18
Locker, A, 1997 'The fish bones', in Thomas, C, Sloane, B, & Phillpotts, C, 234
Nailor, A, 1997 'The leather', in Thomas, C, Sloane, B, & Phillpotts, C, 215–17
Pipe, A, 1997 'The animal bone', in Thomas, C, Sloane, B, & Phillpotts, C, 231–4
de Rouffignac, C, 1997 'Parasite remains', in Thomas, C, Sloane, B, & Phillpotts, C, 247–8
Samuel, M, with de Domingo, C, 1997 'Moulded stone', in Thomas, C, Sloane, B, & Phillpotts, C, 186–95
Sidell, J, 1997 'The eggshell', in Thomas, C, Sloane, B, & Phillpotts, C, 248
Smith, D, 1997 'Insect fauna', in Thomas, C, Sloane, B, & Phillpotts, C, 245–7
Stephenson, R, with Spoerry, P, 1997 'The pottery', in Thomas, C, Sloane, B, & Phillpotts, C, 184–6
Thomas, C, Sloane, B, & Phillpotts, C, 1997 *Excavations at the Priory and Hospital of St Mary Spital, London,* MoLAS Monograph 1

OFF85

Map site: 41
DGLA(N): Robert Cowie
NGR: TQ 3730 8878

413–417 Wick Lane, E3

Excavation in 1985 revealed alluvial deposits provisionally dated to *c* AD200 and overlain by make-up material associated with a rammed gravel layer. This was covered by further alluvial deposits followed by layers of make-up and possible surfaces. Above was late medieval and early post-medieval stratigraphy including two intrusive features.

2–16 Ordell Road, E3

A watching brief in 1988 observed no features earlier than the post-medieval period.

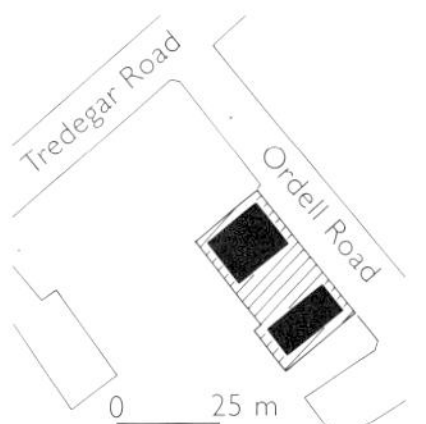

ORD88

Map site: 42
DGLA(N): Naomi Hamilton
NGR: TQ 3700 8318

63–66 Prescot Street, E1

Excavation in 1989 revealed three ditches, possibly representing field boundaries, and predating a Roman cemetery from which four inhumations of the mid–late 2nd-c AD were recovered. The corner of a tile and mortar structure, perhaps part of a mausoleum, was also uncovered, as was a well of the late 1st–early 2nd c AD whose fill contained large quantities of Roman building material and a large fragment of tombstone.

Barber, B, & Bowsher, D, in prep. *The eastern cemetery of Roman London: excavations 1983–1990*

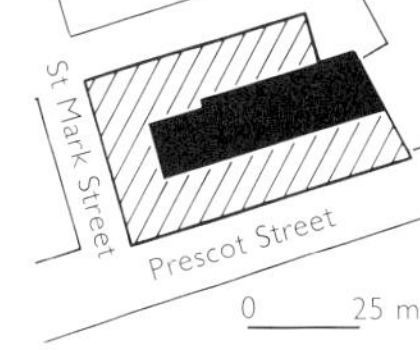

PRE89

Map site: 43
DGLA(N): David Bowsher
NGR: TQ 3400 8100
SMR: 082206–7

Priscilla Road, off Bow Road, E3

Observations in 1977 recorded a flat-bottomed pit cut into gravel and possibly post-medieval in date. Above was a layer of dark, gravelly ploughsoil extending across the whole site.

PRS77

Map site: 44
ILAU: Graham Black
NGR: TQ 3760 8290

Queen Mary and Westfield College, 343–345 Mile End Road, E1

An evaluation excavation in 1990 revealed beneath a ploughsoil a series of cut features of unknown prehistoric–medieval date: a large timber building represented by a series of post-holes was probably medieval. Agriculture probably ceased in the late 18th c.

London Archaeol, 6, 1991, 308; *Medieval Archaeol*, 35, 1991, 156

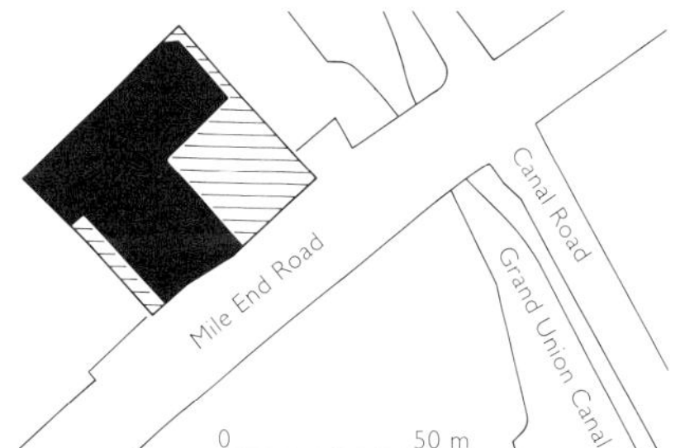

QMC90

Map site: 45
DGLA(N): Kevin Williams
NGR: TQ 3621 8241
SMR: 082333

Royal Mint Square Development, Cartwright Street, E1

Excavation in 1975 revealed the destruction of most of the site's archaeology by post-medieval working and the foundation for a 19th-c railway viaduct. The S part of the site disclosed an 18th-c burial ground.

London Archaeol, 2, 1976, 372

RMS75

Map site: 46
ILAU: Irene Schwab
NGR: TQ 3410 8060
SMR: 080872–3

ROM80

Map site: 47
ILAU: Peter Mills
NGR: TQ 3697 8355
SMR: 080967, 081621–2

Roman Road, Parnell Road, E3

Excavation in 1980 revealed the multi-phase periods of the
London to Colchester Roman road at its approach to the
River Lea. See also AGH90 above, USH76 below.

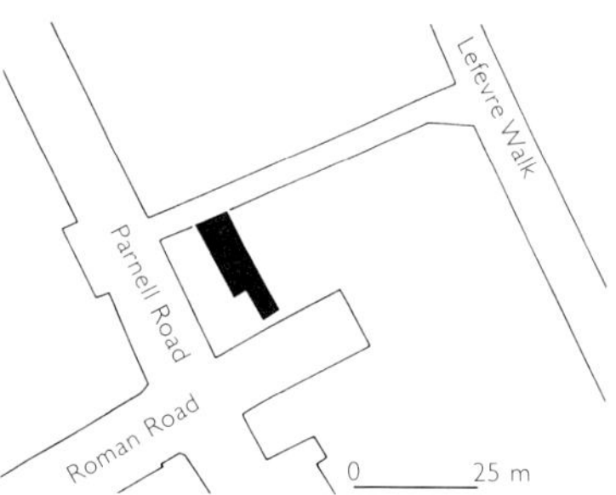

London Archaeol, 4, 1981, 50; *Britannia,* 12, 1981, 353
Bird, J, 1984 'The samian', in Mills, P, 29–30
Dickinson, B M, 1984 'The stamped samian', in Mills, P, 30
Hammerson, M J, 1984 'The coins', in Mills, P, 34
Locker, A, 1984 'The animal bones', in Mills, P, 36
McIsaac, W, 1984 'Roman coarse pottery', in Mills, P, 30–4
McIsaac, W, 1984 'Small finds', in Mills, P, 34–5
Mills, P, 1984 'Excavations at Roman Road/Parnell Road, Old Ford, London
 E3', *Trans London Middlesex Archaeol Soc,* 35, 25–36
Orton, C, 1984 'Abrasive stones', in Mills, P, 35–6

SCS83

Map site: 48
DGLA(N): Robert Ellis
NGR: TQ 3372 8106
SMR: 080880–1, 080917

9 St Clare Street, EC3

Limited excavation in 1983 on the site of Holy Trinity Church revealed on the S side of the site the N
edge of a Roman road of rammed gravel and its ditch, aligned ESE–WNW. A provisional date of the late
1st c is suggested for its construction. To the N of the road was a rectangular pit, at the bottom of
which were traces of a wooden box containing two complete late 1st-c flagons above a quantity of
broken pottery. To the W of the pit were three Roman inhumation burials, and one cremation burial of
the 2nd c; the remains of a later Roman 'plaster' burial were also uncovered. Post-medieval burials had
extensively disturbed the medieval deposits, and only a substantial chalk wall aligned NW–SE survived,
on the S side of the site.

London Archaeol, 4, 1984, 390–1; *Medieval Archaeol,* 28, 1984, 233
Barber, B, & Bowsher, D, in prep. *The eastern cemetery of Roman London: excavations 1983–1990*
Barber, B, Bowsher, D, & Whittaker, K, 1990 'Recent excavations of a cemetery of *Londinium*', *Britannia,* 21, 1–12
Ellis, R, 1985 'Excavations at 9 St Clare Street', *London Archaeol,* 5, 115–21

SHS79

Map site: 49
ILAU: Peter Mills
NGR: TQ 3580 8160
SMR: 080734, 080857, 082211

Stepney High Street, E1

Excavation in 1979 revealed evidence of early occupation in the form of a Saxo-Norman pit and two
late medieval pits. The area had been cultivated from at least the 16th c, and an isolated hearth of the
same period was recorded.

London Archaeol, 3, 1980, 389
Blackmore, L, 1982 'The pottery', in Mills, P, 330–43
Locker, A, 1982 'Animal bones', in Mills, P, 343
Mills, P, 1982 'Excavations at Stepney High Street, E1', *Trans London Middlesex Archaeol Soc,* 33, 324–43

SIN88

Map site: 50
DGLA(N): Chris Thomas
NGR: TQ 3347 8197
SMR: 080934, 082270

15 Spital Square, E1

Excavation in 1988 within the former precinct of the priory and hospital of St Mary without
Bishopsgate revealed a medieval wall aligned E–W, partially robbed at its W end, crossing the N side
of the site. To its S lay a series of dumped soil layers, perhaps representing an open space. No evidence
was found of the Roman cemetery in the area, though many Roman pottery sherds were recovered.
See also SPQ87 below. (For plan, see NRF88.)

London Archaeol, 6, 1989, 79–80; *Britannia,* 20, 1989, 308; *Medieval Archaeol,* 33, 1989, 187

Brehm, B, Shepherd, J D, & Thomas, C, 1997 'The glass', in Thomas, C, Sloane, B, & Phillpotts, C, 210–15

Conheeney, J, 1997 'The human bone', in Thomas, C, Sloane, B, & Phillpotts, C, 218–31

Crowley, N, 1997 'Ceramic building material', in Thomas, C, Sloane, B, & Phillpotts, C, 195–201

Davis, A, 1997, 'The plant remains', in Thomas, C, Sloane, B, & Phillpotts, C, 234–45

Egan, G, 1997 'Non-ceramic finds', in Thomas, C, Sloane, B, & Phillpotts, C, 201–10

Goodburn-Brown, D, 1997 'Conservation', in Thomas, C, Sloane, B, & Phillpotts, C, 248–9

Heard, K, 1997 'Clay tobacco pipes', in Thomas, C, Sloane, B, & Phillpotts, C, 217–18

Locker, A, 1997 'The fish bones', in Thomas, C, Sloane, B, & Phillpotts, C, 234

Nailor, A, 1997 'The leather', in Thomas, C, Sloane, B, & Phillpotts, C, 215–17

Pipe, A, 1997 'The animal bone', in Thomas, C, Sloane, B, & Phillpotts, C, 231–4

de Rouffignac, C, 1997 'Parasite remains', in Thomas, C, Sloane, B, & Phillpotts, C, 247–8

Samuel, M, with de Domingo, C, 1997 'Moulded stone', in Thomas, C, Sloane, B, & Phillpotts, C, 186–95

Sidell, J, 1997 'The eggshell', in Thomas, C, Sloane, B, & Phillpotts, C, 248

Smith, D, 1997 'Insect fauna', in Thomas, C, Sloane, B, & Phillpotts, C, 245–7

Stephenson, R, with Spoerry, P, 1997 'The pottery', in Thomas, C, Sloane, B, & Phillpotts, C, 184–6

Thomas, C, Sloane, B, & Phillpotts, C, 1997 *Excavations at the Priory and Hospital of St Mary Spital, London,* MoLAS Monograph 1

4 Spital Square, E1

SPQ87

Map site: 51
DGLA(N): Barney Sloane
NGR: TQ 3343 8193
SMR: 080934, 082269

Excavation in 1987, probably within the N transept of the priory church of St Mary without Bishopsgate, revealed a Roman ditch cut into the brickearth and overlain by dark earth. Construction layers of crushed stone overlain by layers of clay were cut by five medieval burials. Two pier bases were located, together with much worked stone, including column drums, which had been reused in post-medieval structures. (For plan, see NRF88.)

London Archaeol, 6, 1989, 79–80

Central Foundation Girls School, Spital Square, E1

SPT82

Map site: 52
DGLA(N): Peter Mills
NGR: TQ 3346 8187
SMR: 080934, 081092, 082223

Excavation in 1982 uncovered Roman funerary pottery indicating the presence of a cemetery, though burials had been destroyed by extensive quarrying, possibly of late Roman date. One hundred and eleven medieval inhumations associated with the hospital of St Mary without Bishopsgate were recorded. The hospital buildings appear to have been partly demolished after the Dissolution, and replaced by large houses with formal gardens. Gravel surfaces of this period, possibly yards and paths, were exposed. See SPT85 below.

Medieval Archaeol, 27, 1983, 196

Central Foundation Girls School, Spital Square, E1

SPT85

Map site: 52
DGLA(N): Chris Thomas
NGR: TQ 334 819
SMR: 080934

Excavations within the precinct of St Mary without Bishopsgate revealed four inhumation burials of Roman date, and small pits shortly predating the medieval priory. A levelling dump, probably associated with the construction of the priory, was cut by a total of 305 burials. See SPT82 above.

Britannia, 17, 1986, 409

SSQ88

Map site: 53
DGLA(N): Christopher
Phillpotts, Chris Thomas
NGR: TQ 3341 8190
SMR: 080934, 082272

38 Spital Square, E1

Excavation in 1988 within the site of the former priory and hospital of St Mary without Bishopsgate revealed rubbish pits of Roman date and probably medieval inhumations. A prominent N–S aligned wall of medieval date was noted. (For plan, see NRF88.)

London Archaeol, 6, 1989, 80; 6, 1990, 194; *Britannia*, 20, 1989, 309; *Medieval Archaeol*, 33, 1989, 187; 34, 1990, 185
Brehm, B, Shepherd, J D, & Thomas, C, 1997 'The glass', in Thomas, C, Sloane, B, & Phillpotts, C, 210–15
Conheeney, J, 1997 'The human bone', in Thomas, C, Sloane, B, & Phillpotts, C, 218–31
Crowley, N, 1997 'Ceramic building material', in Thomas, C, Sloane, B, & Phillpotts, C, 195–201
Davis, A, 1997, 'The plant remains', in Thomas, C, Sloane, B, & Phillpotts, C, 234–45
Egan, G, 1997 'Non-ceramic finds', in Thomas, C, Sloane, B, & Phillpotts, C, 201–10
Goodburn-Brown, D, 1997 'Conservation', in Thomas, C, Sloane, B, & Phillpotts, C, 248–9
Heard, K, 1997 'Clay tobacco pipes', in Thomas, C, Sloane, B, & Phillpotts, C, 217–18
Locker, A, 1997 'The fish bones', in Thomas, C, Sloane, B, & Phillpotts, C, 234
Nailor, A, 1997 'The leather', in Thomas, C, Sloane, B, & Phillpotts, C, 215–17
Pipe, A, 1997 'The animal bone', in Thomas, C, Sloane, B, & Phillpotts, C, 231–4
de Rouffignac, C, 1997 'Parasite remains', in Thomas, C, Sloane, B, & Phillpotts, C, 247–8
Samuel, M, with de Domingo, C, 1997 'Moulded stone', in Thomas, C, Sloane, B, & Phillpotts, C, 186–95
Sidell, J, 1997 'The eggshell', in Thomas, C, Sloane, B, & Phillpotts, C, 248
Smith, D, 1997 'Insect fauna', in Thomas, C, Sloane, B, & Phillpotts, C, 245–7
Stephenson, R, with Spoerry, P, 1997 'The pottery', in Thomas, C, Sloane, B, & Phillpotts, C, 184–6
Thomas, C, Sloane, B, & Phillpotts, C, 1997 *Excavations at the Priory and Hospital of St Mary Spital, London*, MoLAS Monograph 1

STS75

Map site: 54
ILAU: David Whipp
NGR: TQ 3660 8330

St Stephen's Road, E3

A trial excavation in 1975 revealed no archaeological features earlier than the post-medieval period.

London Archaeol, 2, 1976, 372; *Britannia*, 7, 1976, 351

THL78

Map site: 55
ILAU: Robert Whytehead
NGR: TQ 3370 8091

Two archaeological
excavations used site code
THL78, because both sites
were examined in association
with the GLC Tower Bridge
Northern Approach Road
Improvement Scheme.

Goodman's Yard, E1

Excavations in 1978 recorded late Roman dumping, probably infilling a quarry for gravel and brickearth, into which an inhumation burial had been inserted. Only the left foot, with remains of a hobnailed shoe, survived later truncation. The stone foundations of a building, perhaps of 16th-c date, were also found. See also GYD75 above.

Locker, A, 1980 'The animal bones', in Whytehead, R L, 44–6
McIsaac, W, 1980 'The other Roman pottery', in Whytehead, R L, 38–41
Marsh, G, 1980 'Samian', in Whytehead, R L, 37–8
Rhodes, M, 1980 'The remains of a Roman hobnailed shoe', in Whytehead, R L, 44
Shepherd, J D, 1980 'The glass', in Whytehead, R L, 42–3
Whytehead, R L, 1980 'Excavations at Goodman's Yard, 1978', *Trans London Middlesex Archaeol Soc*, 31, 29–46

THL78

Map site: 56
ILAU: David Whipp
NGR: TQ 3360 8070
SMR: 081081

Tower Hill, EC3

Excavation followed by a watching brief in 1978 revealed a 6m stretch of the Roman city wall, surviving to a maximum height of 1m and faced with squared blocks of Kentish ragstone. At ground level was a plinth of large sandstone blocks with a chamfered edge, and behind the wall the remains of the earth rampart stretching back at least 9m. Inside the wall were found the footings of a stone turret, partially excavated in 1936.

London Archaeol, 3, 1979, 275; *Britannia*, 10, 1979, 317

Locker, A, 1980 'The animal bones', in Whipp, D, 65–6

McIsaac, W, 1980 'The other Roman pottery', in Whipp, D, 60–3

Marsh, G, 1980 'Samian', in Whipp, D, 57–60

Shepherd, J D, 1980 'The glass', in Whipp, D, 63–5

Whipp, D, 1980 'Excavations at Tower Hill 1978', *Trans London Middlesex Archaeol Soc*, 31, 47–67

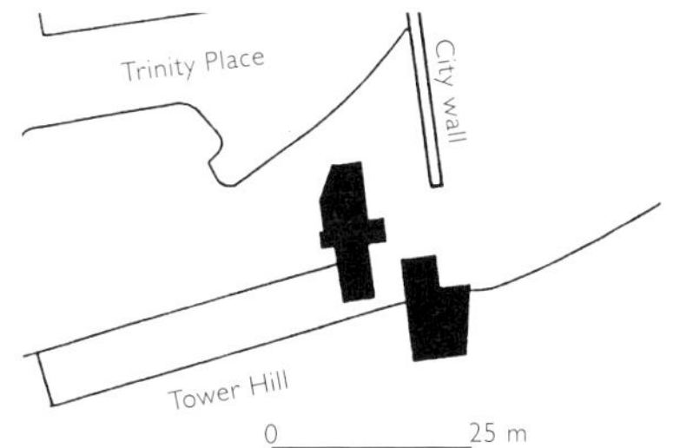

Thomas More Street, E1

Observation in 1988 recorded waterlaid clays above which were marsh deposits, and dump layers consistent with land reclamation.

TMS88

Map site: 57
DGLA(N): Naomi Hamilton
NGR: TQ 3423 8050

Tower Postern, Tower Hill, EC3

Excavation in 1979 revealed the remains of the medieval Tower Postern gate, in the form of a single, S gate tower and fragments of a gate passage to the N, including evidence of a portcullis and two gates; evidence for the N tower was inconclusive. The S tower had been built on a terrace on the N side of the Tower of London moat, into which it had slid (and thus been preserved) some time before the mid-16th c. The walls survived to ground-floor window level, and a basement floor was preserved intact.

London Archaeol, 3, 1980, 388–9; 4, 1981, 49–50

Whipp, D, in prep. 'The postern gate of the Tower of London: excavations 1979'

TOL79

Map site: 58
ILAU: David Whipp
NGR: TQ 3360 8070
SMR: 081079

41–42 Trinity Square, EC3

Excavation in 1985 revealed part of the Roman city wall and internal earth rampart. A deep, regularly recut ditch behind the latter produced late 3rd-c pottery from its latest fill. Also recorded was a gravel pit behind the rampart, filled with building material and subsequently with late 4th-c domestic refuse. Later features on the site included possible medieval property boundaries, and medieval and post-medieval levelling.

London Archaeol, 5, 1986, 164

TRT85

Map site: 59
DGLA(N): Steven Pierpoint
NGR: TQ 3360 8080
SMR: 081084–6, 081530

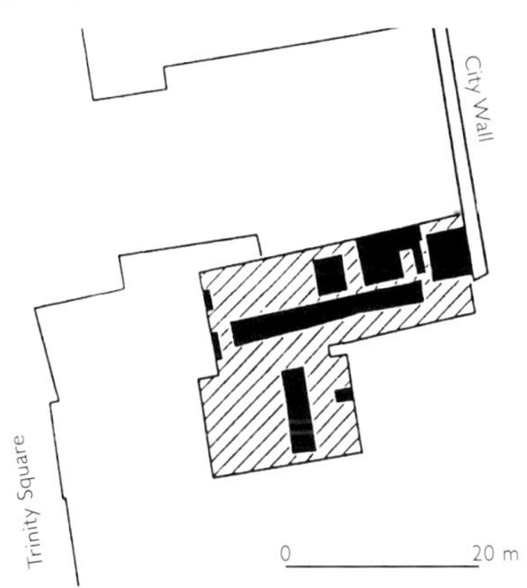

TSG87

Map site: 60
DGLA(N): Stephen Tucker
NGR: TQ 3355 8075
SMR: 082123–9

Tower Hill Station, Trinity Square, EC3

Excavation in 1987 revealed evidence of Roman quarrying and rubbish pits, overlain by a deposit containing Roman pottery. Ragstone wall foundations of uncertain date were also uncovered. A series of backfilled features containing Saxon and early medieval material was recorded; the most extensive being a medieval robber trench aligned E–W, with flat ragstone slabs at the base. Deposits containing 18th–19th-c pottery were also located.

London Archaeol, 5, 1988, 415; *Medieval Archaeol,* 32, 1988, 252

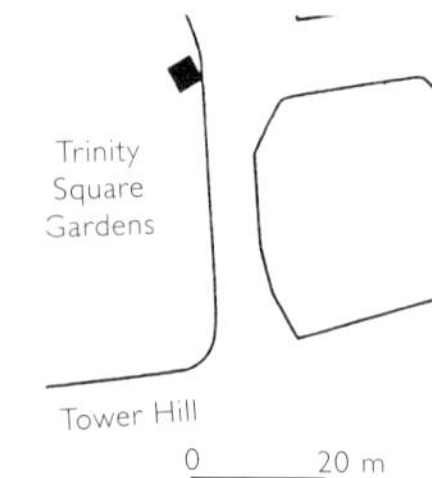

TTL85

Map site: 61
DGLA(N): Paul Falcini,
Robert Ellis
NGR: TQ 3365 8140

The Three Lords public house, 27 Minories, EC3

A watching brief in 1985 on the site of a public house recorded the E side of a V-shaped Roman ditch 1.5m wide and 0.85m deep, aligned N–S and containing 1st- and 2nd-c pottery; a robber trench contained pottery of the late 3rd c. Limited excavation to the S of the house located a late 3rd-c Roman 'plaster' burial overlying a gravel surface and beneath a sandy layer of 2nd-c date.

London Archaeol, 5, 1986, 164
Barber, B, & Bowsher, D, in prep. *The eastern cemetery of Roman London: excavations 1983–1990*
Barber, B, Bowsher, D, & Whittaker, K, 1990 'Recent excavations of a cemetery of *Londinium*', *Britannia,* 21, 1–12

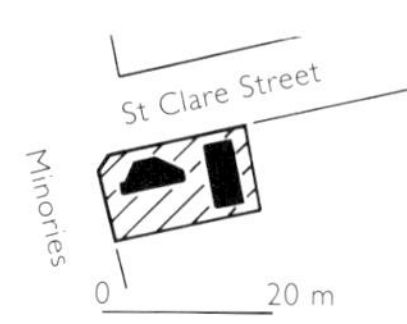

UNC90

Map site: 62
DGLA(N): Carol Williams
NGR: TQ 3620 8246

Queen Mary and Westfield College, 343–345 Mile End Road, E1

Excavation in 1990 revealed no archaeological survival.

London Archaeol, 6, 1991, 308; *Post-Medieval Archaeol,* 25, 1991, 159

UNI83

Map site: 63
ILAU: Peter Mills
NGR: TQ 3430 8010

Union Stairs, Wapping High Street, E1

Observation in 1983 revealed 16th-c foreshore dumping only.

UR74

Map site: not shown
ILAU: Irene Schwab
NGR: TQ 3690 8357

Usher Road, E3

Excavation in 1974 revealed a complex of pits and ditches of the Roman period, to the N side of the London to Colchester road and apparently part of a field-system. The material is of primarily 3rd–4th-c date, though there is evidence of activity from the later 2nd c and extending well into the 4th c. See AGH90, ROM80 above, USH76 below.

London Archaeol, 2, 1975, 259

Usher Road, Armagh Road, E3

Excavation in 1976 revealed several linear features probably of Roman date. See also AGH90, ROM80 above.

London Archaeol, 3, 1977, 39; Britannia, 8, 1977, 409

USH76

Map site: 64
ILAU: David Whipp
NGR: TQ 3690 8370
SMR: 080993, 081070

Wapping Wall, Garnet Street, Monza Street, E1

Observation in 1984 recorded a possible contractors' testpit, the backfill of which consisted of heavy wet clay containing Roman and post-medieval pottery.

WAW84

Map site: 65
DGLA: Robert Ellis
NGR: TQ 3510 8030

Worcester House, Stepney Green, E1

Excavation in 1985 revealed the remains of the octagonal gatehouse tower of the former Worcester House, built in the late 16th c. A substantially constructed range of buildings represented the rear of the gatehouse and the NW wing of the house itself. A less substantial set of structures was also recorded, either ancillary buildings of the E wing or later infilling of the former courtyard. The S wing of the house was outlined by two rooms, though structural differences from other parts were noted. The buildings appear to have been only slightly modified, if at all, before demolition in 1858.

London Archaeol, 5, 1986, 164

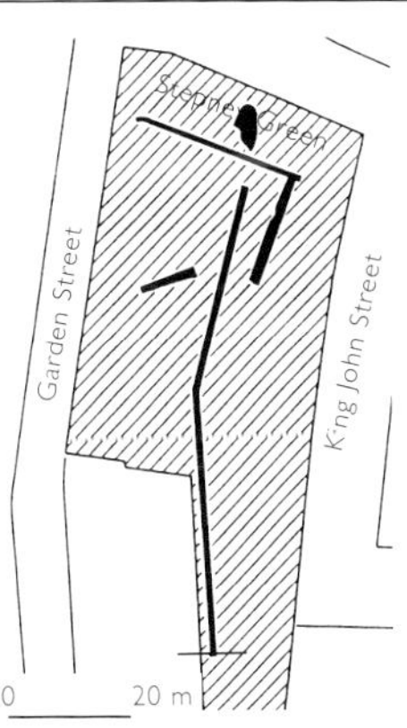

WOR85

Map site: 66
DGLA(N): Paul Falcini
NGR: TQ 3580 8170

29 West Tenter Street, 59 Mansell Street, E1

Excavation in 1990 revealed prehistoric activity in the form of a possible linear feature and a small pit. The site, immediately S of MSL87, recovered further evidence of the Roman cemetery, including nine inhumations, ten cremations, two ditches and two mausolea.

London Archaeol, 6, 1991, 308; Britannia, 22, 1991, 273
Barber, B, & Bowsher, D, in prep. *The eastern cemetery of Roman London: excavations 1983–1990*
Barber, B, Bowsher, D, & Whittaker, K, 1990 'Recent excavations of a cemetery of *Londinium*', *Britannia*, 21, 1–12

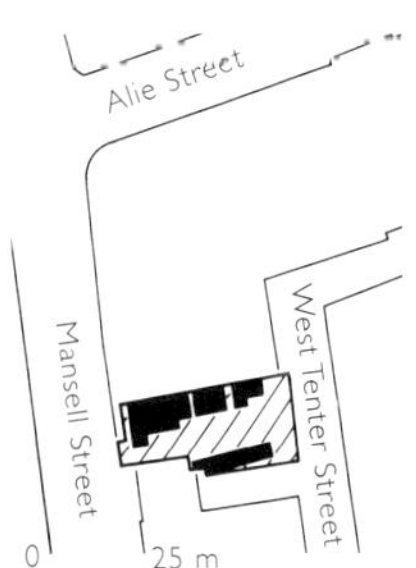

**WTE88,
WTE90**

Map site: 67, 68
DGLA(N): Bruno Barber
NGR: TQ 3384 8108

WTN83, WTN84

Map site: 69
DGLA(N): Robert Whytehead
NGR: TQ 3390 8101
SMR: 080883, 081503–4

West Tenter Street, Scarborough Street, St Mark Street, South Tenter Street, E1

Excavation in 1984 revealed burials cut into natural, and the backfill of gravel pits apparently dug after the area had begun to be used as a cemetery. 110 graves were identified, and 13 cremations. A large circular pit was located, lined at its base with a square wooden construction some of which cut through some of the later graves. Traces of walls associated with burials at the E end of the site may be those of mausolea. The graves were apparently aligned either parallel or at right angles to a N–S ditch, itself possibly aligned on a nearby road-line. Dating of the cemetery appears to range between the late 2nd c and the late 3rd, when material of that date was tipped in a wide spread over graves in the centre of the site. A mid-14th-c coin was found in one isolated feature. Medieval and 17th-c pits had removed some earlier deposits, and medieval ploughsoil had reduced the Roman ground level and cut through the tops of some cremation urns.

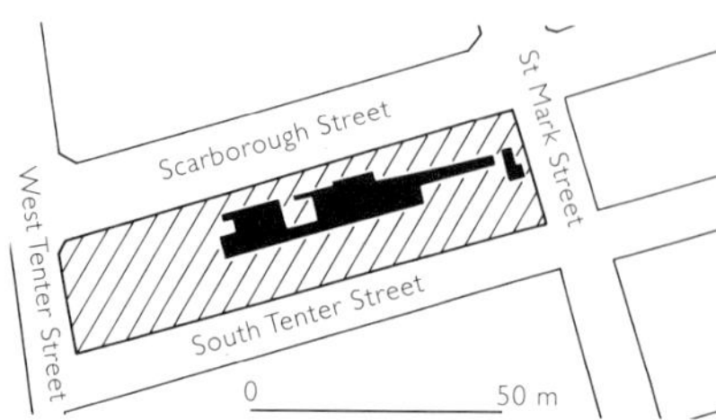

London Archaeol, 5, 1985, 66–7; *Britannia,* 17, 1986, 408

Barber, B, & Bowsher, D, in prep. *The eastern cemetery of Roman London: excavations 1983–1990*

Whytehead, R, 1986 'The excavation of an area within a Roman cemetery at West Tenter Street, London, E1', *Trans London Middlesex Archaeol Soc,* 37, 23–124

WWL85

Map site: 70
DGLA(N): Peter Mills
NGR: TQ 3521 8036

Jubilee Wharf, 76 Wapping Wall, E1

Investigation in 1985 included a timber with a joist notch, found by a contractor on gritty foreshore deposits beneath a modern floor.

WANDSWORTH

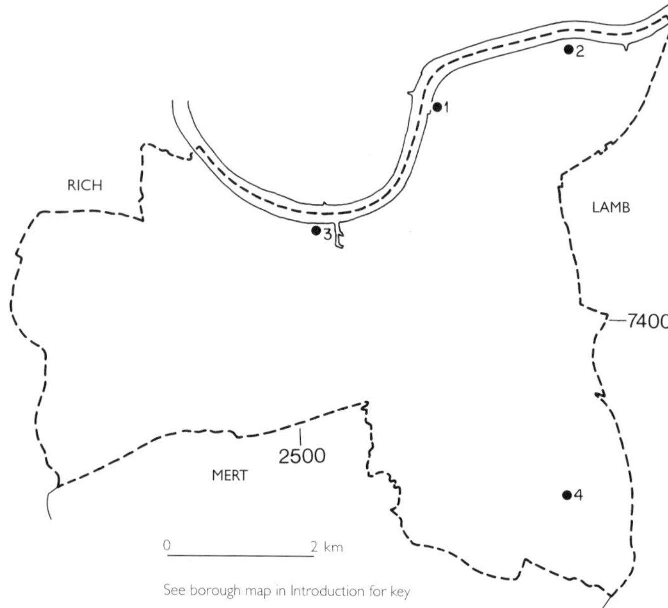

London Borough of Wandsworth

WAND 1 AG75   Althorpe Grove, Westbridge Rd, SW11
WAND 2 BEF89   Battersea Wharf, Queenstown Rd, SW8
WAND 3 PPW89 Point Pleasant, SW18
WAND 4 TBH90   Tooting Bec Hospital, Tooting Bec Rd, SW17

AG75

Map site: 1
SWLT, SAS: Scott McCracken
NGR: TQ 2680 7680
SMR: 031340, 031351, 031385

Althorpe Grove, Westbridge Road, SW11

Excavation in 1975–6 revealed several beam slots which cut into natural, contained Saxon pottery and probably represent trenches for timber buildings. A 13th-c ditch was also located, aligned N–S and perhaps an early boundary. Evidence was also recorded of the post-medieval gardens of Battersea Manor House (c 1760). Excavation further N in 1977 revealed Saxon pits and pottery.

London Archaeol, 2, 1976, 372; 3, 1977, 39; 3, 1978, 162; *Medieval Archaeol,* 22, 1978, 148; *Surrey Archaeol Coll,* 72, 1980, 250
McCracken, J S, 1977 'Wandsworth: Althorpe Grove, Battersea', *Surrey Archaeol Soc Bull,* 139

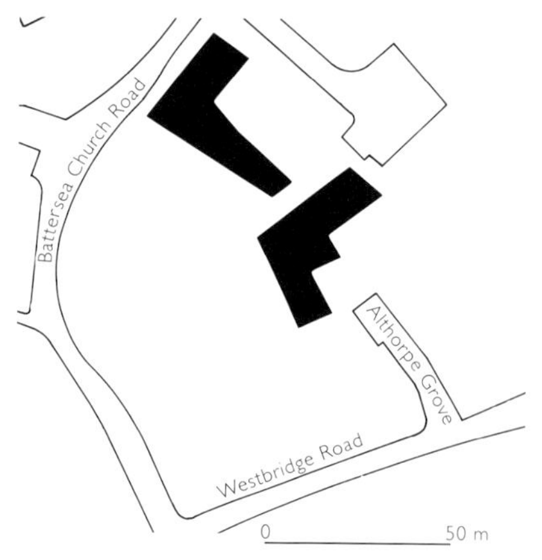

BEF89

Map site: 2
DGLA(N): Gillian Batchelor
NGR: TQ 2866 7757

Battersea Wharf, Queenstown Road, SW8

A trial excavation in 1989 revealed a sand island with no evidence of occupation.

London Archaeol, 6, 1990, 194; *Surrey Archaeol Coll,* 80, 1990, 226

Point Pleasant, SW18

PPW89

Map site: 3
DGLA(N): David Saxby
NGR: TQ 2520 7520
SMR: 021149–50

Excavation in 1989 revealed a layer of grey silt and sand containing probably Mesolithic flints, including a core, flakes and blades. It also produced prehistoric (possibly), Saxon and medieval pottery.

London Archaeol, 6, 1990, 194; Surrey Archaeol Coll, 80, 1990, 226

Tooting Bec Hospital, Tooting Bec Road, SW17

TBH90

Map site: 4
DGLA(N): Timothy Haillay
NGR: TQ 2860 7170
SMR: 021307–9

Excavation in 1990 revealed a series of early 19th-c dumping layers probably relating to Tooting Lodge, built in 1803. A large feature recorded may have been the lodge fishpond, or a depression caused by gravel extraction.

London Archaeol, 6, 1991, 308; Surrey Archaeol Coll, 81, 1991–2, 167

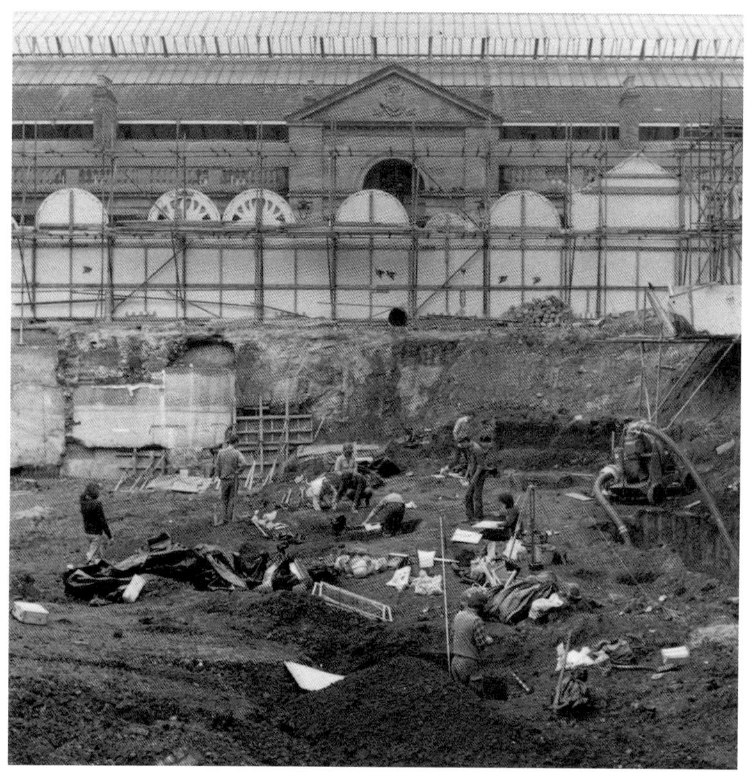

Westminster JUB85 Jubilee Hall, Covent Garden, WC2. Excavations underway, showing the discovery of Saxon features.

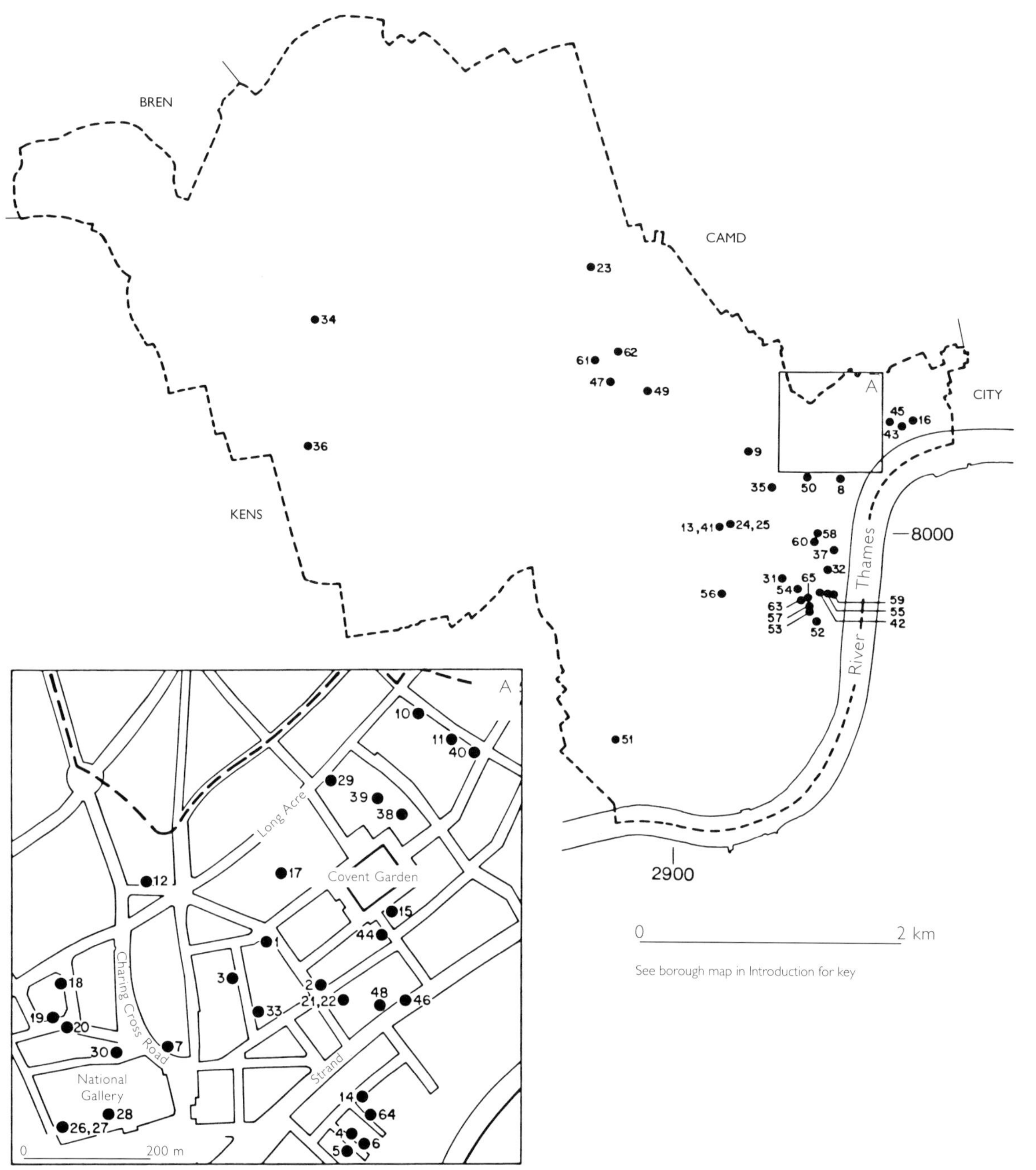

See borough map in Introduction for key

City of Westminster

WEST 1   BDF89   21–26 Bedford St (Moss Bros site), WC2

WEST 2   BDS89   39–40 Bedford St (outside), WC2

WEST 3   BFD88   20–22 Bedfordbury, WC2

WEST 4   BHM88   12 Buckingham St, WC2

WEST 5   BKS87   11 Buckingham St, WC2

WEST 6   BKS88   13–14 Buckingham St, WC2

WEST 7   CAV86   Cavell House, St Martin's Lane, Charing Cross Rd, WC2

WEST 8   CHA87   Charing Cross Station, Villiers St, WC2

WEST 9   CRY89   Criterion Theatre, Piccadilly, W1

WEST 10   DRU88   44–46 Drury Lane, WC2

WEST 11   DRY90   55–57 Drury Lane, WC2

WEST 12   GTS86   10 Great Newport St, WC2

WEST 13   HRH90   St James's Palace (apartment 29), Cleveland Row, SW1

WEST 14   JAD89   17–19 John Adam St, WC2

WEST 15   JUB85   Jubilee Hall, Covent Garden, WC2

WEST 16   KIL90   King's College, 152–158 Strand, WC2

WEST 17   KIN88   35 King St, 17–18 Floral St, WC2

WEST 18   LES89   Leicester Square (electricity substation), WC2

WEST 19   LSQ88   33–34 Leicester Square, WC2

WEST 20   LSQ89   Leicester Square (public conveniences), WC2

WEST 21   MAI85   21–22 Maiden Lane, WC2

WEST 22   MAI86   21–22 Maiden Lane, WC2

WEST 23   MAY90   55–57 Marylebone High St, W1

WEST 24   MRB89   Marlborough House, Pall Mall, SW1

WEST 25   MRB90   Marlborough House, Pall Mall, SW1

WEST 26   NAG86   National Gallery Extension (Hampton site), St Martin's St, Whitcomb St, WC2

WEST 27   NAG87   National Gallery Extension (Hampton site), St Martin's St, Whitcomb St, WC2

WEST 28   NGA87   National Gallery Basement, Trafalgar Square, WC2

WEST 29   ODM77   Long Acre (Odhams Press site), WC2

WEST 30   ONG89   14 Orange St, WC2

WEST 31   OQS81   3–7 Old Queen St, SW1

WEST 32   PAR87   37–46 Parliament St, SW1

WEST 33   PEA87   Peabody site, junction of Bedfordbury, Chandos Place, WC2

WEST 34   PGY90   Paddington Goods Yard, Bishop's Bridge Rd, W2

WEST 35   PML87   123 Pall Mall, SW1

<table>
<tr><td>WEST 36</td><td>POR76</td><td>1–1A Porchester Terrace, 101–103 Bayswater Rd, W2</td></tr>
<tr><td>WEST 37</td><td>RCH80</td><td>Richmond Terrace, SW1</td></tr>
<tr><td>WEST 38</td><td>ROH89</td><td>The Royal Opera House (car park), Bow St, WC2</td></tr>
<tr><td>WEST 39</td><td>ROH90</td><td>The Royal Opera House and Floral Hall, Jubilee Gardens, 45–47 Floral St, 51–54 Long Acre, WC2</td></tr>
<tr><td>WEST 40</td><td>RUS87</td><td>Drury House, Russell St, Drury Lane, WC2</td></tr>
<tr><td>WEST 41</td><td>SJP89</td><td>St James's Palace (apartment 29), Cleveland Row, SW1</td></tr>
<tr><td>WEST 42</td><td>SMW88</td><td>St Margaret's church, St Margaret St, SW1</td></tr>
<tr><td>WEST 43</td><td>SOM88</td><td>Somerset House, Strand, WC2</td></tr>
<tr><td>WEST 44</td><td>SOT89</td><td>26–27 Southampton St, WC2</td></tr>
<tr><td>WEST 45</td><td>STN87</td><td>132–140 Strand, WC2</td></tr>
<tr><td>WEST 46</td><td>STN89</td><td>366 Strand, WC2</td></tr>
<tr><td>WEST 47</td><td>STP79</td><td>Stratford Place, Oxford St, W1</td></tr>
<tr><td>WEST 48</td><td>STR90</td><td>406–408 Strand, WC2</td></tr>
<tr><td>WEST 49</td><td>TEN89</td><td>1 Tenterden St, W1</td></tr>
<tr><td>WEST 50</td><td>TSQ88</td><td>Trafalgar Square, WC2</td></tr>
<tr><td>WEST 51</td><td>VIC90</td><td>Ebury Bridge House, Ebury Bridge Rd, SW1</td></tr>
<tr><td>WEST 52</td><td>WAG88</td><td>Westminster Abbey (College Garden), Great College St, SW1</td></tr>
<tr><td>WEST 53</td><td>WAM75</td><td>Westminster Abbey, 20 Dean's Yard, SW1</td></tr>
<tr><td>WEST 54</td><td>WBS79</td><td>Broad Sanctuary, SW1</td></tr>
<tr><td>WEST 55</td><td>WCG78</td><td>Parliament Square, St Margaret St (Cromwell Green), SW1</td></tr>
<tr><td>WEST 56</td><td>WEL78</td><td>Wellington Barracks, Birdcage Walk, SW1</td></tr>
<tr><td>WEST 57</td><td>WGC88</td><td>Westminster Abbey (Great Cloister), Broad Sanctuary, SW1</td></tr>
<tr><td>WEST 58</td><td>WHI79</td><td>49–51 Whitehall, SW1</td></tr>
<tr><td>WEST 59</td><td>WHL75</td><td>Westminster Hall, St Margaret St, SW1</td></tr>
<tr><td>WEST 60</td><td>WHP76</td><td>Downing St (Treasury Green), SW1</td></tr>
<tr><td>WEST 61</td><td>WIG78</td><td>Wigmore St, W1</td></tr>
<tr><td>WEST 62</td><td>WOT90</td><td>42–46 Wigmore St, W1</td></tr>
<tr><td>WEST 65</td><td>WSA88</td><td>Westminster Abbey (north side), Broad Sanctuary, SW1</td></tr>
<tr><td>WEST</td><td>WST86</td><td>Westminster Abbey (Undercroft Museum), Broad Sanctuary, SW1</td></tr>
<tr><td>WEST 63</td><td>WST88</td><td>Westminster Abbey (north-west tower), Broad Sanctuary, SW1</td></tr>
<tr><td>WEST 64</td><td>YKB88</td><td>18–20 York Buildings, WC2</td></tr>
</table>

Moss Bros site, 21–26 Bedford Street, WC2

BDF89

An evaluation excavation in 1989 revealed a number of pits containing Middle Saxon pottery, and also a ditch of unknown date.

London Archaeol, 6, 1990, 195; *Medieval Archaeol*, 34, 1990, 185
Cowie, R, 1988 'A gazetteer of Middle Saxon sites and finds in the Strand/Westminster area', *Trans London Middlesex Archaeol Soc*, 39, 42 (28)

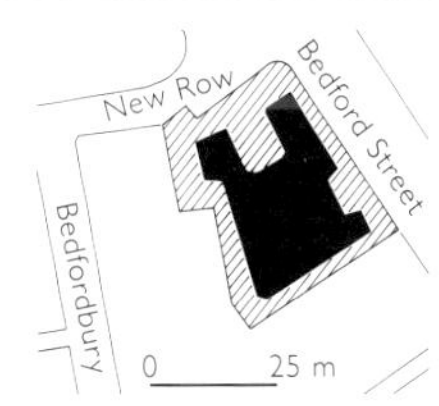

Map site: 1
DGLA(N): Stewart Hoad
NGR: TQ 3020 8079
SMR: 082177–8

Outside 39–40 Bedford Street, WC2

BDS89

A watching brief in 1989 revealed a number of layers of brown sandy clay containing oyster shell and animal bone. There were also several brickearth layers and associated burnt daub containing a sherd of Roman or Saxon pottery.

London Archaeol, 6, 1990, 195; *Medieval Archaeol*, 34, 1990, 185
Cowie, R, 1988 'A gazetteer of Middle Saxon sites and finds in the Strand/Westminster area', *Trans London Middlesex Archaeol Soc*, 39, 42 (26)

Map site: 2
DGLA(N): Robert Cowie
NGR: TQ 3028 8072
SMR: 082176

20–22 Bedfordbury, WC2

BFD88

Excavation in 1988 revealed no archaeological evidence.

Medieval Archaeol, 32, 1988, 253

Map site: 3
DGLA(N): Stephen Haynes
NGR: TQ 3138 0760

BHM88

Map site: 4
DGLA(N): Stewart Hoad,
Andrew Letch
NGR: TQ 3033 8048
SMR: 082174

12 Buckingham Street, WC2

A watching brief in 1988 recorded considerable quantities of waterlogged deposits which included the apparent remains of a wattle fence. Animal bone was also recovered. The levels were perhaps Saxon, though no dating evidence was found.

London Archaeol, 6, 1989, 80
Cowie, R, 1988 'A gazetteer of Middle Saxon sites and finds in the Strand/Westminster area', *Trans London Middlesex Archaeol Soc,* 39, 41 (19)

BKS87

Map site: 5
DGLA(N): Robert Cowie
NGR: TQ 3032 8048

11 Buckingham Street, WC2

A watching brief in 1987 recorded walls of late medieval or early post-medieval date, possibly part of the basement of York House.

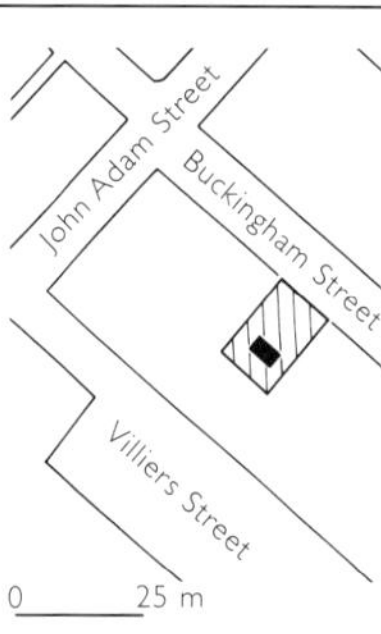

BKS88

Map site: 6
DGLA(N): Niall Roycroft
NGR: TQ 3034 8046

13–14 Buckingham Street, WC2

A watching brief in 1988 produced much evidence of local topography and land reclamation.

CAV86

Map site: 7
DGLA(N)
NGR: TQ 3003 8064
SMR: 082173

Cavell House, St Martin's Lane, Charing Cross Road, WC2

A watching brief in 1986 recorded a pit, or pits, of possible Middle Saxon date.

Medieval Archaeol, 31, 1987, 133
Cowie, R, 1988 'A gazetteer of Middle Saxon sites and finds in the Strand/Westminster area', *Trans London Middlesex Archaeol Soc,* 39, 41 (17)

CHA87

Map site: 8
DGLA(N): Robert Cowie
NGR: TQ 303 804

Charing Cross Station, Villiers Street, WC2

A watching brief on several pits in 1987 recorded good organic preservation in the lower layers, some of which contained quantities of domestic refuse but few artefacts that could be dated accurately. Some pits produced evidence of a late or early post-medieval water channel. In another were noted the impressive remains of a wall of the same period, when the site formed part of the garden of York House.

Criterion Theatre, Piccadilly, W1

CRY89

Map site: 9

Currently there is no further information for this site.

44–46 Drury Lane, WC2

DRU88

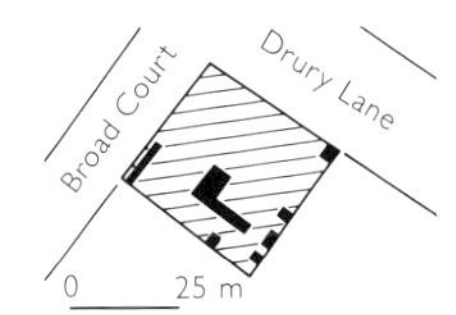

Limited excavation in 1988 revealed Saxon deposits, 0.5m deep and probably dumping, overlain by a thin spread of iron waste and cut by a deep pit or well and a post-hole; probably an ironworking site. The little dating evidence found was all Middle Saxon.

Map site: 10
DGLA(N):
Robert Whytehead
NGR: TQ 3043 8114
SMR: 082108

London Archaeol, 6, 1989, 80; *Medieval Archaeol,* 33, 1989, 188
Cowie, R, 1988 'A gazetteer of Middle Saxon sites and finds in the Strand/Westminster area', *Trans London Middlesex Archaeol Soc,* 39, 44 (45)

55–57 Drury Lane, WC2

DRY90

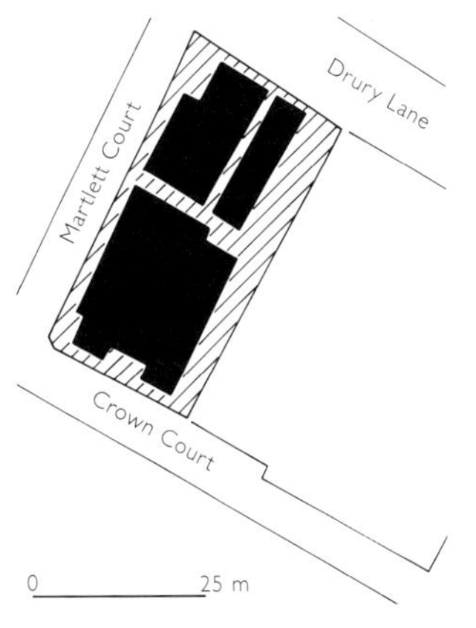

Excavation in 1990 revealed a possible ploughsoil together with ditches, which perhaps served as field boundaries; they contained prehistoric and Roman pottery and coins (600BC–AD350). Evidence of Saxon occupation included several rubbish pits containing domestic material and a Saxon coin *(sceat),* and seven wood-lined storage pits. A rectangular pattern of post-holes indicated the site of a timber structure, close to two wells. Several pits containing rubbish of medieval date were also excavated.

Map site: 11
DGLA(N): Stewart Hoad
NGR: TQ 3048 8110
SMR: 082180, 082329–30

London Archaeol, 6, 1991, 308; *Britannia,* 22, 1991, 273; *Medieval Archaeol,* 35, 1991, 156
Cowie, R, 1988 'A gazetteer of Middle Saxon sites and finds in the Strand/Westminster area', *Trans London Middlesex Archaeol Soc,* 39, 44 (46)

10 Great Newport Street, WC2

GTS86

A watching brief in 1986 recorded the profile of a deep Saxon pit, much damaged in the Victorian period.

Map site: 12
ILAU: Robert Whytehead
NGR: TQ 3001 8091
SMR: 081506

Medieval Archaeol, 31, 1987, 133
Cowie, R, 1988 'A gazetteer of Middle Saxon sites and finds in the Strand/Westminster area', *Trans London Middlesex Archaeol Soc,* 39, 42 (31)

St James's Palace (apartment 29), Cleveland Row, SW1

HRH90

A watching brief in 1990 observed two areas in the location of an earlier excavation (see SJP89 below). A sleeper wall was removed from the fireplace in the SE corner of the cloakroom to reveal the original palace brickwork. In the second area, the joists of the modern floor were seen to have been laid on a flagged pavement, beneath which were recorded a post-hole and demolition debris which included a quantity of Reigate stone fragments, thought to be rubble from the medieval hospital which had preceded the palace on the site.

Map site: 13
DGLA(N): Carol Williams
NGR: TQ 2936 8100

London Archaeol, 6, 1991, 309; *Post-Medieval Archaeol,* 25, 1991, 134

JAD89

Map site: 14
DGLA(N): Chris Thomas
NGR: TQ 3033 8054
SMR: 082175

17–19 John Adam Street, WC2

Excavation in 1989 revealed, on the W side of the site, part of an 18th-c wall with related tile floor. In the N, natural was cut by two possible gravel-extraction pits of probable 17th-c date. Other features included walls and further pits.

Cowie, R, 1988 'A gazetteer of Middle Saxon sites and finds in the Strand/Westminster area', *Trans London Middlesex Archaeol Soc*, 39, 41 (20)

JUB85

Map site: 15
DGLA(N): Robert Whytehead
NGR: TQ 3040 8085
SMR: 081235, 081505

Jubilee Hall, Covent Garden, WC2

Observation in 1985 recorded evidence of Middle Saxon occupation and industrial activity on the Strand foreshore of the Thames in the form of buildings, fireplaces, hearths and at least one well. Finds included pottery of the mid-7th–9th c, circular loom-weight fragments and a *sceat* of *c* 720.

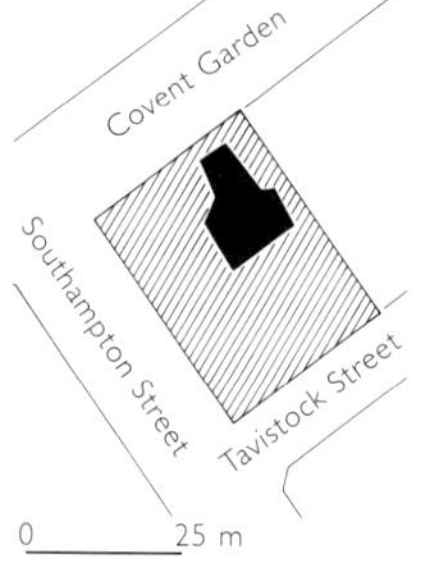

London Archaeol, 5, 1986, 164; *Medieval Archaeol*, 30, 1986, 143
Cowie, R, 1988 'A gazetteer of Middle Saxon sites and finds in the Strand/Westminster area', *Trans London Middlesex Archaeol Soc*, 39, 43 (37)
Cowie, R, Whytehead, R L, & Blackmore, L, 1988 'Two Middle Saxon occupation sites at Jubilee Hall and 21–22 Maiden Lane', *Trans London Middlesex Archaeol Soc*, 39, 47–163
Whytehead, R, 1985 'Saxons in Covent Garden', Mosaic, *London Archaeol*, 5, 112
Whytehead, R, 1985 'The Jubilee Hall site reveals new evidence of Saxon London', *Rescue News*, 37

KIL90

Map site: 16
DGLA(N): Gordon Malcolm
NGR: TQ 3085 8086
SMR: 082324–6

King's College, 152–158 Strand, WC2

A watching brief in 1990–1 recorded a possible Saxon rubbish pit and waterlogged deposits of what appeared to be part of the medieval waterfront or related features. Extensive Tudor remains were observed, including foundations and indications of earlier robbed-out features.

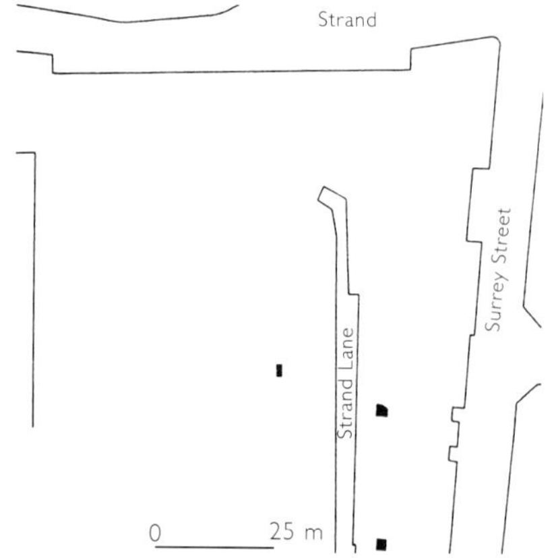

London Archaeol, 6, 1991, 308; *Medieval Archaeol*, 35, 1991, 156
Cowie, R, 1988 'A gazetteer of Middle Saxon sites and finds in the Strand/Westminster area', *Trans London Middlesex Archaeol Soc*, 39, 44 (54)

KIN88

Map site: 17
DGLA(N): Kevin Williams, Carol Williams
NGR: TQ 3023 8088
SMR: 082109, 082118–19

35 King Street, 17–18 Floral Street, WC2

The excavation of 17 testpits in 1988 located archaeological material in five of them, at either end of the site. Two cut features were identified as Saxon, and three others as post-medieval.

London Archaeol, 6, 1989, 80; *Medieval Archaeol*, 33, 1989, 188
Cowie, R, 1988 'A gazetteer of Middle Saxon sites and finds in the Strand/Westminster area', *Trans London Middlesex Archaeol Soc*, 39, 43 (35)

Leicester Square (electricity substation), WC2

Excavation in 1989 revealed four ditches, three aligned N–S and one NW–SE. Only one contained datable material, which consisted of worked flint of the Late Mesolithic/Early Neolithic period, and sherds of pottery. A group of post-holes was also found.

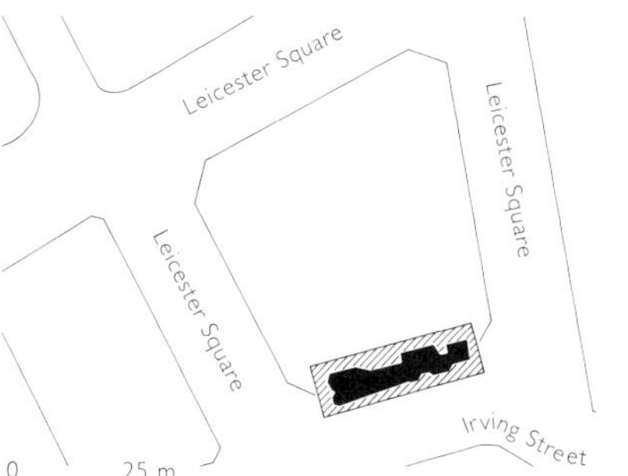

London Archaeol, 6, 1990, 195

Cowie, R, 1988 'A gazetteer of Middle Saxon sites and finds in the
  Strand/Westminster area', *Trans London Middlesex Archaeol Soc,* 39, 41 (16)

LES89

Map site: 18
DGLA(N): Stewart Hoad
NGR: TQ 2985 8068
SMR: 082170–2

33–34 Leicester Square, WC2

Excavation in 1988 revealed a deep stratigraphy beneath the Square, indicating much post-medieval activity and the possibility of the undisturbed survival of Saxon material beneath these deposits.

LSQ88

Map site: 19
DGLA(N): Gordon Malcolm
NGR: TQ 2988 8066

Leicester Square (public conveniences), WC2

Excavation in 1989 revealed large undated features cutting natural.

London Archaeol, 6, 1990, 195

LSQ89

Map site: 20
DGLA(N): Robert Cowie
NGR: TQ 2983 8073
SMR: 082231

21–22 Maiden Lane, WC2

Trial work in 1985 and excavation in 1986 exposed Saxon stratigraphy including evidence of 8th–9th-c settlement in the form of rubbish pits, dump layers, stake-holes and post-holes. A large ditch more than 2m wide and 2m deep after truncation ran E–W across the site, cutting a pit containing a coin of 769–821 and itself containing pottery provisionally dated to the 9th c: the shape and date of the ditch suggest that its purpose was defensive. An area of tiled paving was uncovered in the SE corner, laid in the Middle Saxon period and composed of Roman roof tiles and possibly *pilae.*

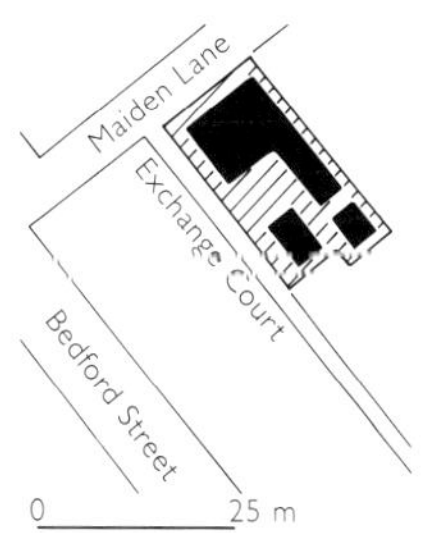

London Archaeol, 5, 1987, 278; *Medieval Archaeol,* 31, 1987, 133

Cowie, R, 1988 'A gazetteer of Middle Saxon sites and finds in the Strand/Westminster area', *Trans London Middlesex Archaeol Soc,* 39,
  42 (25)

Cowie, R, Whytehead, R L, & Blackmore, L, 1988 'Two Middle Saxon occupation sites at Jubilee Hall and 21–22 Maiden Lane', *Trans
  London Middlesex Archaeol Soc,* 39, 47–163

MA185, MA186

Map site: 21, 22
DGLA(N): Robert Cowie
NGR: TQ 3031 8072
SMR: 081315, 081454

MAY90

Map site: 23
DGLA(N): Bruno Barber
NGR: TQ 2836 8200
SMR: 081218

55–57 Marylebone High Street, W1

A watching brief in 1990 observed a wall which was possibly part of the 13th-c Marylebone manor house, or one of its post-medieval rebuilds. Large quantities of demolition debris suggested that the medieval and post-medieval structures stood on or close to the site.

London Archaeol, 6, 1991, 309

MRB89, MRB90

Map site: 24, 25
DGLA(N): Mark Barratt
NGR: TQ 2946 8009
SMR: 081278, 206564

Marlborough House, Pall Mall, SW1

A watching brief in 1989 on contractors' testpits in the basement and grounds of Wren's town house (1709), followed by excavation and further observation in 1990, revealed the remains of buildings that preceded the house: the foundations of the kitchen ranges of Henry VIII's St James's Palace (1538), destroyed by fire in 1809; and a wall of the 17th-c Capuchin friary that stood to the E of Inigo Jones's Queen's Chapel (1627). Inside the house, the walls and floors of Wren's original building, altered in the 1770s and in 1861–3, were recorded beneath later basement floor levels. Finds included several pottery sherds and two fragments of decorated floor tile from deposits dated between 1150 and 1350, perhaps from the hospital of St James the Less, demolished *c* 1538.

London Archaeol, 6, 1991, 308; *Medieval Archaeol,* 35, 1991, 157; *Post-Medieval Archaeol,* 25, 1991, 133

NAG86

Map site: 26
DGLA(N): Robert Cowie
NGR: TQ 2989 8051

National Gallery Extension (Hampton site), St Martin's Street, Whitcomb Street, WC2

Excavation in 1986 revealed intrusive features, often cutting into natural gravels and filled with sandy clays that were overlain in places by layers of similar material. The larger features cutting the gravel are provisionally interpreted as quarry pits. Only a few sherds of Roman, Saxon and medieval pottery and a small quantity of animal bone were recovered. Post-medieval stratigraphy was located, including brick walls and concrete slabs.

NAG87

Map site: 27
DGLA(N): Robert Cowie
NGR: TQ 2989 8051

National Gallery Extension (Hampton site), St Martin's Street, Whitcomb Street, WC2

Excavation in June–September 1987 revealed large Saxon gravel quarries up to 15.5m long, the sparsity of domestic refuse suggesting that they lay outside the area of Middle Saxon occupation, and that the W boundary of the settlement was located near the middle of what is now Trafalgar Square. The large size of the pits implies that they were communally operated, probably for road and yard surfacing (see also JUB85, MAI86 above, PEA87 below). A number of features cut into the upper layers filling one of the pits provided evidence of activity in the 11th and 12th c.

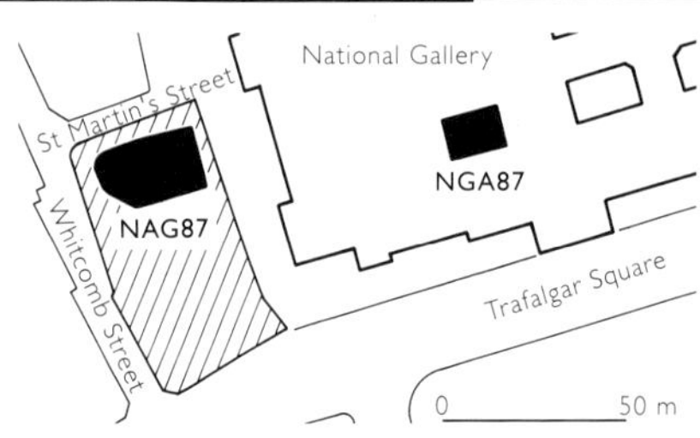

London Archaeol, 5, 1988, 415
Cowie, R, 1988 'A gazetteer of Middle Saxon sites and finds in the Strand/Westminster area', *Trans London Middlesex Archaeol Soc,* 39, 41 (13)
Whytehead, R L, Cowie, R, & Blackmore, L, 1989 'Excavations at the Peabody Site, Chandos Place, and the National Gallery', *Trans London Middlesex Archaeol Soc,* 40, 35–176

National Gallery Basement, Trafalgar Square, WC2

Excavation in February 1987 revealed pits containing large quantities of domestic refuse (in contrast with NAG87 above). The initial function of two larger pits was unclear, though they may have been wells or quarry pits. (For plan, see NAG87.)

London Archaeol, 5, 1988, 415; *Medieval Archaeol,* 32, 1988, 252
Cowie, R, 1988 'A gazetteer of Middle Saxon sites and finds in the Strand/Westminster area', *Trans London Middlesex Archaeol Soc,* 39, 41 (14, 15)
Whytehead, R L, Cowie, R, & Blackmore, L, 1989 'Excavations at the Peabody Site, Chandos Place, and the National Gallery', *Trans London Middlesex Archaeol Soc,* 40, 35–176

NGA87

Map site: 28
DGLA(N): Robert Cowie
NGR: TQ 2996 8054
SMR: 081507, 081812

Odhams Press site, Long Acre, WC2

Observations in 1977 recorded evidence of a plague pit of probable 17th-c date.

ODM77

Map site: 29
ILAU: Irene Schwab
NGR: TQ 3030 8110
SMR: 081459

14 Orange Street, WC2

Excavation in 1989 revealed various industrial dump layers containing bone pinmaking handles of 17th-c date. Sealed by these was a clay floor surface and a N–S beam slot dating to the 16th–17th c and probably associated with a post-medieval coachworks.

London Archaeol, 6, 1990, 195; *Post-Medieval Archaeol,* 24, 1990, 206

ONG89

Map site: 30
DGLA(N): Trevor Cox
NGR: TQ 2985 8065
SMR: 082232

3–7 Old Queen Street, SW1

Observation in 1981 recorded the destruction of most of the site by Victorian basements; from one surviving corner was recovered 13th–16th-c pottery, presumably part of the bog deposits around Thorney Island.

OQS81

Map site: 31
ILAU: Robert Whytehead,
Peter Mills
NGR: TQ 298 796
SMR: 082168

37–46 Parliament Street, SW1

Excavation in 1987 on the N edge of the former Thorney Island revealed three features predating a flood layer thought to be Roman in date. After subsequent flooding two drainage channels had been dug, one of them recut twice and revetted with wooden stakes. Silting of the area apparently continued until the 13th and 14th c; two 15th-c stake and wattle fences up to 10m long and joining at their W ends, perhaps fish traps, were encountered at the W end of the site. The area seems to have remained marshy until the end of the medieval period, when drainage and consolidation by dumping took place. A wall of reused sandstone and Reigate stone was constructed upon one of these deposits.

London Archaeol, 5, 1988, 415; *Medieval Archaeol,* 32, 1988, 253

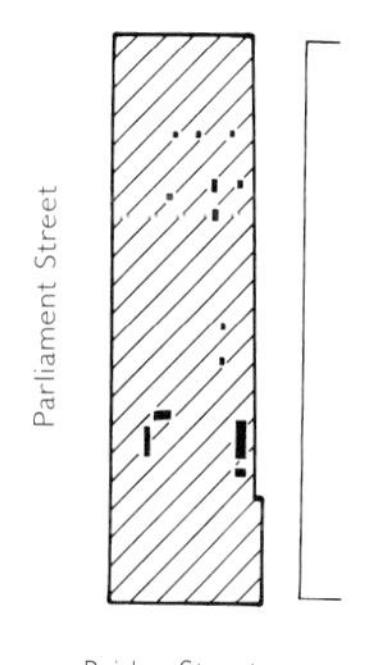

PAR87

Map site: 32
DGLA(N): Chris Thomas
NGR: TQ 302 797
SMR: 082124, 082130–6

PEA87

Map site: 33
DGLA(N): Robert
Whytehead
NGR: TQ 3019 8070
SMR: 081813

Peabody site, junction of Bedfordbury, Chandos Place, WC2

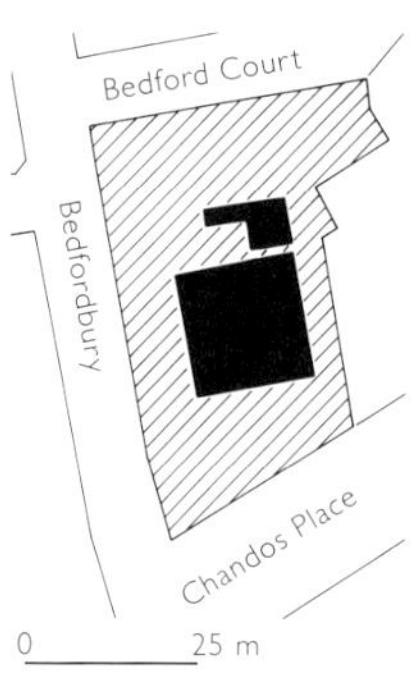

Excavation in 1987 revealed evidence of a Middle Saxon structure with a barrel-lined well set in a gravelled yard, the building having eventually collapsed and the yard gone out of use. An adult grave was found, oriented E–W and containing an iron spearhead. A sequence of stake-built, earth-floored pits, numerous rubbish pits, two cesspits and a possible wall was recorded. The sequence, where it survived, was capped by dark earth.

London Archaeol, 5, 1988, 415
Cowie, R, 1988 'A gazetteer of Middle Saxon sites and finds in the Strand/Westminster area', *Trans London Middlesex Archaeol Soc,* 39, 42 (23)
Whytehead, R L, Cowie, R, & Blackmore, L, 1989 'Excavations at the Peabody Site, Chandos Place, and the National Gallery', *Trans London Middlesex Archaeol Soc,* 40, 35–176

PGY90

Map site: 34
DGLA(N): James Hunter
NGR: TQ 262 814
SMR: 082328

Paddington Goods Yard, Bishop's Bridge Road, W2

An evaluation excavation in 1990 revealed 19th-c pottery dumps only.

London Archaeol, 6, 1991, 309

PML87

Map site: 35
DGLA(N): Robert
Whytehead
NGR: TQ 298 803

123 Pall Mall, SW1

Observation of central and N rooms in 1987 revealed 18th-c brick footings and a well. In the rear rooms, traces were found of one or more deep pits backfilled with medieval material and interpreted as clay or sand and gravel pits.

POR76

Map site: 36
ILAU: Irene Schwab
NGR: TQ 261 807
SMR: 081458

1–1A Porchester Terrace, 101–103 Bayswater Road, W2

A trial trench examined in 1976 revealed no trace of the Roman road from London to Silchester; natural sand found to be overlain by a layer of brown ploughsoil, was covered in turn by modern debris.

London Archaeol, 3, 1977, 39

RCH80

Map site: 37
ILAU: Peter Mills
NGR: TQ 302 719

Richmond Terrace, SW1

Limited trial trenching in 1980 indicated that the site, frequently flooded by the Thames, was possibly used as a refuse dump in the late medieval period.

London Archaeol, 4, 1981, 50

The Royal Opera House (car park), Bow Street, WC2

A trial excavation in 1989 revealed several Middle Saxon rubbish pits.

London Archaeol, 6, 1990, 195; *Medieval Archaeol,* 34, 1990, 185

Cowie, R, 1988 'A gazetteer of Middle Saxon sites and finds in the Strand/Westminster area', *Trans London Middlesex Archaeol Soc,* 39, 43 (38)

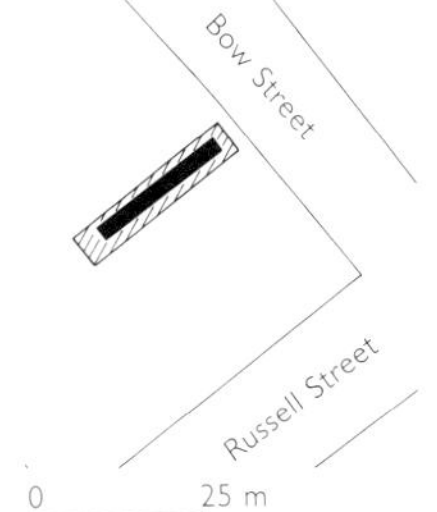

ROH89

Map site: 38
DGLA(N): Robert Cowie
NGR: TQ 3043 8099
SMR: 082179

The Royal Opera House and Floral Hall, Jubilee Gardens, 45–47 Floral Street, 51–54 Long Acre, WC2

Evaluation excavations in a testpit in the Royal Opera House in 1990 revealed a brick floor that was probably part of the theatre built by Robert Smirke in the early 19th c, or possibly the first Covent Garden Theatre of 1731–2. Several pits cut into the river gravel beneath the Floral Hall contained large fragments of brickwork, including demolition debris from a floor; probably from one of the earlier theatres. Further excavation revealed strata provisionally dated to the Middle Saxon period and including pits and a well. Post-medieval strata included a large intrusive feature, brick walls, a brick-lined cesspit and a well. Two inhumation burials of possible 14th-c date were found during the excavations.

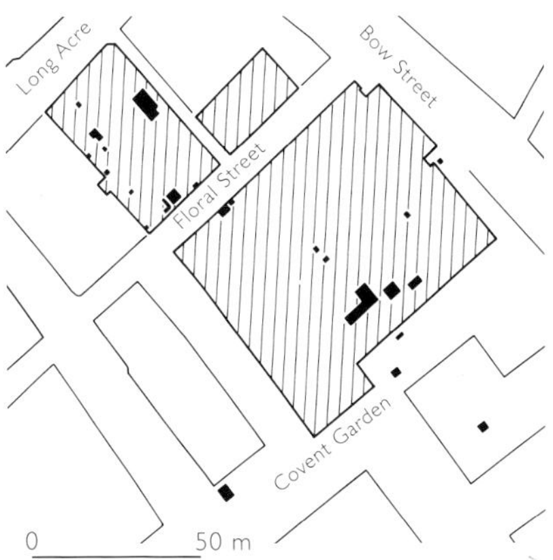

London Archaeol, 6, 1991, 308; *Medieval Archaeol,* 35, 1991, 156; *Post-Medieval Archaeol,* 25, 1991, 133

Cowie, R, 1988 'A gazetteer of Middle Saxon sites and finds in the Strand/Westminster area', *Trans London Middlesex Archaeol Soc,* 39, 43 (39)

ROH90

Map site: 39
DGLA(N): Robert Cowie
NGR: TQ 3031 8104
SMR: 082316–21

Drury House, Russell Street, Drury Lane, WC2

Excavation in 1987 revealed two probable pits containing pottery of possible Middle Saxon date.

Cowie, R, 1988 'A gazetteer of Middle Saxon sites and finds in the Strand/Westminster area', *Trans London Middlesex Archaeol Soc,* 39, 44 (47, 48)

RUS87

Map site: 40
DGLA(N): Robert Whytehead
NGR: TQ 3051 8106
SMR: 082139–40

St James's Palace (apartment 29), Cleveland Row, SW1

Excavation in 1989 revealed probable medieval deposits most likely relating to the hospital of St James, founded before 1100 (see HRH90 above). The best-preserved evidence was from the Tudor period, including the remains of a garderobe. Other features included stake-holes and post-holes, probably relating to the construction of the palace and possibly also to subsequent maintenance.

SJP89

Map site: 41
DGLA(N): Alex Mackie
NGR: TQ 2936 8100

SMW88

Map site: 42
DGLA(N): Kenneth Pitt
NGR: TQ 3013 7953

St Margaret's church, St Margaret Street, SW1

Excavation in 1988–9 related chiefly to the vestry. Some pre-vestry features were located, notably a chalk wall which was probably the outer wall of one of the buildings shown on Morgan's map of 1682 and Rocque's map of 1746, and apparently marking the E boundary of the graveyard. Burials associated with the graveyard were heavily disturbed, much disarticulated human bone being found, by the construction of the vestry and other earlier and later activity.

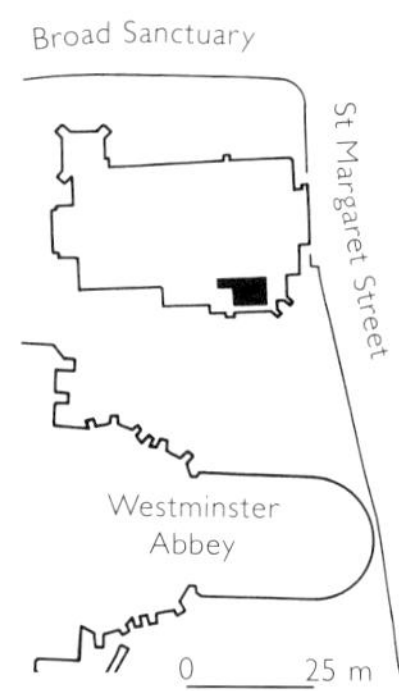

SOM88

Map site: 43
DGLA(N): Robert Cowie
NGR: TQ 3077 8083

Somerset House, Strand, WC2

Observation of underpinning work in 1988 revealed that heavily disturbed Saxon pits had survived basementing, which over a large area reached the level of the natural gravel.

London Archaeol, 6, 1989, 80; *Medieval Archaeol*, 33, 1989, 188
Cowie, R, 1988 'A gazetteer of Middle Saxon sites and finds in the Strand/Westminster area', *Trans London Middlesex Archaeol Soc*, 39, 44 (54)

SOT89

Map site: 44
DGLA(N): Robert Cowie
NGR: TQ 3037 8080
SMR: 082169

26–27 Southampton Street, WC2

An excavation and watching brief in 1989 revealed evidence of Middle Saxon occupation, including rubbish pits, dump layers and traces of a post structure aligned E–W. The pottery assemblage comprised Ipswich ware, shelly ware, chaff-tempered pottery and continental wares.

London Archaeol, 6, 1990, 195; *Medieval Archaeol*, 34, 1990, 185
Cowie, R, 1988 'A gazetteer of Middle Saxon sites and finds in the Strand/Westminster area', *Trans London Middlesex Archaeol Soc*, 39, 43 (36)

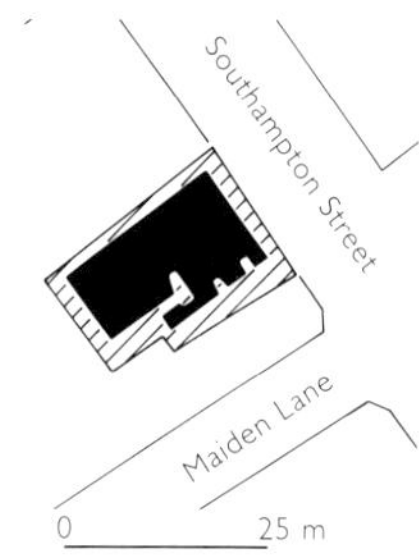

STN87

Map site: 45
DGLA(N)
NGR: TQ 3066 8084

132–140 Strand, WC2

A watching brief in 1987 observed two cut features: one containing a sherd of Ipswich ware, and the other domestic debris.

Cowie, R, 1988 'A gazetteer of Middle Saxon sites and finds in the Strand/Westminster area', *Trans London Middlesex Archaeol Soc*, 39, 44 (53)

STN89

Map site: 46
DGLA(N): Robert Cowie
NGR: TQ 3053 8079

366 Strand, WC2

Investigation in 1989 noted deposits mostly of probable Middle Saxon date.

Cowie, R, 1988 'A gazetteer of Middle Saxon sites and finds in the Strand/Westminster area', *Trans London Middlesex Archaeol Soc*, 39, 44 (49)

Stratford Place, Oxford Street, W1

A watching brief in 1979 recorded an undated rectangular masonry structure, possibly the cistern of the Lord Mayor's Banqueting House shown on various maps and engravings.

London Archaeol, 3, 1980, 389

STP79

Map site: 47
ILAU: Wendy McIsaac
NGR: TQ 285 812

406–408 Strand, WC2

A watching brief in 1990 recorded no archaeological survival.

London Archaeol, 6, 1991, 309; Post-Medieval Archaeol, 25, 1991, 134

STR90

Map site: 48
DGLA(N): Chris Thomas
NGR: TQ 3038 8071
SMR: 082327

1 Tenterden Street, W1

An evaluation excavation in 1989 revealed 18th-c truncation on the W part of the site, archaeological evidence being confined to two ditches of probable Roman date.

TEN89

Map site: 49
DGLA(N): Aileen Connor
NGR: TQ 287 810
SMR: 082182–3

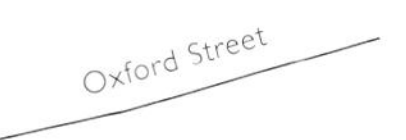
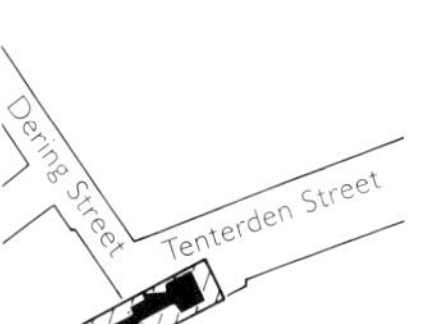

Trafalgar Square, WC2

A watching brief on drain trenches in 1988 recorded two barrel-wells, possibly Roman or Saxon in date, and a deep feature in the NW corner of the Square containing waterlogged wood, possibly a Saxon gravel pit. Saxon rubbish pits were observed in the W half of the Square, and a large medieval gravel pit was noted in the SE corner. Medieval N–S wall foundations were noted on the N and S sides of the Square, probably footings of the King's Mews.

London Archaeol, 6, 1989, 80; Medieval Archaeol, 33, 1989, 187
Cowie, R, 1988 'A gazetteer of Middle Saxon sites and finds in the Strand/Westminster area', *Trans London Middlesex Archaeol Soc, 39*,
40–1 (12)

TSQ88

Map site: 50
DGLA(N): Robert Cowie
NGR: TQ 3005 8044
SMR: 081343, 082111–14

Ebury Bridge House, Ebury Bridge Road, SW1

A watching brief in 1990 revealed a single undated feature recorded in section.

London Archaeol, 6, 1991, 308

VIC90

Map site: 51
DGLA(N): Gordon Malcolm
NGR: TQ 2859 7845
SMR: 082323

WAG88

Map site: 52
DGLA(N): Alex Mackie
NGR: TQ 3010 7935
SMR: 082273

Westminster Abbey (College Garden), Great College Street, SW1

An auger survey in 1988 indicated a probably natural channel of the River Tyburn, and early occupation of uncertain date, possibly Roman or Saxon. At least 13 medieval and numerous post-medieval features were also located, showing intensive use of the garden area into the 17th c.

London Archaeol, 6, 1989, 80; Medieval Archaeol, 33, 1989, 188

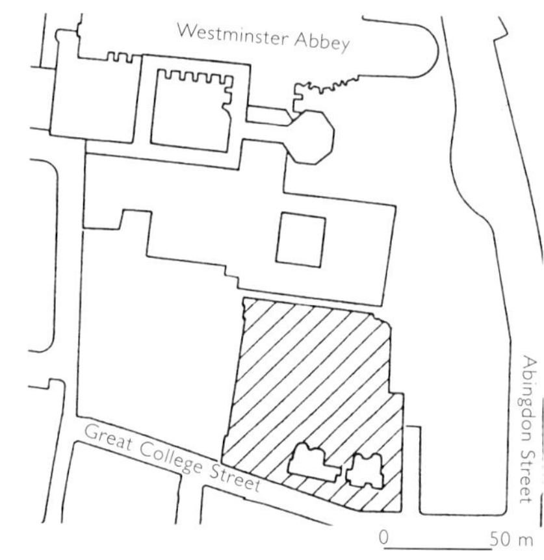

WAM75

Map site: 53
ILAU: Graham Black
NGR: TQ 300 794
SMR: 081244, 081250, 081263

Westminster Abbey, 20 Dean's Yard, SW1

Excavation in 1975 revealed evidence of the pre-Norman minster, notably the possible footings of a timber building. In the post-conquest period the site remained as an open court between the monastic kitchen and frater until the insertion of the misericord and its sub-vault in the first half of the 13th c. These buildings were demolished in the late 16th c.

London Archaeol, 2, 1976, 372; Britannia, 7, 1976, 351; Medieval Archaeol, 20, 1976, 166, 179; 21, 1977, 228
Black, G, 1975 'Excavations at the misericord of Westminster Abbey', *London Archaeol*, 2, 314–16
Black, G, 1977 'The redevelopment of 20 Dean's Yard, Westminster Abbey 1975–1977', *Trans London Middlesex Archaeol Soc*, 28, 190–210
Cowie, R, 1988 'A gazetteer of Middle Saxon sites and finds in the Strand/Westminster area', *Trans London Middlesex Archaeol Soc*, 39, 40 (2)
Eames, E, 1977 'The tiles', in Black, G, 202–3
Evans, J, 1977 'Analysis of mortar samples from the sub-vault', in Black, G, 204–9
Rigold, S E, 1977 'Sculptured block from the sub-vault of the misericord, Westminster Abbey', in Black, G, 200–2

WBS79

Map site: 54
ILAU: Peter Mills
NGR: TQ 2995 7692
SMR: 081365, 081419–22

Broad Sanctuary, SW1

Excavations in 1979 exposed a series of drainage ditches showing that the area had been reclaimed from the surrounding marshes in the 16th c.

London Archaeol, 3, 1980, 389
Locker, A, 1982 'The animal bones', in Mills, P, 357–9
McIsaac, W, 1982 'The small finds', in Mills, P, 355–7
Mills, P, 1982 'Excavations at Broad Sanctuary, Westminster', *Trans London Middlesex Archaeol Soc*, 33, 345–65
Platts, E, 1982 'The pottery', in Mills, P, 352–5
Scale, R G, 1982 'Pollen report', in Mills, P, 360–4

Parliament Square, St Margaret Street (Cromwell Green), SW1

WCG78

Map site: 55
ILAU: Peter Mills
NGR: TQ 3018 7953
SMR: 081149, 081395–9

Excavation in 1978 revealed a number of prehistoric, possibly Late Iron Age, gullies and post-holes. Roman and possibly Saxon watercourses were recorded. Some late medieval drains were also found, though most of the medieval deposits had been removed in the 19th c.

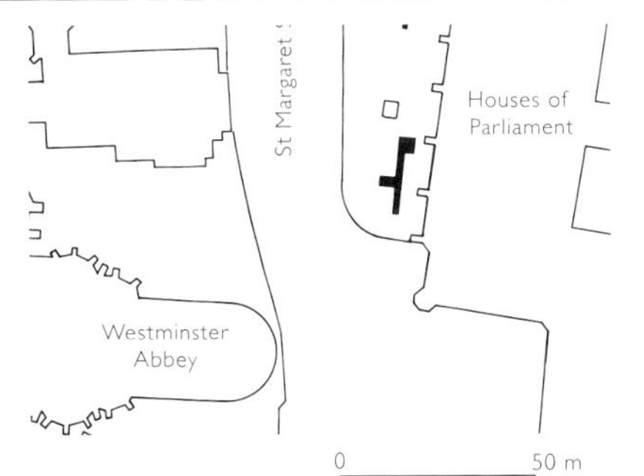

London Archaeol, 3, 1979, 275; Britannia, 10, 1979, 317; Medieval Archaeol, 23, 1979, 241

Collins, D, 1980 'Flints', in Mills, P, 27–8

Cowie, R, 1988 'A gazetteer of Middle Saxon sites and finds in the Strand/Westminster area', Trans London Middlesex Archaeol Soc, 39, 40 (5)

Mills, P, 1980 'Excavations at Cromwell Green in the Palace of Westminster', Trans London Middlesex Archaeol Soc, 31, 18–28

Platts, E, 1980 'The pottery', in Mills, P, 26–7

Wellington Barracks, Birdcage Walk, SW1

WEL78

Map site: 56
ILAU: Irene Schwab
NGR: TQ 294 795

Observation in 1978 recorded several sections, one of them revealing the remains of brick buildings of probable 16th–17th-c date.

Westminster Abbey (Great Cloister), Broad Sanctuary, SW1

WGC88

Map site: 57
DGLA(N): Gordon Malcolm
NGR: TQ 3006 7945

Examination took place in 1988 of deposits, which included disturbed human bone and fragments of medieval worked stone, indicating levelling up within the cloister garth in the early 17th c.

45–51 Whitehall, SW1

WHI79

Map site: 58
ILAU: Peter Mills
NGR: TQ 301 800
SMR: 081460

Excavation in 1979 showed that the Taplow Gravels did not extend as far S from Trafalgar Square as this site, which lay on alluvial deposits. Modern buildings had destroyed any later archaeological strata.

London Archaeol, 3, 1980, 389

Westminster Hall, St Margaret Street, SW1

WHL75

Map site: 59
ILAU: David Whipp
NGR: TQ 303 795
SMR: 081245

Excavation in 1975 confirmed that 19th-c construction had destroyed nearly all trace of a 13th-c stone building. A number of pits and gullies and the footings of a medieval wall were revealed. One pit produced an assemblage of coarseware cooking pots.

London Archaeol, 2, 1976, 372; Medieval Archaeol, 20, 1976, 193

Whipp, D, & Platts, E, 1976 'Westminster Hall excavations', London Archaeol, 2, 351–5

WHP76

Map site: 60
ILAU: David Whipp
NGR: TQ 3010 7995

Downing Street (Treasury Green), SW1

Observation in 1976 indicated no surviving archaeological features.

WIG78

Map site: 61
ILAU: Irene Schwab
NGR: TQ 284 813

Wigmore Street, W1

Observation in 1978 recorded the possible fill of the River Tyburn, or an associated channel.

WOT90

Map site: 62
DGLA(N): Gordon Malcolm
NGR: TQ 2855 8137

42–46 Wigmore Street, W1

A watching brief in 1990 revealed undated archaeological deposits.

London Archaeol, 6, 1991, 309

WSA88

Map site: 65
DGLA(N): Gordon Malcolm
NGR: TQ 3000 7951

Westminster Abbey (north side), Broad Sanctuary, SW1

A testpit survey took place in 1988.

WST86

Map site: not shown
DGLA(N): Peter Mills
NGR: TQ 3008 7942
SMR: 081317, 081451–3,
082137, 082164

Westminster Abbey (Undercroft Museum), Broad Sanctuary, SW1

Excavation within the late 11th-c undercroft and near the S edge of Thorney Island in 1986 revealed stratified deposits up to 2m deep, recording evidence of occupation from the 10th c onwards and residual Roman material. A large, irregular feature, probably a quarry, at the S edge of the site silted up in the 10th c and was sealed by waterlaid, probably riverine, deposits. Cut through these was a ditch 7m wide and 2m deep that turned 90 degrees within the excavation and possibly defined the S limit of the abbey precinct. Possibly contemporary was a rammed gravel surface, twice renewed. The top of the ditch was backfilled with clay and sand, which was cut by a series of post-holes for a timber building 6m wide and more than 10m long. Most of the occupation levels had been destroyed, but it was probably built in the mid-11th c; after its removal a shallow ditch cut through the centre of its site and contained a rare polychrome tile. The present undercroft was begun c 1060, probably for storage originally, but it was converted into a series of rooms, including a warming house, from the 12th c onwards. Details of the undercroft's construction and underpinning were recorded.

London Archaeol, 5, 1987, 278

Betts, I, 1995 'Early ceramic tiles', in Mills, P, 100–2

Betts, I, 1995 'Hones', in Mills, P, 91

Blackmore, L, 1995 'The Middle Saxon pottery', in Mills, P, 80

Cotton, J, 1995 'Flints', in Mills, P, 90

Cowie, R, 1988 'A gazetteer of Middle Saxon sites and finds in the Strand/Westminster area', *Trans London Middlesex Archaeol Soc*, 39, 40 (3)

Davis, A, 1995 'Plant remains', in Mills, P, 113–20

Goffin, R, 1995 'Introduction' to 'The pottery', in Mills, P, 79–80

Goffin, R, 1995 'The accessioned finds', in Mills, P, 87–90

Goffin, R, 1995 'The medieval and later pottery', in Mills, P, 80–7

Goffin, R, & Crowley, N, 1995 'Building material', in Mills, P, 97–100

Locker, A, 1995 'The fish bones', in Mills, P, 111–13

Mills, P, 1995 'Excavations at the dorter undercroft, Westminster Abbey', *Trans London Middlesex Archaeol Soc*, 46, 69–124

Mortimer, C, 1995 'Chemical analysis of No. 175', in Mills, P, 97

Mortimer, C, & Shepherd, J D, 1995 'Introduction' to 'Window and vessel glass', in Mills, P, 92

Pipe, A, & West, B, 1995 'The animal bones', in Mills, P, 104–11

Samuel, M, 1995 'Worked stone', in Mills, P, 102–4

Shepherd, J D, 1995 'Catalogue', in Mills, P, 92–6

Shepherd, J D, 1995 'Vessel glass', in Mills, P, 96–7

Swain, H, 1995 'The prehistoric pottery', in Mills, P, 80

Waugh, K, 1995 'The Roman pottery', in Mills, P, 80

Williams, D F, 1995 'Lava quern fragments', in Mills, P, 91

Westminster Abbey (north-west tower), Broad Sanctuary, SW1

WST88

Map site: 63
DGLA(N): Stephen Haynes
NGR: TQ 3000 7951

Excavation in 1988 exposed medieval walls and evidence of dumping and truncation.

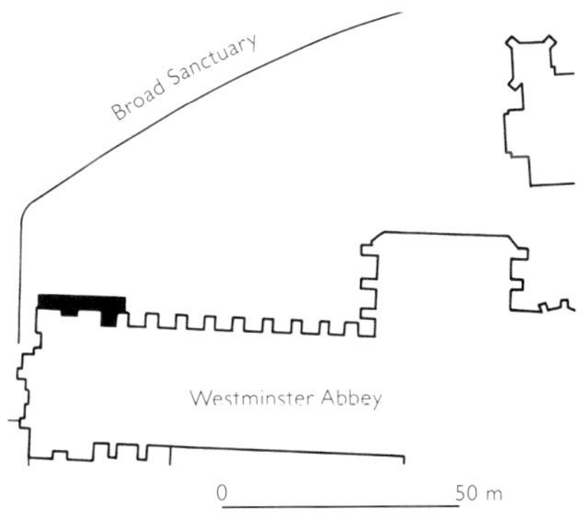

18–20 York Buildings, WC2

YKB88

Map site: 64
DGLA(N): Robert Cowie
NGR: TQ 3036 8054
SMR: 082115–17, 082274

Excavation in 1988 revealed a small area of Middle Saxon waterfront, possibly an embankment, and a row of stakes. This was overlain by sand and cobbles, sealed in turn by waterlaid clay from the top of which pottery was recovered. To the N was a row of vertical oak planks, aligned N–S and surrounded by brushwood and stakes dated by dendrochronology to the late 7th c. A medieval boundary wall on the NE side of the property survived to at least 4.26m in height, and belonged to either Durham or York House.

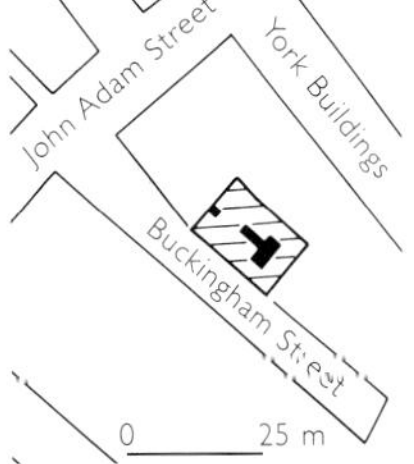

London Archaeol, 6, 1989, 80; *Medieval Archaeol*, 33, 1989, 188

Cowie, R, 1988 'A gazetteer of Middle Saxon sites and finds in the Strand/Westminster area', *Trans London Middlesex Archaeol Soc*, 39, 41–2 (22)

INDEX

Compiled by S Atkin

Page numbers in **bold** refer to maps. Subjects may occur more than once on a page.

276